TORTURED SUBJECTS

Tortured Subjects

Pain, Truth, and the Body in Early Modern France

Lisa Silverman

THE UNIVERSITY OF CHICAGO PRESS
CHICAGO AND LONDON

Lisa Silverman received her B.A. from Swarthmore College in 1984 and her Ph.D. from Rutgers University in 1993. A scholar of early modern French history and the history of the body, she has taught at the University of Southern California.

The University of Chicago Press, Chicago 60637
The University of Chicago Press, Ltd., London
© 2001 by The University of Chicago
All rights reserved. Published 2001
Printed in the United States of America
10 09 08 07 06 05 04 03 02 01   1 2 3 4 5
ISBN: 0-226-75753-6 (cloth)
ISBN: 0-226-75754-4 (paper)

Library of Congress Cataloging-in-Publication Data
Silverman, Lisa.
    Tortured subjects : pain, truth, and the body in early modern France /
Lisa Silverman.
        p. cm.
Includes bibliographical references and index.
    ISBN 0-226-75753-6 (cloth : alk. paper) — ISBN 0-226-75754-4 (pbk. :
alk. paper)
    1. Torture—France—History.   2. Criminal justice, Administration of—France—
History.   I. Title.
    HV8599.F7 S55 2001
    364.6'7—dc21
                                                                                        00-009586
⊚ The paper used in this publication meets the minimum requirements of the American National Standard for Information Sciences—Permanence of Paper for Printed Library Materials, ANSI Z39.48-1992.

CONTENTS

ILLUSTRATIONS

This book has its origin in the hospital bed where I once lay for several weeks in enforced contemplation of the meanings and limits of embodiment. Although those days are far behind me, their intensity has echoed through my life, insisting that I find a way to express the personal and cultural significance of bodily experiences.

I hope to contribute to our understanding of the human body as one of the many environments of human history, in a kind of extension of the *Annales* project, if you will. While the environments in which we live exert subtle pressures on us, what is most significant about those environments is our interaction with them, the ways in which we choose to respond to their constraints. This book, then, is an examination of the constraints of the body, of the ways in which those constraints inspire cultural responses and, most specifically, of the ways in which the meanings of pain resonated in early modern culture. Despite my employment of primary sources and secondary literatures having to do with the histories of law, religion, and medicine, I am not principally a historian of those phenomena. I have chosen to explore those areas largely because of the ways in which they illuminate the history of the body. I hope that I have not strayed too far afield or stumbled too badly in my path; no doubt there are passages here that specialists in those fields will find lacking. I hope that they will nonetheless find their subjects cast into new light by an approach that places the body at the center of everything—where it was and is.

But this book is also an attempt to come to terms with the ways in which human bodies can be caught in struggles between individuals and state systems, each asserting that they have rights over the bodies in question. When I embarked on this study, it seemed to me that there were a number of issues at stake in such conflicts; translated into the early modern moment, these issues seemed to be expressed most powerfully in debates over suicide, execution, abortion, and torture. For a variety of reasons both personal and political, I chose to focus my attention on the last of these issues.

In the modern world, torture has come to mean the illegal use of force by state actors. Of late, some human rights advocates have tried to broaden that definition to include the legal use of force, thereby including in the definition of torture corporal and capital punishments; others, to include nonstate actors, thereby including acts of domestic violence. These definitions are politically motivated: they lie at the heart of a profoundly important effort to extinguish human suffering. But the imposition of modern understandings of torture is unlikely to illuminate the functions and meanings of torture in the past. Part of the historian's task—part of my task—is to do justice to the past and its vanished peoples by seeking to comprehend it on its own terms. For the purposes of this exploration, therefore, I have chosen to adopt the definition of torture employed in early modern French law. When I speak about torture, I am speaking about the legal practice of torture that permitted the infliction of pain by officers of the state on the bodies of suspects in capital cases. While modern readers may well see torture in the public punishments of floggings and brandings, hangings and beheadings, all the evidence I have seen suggests that the people of early modern France did not—although they did see suffering. This book is an effort to leave behind our certainties and to enter instead into their world and see, as much as we can, through their eyes.

As the foregoing suggests, this book is about a dense tangle of things that a wiser scholar might never had the temerity to take on. If I have been able to tease any meaning out of that tangle, it is thanks to the following people who have assisted me over the years with graciousness and generosity.

My own teachers are foremost among this group. At Swarthmore College, Robert S. DuPlessis and Mary Poovey taught me to take nothing for granted. At Rutgers University, Rudolph Bell exercised both a remarkable patience and a brashly critical sensibility; thereafter, he served as an important source of support during the writing of this book.

Scholarly groups that heard me out and encouraged me to refine my thoughts include the Wesleyan Renaissance Seminar, the Los Angeles Early Modern France Group, the Law and Humanities Reading Group, and Dialogica. I was privileged to participate in the interdisciplinary conference held at the University of Chicago in March 1999 entitled "Investigating and Combating Torture: Explorations of a New Human Rights Paradigm," where I received enormous inspiration from colleagues working in many different disciplines. My colleagues at the University of Southern California, and elsewhere in Los Angeles, challenged me to reformulate the presentation of my ideas: thanks to Marjorie Becker, Florine Bruneau, Charlotte Furth, Brendan Nagle, Ed Perkins, Amy Richlin, and Martha Tocco.

I have worked at many libraries over the years, but nowhere was I received with greater kindness than at the History and Special Collections Division of the Louise M. Darling Biomedical Library at the University of California–Los Angeles. Katharine E. S. Donahue, the head librarian of that collection, represents the scholarly community at its best: warm, knowledgeable, and accommodating.

Research support provided by Rutgers University, by the University of Southern California, and by the Arnold L. and Lois S. Graves Foundation was crucial in allowing me to travel to archives, to read broadly, and to think carefully.

At the University of Chicago Press, I was remarkably fortunate to work with Doug Mitchell and Robert Devens, whose unflagging belief in this project sustained me through times of doubt. Thanks, too, to the anonymous readers for the Press, whose comments gave me an opportunity to see my work from new perspectives and to clarify my meanings.

The teachers at the Anna Bing Arnold Child Care Center and the Hilltop Nursery School cared lovingly for my son when my work took me away from him—a debt I can never repay.

Among my friends, I would particularly like to thank Joshua Gamson and Photini Sinnis, each of whom offered me very different kinds of support when I needed it most.

And my grateful thanks to and for those who have sustained me in body and soul: my parents, Eliane Leslau Silverman and Sheldon Silverman; my sister, Monique Silverman; and most of all, my companion, Mitchell Hartman, and our children, Jeremiah and Amalia.

A NOTE ON FOREIGN TERMS

Early modern French courts, officers, and procedures were markedly different from their English equivalents. For that reason, I have chosen to retain the French wherever possible, offering preliminary definitions here for those readers unfamiliar with these terms. More descriptive accounts may be found in the text. Readers interested in further examination of these institutions may wish to consult Marcel Marion, *Dictionnaire des institutions de la France, XVIIe–XVIIIe siècles* (1923; reprint, Paris: Picard, 1984).

French Courts

The French courts were organized in a strict hierarchy whose order was complicated by the creation of new courts at intermediary levels throughout the early modern period. I make reference to the municipal court of the city of Toulouse, the *capitoulat,* and its officers, the *capitouls,* the elected officials responsible for the administration of the city and of justice in specific instances. The *capitoulat* coexisted with a complex series of "ordinary" royal courts, including the *sénéchaussées* and *bailliages,* courts of first instance for civil and criminal cases whose decisions could be appealed to the *présidiaux* and *parlement.* The *présidiaux* were courts of first instance for specific kinds of civil and criminal cases, some of whose decisions could be appealed to the *parlements,* which also served as courts of appeal for the *sénéchaussées* and *bailliages.* The *parlements* themselves, composed of thirteen superior courts, had responsibilities that encompassed the political and the judicial. Each *parlement* was divided into four regular chambers: the *chambre des enquêtes,* the *chambre des requêtes,* the *grand' chambre,* and the *tournelle,* which heard criminal cases in the first instance for those who possessed the privilege of *committimus au petit sceau* and on appeal for all others. "Extraordinary" royal courts had more limited jurisdictions, generally defined as encompassing specific geographies and/or populations, and included such courts as the *Grands Maitres des Eaux et Forêts,* which heard cases involving royal rivers and forests; the *chambre de l'edit,* which heard cases involving Protestants; and the *maréchaussées,* which heard cases involving public highways, soldiers, and vagabonds. The proliferation of courts in France often resulted in jurisdictional battles among the courts.

Court Officials

The personnel of the courts included the *huissiers,* bailiffs responsible for maintaining order in the court and for delivery of court documents like warrants. Also among the personnel were the *greffiers,* court clerks who recorded court decisions, depositions, and interrogations and prepared warrants, inventories, and any other documentation required by the court. Some modern authors include these minor officials in the category of the *gens de loi;* others do not, restricting the term to mean officers of the court trained in the law, including *avocats* and *procureurs,* roughly equivalent to the English barrister and soliciter, respectively, although the *procureur du roi* or *procureur-général* held an office more like that of the public prosecutor.

Conseillers existed in all courts. The term *conseiller* is an imprecise one that designates little more than an official of the court in question. *Magistrats* were judges responsible for rendering judgments. Within the *parlements,* titles were more specific and could indicate both the chamber to which the officeholder was attached, and the level of the hierarchy to which he had ascended; hence among the *parlementaires* (judges of the *parlements* in general) there were *premiers présidents, présidents à mortier,* and so on. Each case in the *parlements* was assigned a *rapporteur,* a judge responsible for collecting and summarizing all relevant data for the benefit of his fellow judges.

Legal Documents and Procedures

Court officers were responsible for generating a variety of documents in the course of investigating and judging cases, from arrest warrants to final judgments. The nature of the French legal system was such that judges in the *parlements* could issue two kinds of *arrêts* (sentences): interlocutory sentences, which ordered some action be taken before final judgment was rendered; and definitive sentences, which determined the guilt status of the accused and the penalty, if appropriate.

Sentences to the *question* (torture) could be the result of either interlocutory or definitive sentences, because the kind of torture ordered—the *question préalable* or the *question préparatoire*—depended on the legal status of the accused. The *question préalable* was the result of an interlocutory sentence, pronounced before the court had rendered a decision as to the guilt status of the accused. The *question préparatoire* was the result of a definitive sentence and sought information concerning the accomplices of the condemned. Torture was distinguished not only in relationship to the legal status of the accused but also according to its physical form. In Toulouse, the *parlement* relied on three forms of torture—the *estrapade* (the strappado), the *question d'eau* (the water torture), and the *brodequins* or *mordaches*. Each method is described in detail in the text. Records of interrogations conducted under torture or before execution were known as *procès-verbaux*.

All translations from the original French are my own unless otherwise noted.

TORTURED SUBJECTS

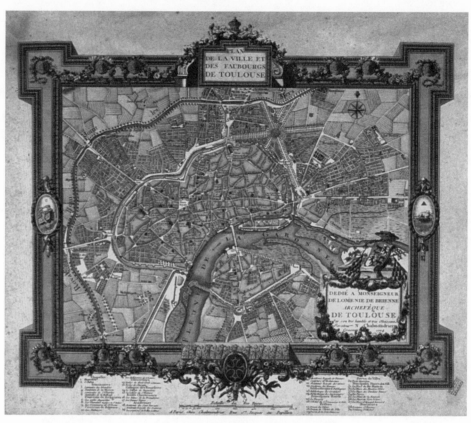

Map of Toulouse by Chalmandrier, no. 2.017. Courtesy of Musée Paul-Dupuy, Toulouse, Cliché S.T.C.

INTRODUCTION

In 1762, Jean Calas died, broken on the wheel, convicted of the murder of his eldest son. Tortured before his execution to reveal the names of his accomplices, he remained silent. Calas was a Protestant living in Toulouse who stood accused of having murdered his son to prevent the latter's conversion to Roman Catholicism. After his execution, his youngest surviving son fled to Geneva to elicit the support of Voltaire in his quest to clear the family name. What began as a simple charge of murder became an international cause célèbre, a challenge to the justice system and to its methods.[1] Through the Calas case, Voltaire and other philosophes embarked on a searching critique of old regime justice.

Thirty-six years before the Calas case was heard, another man stood accused in the *parlement* of Toulouse. Jean Bourdil, charged with the murder of two soldiers, was tortured on the presumption of his guilt. Like Calas, Bourdil denied any guilt in the case; like Calas, he was sentenced on the strength of the evidence against him despite his protestations of innocence.[2] Yet no one came to Bourdil's defense; no one decried his torture. What happened during the intervening years that judicial torture came to represent the inequities of the justice system and, as such, came to arouse public outrage?

In the last third of the eighteenth century, after centuries of the legal practice of torture, *parlementaires* and philosophes were engaged in a debate about the meaning and function of torture. *Parlementaires* defended the practice in language inspired by theology; philosophes attacked it in terms drawn from science and medicine. Yet the debate over torture was more than a debate about the nature of legal evidence. It was a debate about the meaning of human experience. At its heart was a reevaluation of the experience of pain, the uses of the body, and the definition of truth. The formal resolution of the debate through the abolition of torture and the rejection of human suffering as a means to knowledge has remained with us as one of the fundamental legacies of the Enlightenment.

This book explores the extraordinary shift from a generalized acceptance to a generalized rejection of coerced testimony, of judicial torture, and of pain itself through an examination of sources produced in Toulouse and elsewhere in France between 1600 and 1788. The argument, in essence, is the following: that torture at one time was a meaningful cultural practice as well as a functional legal practice. As such, it rested upon an implicit consensus concerning the nature of pain, of truth, and of the body. As that consensus broke down, as the definitions of these three terms shifted and eroded over the course of the seventeenth and eighteenth centuries, so too did the epistemological foundation of torture shift and erode until, by the late eighteenth century, it had come to be a culturally indefensible practice.

Although the debate about torture was conducted by elites, the abolition of torture and all that it implied was a legal and cultural change not confined to their experience. Members of the popular classes, far more often the victims of torture than were those engaged in defining the terms of the debate, were most directly affected by legal reforms, despite the fact that they avoided the state justice system whenever possible. Private justice remained for them an important method of settling disputes.[3] Judgment in the courts was a last resort for nonelites, a method as often imposed on them by officers of the state as it was freely chosen by them. Lacking the formal training of *parlementaires* and philosophes, nonelites were excluded from the debate about torture. Their ideas and opinions counted for little. Today, individual and collective understandings among the populace of the justice system and its methods, of the place of pain in human experience, are less accessible to us than those among the elites.

Yet while barred from active participation in political processes and the *parlement*, attitudes among the populace nonetheless formed an important part of the changing consensus regarding the practice of torture. Even as it appears that the lived experience of the popular and elite classes grew ever more distinct over the course of the seventeenth and eighteenth centuries, it would be artificial to overemphasize the separation of popular and elite cultures in early modern France. Although peasants and artisans were shut out of learned debate, *parlementaires* and philosophes continued to participate in popular rituals in ways that reflected their support of and belief in popular traditions. Engaged in and aware of both the little and the great cultural traditions, *parlementaires* and philosophes brought to the debate about torture attitudes, ideas, and opinions that they shared with nonelites.[4] In the context of a culture that cared deeply about the problems of embodiment and disembodiment, torture aroused deep passion.[5]

In early modern France, there were competing and overlapping discourses of pain to which to subscribe, discourses that gained and lost dominance but that never entirely disappeared. In the realm of the professions, jurists, theologians, and medical practitioners disagreed as to the relative meanings and merits of pain: should pain be understood as a just punishment from God, as a spiritual opportunity, or as a simple symptom of underlying corruption? These understandings coexisted in the culture, and it was incumbent upon individuals to negotiate their inconsistencies. The evidence suggests that the people of early modern France endorsed different interpretations of pain in different spheres of their lives. That the same jurists who ordered and were present at interrogations under torture themselves engaged in ascetic religious practices including self-flagellation and sought medical relief for pain should suggest that while they were reasonable men, they were not always entirely rational men. Their lives reflected some fundamental inconsistencies, inconsistencies that they shared with the culture at large. To seek pure rationality in the actions of the dead is to seek to diminish the complexity of the past.

Parlementaires thinking about pain employed some of the cultural tools available to them. They understood pain in part through the perspective of religion, surrounded as they were by images of suffering in their churches and confraternal chapels. The philosophes with whom they argued, by contrast, sought to combat these sacramental understandings of pain, understandings that these judges shared with the peasants on whom they sat in judgment. The fierce debate in which these elites were engaged persisted because there was no broad agreement about how to understand suffering or how to treat pain, no agreement as to whether pain and suffering were one and the same, no agreement as to whether human suffering served some metaphysical purpose. A chorus of voices argued for competing interpretations. Yet in the Toulousain context they came to the debate from a common history.

Although judicial torture was everywhere an integral part of the early modern French criminal procedure, Toulouse is arguably the best place to study the practice of torture because it was distinguished among French cities by its possession of the longest and most infamous history of this form of interrogation. During the eighteenth century it was publicly identified as the city and the *parlement* most committed to and engaged in the practice of torture. Indeed, in letters concerning the Calas case, Voltaire wrote of the Languedoc as "the land of fanaticism."[6] Whatever the truth of that assertion, from the establishment of municipal inquisitors in the thirteenth century to the notorious Calas case in the eighteenth century, Toulouse witnessed an intense struggle about the meaning of the body and bodily experience in the context of secular culture.

Judicial torture was first employed in Toulousain courts during the thirteenth century by the town consuls, when they began to supplement accusatorial procedure with inquisitorial procedure and to suppress private panels of arbitrators in favor of judges who received their authority from the consuls.[7] The use of torture was, in fact, viewed by the consuls as a municipal privilege to be guarded against the seigneurial incursions of the counts of Toulouse and their vicars, an indispensable aspect of the right of courts that relied ever more on traditions of Roman law.[8] In the thirteenth and fourteenth centuries, the right to inflict pain on those accused in criminal cases became as much a mark of the political autonomy of the municipal consuls from lordly domination as it was a tool of domination and discipline of local populations, a political issue in the struggle among the consuls, the counts of Toulouse, and the Capetian kings. The effort to maintain local autonomy in the face of seigneurial and royal aggression was not, of course, particular to Toulouse and the Languedoc, but was replicated in other cities.

During this period of political instability, the employment of Roman law by municipal courts and consuls in the Languedoc was supported by the French crown, which treated Roman law in the south of France as a form of local customary law to be upheld by royal courts. Support of municipal courts and customs was, therefore, a tool employed by the French crown to undermine local nobles by granting greater autonomy to municipalities theoretically under independent noble control and seigneurial law in an effort to win their support. At the same time, the crown, in the process of creating a new court of appeals in the *parlement* of Paris, itself came to rely on traditions of canon and Roman law.[9] Through the *parlement* of Paris and, ultimately, through all of the provincial *parlements*, the employment of inquisitorial procedures, including torture, based in Roman law—procedures employed in the Languedoc before its incorporation into the possessions of the French kings—were confirmed and spread throughout the realm. With the adoption of Roman law, the crown, too, was enabled to employ torture as an evidentiary procedure. And by gradually limiting the independent employment of specific procedures permitted under Roman law to the *parlement*, like the use of judicial torture, the crown further subordinated local courts to its control without curtailing their right to pronounce sentences.

Torture in the Languedoc was associated not only with municipal and royal courts but also with the ecclesiastical courts of the Albigensian Crusades of the thirteenth century and with the continuing attempt by the Capetian kings to incorporate the region into the kingdom of France, with an intended loss of local authority and local custom.[10] The Crusades were, in fact, unsuccessful in ending local political authority through their attacks on local elites. Indeed, as noted above, in Toulouse they served to expand municipal liberties at the expense of the rights of the counts of Toulouse.

And although it is true that Dominican inquisitors were infamous for their use of torture as a tool against heresy, they seem to have adopted the use of torture only after its employment by municipal authorities.[11] Given the church's prohibition on bloodshed by its officers, ecclesiastical authorities faced different questions than did secular authorities when considering the legitimacy of the use of torture and carried on debates independent of state officials concerning the appropriateness of physical coercion.[12] There were, therefore, important differences between the secular and ecclesiastical uses of torture that today demand independent investigations.

Judicial torture was introduced into the Languedoc at a moment of political crisis and was employed by a wide variety of courts. Its institutionalization in the royal courts testified to the resolution of that crisis. Torture was one of many legal tools employed by municipal consuls and by the Capetian kings in their joint effort to undermine the power of local nobles. Yet it was not so much a simple tool of coercion as it was a means of gathering evidence, which reflected a new methodology and a new epistemology.[13] The employment of judicial torture must therefore be understood not only within this political context but also within a legal and institutional context that recognized the existence of the patchwork of law that included oral custom, written custom, and the learned law, each of which developed with reference to Roman law, each of which was incorporated and enforced by royal courts.[14] Judicial torture became available as a legal procedure when the gradual adoption of principles and practices of Roman law were found to be useful by those who sought to govern the Languedoc. As a legal institution, therefore, judicial torture testified to the political struggles among municipal, seigneurial, ecclesiastical, and royal courts. It came into common usage as those who sought to govern turned to written codes of law to define the boundaries of their legal control, and it served to announce the independence of local political elites from seigneurial control as much as it served to curtail local political conflict through coercion.

But the political and institutional utility of judicial torture is not enough to explain its employment, especially after the thirteenth century, when these questions of political control and loyalty had been answered in theory. The simple availability of torture within the context of Roman law procedure did not require its actual employment. Judicial torture was employed not only because it made political and legal sense but also because it made cultural sense. The legal employment of torture is, therefore, an outstanding instance of the way in which legal institutions reflect broader cultural values. Judicial torture possessed not only an institutional logic but also a cultural logic. It made sense not only as a tool of government but also as a form of testimony. As a cultural institution, torture testified both to the meaningfulness of human suffering and the corresponding valuelessness of human volition, and to the intimate connections among pain, truth, and the body. And it was on these cultural grounds that the eighteenth-century debate was argued. Five hundred years after torture was first employed in Toulouse, *parlementaires* and philosophes came to debate whether human suffering held any meaning; whether truth was produced with or without self-consciousness, whether it existed prior to consciousness or whether it was self-consciously fashioned; and whether the body could produce legal evidence independent of the mind or soul.

For centuries associated with political rebellion, religious dissent, and the use of torture to protect local autonomy and produce testimony, Toulouse is therefore the paradigmatic city from which to view the practice of torture, at once distinct in its own experience and representative of the experience of other provincial *parlements*. The deliberate infliction of suffering in the cause of truth is a history that is peculiarly located in the south of France but that had resonance for all of France.

Suffering is ordained as the essential human condition in Genesis, the price of knowledge. Within the Christian tradition, therefore, suffering is one of the essential ways in which we know that we are human. And as the sin of Adam—the sin of free will—plunged humanity into the world of suffering, so the suffering of Christ holds out the promise of redemption from sin. The promise of Christ—the new Adam who voluntarily takes on human suffering in order to relieve it—is that redemption means salvation from the human condition of pain, suffering, and mortality, in addition to salvation from sin.[15]

But what of the mundane experience of pain and suffering? How were the faithful to understand the pain that they daily endured? In the early modern period, suffering was represented by the Roman Catholic Church as an ennobling experience that permits the faithful to identify with the Savior through imitation—and by heretics, as an experience that permits the enthusiast, like Christ, to redeem suffering by choosing suffering.[16] In specific religious contexts, physical suffering was viewed as a positive technique for the destruction of selfishness, of ego, so as to make room in the heart for God.[17] To suffer was to eliminate the self, the will, and self-consciousness in order to make room for God, God's will, and consciousness of the divine. Intentionally to reenact the pain of Christ, through ascetic practices ranging from retrenchment of sleep to self-flagellation, was also to relieve the burden of the Savior by taking back the suffering that defines humanity. Suffering thus performed many functions: it served to permit identification with Christ; to relieve the burden of Christ; like him, to redeem the suffering of others; and to destroy the self and the will. This religious understanding of pain is one that the *parlementaires* drew on in the courts, in their discussions of the meaning and function of torture, and in the streets, in religious devotions that included their participation in penitential processions.

Much as chosen suffering sought to crush the rebellious will and thereby to make spiritual space for the indwelling truth of God, so too did judicial torture, by inflicting pain on an accused, seek to destroy the willfulness that diminished the truth of testimony. Truth was, by implication, a spontane- ous production, not a composed one. The theology of original sin suggests that human will is always tainted, that what is willed by human beings is always already corrupt. In this context, to tell the truth voluntarily is a near impossibility, precisely because it is human will that is suspect. As a logical extension of this theology, French criminal procedure implied that only by bypassing the will, by eliciting testimony that is not willed, that is not the product of human intent, could pure truth be achieved. Judicial torture therefore sought not only verbal testimony but also bodily evidence that escaped the willful control of the self, evidence that might take the physical form of blushes, silences, and tears. Torture inflicted pain as a means of achieving the spontaneous truth of the body rather than the composed truth of the mind. Torture sought the evidence of an animate body that could not dissimulate.

And it was precisely this attempt to destroy human will through pain as a means of achieving truth that aroused the objections of the philosophes. In their attacks on torture, Enlightenment writers posited a compelling chain of assertions regarding bodily experience, assertions that continue to underlie our understanding of the relationship of human agency and hu- man experience. The philosophes asserted not that will and truth were op- posed but that will and the body were opposed, that pain and personal agency could not coexist in one body, that personal agency was the highest cultural good, and that pain was therefore profoundly opposed to per- sonhood, to politics, and to culture itself.[18] Protest against torture came from a growing sense that physical pain could serve no good or useful pur- pose. The protest against torture in this way was part of a broader protest against the penal system, public execution, and other physical punish- ments, including branding and flogging. Seen in this light, the end of legal torture was bound up with a reevaluation of the ontological status of pain, of the very utility of pain.

The early modern period was, therefore, a moment during which both the body and pain were self-consciously reconceptualized. By the end of the eighteenth century, the body was no longer understood as a vehicle connecting the sacred and the profane. The active pursuit of physical pain was no longer understood as a form of spiritual perfection, of *imitatio christi*, but as a sickness or a form of sexual perversity.[19] Pain itself was likewise understood as an empty or negative response to physical stimuli even as spiritual and psychic pain continued to be valued through the doctrine of sensibility.[20] Once associated with spiritual perfection and ultimate meaning, pain came to be associated with physical corruption and meaninglessness.[21]

The Enlightenment vision was therefore deeply at odds with the Christian evaluation of the relationships among pain and truth, will and the body, and must be understood as part of the desacralization of the eighteenth century. From viewing the infliction of pain as a positive technique for the destruction of selfishness to viewing pain as a negative technique for the destruction of the self, from viewing pain as a human experience that is central to culture and that expresses human longing for closeness to or imitation of divinity to viewing pain as an animalistic experience that shuts people out of culture and even out of their true identities and that must therefore be avoided at all costs—this is the shift in thinking that this book will explore.

These changes proceeded slowly and unevenly. The sacramental embrace of pain, which was predominant in the seventeenth century and implicitly endorsed by the courts, was challenged as early as the 1650s.[22] The secular vision of pain, which had the support of both surgeons and philosophes and which became the lens through which torture was viewed, emerged no later than the 1680s. But it must again be emphasized that these two distinctive styles of understanding coexisted for a long period of time before the tensions between them became unbearable. It was only when those differences were made public and explicit—certainly by the 1760s in the published protests over the Calas affair—that the French were forced publicly to reevaluate the status of pain.

The principal sources for this study include the dossiers compiled in criminal cases, the sentences to torture, and the interrogations under torture produced by the *parlement* of Toulouse from 1600 to 1788, the year in which torture was formally abolished. But how far can we trust these sources, written by the very jurists who ordered the torture of persons accused of capital crimes? Studies of torture raise the problem of evidence most pointedly. Torture is always at the center of an epistemological crisis because it always forces us to reconsider the relationship between coercion and truth, between free will and evidence. Torture demands that we consider what it is we mean by documentary proof. It requires that we examine our easy elision of truth, evidence, and proof.

Torture raises this epistemological problem on a number of levels. First, there is the question of the preservation of documents pertaining to torture, whether those documents are the physical implements of torture, the written records of interrogations, or the written or oral recollections of those who witnessed, participated in, or suffered acts of torture. Why are such documents created in the first place, and preserved, in the second place? What does the preservation of such documents mean? Second, there is the question of the nature of the evidence sought through torture. Do torturers look for new information, for confirmation of information already possessed, or is the process utterly unconnected to the collection of information? And where is this information located—in words or in gestures? Finally, there is the question of truth. If we can demonstrate the accuracy of the records of torture, can we also demonstrate that victims tell the truth under torture? When they impart accurate information, is that the same thing as telling the truth? When they impart inaccurate information, is that the same thing as lying?

Historians of early modern Europe have taken up the problem of evidence with great energy, inquiring into the purposes of writing, the problems of preservation, and the relationship between the written and the lived. Historians who work with official documents produced by notaries, whether those documents are marriage contracts, minutes of guild meetings, or criminal court records, have been in the forefront of those considering the problems raised by the creation and preservation of written documents.[23]

In the regions of Roman law, notarial transcriptions are judged to be accurate representations of oral events, despite the fact that they did not always record dialogue verbatim.[24] On some occasions, rather than record each speaker, notaries imposed a verbal order where none existed, representing speech as an impersonal and collective enterprise. In the event that notaries did record dialogue verbatim, as in Italian criminal court proceedings, these transcriptions are as close as we can come to the oral culture and the specific and personal perspectives of the illiterate.[25]

If notarial transcriptions are accurate records of oral events, are they also accurate records of the truth? Historians are divided on this question. Some historians assert that people lied to judges in interrogations so as to shield themselves from the law; some have argued with great sensitivity that such "lies" need to be read not as devices to protect individuals from further prosecution but rather as instances of cultural and moral conflict.[26] Others note that denials of self-incriminating evidence disappear after oath-taking; in other words, that people took oaths with great seriousness and strove not to perjure themselves, but to tell the truth whatever the cost to themselves.[27]

Documentary evidence produced not by notaries but by private individuals caught up in criminal proceedings also presents an ambiguous picture. It appears from these sources that sometimes people told the truth as they knew it, a truth sometimes unlike the truth of the jurists and notaries; that sometimes they lied deliberately; and that sometimes they were themselves convinced by the legal proceedings that the truth was not what they said of their own volition but was what they said under torture.[28]

When we study torture, we are studying documents produced by *greffiers* (clerks of the courts), which are, like other notarial records, accurate records of oral events. The question of truth or falsity does not arise at the documentary level. As they sat at their desks in the prisons, quill, ink, paper, and sand arrayed before them, the *greffiers* did not produce complete confessions awaiting only a coerced signature. They accurately recorded the verbal exchange of the interrogation, writing to keep pace with the interrogation as it progressed. Whether defendants spoke the truth—and what truth means in the context of torture—is less apparent. But here I am less concerned with whether the events reported and the deeds confessed actually occurred, less concerned with whether defendants told the truth, than I am with their truth status in the courts. In other words, I am less interested in whether a given defendant committed murder than I am in whether confessions to murder given under torture were taken to be truthful.

The sources available for the study of the practice of torture were generated at successive stages of an investigation by various officials of the justice system. Three kinds of documents exist: *dossiers*, containing items ranging from arrest warrants to witness interviews to experts' reports; interlocutory and definitive sentences pronounced by the *parlement;* and interrogations conducted under torture. In addition, seventeenth- and eighteenth-century legal manuals occasionally reprinted sentences and interrogations to serve as examples of procedure for their readership. I deal with documents that were produced by the *parlement* of Toulouse, with sentences to torture and with interrogations conducted under torture.[29] Sentences and interrogations are written records of oral events, whose purpose was not only to record the event so that there would be documentary evidence that demonstrated that the event had in fact occurred, but also to communicate specific information derived through oral exchange to persons not present at the event.[30]

Sentences were prepared and preserved in multiple drafts and copies.

The first draft copy, written on a loose folio of paper and often stamped with the seal of the examining court, was placed in the dossier and assigned a letter and a descriptive tag on the verso that helped to identify its proper location in the file. A large dossier might run through the alphabet several times, for example, from "A" to "ZZZ." If the sentence pronounced by the examining court required review by the *parlement,* a second draft copy of the sentence was added to the registers of the criminal chamber of the *parlement.* This second draft copy began with an accounting of the legal history of a case, a listing of all the previous sentences and documents involved in the case, as a means of providing a paper trail. It next incorporated whatever changes in the sentence were deemed necessary by the *parlement* after review of the evidence as represented by the dossier. In many instances, no changes were required, and the *parlement* simply confirmed the sentence of the lower court with the phrase "la Cour ordonne que ladite sentence sortira son plein et entier effet et sera executée suivant sa forme et teneur" (the Court orders that the said sentence will have its full and entire effect and will be executed following its form and terms). This kind of shorthand means that some cases of torture are invisible in the registers, because there is no explicit reference in the sentence to torture.

Sentences were made to serve both as historical records of the decision of the court and as administrative communications to the persons whose task it was to carry out the terms of the sentence. On occasion, sentences also served as communications to persons witnessing the fulfillment of the terms of the sentence because sentences were read aloud at public executions, if at no other public punishments. This reading aloud was not an essential act in the eyes of the law and did not contribute to the legal force of the sentence. As proof of this, one might cite the use of *retentums.* Many sentences had attached *retentums* to them, instructions appended to the main body of the sentence that were to remain secret by not being read aloud but that were nonetheless legally binding. It was the written form of the sentence, therefore, that carried legal weight, not the act of reading the sentence aloud. The written sentence was not simply a record of a completed event, but instructions for an event that had not yet occurred.

In theory, these sentences also served as administrative references that could be consulted as a guide to the practice of the *parlement.* In fact, the bound registers of the criminal chamber virtually prohibit use of their contents as effective administrative reference sources. Although the contents of the registers are arranged chronologically, since each entry was added in turn to the empty register, the volumes have no system of indexing whatsoever. Cases could not be relocated by the names of the accused, by the crimes of which they were accused, or by the punishments meted out. The only way to search these registers was by the date of the sentence, so that one would have to be familiar with a specific case before these registers could be of any practical reference use. Once a given case was located in the register, however, the careful notation of the legal history of the case that opened each sentence provided a clear path to search out the legal history of that case. As documents, then, the function of the sentences was to communicate a series of instructions and to record the fact of those instructions. They were not intended to provide an easily employed guide to the general practice of the court, although they did provide clear information as regards specific sentences.

Interrogations were preserved in a single copy.[31] They, too, were assigned a letter and a descriptive tag on the verso, so that they could be placed in the dossier for judicial review of the entire case. Upon completion of the trial, they were intended to remain with the *dossier*. They constituted, therefore, one of many pieces of evidence to be found in the *dossier* and were not seen as exceptional in any way. They were not intended to be consulted as a class of documents unto themselves but were intended to be read only in the context of the specific case. Many *dossiers* that originated in lower courts have been lost. Among those that remain, the majority are bundled together by year. As is the case with sentences, they are not indexed in any way and are difficult to consult. In the nineteenth century, an archivist at the Archives Départementales de la Haute Garonne systematically removed extant interrogations and *procès-verbaux d'exécution* from their *dossiers* and bound them together in a single subseries. Both kinds of documents can be resituated in their original *dossiers* thanks to their identifying letters and descriptions.

Like sentences, interrogations served as both historical records and as administrative communications. After the interrogation was concluded, it was read aloud to all its participants, who were then required to countersign the record of the interrogation both to confirm that the preceding events had occurred as the document recorded them and to indicate their willingness to support the legality of the document. The documents also served as communications: as not all judges in a case were required to be present when the accused was tortured, it was the responsibility of the *rapporteur* to create a record of the interrogation so that his fellow judges could be privy to all the information that was derived through torture.

There is no evidence to suggest that interrogations served as administrative references to provide guidance as to past practice. Interrogations seem not to have been consulted once a case was closed. They were of use only for the duration of a specific case. The one instance in which interrogations might have been used as a guide to past practice is reported by Pierre

Barthès, a Toulousain diarist who wrote between 1737 and 1780.[32] In 1778, he notes that a woman had been sentenced to be tortured and that no one could remember the procedure for the torture of women. He writes that "they were at pains to know what this sort of *question* was, because it had been forty-three years since they gave the *question* to a woman, but after some searching, they found an instrument called the *mordaches.*"[33] Barthès's account indicates the uselessness of interrogations as administrative references in the utter failure to locate court documents as a guide to practice at the same time as it suggests the length of the living memory of the court.

Sentences and interrogations, like other legal documents produced by notaries, were accurate records of oral events. They were produced to serve as essential communications to interested parties and as records of past events. They were not produced to provide an accessible guide to past practice. They were preserved almost accidentally, tucked into *dossiers* that were tossed into storage rooms, of no particular interest to anyone upon the conclusion of a case.

At the same time, the way in which these documents were recorded changed over time, as different pieces of information were gradually inserted and as different linguistic formulas were seen to be essential. In other words, once the form of the sentence or interrogation was standardized, changes in that standardized form reflect cultural concerns not to do with the preservation of evidence per se. Changes in the written form of interrogations point to changes in the requirements of the judges, changes in their understandings of what was significant in a criminal case. Sentences and interrogations are therefore useful not only in establishing the frequency and method of employment of specific legal practices but also in ascertaining changing elite understandings of crime, law, and proof. On the rare instances where they record dialogue verbatim—which, for the purposes of this study, is taken to mean moments where dialogue is reported in direct rather than indirect discourse, in the first rather than in the third person—they may also be useful in elucidating the perspectives of the popular classes.

Why is this study significant? In the first place, examination of the practice of torture matters because it reveals ways in which the early modern body was believed to be possessed of different proportions and capabilities than is the modern body. Historians have already suggested that during the early modern period, the body was seen to be permeable, open to universal influences, and grotesque in its openness.[34] It was this permeable body that was at the core of numerous early modern debates concerning the nature of authority, from debates over the nature of the Eucharist to debates about the nature and location of monarchical authority.[35] And it was this body that was gradually reconceptualized and redefined over the course of this period. Despite important differences between the early modern and the modern conceptions of the body, some of the language used to describe the body, bodily experience, and the relationship of the body to the self is employed in both periods. For this reason, it is essential that we uncover the origins of the language we use to describe the human body, its relationship to the individual agent and to the body politic.

In the second place, this study opens up legal documents for cultural analysis.[36] The practice of torture has traditionally been examined within a legal historiographical context. Legal historians have treated the problem of torture as a problem wholly internal to the law and have argued that legal reforms of the seventeenth century rendered torture obsolete. They therefore fail to account for the continued use of torture over the course of the eighteenth century. For while it is unquestionably the case that torture was employed with diminishing frequency over the centuries, thanks in large measure to new standards of proof and new forms of punishment, it is also true that judges continued to sentence individuals to torture for more than a century after its proclaimed obsolescence. And so, given the real strengths of this legal historical argument, we must examine phenomena other than the law to account for torture's persistence. The documents examined here—from legal manuals and trial records, to confraternal statutes and surgical texts, to causes célèbres and philosophical tracts—are extraordinarily rich sources that contain a wealth of information about the meaning of torture. By placing torture within a cultural context, I argue that cultural changes *as well as* legal changes undermined the use of torture.

Finally, in the broadest and most tentative sense, this study has something to contribute, if only indirectly, to our own understandings of the problem of the body. Many of our own uncertainties about the nature and limits of the body find their origin in these seventeenth- and eighteenth-century struggles to articulate a new understanding of the body. Our own efforts to shape a cultural consensus around such issues as the patenting of cell lines and the sale of organs, abortion and surrogacy, suicide and capital punishment—each of which is centrally concerned with the question, who owns the body?—owe a tremendous amount to these earlier discussions of the body.

Despite its importance within the early modern French legal system, torture has only recently become a focus of historical attention.[37] This is perhaps in part because of the difficulties scholars encounter when trying to define torture. Do we mean by torture the legal or the illegal use of force? The use of force by state or nonstate agents? As a historian, my training urges me to take seriously the ways in which my sources—my subjects—define matters. In early modern France, torture had a clear legal definition that distinguished it from other painful practices. When early modern French jurists spoke about torture, they referred to the legal employment of pain by state agents in the context of a carefully regulated evidentiary procedure. They did not include in this definition the legal employment of pain for punitive purposes or the extralegal employment of pain by state or nonstate agents. This book, which seeks to understand the meanings of torture in the early modern context, adopts this definition. My decision to employ early modern definitions as a means of coming to terms with the prejudices of the elites who devised them, of respecting the peculiarities of my subjects, sets my work apart from that of scholars who use the word *torture* to refer to the many uses of violence in early modern society.[38] Although this is, therefore, a somewhat different approach from that employed by many other scholars, I hope it will be carefully considered because I believe that one way of honoring the suffering of the past is to take it seriously on its own terms, however repugnant those terms may be to us. That said, I would like to briefly examine the historical literature as it pertains to torture per se.

There are several characteristic approaches to the study of torture. Social historians, for example, turn to legal documents to place torture within a context of statistical analyses of crime and punishment. More concerned with social relations as expressed through criminal behavior than with elite ideas concerning the nature of evidence, these studies do not consider torture as a distinct problem. They therefore fail to distinguish clearly the public form and punitive purpose of punishment from the private form and interrogative purpose of torture.[39] But torture needs to be addressed as a separate issue because the expressed purpose of torture differed from that of punishment. Furthermore, the problem of torture engages questions of the body and of epistemology that studies of crime and punishment cannot. These epistemological questions have little to do with the statistical profiles constructed by scholars in regional studies of crime and punishment but take as their point of departure the meaning of the practice of torture.

Institutional historians, on the other hand, straightforwardly describe the regulated use of torture as one aspect of early modern criminal procedure.[40] They clarify the function of torture within this procedural model, occasionally imputing social values to the justice system as a whole. David Jacobson, for example, represents torture as illustrative of old regime

brutality and authoritarianism; Adhemar Esmein condemns it as a violation
of human dignity corrected by the reforms of the Revolution.[41] Their conclusions are supported by other historians who hold that the philosophic goals
of the Enlightenment were the driving forces behind legal reform.[42] Drawing on the writings of jurists and reformers, these authors locate the abolition of torture within a progressive interpretation of law and society.[43]

Legal historians oppose themselves to both of these readings. Rejecting
the view that torture was abolished primarily on philosophic grounds, John
Langbein argues that the formal abolition of torture in the eighteenth century—not only in France but also throughout Europe—simply capped two
centuries of de facto legal reform by magistrates.[44] He suggests that new
legal penalties, formally introduced in the seventeenth century, which required lower standards of proof, paved the way for the abolition. When
criminal convictions could be brought without full proof, the need for coerced confessions was obviated. Langbein posits a disjunction between the
theory and practice of criminal law, noting that jurists routinely punished
individuals without complete proof before legal mechanisms regulated such
action. The abolition of torture in the 1780s, he argues, was simply the
formal legal recognition of this change in actual practice.

Archival evidence has modified this thesis. Scholars have been able to
demonstrate that while the use of torture most certainly diminished over
time, that trend began before the introduction of formal legislation that
provided for criminal penalties in the absence of full proof.[45] In Paris, the
use of torture declined steadily, from an annual mean of four cases of the
question préalable from 1539 to 1542, to only one or two cases a year by the
early seventeenth century.[46] Confessions under torture likewise declined,
from 8.5 percent of cases around 1540 to 2.3 percent of cases by the beginning of the seventeenth century.[47] In his studies of Parisian courts, Alfred
Soman asserts that after 1670, torture was employed as a means of fright-
ening prisoners into confessions rather than actually extorting confessions
from them, despite the fact that he finds a diminishing rate of confession.[48]
In Brittany in the seventeenth century, there was a comparable pattern of
diminution: from 1600 to 1650, the *parlement* of Brittany pronounced an
annual mean number of 27.6 sentences to the *question préalable* and 4.8
sentences to the *question préparatoire;* and from 1651 to 1700, an annual
mean number of 12.7 sentences to the *question préalable* and 0.72 sentences
to the *question préparatoire.* Here, too, rates of confession were low; in only
8.3 percent of cases in which the *question préparatoire* was employed did
individuals confess legally useful information.[49]

In delineating the decline in both the use of torture and in the rate of confession, scholars have failed to account for the continued reliance on torture. Indeed, most stress the illogic of the continuing practice of torture.[50] While the diminished use of torture is undisputed—my own evidence also supports this finding—the fact remains that jurists did continue to employ it, albeit sparingly, long after scholars argue that it was obsolete. This continued usage suggests two possible conclusions: either capital convictions satisfied judicial officials in a way that afflictive punishments did not and torture thus retained a strict legal significance in achieving such convictions in the very few cases in which confessions were achieved, or torture in itself possessed a cultural significance unacknowledged by many historians.

Michel Foucault implicitly regards torture not only as a legal but as a social practice, though he subsumes his discussion of the practice within a larger study of punishment.[51] He suggests that legal practices must be examined not only for their punitive effects but also for their positive effects, for the ways in which they construct and consolidate communities. In his analysis, torture has significance beyond its immediate function in law.

Over the course of the last twenty years, scholars from disciplines other than history have begun to turn their attention to the problem of torture. They concur with Foucault's contention that torture has a cultural meaning that transcends its legal function. These writers therefore use the study of torture as a means of exploring philosophical problems implicit in the practice of torture.

The classicist Page DuBois, for example, studies torture in ancient Greece because, as the extreme instance of truth-seeking, it permits her to examine classical conceptualizations of truth.[52] Her study is grounded in literary texts as no legal documents involving the use of torture have survived. Torture was legal in the Greek city-states, although it could be employed only on the bodies of slaves. DuBois asserts that torture was fundamental to classical society in that it helped to delineate not merely a social but an epistemological boundary between slaves and citizens: slaves were assumed to speak the truth only under torture because, lacking the ability to reason, they lacked the ability to dissemble as their citizen-masters might. In this formulation, the slave body becomes the site of the truth, which lies outside the community of free men. The search for truth is therefore conceptualized as a heroic voyage beyond this known community. Truth is an artifact to be sought outside the bounds of civilization, beyond reason, whole in itself. This, she concludes, is our classical legacy, this mystical conceptualization of truth: rather than truth as process, built up within a community of speakers, created through shared observation and consensus, we have truth as product, an artifact to be discovered. In her study, torture is treated as a vehicle for examining these competing conceptualizations of the truth, rather than as a legal or cultural institution in itself.

Elaine Scarry, on the other hand, writing about the nature of pain and imagination, examines torture as the extreme example of pain infliction.[53] The primary function of torture is, in her analysis, to rob the victim of an authentic voice and to transfer the incontestability of pain from the suffering body to the unstable regime. Illegal state torture thus functions not only politically to suppress vocal opposition but grammatically to appropriate the voice of the people for the regime, thereby stripping the populace of its own voice, forced to mouth the words of the regime. She equates the infliction of pain with the suppression of language and the diminution of pain with its expression through language, thereby positing a constant relationship between expressing pain and eliminating pain. Thus, the end of suffering is achieved in the articulation of pain, by the victim or by those speaking on the victim's behalf. The infliction of such pain through torture is "an absolute of immorality," distinguished from pain inflicted by war only by its lack of consent.[54] She further identifies both torture and war as "the two events in which the ordinary assumptions of culture are suspended."[55] She concludes her analysis by suggesting that if human labor is the extension of the self in the world, then pain, by making the body so persistently present as to extinguish the imagination, is the experience that prevents such self-extension.

Scarry's study is unquestionably the most humane and thoughtful examination of the contemporary practice of torture, but she overextends her interpretation in her consistent representation of torture as a cross-cultural and transhistorical phenomenon.[56] In her examination of the international proliferation of euphemisms for torture ("the telephone," "the birthday party," "the parrot's perch") and torture rooms ("the production room," "the blue-lit stage," "the guest room"), for example, Scarry astutely identifies "the torturer's idiom [that] not only indicates but helps bring about the process of perception in which all human reality is made, no matter how screamingly present, invisible, inaudible."[57] Yet she fails to acknowledge explicitly that her analysis is based on the contemporary and illegal practice of torture. In France in the eighteenth century, there were no euphemisms for torture because there was no need to render the reality of pain invisible, no need to deny the process: the publicly and legally acknowledged purpose of judicial torture was precisely to render truth visible and audible through the infliction of pain.

Similarly, in her assertion that what distinguishes torture from war is the lack of consent of its "participants," she states that "in war, the persons whose bodies are used . . . have given their consent over this most radical use of the human body while in torture no such consent is exercised."[58] If the consent of soldiers to fight and die is understood to be a generalized cultural consent rather than a particular and individual consent, then the contemporary illegal practice of torture is truly a nonconsensual practice. But in early modern France, torture differed in no way from other components of the legal system in that as a legal procedure it, too, partook of such a general cultural consent.[59] The issue of consent is an issue grounded in the contemporary moment; it is not a transhistorical feature of torture. Or again, when Scarry states that torture and war are "the two events in which ordinary assumptions of culture are suspended," her statement functions to place these practices outside of contemporary culture. Yet the practice of torture did not always require such a suspension of cultural assumptions: indeed, in the early modern practice of judicial torture many ordinary assumptions of early modern culture are not merely present but are most readily grasped.

In Scarry's discussion, pain, perhaps owing to its physiological universality, is denied cultural mutability. For Scarry, pain has a primary meaning, and that meaning is the negation of the essence of humanity in its suppression of imagination. Yet pain, like truth, is grounded in culture and history, and it has many meanings, which vary according to time and place.[60] Indeed, Scarry herself briefly acknowledges this in an examination of the penitent. She acknowledges a deliberate search for pain in penitential practices like self-flagellation and raises the issue of self-inflicted pain in order to distinguish it from the extreme negativity of other-inflicted suffering in their differing degrees of duration, control, and purpose.[61] That is to say, she raises for a moment the possibility of pain as a chosen experience that has real and acknowledged cultural value, only to return to her dominant vision of pain as pure negativity associated with the loss of autonomy. The distinctions Scarry creates between the experiences of willing penitents and unwilling victims are important and deserving of further consideration. In a culture in which the ritualized infliction of pain has ceased to be meaningful, the experience of pain may well be one of intense negativity. However, in any culture in which pain continues to be highly valued in the sacred sphere, it must be carefully assessed when it appears in secular practice.

Theorizing about the reappearance of torture in the modern world, Scarry notes that the infliction of pain occurs most frequently at moments of political instability, suggesting that pain is used to stabilize regimes by lending them its incontestability. Drawing from this twentieth-century model, one might therefore anticipate that the practice of judicial torture in early modern France would peak at moments of political crisis—perhaps

in the 1630s and 1640s during the Fronde, and again in the years immediately preceding the revolution. But in fact, the use of judicial torture in the
Languedoc declined steadily from 1600 on and experienced a dramatic
drop around 1650.

In the discussions of torture provided by DuBois and Scarry, the problem of truth has become the province of the historian, and the problem of
pain, that of the philosopher. But torture is—or was—both truth seeking
and pain inflicting. It needs, therefore, to be studied not in terms of one of
these features, either truth seeking or pain infliction, but as and in itself.
And it must be studied in this way because our very ability to distinguish
these two central features *as* separate features depends upon epistemological changes that occurred in the eighteenth century. As long as pain was
viewed as a meaningful experience connecting body and soul, the sacred
and the profane, torture was construed as a single metaphysical activity, an
activity grounded in the physical body that had ramifications for the
"ghostly" body. But once pain was reconceptualized and represented as a
meaningless and mechanical physiological response devoid of social meaning, torture lost its integrity and its perceived ability to draw the truth from
the body. The task, therefore, is to redraw the connections between truth
and pain, the body and language, to refashion the judicial world in which
the infliction of pain could indeed draw truth from the body just as a knife
draws blood.

PART ONE

An Epistemology of Pain

When we think and talk about torture in the modern moment, we tend to imagine situations in which pain is inflicted on a victim cruelly and arbitrarily by a governing regime for no purpose other than the physical and psychological destruction of its enemies. We do not believe that torture produces reliable evidence, despite our acknowledgment that some truths are spoken under torture. The only certain product of torture, we believe, is pain, and the fear it leaves in its wake.

In early modern France, by contrast, torture was not employed arbitrarily at the will of interrogators. Rather, carefully considered procedural rules suggested its use in specific circumstances and with the authority of specific courts. Although judges exercised considerable discretion in determining which cases met these rules and, hence, in determining which prisoners to torture, they were not free to choose the specific methods of torture or the length of each session of torture, as they were bound in these matters by legal codes. As the first part of this book examines the legal practice of torture, it explores the meanings, functions, and limits of pain in the context of early modern French law and legal practice.

Chapter 1 employs a single case—the murder trial of a minor municipal officer named Jean Bourdil—to provide a picture of conviction to torture and to elucidate the specific rules governing the practice of torture. This case was chosen because it demonstrates one of the central features of cases that culminated in torture: it was a capital case so confusing, so laden with conflicting evidence that only torture could resolve its ambiguities. Rather than present a tidy narrative of the case, therefore, it will be presented as it appeared to and was recorded by the judges themselves, in all its convoluted chronology.

What guided Bourdil's judges? How did they decide that this was a case in which torture might usefully be employed? Chapter 2 answers this question by providing close readings of the legal manuals on which judges relied. I argue both that judicial understandings of pain and its relationship to truth and the body as expressed in these texts explains their reliance on torture as a meaningful practice, and that legal reforms were therefore the necessary but not the sufficient conditions for the abandonment of torture. The end of torture as a legal practice reflects not only important changes in proof and penalties but also a changed understanding of the desirability of inflicting pain.

Did the practice of torture correspond to the theory outlined in these manuals? My evidence, like that of other historians, demonstrates a dramatic decline in the employment of torture from the beginning of the seventeenth century. But my evidence also demonstrates a continued employment of torture—as does theirs. What supported this continuing practice? Chapter 3 suggests that there were some important differences between theory and practice, differences that hung on the ritualized qualities of the practice of torture. While some historians have discussed the illogic of the practice of torture in the context of the law as problematic, I would point to that illogic in a more positive vein. Torture was intended precisely to move beyond the bounds of logic. Never required by law, rarely successful in achieving confessions, torture was, nonetheless, a regular practice in the *parlements* because only through the practice of torture could judges explore the interconnections among pain, truth, and the body in cases in which truth, proof, and evidence had become elusive and entangled. In their absence, torture persisted because it had a powerful cultural significance.

The *estrapade*. From Jean Milles de Souvigny, *Praxis criminis persequendi* (Paris, 1541). Courtesy of New York Public Library, Spencer Collection.

I

Murder in the rue Noue: The Trials of Jean Bourdil
and the Legal System of Old Regime France

By the spring of 1726, Toulouse was a city of fading grandeur. The city walls enclosed streets of brick facades and stone pavers, rose and dove-toned in the shade, rust and cream-colored in the sun. Long ago those streets had been filled with pilgrims and heretics, with merchants and with rebels. Once the preeminent European supplier of pastel, still an important regional entrepôt, Toulouse had come to rely on the *parlement* and other courts located in the city for its livelihood: the *sénéchal-présidial*, the *Grand Maitres des Eaux et Forêts*, the *grenier à sel, cour des monnaies, capitoulat, bourse des marchands*, and *bureau des finances*. By the early eighteenth century, the city was a more prosaic place than it had once been, an administrative city par excellence that drew immigrants in scores, looking for work and for charity.[1]

In bustling streets too anonymous for residents to greet one another by name, the corporate conventions of early modern French society still permitted them to recognize one another by their dress and by their manner: priests in their black cassocks and prostitutes in their yellow gowns, sooty chimney sweeps and laundresses with their water-roughened hands, professors in their black robes and lawyers in their scarlet ones, tanners stinking of urine and butchers of blood, staggering tailors and trembling hatters, liveried servants, uniformed soldiers, and ragged beggars.[2] Dress served to express not only the gender, the estate, and the occupation of the wearer but also occasioned opportunities for honor and insult: hats respectfully doffed and mockingly torn off, gloves removed as a sign of favor for cere-monial kisses of the hand or insultingly slapped across the face, swords worn elegantly or boorishly, reflecting the true estate and false pretensions of their possessors.[3] Dress likewise served to mask to some small degree the histories etched in the flesh: the weather-reddened skin of peasants and the pallor of woolwashers; the bleeding gums of those suffering from scurvy, the missing teeth of women who had undergone many pregnancies inadequately nourished, and the excessive salivation of syphilitics under-going mercury treatments; the brands burned into the shoulders of con-demned criminals, the slit ears and noses of deserters from the king's armies.[4] The streets were the theater in which identity was performed, and the body was its stage.

By day these streets rang with the calls of merchants and peddlers, the shouted warnings of carters and watercarriers, and the songs of street musicians; with ribald gossip, shared laughter, and whispered threats. As dusk fell and the city faded to gray, the riot of the day ebbed. Dark and murmuring, the streets were transformed.

On the night of 17 April 1726, between eight and nine o'clock in the evening, Etienne Bourret, a hosier's apprentice, heard a commotion in the street outside his window: running footsteps and shouts, and a voice that cried "Tuë, tuë!"[5] Looking out of his window in the rue Noue, in the faubourg Saint Cyprien, he saw five or six men with naked swords in their hands, and another man with a dragoon's saber, all of them running like madmen, some shouting, "I'll kill him," and another, "Here he is!" In the confusion, he heard a voice he knew. Delisle, one of the *archers* attached to the Hôpital de la Grave, whose job it was to round up and detain the indigent poor, was speaking to a soldier: "It's you that I want," the soldier replying, "Messieurs, I'm not here to insult you." Then all together they threw themselves on the soldier. Bourret saw Delisle stab the soldier in the belly, and Bourret cried out the window, "Wretches, I know you all!" The attackers fled, and at the same time Bourret heard the soldier in the street below cry out, "Alas, is there no one in this neighborhood who wants to help a poor person?!"[6]

Bourret's neighbor also overheard the crime. Lying in bed, he heard Pedron, another *archer*, shout, "Come here, you damn bugger!" and then a slap, and the sound of many people running, and a voice that cried, "My God, our Lady of the Rosary, have pity on me! Won't anyone come to help me?"[7]

Shortly thereafter, Jean Anglade, a carder, who was walking home from work with a friend, found a man lying face down on the pavement near the Pont Neuf, his sword sheathed beside him. Thinking that he was drunk, the two men helped him to his feet, but finding that he showed no signs of life, they examined him in the moonlight, and saw that his chest was all bloody and that he was dead of a wound to the stomach. Leaving his friend to guard the corpse, Anglade went for help. Walking in the direction of the Hôpital de la Grave, he ran into Jean Bourdil, yet another of the *archers* attached to the hospital, and told him that he had just found a dead body. Then Anglade went home.

Eventually, the crime was reported to François de Turle de Labresprin, one of the *capitouls*, the municipal judges and governors of Toulouse, probably by Desdassan, the carder Anglade's friend, though the documents are not precise on this point. Two men arrived at the home of de Turle de Labresprin in the rue des Gestes to report that two murders had been committed on the persons of two soldiers.[8] De Turle de Labresprin accordingly summoned François Dutoron, his legal assistant, Jean François Malassus, the clerk of the criminal court, and Jean Baptiste Duclos, captain of the watch, and with an armed guard to accompany them, they set out to begin their investigation.

Near the Pont Neuf, they found the body of a man, dressed in light gray with blue collar and cuffs and gilded leather buttons and a coffee-colored jacket, lying on his back on the pavement, his sword still sheathed beside him. Anglade and Desdassan had evidently turned the body over in the course of their examination. As de Turle de Labresprin examined him, he was informed that there was a second victim not yet dead of his wounds who might still tell him who had committed the crime. Four men were assigned to guard the corpse, while the rest of the company transferred the dying man to the Hôpital St. Jacques, on the banks of the Garonne.

A porter at the hospital put the dying man to bed, where he lay motionless after having received extreme unction. De Turle de Labresprin asked him his name and *qualité*, but the man could neither hear nor respond to the questions. He died within a quarter of an hour. The captain of his regiment, the Flanders Infantry, present by now, asked and was granted permission to search the dead man's clothes and to inventory any money and personal effects. Among those effects was a key to a chest that the soldier kept at his lodgings, in the place de Chayredon, just across the Pont Neuf.

The investigators returned therefore to the *citie* to retrieve the dead man's possessions and to investigate the crime. Bertrand Ignard, the innkeeper at the soldier's lodgings, led them to a room at the back of the second floor and showed them the chest he had lent the dead man, whose name was Pierre Verdieu. In it they found the regimental monies with which he had been entrusted, along with some used clothes, and in the stable they found the dead man's horse, a chestnut with two white feet. They asked Ignard if he knew who had killed his lodger, threatening to search the premises for the assailants, whereupon Ignard denounced the *archers* of the Hôpital de la Grave.

And so de Turle de Labresprin and his entourage crossed the river for a third time that night, returning to the faubourg Saint Cyprien to speak with the *archers*. At the Hôpital de la Grave, they were admitted by a porter, who led them to the guardroom, where they found Louis Prieur, *sous-brigadier*, and Jean Bourdil, *archer*, asleep in bed. The two men were roused and made to dress in the clothes at hand: Prieur in his regulation overcoat, Bourdil in a gray overcoat. A sword lay on a table in the room that, when unsheathed, was discovered to be bloody and nicked along the blade. Bourdil acknowledged the sword as his own but said he did not know where the blood had come from. He had lent the sword to a friend—Delisle—earlier that day, clean, and it had been returned to him within half an hour of its loan. A bloody sword belonging to Prieur was also found, though he said that the blood that covered it was his own, the result of an injury sustained during a disturbance that had disrupted his duties two weeks earlier. Both men were seized and asked to name their accomplices in the crime, and guards were dispatched to search for anyone they might name.

The group now made their way back to the Pont Neuf, where the first corpse, still under guard, was shown to the suspects. Bourdil recognized him as the man with whom he had shared a drink in the tavern Chez Perruque at about eight o'clock the previous evening. Prieur did not recognize him. Bringing the corpse along with them, the group proceeded to the Hôpital St. Jacques. The body of Pierre Verdieu, the man who had died in the hospital, was then shown to them, but neither suspect recognized him. Both Prieur and Bourdil were placed under arrest in order to submit to an official interrogation.

Before concluding their investigation that night, de Turle de Labresprin and the clerk of the court made one last stop. Shortly before dawn they went to the home of Pierre Bagneres, the *brigadier* of the *archers* attached to the hospital, whom they found with a head wound.[9] He explained that he had been injured the day before—that is, during the afternoon preceding the murders in the faubourg—during a riot that arose around the transportation of a beggar to the hospital.[10] Such struggles were by no means uncommon. The *archers,* as petty government officials, were literally in the forefront of the state's attempt to control the urban poor and were, therefore, the immediate targets of popular resentment directed at government interference in local communities. No wealthier than the majority of the laboring classes, prone to dismissal themselves in times of governmental insolvency, patrolling the city streets on foot and armed only with swords, the *archers* nonetheless represented the strong arm of the state and aroused hostility and resentment wherever they went—so much so that they sometimes needed the assistance of other government officials, from the municipal watch to the intendants themselves, to rescue them from the violence they suffered in the course of their duties.[11]

Indeed, Jean Baptiste Duclos, the captain of the watch, who had accompanied de Turle de Labresprin for much of the evening, had filed a report of this disturbance.[12] At about half past two in the afternoon of 17 April, on the orders of de Turle de Labresprin himself, eighteen men of the watch had set out to rescue a group of *archers*. They were besieged in the towers of the Pont Neuf by a disorderly group, including some soldiers, who wanted them to release the beggar they were escorting to the hospital. In the ensuing scuffle, Bagneres was hit over the head by a lackey wielding a club. But having returned home via the surgeon's, Bagneres swore that he had not set foot outside of his house since five o'clock in the evening. He was arrested, nonetheless, and escorted to the prisons of the *hôtel de ville*. Three *archers* had been arrested for the murder of two soldiers, but whether they had indeed committed these crimes, and why, was still unknown. It was not yet dawn of the morning of 18 April.

On 18 April, the day after the murders in the faubourg Saint Cyprien, the *procureur du roi* formally notified the municipal judges of the city, the *capitoulat*, of the crime, at the same time ordering an autopsy to be performed on the man who had died in the street.[13] Over the next two days, the *capitoulat*, as the body conducting the preliminary findings, conducted interviews with six *archers*, all linked circumstantially to the murders, issued a series of witness subpoenas, and conducted a thorough search of Pierre Berger's tavern in the faubourg Saint Cyprien.[14]

The *capitouls* spoke first with Jean Bourdil, the *archer* under arrest. He testified that between eight and nine o'clock on the evening of 17 April, he was drinking with two friends—Delisle and Dufaur—in the tavern Chez Perruque located in the rue Noue in the faubourg Saint Cyprien. A soldier sat drinking at another table, in the company of two or three other men, the same soldier later found dead at the Pont Neuf. When they had finished, Bourdil and his friends left. In the street, as they were leaving the tavern in some confusion, Dufaur turned on another soldier with a naked sword, saying to him, "You bugger, it's you that wants to kill me," and, hitting the soldier with the flat of his sword and once with the point, drove him into the tavern. Bourdil himself was unarmed, he said, having earlier lent his sword to Delisle, who had in turn lent it to Dufaur—so it was Bourdil's sword that was used to drive this second soldier into the tavern to join the first.

The rest of the *archers* gave their testimony. Louis Prieur, the *sousbrigadier* under arrest who denied having ever been in the tavern with the soldiers—an allegation supported by all witness testimony—said that Bourdil had arrived at the hospital just after dusk and had reported that he had been in a fight near the Pont Neuf, where some people had been hurt.

Anthoine Bajou, *archer,* said he had gone home at six o'clock. Bernard Lauzere, *sousbrigadier,* said he had not been near the bridge all day, since he had been performing his Easter duty—his annual confession. Pierre Bagneres, *brigadier,* said again that after being injured in the disturbance on the Pont Neuf, he had visited the surgeon and gone home to bed around five o'clock and that he had not left the house until his arrest. And Jean Puntis, the last of the *archers* to be questioned, said that he had helped Bagneres home from the surgeon's and then gone home himself around eight o'clock.

The judges, certain that the murder was connected to the disturbance on the Pont Neuf earlier the same day, strove through questioning to establish such a connection. They asked Anthoine Bajou if the *archers* had not participated in the assault "in hatred, to avenge themselves for a certain quarrel that they had had five hours earlier"[15] and asked Bernard Lauzere if the *archers* had not effected a reconciliation with the soldiers at the tavern as part of an elaborate plan to avenge themselves for "certain insults" they had suffered.[16] The *archers* denied these imputations, and all but Bourdil denied having been near the bridge that night.

The first nine witnesses to be called, all Toulousain residents, confirmed the information given earlier by the *archers* and expanded on it, helping the judges to fashion a more coherent narrative of events.[17] Jean Moulinier and Louise Savés, husband and wife, kept the tavern in the faubourg Saint Cyprien called Chez Perruque. They testified that on the night in question, between seven and eight o'clock, three silk workers—Guilhaume Taules, Jean Bernard, and Pierre Loyseau—and a soldier dressed in a gray coat with blue trim, named Pintous, ordered some wine from Savés. A short while later, three *archers* from the Hôpital de la Grave—Bourdil, Delisle, and Pedron—arrived with their friend Dufaur. They sat down at another table and ordered something to drink. By this time the silk workers at the first table had finished and asked for more to drink, but Moulinier refused it because it was late. The soldier in gray said to the *archers,* "Messieurs, I'd like to drink a bit of your wine; give some to me." And so they drank together, toasted each other, and shared their tobacco, "ce faisant des honnêtetés réciproques." The *archers* left before anyone else, and just as they were leaving the tavern—or was it a bit later when Moulinier and Savés were closing up?—another soldier came in, complaining that he'd been struck with a stone on entering. But by then it was late, and the couple didn't want to serve anyone else, so they made everyone leave and they closed the door. That was just before they heard a terrible noise in the street. Later, of course, they'd heard that one of the soldiers had been killed, but at the time they knew nothing about it—although Savés did remember noticing that

Delisle had worn a sword under his arm, perhaps the one lent to him by Bourdil.

The accounts of the silk workers who were there that night concurred in large measure. They had indeed drunk with the soldier Pintous and watched him drink with the *archers*, too. The *archers* left the tavern first, then the silk workers with their soldier-companion. They parted company with him in front of the tavern. Only Loyseau remembered the second soldier: he recounted that they left two soldiers standing in the street. All three remembered that at least one, if not two, of the *archers* were armed, but they could not agree as to which of them had been—all three *archers* were named as the armed man. And both Loyseau and Bernard remembered that one of the armed *archers* wore a gray coat, like the soldier Pintous, rather than his regulation overcoat.

As the *capitouls* continued to question witnesses, they found that the two murders under investigation seemed to have had their beginnings in two locations: in the faubourg and in the *citie*. The route that led to the murder of Pierre Verdieu, the soldier who died in the hospital, began at his lodgings in the inn of Bertrand Ignard. Bertrand Loubens, a mason, testified that at around eight o'clock he had been walking past Pierre Berger's tavern in Saint Cyprien. Berger told Loubens to walk across the bridge and into the *citie*, to Ignard's inn, to tell Pierre Verdieu, one of Ignard's lodgers, to come to the tavern, which Loubens did. The innkeeper himself confirmed this evidence. Around eight o'clock, he said, a mason knocked on his door, asking for Verdieu, a soldier in the Flanders Regiment, saying that the tavern keeper Berger was asking for him. Within about forty-five minutes Verdieu left Ignard's inn with Etienne Samouillan, a fellow soldier.

Samouillan testified in his turn that Loubens had performed his errand and that Verdieu had initially set out alone but then returned, and asked Samouillan to go with him. There was a man lodging in the faubourg Saint Cyprien, he said, who owed him thirty sols, though when they got to the debtor's lodgings there was no one in. On their way back to the city, they passed through the rue Noue, where they were set upon by a group of fourteen or fifteen armed men, one of whom was dressed in gray. Samouillan himself was hit on the head with the flat of a sword and took flight, and heard Verdieu cry out, "I am dead!" Samouillan was pursued all the way back to Ignard's, but a short time later he returned to the bridge where he found Verdieu mortally wounded and beside him, Pintous, another soldier of his regiment, dead on the pavement—the same man who had been drinking with the silk workers earlier that night. How or by whom Pintous had been murdered, Samouillan could not say.

One of the witnesses, Sieur Jacques Puget, saw Samouillan in his flight toward the place de Chayredon. It was between nine and ten o'clock, he thought, and he had been walking his mother-in-law home after having supper with her. On his way home alone, he noticed two *archers* with naked swords in their hands—Delisle and a man he identified as the "Spaniard's husband"—and another man he said he would recognize if he saw again. He asked the three of them what they wanted, at which they put away their swords, explaining that they had quarreled with some people who owed them money. This certainly suggested that these *archers* were among the men in pursuit of Pierre Verdieu and Etienne Samouillan in an argument over debt—and that they were perhaps the murderers of Pierre Verdieu. But then who had killed Pintous? The *capitouls* were no closer to answering this question than they had been at the outset.

These preliminary findings resulted in the *capitouls* issuing an arrest warrant to be formally served by the bailiff on Jean Bourdil and Louis Prieur, already in the prisons of the *hôtel de ville*. They also empowered the bailiff to search the residences of Delisle, Pedron, and Dufaur and to transport them to the *hôtel de ville* if found. Because none of the three could be found at home, their wives were served with papers that demanded that the three men give themselves up within two weeks.[18]

At this point, three days after the assault, Jean Bourdil and Louis Prieur were the official suspects and were duly questioned, without formal knowledge of the charges against them. Of course, each of them had seen the bodies of the two dead men, and the leading questions of the judges must have given them an uneasy certainty of the charges as each man was asked explicitly about his role in the murders of the two soldiers.

In the first formal questioning of the two suspects, Jean Bourdil admitted to wearing a gray coat on the night of the murders. Indeed, he said that he had changed out of his uniform overcoat so that he would not himself be assaulted as he moved through the city, as he had been earlier that day on the Pont Neuf. But he insisted that he had not been armed, that he had lent his sword to Delisle, who had in turn lent it to Dufaur.[19] Prieur seemed to support Bourdil's evidence, stating that when he saw Bourdil at the hospital that night he was not carrying a naked sword. But the judges were not satisfied. Why, they reasoned, would Delisle ask to borrow Bourdil's sword when he had one of his own, and having done so, why return it bloody to the man who lent it in good faith?[20]

On 24 April, having reviewed the evidence gathered over the course of the week, the *procureur* recommended that the case proceed according to extraordinary procedure, employing *recollement* and confrontations of witnesses with the accused.[21] The *capitouls* were in agreement and passed sentence accordingly.[22] An order was again issued for the seizure of Delisle, Dufaur, and Pedron, and for Pierre Berger, known as Lapierre, the inn-keeper who had sent the message through the mason Loubens to Pierre Verdieu, the message that had led him to his death.

Subpoenas were issued for a second time.[23] The first group of witnesses were asked to confirm their evidence in the *recollement*, which they did without adding any new details.[24] Four new witnesses were heard: the apprentice Etienne Bourret and his neighbor, who overheard the crime from their rooms; Jean Anglade, the carder who found the dead men; and the noble Jean George Mathias Sens.[25] Sens witnessed three men in bourgeois dress emerge from the tavern Chez Perruque; he then saw four or five men appear from the street leading to the Hôpital de la Grave and an equal number of men from another street converge upon them. The three soldiers were attacked by the mob: one man was killed in flight; another mortally injured; and the third took flight in the direction of the place de Chayredon, pursued by two armed men who threw stones at him. Sens recognized six or seven of the attackers as *archers* by their uniforms. His testimony brought the murders together for the first time, placing all three soldiers together at the tavern—Pintous who had been drinking inside, with Pierre Verdieu and Etienne Samouillan—in the company of the band of armed men who converged and scattered in the midst of the attack.

Once all thirteen witnesses had confirmed their initial testimony, six of them were selected to be confronted with Louis Prieur and ten of them with Jean Bourdil.[26] The two suspects were informed that any objections they wanted to pose to the witnesses must be made before the previous testimony of the witnesses was read to them; in other words, they could object to the simple presence of specific witnesses who they felt might be prejudicial to them and, therefore, to their testimony, but not to the testimony itself. The confrontations between Louis Prieur and the six witnesses were uneventful. Prieur challenged none of the witnesses. Of the six, he knew only Jean Moulinier, the tavern keeper of Chez Perruque, who affirmed that Prieur had not been in his tavern on the night of the murders.

The confrontations between Jean Bourdil and the ten witnesses did not proceed as smoothly. Bourdil and the three silk workers acknowledged their mutual recognition. Jean Bernard maintained that Bourdil was armed that night, testimony that Bourdil formally denied, and Pierre Loyseau identified him as the man in the gray coat, the same coat he was wearing during their confrontation. The noble Sens, who did not know Bourdil, said that he resembled the man in the gray coat he had seen pursuing the third soldier in the direction of the place de Chayredon. But Samouillan, the very man who had been pursued, said that he had not seen Bourdil that night. Etienne Bourret, the hosier's apprentice, who had seen the first group of men descend upon the soldiers and who knew Bourdil, said that he had not seen him among the group. Likewise, Jacques Puget, the merchant who had also seen Samouillan in flight, said that he had not seen Bourdil that night. All in all, the testimony appeared to be rather inconclusive. Bourdil had clearly been present in the tavern dressed in a gray coat, but no one had seen him attack either of the dead men and no one could definitively identify him as one of the men who pursued Samouillan.

The *capitouls* questioned Bourdil for a third time before passing the whole *dossier* on to the *procureur*, de Carriere.[27] Having reviewed the case, de Carriere noted his opinion in his report:

> Concluded that before passing judgment definitely . . . it should be ordered that the named Jean Bourdil called Police, one of the accused, should be, reserving the proofs and evidence of the whole trial, applied to the ordinary and extraordinary *question* in order to know the truth from his mouth, if he did not commit the said murders, and his accomplices, and with regard to Louis Prieur, also accused, it should be ordered that judgment will be suspended in his case until the report of the *procès-verbal* of the *question* . . .[28]

The *procureur* was evidently of the opinion that there was not adequate evidence to condemn the accused men to death, the appropriate penalty in such a serious affair, but that there was sufficient evidence to support a sentence to torture.

Three days later, the *capitouls* formally questioned Bourdil and Prieur for a fourth and final time and confronted them with each other.[29] It was time to deliberate the sentence. The evidence had been difficult throughout: witnesses had failed to support one another's evidence, and the two men accused had insisted on their innocence. The only incidents that stood out with any certainty were the disturbance on the Pont Neuf when the *archers* were attacked in the performance of their duties; the meeting of the *archers* and the soldier Pintous in the tavern Chez Perruque; the message that sent Verdieu and Samouillan into the faubourg; the assault of one or more soldiers in the street by an armed band of men, some in the uniform of the *archers;* and the flight of Samouillan across the Pont Neuf pursued by the man in gray.

Dutoron, the *rapporteur* for the case, was of the opinion that Jean Bourdil should be condemned to an *amende honorable* and to death by breaking on the wheel and that Louis Prieur should be released. His fellow judges— Fitte, de Turle de Labresprin, Guerard, and Cormouls—concurred.[30] Accordingly, they passed sentence on the two accused:

> By our present sentence, ruling definitively with regard to the said Jean Bour-
> dil, we declare that the said Jean Bourdil is convicted of the crime of murder
> with which he was charged, in reparation for which we condemn him to be
> delivered to the *exécuteur de la haute justice*, who shall lead him, bareheaded
> and barefoot, in a penitent's shirt, holding a burning candle, into the court-
> room where on his knees he will beg pardon of God, the king, and justice for
> the said crime and will say that he repents it; this done, he will be put into a
> cart that will follow the accustomed route to the church of St. Etienne, where
> he will make the same apology; and will then be driven to the Pont Neuf,
> near the Hôpital St. Jacques, where, on a scaffold that will be erected there,
> the *exécuteur de la haute justice* will break his arms, legs, and breast; after which
> he will be placed on a wheel where he will stay for as long as it pleases God
> to give him life; and after his death, his body will be exposed in the gallows
> to inspire fear in the wicked . . . and with regard to the said Louis Prieur, we
> dismiss the charges against him.[31]

The case had progressed through every required stage of an investigation: the initiation of proceedings by the *procureur;* the preliminary investigation leading to the formal arrest of suspects; the questioning of those suspects without formal knowledge of charges and without benefit of counsel; the recommendation for prosecution according to extraordinary procedure by the *procureur;* the *recollement* and confrontations with the accused; the report of the *procureur;* and the final deliberations of the judges leading to sentencing.

The *capitouls* read their sentence aloud to the two accused. But they were not empowered to carry out such a sentence before automatic and mandatory review by the *parlement.* The entire *dossier* would have to be sent on to the judges of the *parlement.* Bourdil and Prieur were returned to the prisons of the *hôtel de ville* pending review of their appeal, and the *dossier* was returned to the *procureur* to present to the *parlement* for review. Bourdil still had a chance to save his life, and Prieur, to lose his.

This sentence strikes many modern readers as a barbarity, a betrayal of everything that the law stands for. Yet in early modern France sentences to public execution, like sentences to torture, were legal if specific tests of proof and rules of procedure were met. Perhaps the question that troubles us is not, then, were such sentences lawful but rather, were they just? If by justice we mean that judicial decisions conform to the rules of a given legal system, then this sentence was, in fact, just. In order to sustain this particular understanding of justice, it is essential that we understand both the criminal procedure that was common to all these courts and the hierarchy of the court system so as to understand which courts were empowered to order the actual performance of torture as opposed to pronounce sentences to torture. Only then we can assess whether sentences were justly administered in the terms of the courts of early modern France.[32] But if by justice we mean that the dignity of the person of the accused is respected by officers of the court—in other words, if we seek to impose contemporary definitions of justice on legal systems removed from us in time and place—then these sentences were manifestly unjust. But it seems equally apparent that employing contemporary definitions of justice cannot deepen our understanding of the past. For the moment, then, let us set aside this definition of justice and instead focus on the question of whether early modern French criminal courts were just in their own terms at the same time as we begin to come to terms with what was meant by justice in those courts. We can return to more familiar definitions of justice later when we examine the responses of the philosophes to the institution of torture.

The criminal procedure of the *capitoulat* resembled that of the ordinary justice system as a whole.[33] Criminal proceedings in the first instance were initiated when the *procureur-général,* the crown's representative in the courts, denounced a suspect to the court alone or in conjunction with a private party. The court then appointed a commission to determine whether the evidence supported further proceedings. The commission was empowered to examine physical evidence and to interview witnesses.

These preliminary findings, recorded by the *greffier,* were handed back to the *procureur,* who offered an opinion as to prosecution. If the *procureur* recommended for prosecution, the court issued a writ for the summons or arrest of the suspect.

When the suspect answered the summons, one judge was nominated to examine the case in the role of *rapporteur.* The suspect was questioned by this judge, without knowledge of the charges in the case and without benefit of counsel. The judge was to presume neither the guilt nor the innocence of the suspect. Responses to this interrogation were recorded by the *greffier.* If the suspect admitted guilt, a written confession was submitted to the *procureur,* who recommended sentence. At this point, the accused was informed of the charges and offered an opportunity to plead extenuating circumstances.

If, however, the crime required capital punishment or if the accused protested his or her innocence, proceedings continued. The *procureur* presented the case for the prosecution and usually requested that the trial continue in accordance with extraordinary procedure. Two main forms of criminal procedure were established by the Ordinance of Blois (1498): "ordinary" and "extraordinary." Ordinary procedure indicated a trial conducted in public, with provision made for defense counsel and without recourse to torture. Extraordinary procedure, on the other hand, involved a secret trial in which the accused had no right to counsel and in which the use of torture was permitted if specific criteria were met.[34]

During extraordinary procedure, the witnesses who had been interviewed in the preliminary hearing were recalled in a procedure known as *recollement* and asked to confirm on oath their previous depositions. Deviations from prior testimony opened witnesses to perjury charges. Witnesses were then confronted with the accused, who could offer objections to the testimony of witnesses who they had reason to believe might be prejudicial to them prior to hearing such testimony.

The *dossier*, with reports of preliminary hearings, interrogations of the accused, witness depositions, and confrontations with the accused, was presented to the *procureur*, who wrote a report that summarized the case and offered recommendations for sentencing. The *procureur* then passed the *dossier* on to the *rapporteur* to analyze the documents and suggest a judgment. In a capital case, if the *rapporteur* found that the evidence was inadequate for conviction, he might recommend for the *question préparatoire*, torture designed to elicit details of the crime known only to the guilty party. In this case, the *rapporteur* informed the accused of the sentence to torture and questioned him both before and after the interrogation under torture. In theory, torture was to be administered immediately to prevent the accused from preparing for it; in fact, appeal from the sentence was automatic if pronounced by judges not attached to a sovereign court. As a result, any case originating in a lower court in which there was a sentence to torture would automatically be appealed before the *parlement*.

The *capitoulat* of Toulouse, the court that initiated proceedings against Jean Bourdil, was one of a few municipal courts that still functioned in France, though such courts had once been commonplace. Until the thirteenth century, administration of justice outside the royal domain had been delegated to nonroyal courts, including seigneurial, municipal, and ecclesiastical tribunals.[35] From the 1400s on, the competence of these nonroyal tribunals was gradually reduced, though not actually abolished. This transformation in the administration of justice was achieved through the introduction of three legal concepts: *cas royaux, prévention,* and *justice retenue.*

The theory of *cas royaux* held that the royal courts exercised sole jurisdiction over those crimes that threatened the peace, the person, the property, and the rights of the king. The concept of *cas royaux* brought many capital crimes under the jurisdiction of royal courts, including lèse-majesté, sacrilege, heresy, resistance to the orders of the king or his officials, illegal bearing of arms, unlawful assembly, popular disturbance, crimes committed by royal officials, counterfeiting, forgery, usury, false bankruptcy, rape, adultery, abortion, kidnapping, suicide, arson, crimes committed on public roads, and offenses committed by Protestants. The theory of *prévention* further expanded the caseloads of the royal courts by recognizing that the king, as the source of all justice, had a responsibility to deliver justice within a reasonable period of time. As a result, if proceedings were not promptly initiated within a nonroyal court, a case could be transferred to one of the royal courts. The theory of *justice retenue* held that because the king delegated his authority without ever giving that authority away, he retained the right to intervene in the judicial process at any point. The practical consequence of these three principles was to undermine greatly the power of nonroyal courts. Yet a handful of nonroyal courts clung to their powers and privileges, among them the *capitoulat* of Toulouse, whose jurisdiction extended over crimes, excluding *cas royaux*, committed in the city and *gardiage* of Toulouse.

Royal justice was administered through two kinds of courts, the *tribunaux d'exception* (extraordinary courts) and the *tribunaux ordinaires* (ordinary courts). The extraordinary courts judged specific kinds of cases or cases involving specific classes of individuals. Thus, the *Grand Maîtres des Eaux et Fôrets* heard civil and criminal cases involving waterways and forests, while the *prévôtés des maréchaux* heard cases involving certain classes of persons—primarily vagabonds and soldiers—as well as cases involving the public highways.

The ordinary courts comprised a judicial hierarchy competent to hear civil and criminal cases in the first instance and on appeal. The lowest of these royal courts were the royal *prévôtés*, whose competence extended only over those cases not specifically attributed to higher royal courts. By the eighteenth century, these courts were largely superseded by the *sénéchaussées* and the *bailliages*, the most common courts of first instance for all *cas royaux* committed within their jurisdiction. The next rank in the judicial hierarchy was occupied by the *présidiaux*, whose primary functions were to hear civil appeals and to render judgments of competence in criminal cases in order to determine if the case at hand should be heard by the *sénéchaussées* or by the *prévôtés des maréchaux*.

The highest of the ordinary courts were the *parlements*, which heard civil and criminal cases in the first instance for those whose privilege of *committimus au petit sceau* exempted them from judgments rendered by lower courts, as well as cases on appeal.[36] The *parlement* of Toulouse was traditionally considered the second most important of the *parlements* of France, both because it was the second oldest, founded in 1437, and because its jurisdiction was the second largest, surpassed only by the *parlement* of Paris.[37] This court, like the other *parlements*, was composed of three permanent chambers: the *grand' chambre*, for the most serious cases or for those involving the most important persons; the *chambre des requêtes*, for civil cases in the first instance; and the *chambre des enquêtes*, for civil cases on appeal as well as for criminal cases on appeal when they involved fines rather than corporal punishments. Other chambers could then be composed by rota as needed. The *parlements* regularly assembled the *tournelle* by rota to hear criminal cases.[38] In Toulouse, this chamber assembled at least four days a week, on Monday, Wednesday, Thursday, and Saturday and on the eves of all festivals. Only one trial per day per member was held, for which each member received a standard fee: *présidents* received 6 livres 10 sous; *présidents à enquetes*, 4.5 livres, 7.5 sous; and *conseillers*, 3 livres, 5 sous. In theory, therefore, the *tournelle* could hear no more than thirteen cases in each session, or fifty-two cases per week. From the perspective of his judges, Bourdil's case was one among many.

On 3 May 1726, the *parlement* of Toulouse received the Bourdil *dossier* from the *capitouls* and began to examine the assembled documents that had prompted the lower court to pronounce the death sentence, which required automatic appeal to the high court. One week later, on Friday, 10 May 1726, the *président* Celez and his fellow *parlementaires* filled their benches in the criminal chamber of the *parlement*. Seated on the *sellette* placed in front of them, Jean Bourdil waited to hear his sentence, as did his codefendant, Louis Prieur, who stood behind the *barre*.[39] The *parlement* adopted the *procureur's* recommendation of 24 April in its own interlocutory sentence:

> The Court, without regard to the two reports made by the said *capitouls* on 17 April last and by du Touron, *assesseur*, on 18 of the said month of April rejects the confrontation of Etienne Bourret, witness, with Louis Prieur, on 27 of said month of April last, before ruling definitively on the said appeal, reserving the proofs and evidence of the case, ordered and orders that the said Jean Bourdil will be applied to the *question ordinaire et extraordinaire* to hear the truth from his mouth, and with regard to the said Louis Prieur, orders that judgment be reserved until the report of torture of the said Bourdil is returned, and to carry out the present sentence sends it before the *capitouls*.[40]

Not satisfied with the evidence presented in the case, the judges of the *parlement* had overturned the death sentence pronounced by the *capitouls* on Jean Bourdil. More evidence was needed, and torture was to be the means of achieving that evidence. Led from the courtroom, Bourdil and

Prieur were returned to their cells in the prison in the *hôtel de ville* to await the fulfillment of this sentence.

It must be stressed that judges could not employ torture at will. Like every phase of the judicial process, torture was hedged about by rules that, over time, were altered by major pieces of legislation that addressed the criminal justice system. Important ordinances governing criminal legislation included the Ordinance of Blois (1498), the Ordinance of Villers-Cotterets (1539), and the new criminal ordinance of 1670.[41]

The Ordinance of Blois requested—but did not require—that judges engage in careful deliberation before sentencing to torture, prevented the repetition of torture until new evidence was brought to bear in a case, required that a written report of the interrogation be drawn up, and provided a twenty-four-hour waiting period between torture and the requisite "voluntary" reiteration of confession. Confession of guilt under torture and subsequent reiteration of confession yielded capital sentences. If the accused did not confess under torture, he or she could not be subject to a capital sentence. The Ordinance of Villers-Cotterets required that protestations of innocence under torture purge all evidence against the accused. In theory, therefore, this ordinance required that individuals who protested their innocence under torture be set free without any criminal penalty. In practice, judges could "reserve" proofs against the accused, so that even in those cases in which such protestations were made, the accused might nonetheless be sentenced to criminal penalties.

The criminal ordinance of 1670 went on to create two kinds of distinctions between modes of torture: a distinction between the *question préparatoire*, the torture of an accused for a full confession or for details of a crime only the guilty party could know, and the *question préalable*, the torture of a convicted criminal for the names of his accomplices, as well as a distinction between "ordinary" and "extraordinary" torture, largely a difference of degree of intensity. It also allowed for afflictive punishments following torture on the basis of the evidence already existing against the accused, even after protestations of innocence under torture, even without reserve of proofs. These afflictive sentences included temporary or perpetual banishment from the jurisdiction, temporary or perpetual confinement to galleys for men and hospitals for women, corporal punishment, and the *amende honorable*, or public confession of guilt.

In theory, anyone could be subject to torture: "In France, all persons can be sentenced to the *question*, men and women, boys and girls, old and young, nobles and commoners, priests, clerics, monks, nuns, etc."[42] In practice, judges were encouraged to sentence individuals to torture with close attention to their physical abilities; those who should not be subject to torture included the following:

> prepubescents; the mad; the deaf and dumb, because one must interrogate them by means of signs and gestures, which would not be feasible in the midst of torment; the sick and infirm, and those who are not in a state to suffer the *question* without danger to their lives, which must be certified by the reports of doctors and surgeons; women with child during their pregnancies and for forty days after to give them time to regain their strength, for fear that they or their fruit should perish because of the torments.[43]

The accused could be tortured only once, unless new evidence came to light; once removed from the instruments of their torture, they could not be returned to them. Judges were required to limit these single sessions of torture to a maximum of an hour and a quarter.[44] In addition, the ordinance of 1670 sought to impose some measure of uniformity on the practice of torture, but without specifying the actual physical practice of torture. Pussort, one of the authors of the ordinance, observed in the written deliberations that "it was difficult to make the *question* uniform, because the necessary description would be indecent in an ordinance."[45] The ordinance, therefore, required only that each *parlement* employ its customary form of torture.

What was the purpose of torture? What did judges seek through the infliction of pain that they could not otherwise obtain? They sought incontrovertible proof of guilt; and within the context of early modern French law and understandings of the nature and relationships of truth and proof, torture was, in theory, an effective means of proving guilt by adding the weight of confession to the proofs already possessed by the court. After 1670, in the absence of such a confession, judges were still empowered to sentence the accused to afflictive punishments on basis of the very proofs that had empowered them to sentence the accused to the torture that had yielded no further evidence. Torture could never prove that the accused was innocent per se because the failure to confess did not of necessity undermine the evidence gathered before the interrogation; indeed, the criminal ordinance of 1670 institutionalized the inability of torture to purge proofs.

The place of torture within the justice system was closely tied to the role of proof in early modern law.[46] Conviction in criminal cases required material certainty of guilt: to convict an accused, specific kinds of proof had to be present. In the presence of these proofs, conviction was obligatory. Judges could not exercise mercy within this justice system; that privilege was reserved for the king.

To warrant conviction, two things had to be proven: that a crime had been committed, and that the accused was the perpetrator of that crime. To that end, four methods of proof were marshaled: the confession of the accused; witness testimony; written documents; and presumption. Confession and testimony constituted vocal proof; documents constituted instrumental proof; and presumption constituted conjectural proof. Proofs were assessed not only by method, but also by value. Thus, there were complete proofs, necessary for conviction in capital cases; proximate proofs, or presumptions, popularly known as half-proofs; and remote presumptions. The value of proof corresponded informally to the level of punishment that could be applied in a given case.

Complete proofs were provided by two reliable eyewitnesses who had no interest in the case, by certain kinds of written evidence, or by inferences drawn from this evidence. These proofs, required for capital convictions, were sometimes difficult to acquire. Qualified disinterested witnesses were hard to find in this society of small communities. Complete proofs obviated the need for torture.

Proximate proofs were sufficient only for conviction to corporal and pecuniary punishments. They could, in theory, be added together to create full proofs. Thus, half-proofs, which by themselves were sufficient only for corporal or pecuniary sentences, could be used in combination to create complete proofs adequate for capital conviction. Yet even the criminal ordinance of 1670, the last major revision of the old regime legal system to address the question of proof, did not specify what constituted a proximate proof. Precedent alone indicated that the testimony of one reliable eyewitness, certain kinds of written evidence, or extrajudicial confession by the accused attested by two witnesses were adequate proximate proofs. The presence of proximate proof was required before ordering torture.

Remote proofs could be used in sentencing to pecuniary punishments or for ordering further investigation. Remote proofs included the physical appearance of the accused during the initial interrogation, the reputation of the accused, and the proximity of the accused's dwelling to the place of the crime.

Jurists debated the place of confession in this hierarchy of proofs. Some held that judicial confession was a complete proof, adequate in itself for capital conviction; others, that it had to be added to proximate proofs to yield conviction. Until the criminal ordinance of 1670, the absence of a complete proof in a criminal case meant that, in theory, no conviction was possible and that, in practice, no capital conviction was possible. As a result, whether confession was understood to provide a complete or a proximate proof, torture occupied a central position in the judicial system, providing capital convictions that would otherwise have been unattainable.

But there were important limits on the use of torture. The ordinances of Blois and Villers-Cotterets and the criminal ordinance of 1670 together provided for a practice that was governed by the following laws. Torture could be employed only in capital cases. It could be employed only as a last resort. If a full proof existed, torture could not be employed since conviction was already assured. Torture could therefore be employed only when a proximate proof existed, providing grounds for grave suspicion. Suggestive or leading questions during interrogations under torture were not allowed. Confession under the *question préparatoire* had to be substantiated by voluntary reiteration of confession within twenty-four hours of the interrogation. Specific modes of torture were not regulated, but varied regionally and according to custom.

In theory, changes in the standards of proof dictated by the ordinance of 1670 rendered the use of torture legally obsolete in that sentences short of death could be pronounced in the absence of full proof. But the fact is that judges continued to sentence suspects to torture in capital cases until the 1780s, albeit with diminishing frequency, when all forms of torture were formally abolished.

On the morning of 25 May 1726, three men met in the *chambre de la gesne et question* (torture chamber) of the *hôtel de ville* of Toulouse. François Joseph Cormouls, *avocat* and *capitoul,* Bernard Loubaissin, cloth merchant and *capitoul,* and François du Toran, *avocat,* had assembled there to execute the sentence of *question préparatoire* pronounced two weeks earlier by the *parlement* of Toulouse on Jean Bourdil.[47] Before the end of the day, they were joined by the accused, the *greffier,* and the *exécuteur de la haute justice* and his assistants. Outside the room, a physician and a priest stood by should their services be required.

Upon the order of the *capitouls,* the *exécuteur de la haute justice* brought in Jean Bourdil, then held in the prisons of the *hôtel de ville.* His hands placed on the Bible, Bourdil was sworn to tell the truth in response to all questions put to him. Seated amid the instruments of his torture, Bourdil heard the *greffier* read the sentence that brought him there that day:

> The Court ... before ruling definitively on the said appeal, reserving the proofs and evidence of the case, ordered and orders that the said Jean Bourdil will be applied to the *question ordinaire et extraordinaire* to know the truth from his mouth ...

Although Bourdil sat alone with his interrogators, he had a codefendant, Louis Prieur, whose own fate was to be determined by the testimony Bourdil gave that day:

... and with regard to the said Louis Prieur, orders that judgment will be suspended until after the report of the torture of the said Bourdil, costs reserved, and to carry out the present sentence, sends it before the said *capitouls*.[48]

The interrogation had begun.

Jean Bourdil was prepared for his torture as were all those condemned to suffer the *question*. First he was made to swear an oath that he would tell the truth under interrogation. The *exécuteur de la haute justice* and his assistants swore a corresponding oath that they would keep secret all that was said during the interrogation. Then, in the presence of the *capitouls* conducting the interrogation, the *exécuteur de la haute justice* and his assistants stripped Bourdil to the waist, then shaved and searched him to ensure that he carried no charms on his body. Certain charms, it was believed, could protect from pain. Their presence on the body of the accused would therefore obstruct justice by rendering torture painless, and the accused, willfully mute.

Thus sworn, stripped, shaven, and searched, Bourdil was ready to be put to the *question*. In Toulouse, the *question* was given in one or more of three ways: the *estrapade*, applied to both men and women as "ordinary" torture; the *question d'eau*, applied only to men as "extraordinary" torture; and the *brodequins*, applied only to women, also as "extraordinary" torture. The accused was referred to as the *patient*.[49]

The *estrapade* required that the wrists of the accused be bound behind the back. A rope, attached at one end to a hook or a pulley in the ceiling, was attached to the bound wrists, and the accused was drawn into the air. The entire weight of the accused's body was thus brought to bear on the shoulder joints. Weights might be attached to the feet to increase this pressure. Questions were put to the accused while he or she hung in the air. Only an indication of willingness to respond to the judge's questions brought release. Although this method of torture was employed by several *parlements*, it was referred to in a sixteenth-century legal work as the *quaestio Tholosana*.[50] The *question d'eau* consisted of fastening the wrists of the accused to an iron ring bolted into the wall at waist height, and the feet, to another ring embedded in the floor, thus extending the prisoner's body to its full length at a slant. Trestles of varying heights were then wedged under the prisoner's back, forcing a further extension of the body. Finally, his face covered by a linen napkin, water was forced down his throat through a cow's horn, as much as sixteen liters at a time.[51] Use of the *brodequin* involved binding the prisoner to an iron chair. To each shin was attached a vice. Four to eight wedges were inserted between the vice and the leg and pounded into place with a hammer.

Other *parlements* had different customary procedures: in Rennes, the *question* was given by drawing the feet of the accused toward a fire; in Rouen, by a sort of thumbscrew; in Autun, by pouring boiling oil on the legs of the accused.[52] Most *parlements*, however, employed the *question d'eau* and the *brodequin*.[53]

These, then, were the tortures endured by Jean Bourdil: the *question ordinaire* in the form of the *estrapade* three times on 25 May and once again on 27 May, followed by the *question extraordinaire* in the form of the *question d'eau* five times.[54] Raised for the first time,

> The same questions and remonstrances as above were put to him, and we exhorted him to tell the truth and say if he is guilty of the murder of the said two soldiers who were killed, or if he is an accomplice of the murderers, or if he knows the guilty murderers or accomplices. Answered [that] he told the truth and that he is innocent of the murder of the said two soldiers, and that he knows neither the murderers nor the accomplices.[55]

The questions put to him during the physical infliction of his torture continued in this ritualized and repetitive way. Again and again, he was asked nothing more than to confess his guilt in the matter of these murders. Yet throughout his interrogations, Jean Bourdil insisted on his innocence, never once confessing to the kind of specific knowledge of the crimes that only the perpetrator could know. Finally, he was removed from the instruments of his torture.

In accordance with the laws governing the practice of torture, the transcript of the interrogation was read aloud, and Bourdil was made to sign it to signify that he had indeed spoken the words contained in the official record. Although the court documents are silent on this point, he should next have been laid on a mattress before a warming fire and attended to by a physician.

We know that Jean Bourdil was returned to his cell on 27 May 1726 after suffering the *question ordinaire et extraordinaire*. In each of two sessions of torture, on 25 May and then on 27 May, he had failed to confess to the murders of the two soldiers and had failed, too, to offer any new evidence that might shed light on the crime. Adding the *procès-verbal* of his torture to the dossier assembled by the *capitouls*, the *parlement* continued its deliberations for almost two weeks. On 6 June 1726, it reached its final verdict:

> The Court, pronouncing judgment definitely on the interlocutory sentence of the said day 10 May last, condemned and condemns the said Jean Bourdil to serve the King by force in his galleys in perpetuity, warning him against escaping from them on pain of death, declares his goods acquired and confiscated to those who have right of them, setting aside one-third of them for his wife and children, if he has any; acquits the said Louis Prieur; and, moreover,

condemns the said Bourdil to costs, those concerning the said Prieur being compensated.[56]

The torture Bourdil had endured had indeed served its stated purpose: it had provided Bourdil an opportunity truthfully to confirm or deny his knowledge of the murders; and he had clearly and consistently failed to confess. On the basis of the evidence acquired under torture, the *parlement* definitively rejected the original decision of the *capitoulat* to break him on the wheel. Life in the galleys was the sentence they imposed on him. The use of torture had spared Bourdil's life—and condemned him to a life of forced labor.

Bourdil would have joined the Guyenne chain of galley convicts that began its journey in Bordeaux, swung through Toulouse, and continued overland to Perpignan or straight on to the port of Marseilles.[57] Branded on the right shoulder with the letters GAL, wearing an iron collar and chains that shackled him in single or double file to the other condemned men—the army deserters who made up the largest group of galley convicts, branded not only with the letters GAL but also on each cheek with the fleur-de-lis, and their noses and ears cut off; the Protestants punished for public observation of their religion; the thieves and rapists; the salt and tobacco smugglers; the blasphemers and perjurers; the gypsies and vagabonds—he marched the long route in company.

Had he but known, he might have counted himself the fortunate recipient of recent crown reforms. Such reforms sought to regularize the movement of galley chains and to preserve the lives of galley convicts by allowing them to travel only in the months of April and September. Transportation in the winter months had produced terrible deaths among the convicts. If the new regulations were indeed observed in 1726, Bourdil would have remained in prison for three months after final sentencing. He might have been able to forestall the necessity of selling his clothes to his jailers for bread in the hopes of retaining them for the long journey ahead. Once en route, he might have been grateful for the regulated diet he received. And he might also have counted himself fortunate to have been sentenced only after the plague had visited Marseilles for the last time in 1721, when men serving in the galleys were pressed into service in the crisis that followed, tending the sick and burying the dead, and themselves dying in extraordinary numbers. Officially forbidden to do so, his wife and children might have followed the galley chain, taking up residence in Marseilles at the conclusion of their journey in hopes of seeing him in port or helping him to escape. Undoubtedly too poor to supply a slave to take his place at the oars, especially after the confiscation of the bulk of his property, Bourdil would have served out his sentence, laboring in the galleys until his death. But all of this is speculation.

The case against Bourdil's alleged accomplices—Pedron, Delisle, and Dufaur—would drag on until January 1727, by which time all three men would be sentenced to death by the *capitoulat*, and all monies due to the various parties to the case—from Bertrand Ignard, Pierre Verdier's innkeeper, who had been requesting compensation for maintaining Verdier's horse in his stables, to the *capitouls* themselves, who required additional payment for the *greffier* in the case—had been settled, and justice had been served.[58]

The *question d'eau.* From Jean Milles de Souvigny, *Praxis criminis persequendi* (Paris, 1541). Courtesy of New York Public Library, Spencer Collection.

2

"If he trembles, if he weeps, or sighs . . .":

Judges, Legal Manuals, and the Theory of Torture

How did Jean Bourdil's judges arrive at the decision to overturn the death sentence pronounced by the *capitouls* and order torture instead? This chapter will answer that question by providing a brief sketch of the judges and of their legal training in an effort to evoke the legal world within which they worked and by offering a reading of the key legal manuals that addressed torture.

The *parlementaires* were the elite of Toulouse.[1] Wealthier and more numerous than the once-dominant merchants of the cloth and dyeing trades, these men claimed political and cultural dominance of the city. They outnumbered merchants in all urban administrative posts and formed the core membership of the city's cultural organizations.[2] They lived in private homes sumptuously furnished, dressed in the finest clothes—they were the great of this provincial capital and were greatly concerned to maintain their positions. The *parlementaires* proclaimed their roles in both urban and national affairs, proud of their association with the oldest of the provincial *parlements*.

Jean Bourdil's first contact with the *parlementaires* may have occurred during Holy Week, the week of his arrest, before the *capitouls* pronounced sentence on him. Each Easter, the *parlement* of Toulouse observed a tradition known as the *Reddes*, when the members of the court visited the prisons of the city to offer temporary charitable releases to those detainees whose crimes were deemed relatively inoffensive.[3] In 1726, the year of Jean Bourdil's trials, Easter was celebrated on 21 April. Jean Bourdil was under arrest from the night of 18 April 1726 and so may have been in contact with those *parlementaires* who participated in the *Reddes*.

If Bourdil did not see the judges in the prisons of the *hôtel de ville* that Easter, he would certainly have seen them on other occasions prior to his arrest. "Toulouse is a city where there are many holidays and processions": so said one of the anonymous chroniclers of the court.[4] In addition to the observation of the *Reddes*, the entire *parlement* marched in procession on the festivals of Corpus Christi, the Assumption of the Virgin, and on 17

May, the holiday that marked the destruction of the Toulousain Protestant community during the wars of religion.[5] Secular holidays were also observed by the *parlement*, including the festivities marking the opening session of the *parlement*, which took place on Saint Martin's Day, 12 November.[6] The officers of the court processed on that day to celebrate and commemorate the annual opening of the court, each garbed in their particular robes—the magistrates in long scarlet robes decorated with miniver and braid, the *procureur-général* in his miniver-trimmed scarlet robe with its matching shoulder piece, the chief *greffier* in unadorned scarlet, the *huissiers* in violet-purple—each man identified in his office by his dress.[7] The streets must have been awash in scarlet and black: at one time, the *parlement* of Toulouse included 116 *magistrats*, 117 *procureurs* with their clerks, and nearly 300 *avocats* with their secretaries. In addition, this *parlement* employed six chief *greffiers* with forty assistants, as well as numerous royal secretaries and other chancellery officials, notaries, *huissiers*, and *sergents*.[8]

Despite their varied functions and unequal status, these officers of the court maintained a sense of corporate identity. This identity was reinforced not only by the common performance of ritual acts, like the annual procession that marked the opening session of the court, and by shared occupational experiences, but also by more quotidian social contact.[9] The officers of the court tended to live together, concentrated in two of the eight urban parishes, near the buildings of the *parlement*.[10] For the moment, however, it is not the corporate body of judicial officials as a whole, but the *magistrats*, *avocats*, and *procureurs* who are of particular interest, as they were the officials most directly involved in review of lower court decisions like that of the *capitoulat*. Despite the corporate unity of these officials, real differences existed among them, differences based in education and experience.

Judges differed from *avocats* in several ways: judges saw themselves as men of action rather than men of learning, whose power derived from institutional structures and monarchical authority rather than from education.[11] Their outlook was shaped by an awareness of their reliance on this institutionalized power base in combination with their reliance on the stability of society itself to create obedience, lacking effective means to coerce obedience on a mass scale.[12] At the same time, judges experienced a decline in their ability to express themselves on issues of public law during the seventeenth and eighteenth centuries.[13] Despite this decline, their role in the sphere of criminal appeals remained constant. Examination of criminal cases, therefore, permits a unique opportunity to study the judges' outlook because of the unusual degree of freedom and authority they possessed in these cases. The judicial decision to implement torture, I would suggest, must likewise be understood as an important opportunity for direct and independent action by judges in an era of diminishing political power and inadequate police power.

The institution of judicial torture was not only an integral part of the early modern French legal system; it was also an important instance for the exercise of judicial authority. No formal defenses were mounted on its behalf until it came under widespread attack by *avocats* and philosophes in the 1760s. Prior to that time, the theory of torture—that is to say, both the legal rationale of the practice and the proper methods for its use—was laid out in legal manuals for the officials of the courts.

In these manuals, which were published in many cities across the realm, the theory of torture was consistently and coherently articulated. For two centuries, while the laws governing the practice of torture changed, the epistemological foundations of the law as represented in these reference works remained solid. Torture was part of the common legal culture of France. It played an integral role in criminal cases in which evidence was lacking. How, then, did judges and lawyers come to understand the role and function of torture in the legal system? In the legal realm of the seventeenth and eighteenth centuries, what did torture look like? To answer these questions, we will first examine the nature of legal training and then turn to the legal manuals employed by jurists.

Both *avocats* and judges required licenses in order to practice law. The acquisition of the license required three years of study at a law faculty, the first two taken up with lectures on civil law and the last, with French law and royal ordinances, decrees, and their commentaries. Two exams had to be passed, as well, before the prospective *avocat* could present himself to the magistrates of a court to take his oath of profession. He was then required to attend court sessions and lectures for a further two years, a period of apprenticeship during which he was known as an *avocat écoutant.* A minimum age of twenty-five was the final requirement.[14] The *procureurs,* on the other hand, required no formal university training, but rather a ten-year apprenticeship with a *procureur,* culminating in an exam. Once again, the minimum age limit of twenty-five was imposed.[15]

These trainings produced officials with differing areas of expertise: the *procureurs* possessed a procedural expertise, the *avocats,* a legal one. It was the *procureur* to whom litigants addressed themselves, the *procureur* who guided a case through the system from beginning to end. The *avocat,* on the other hand, was called in to plead on behalf of litigants, though not to represent them: the *avocat* served the law rather than the person. Through his erudition and eloquence, the *avocat* sought to move the judges—as well as the audience in the chamber—on behalf of his client.[16]

A recent study of French higher education in the old regime suggests that the formal legal training of *avocats* was superficial at best.[17] Law classes were offered twice daily, each class lasting no more than an hour and a half.[18] The professor would read from his text for the first half-hour, explain his argument for the following half-hour, and conclude with a roll call or question-and-answer session. Students were expected to attend these classes regularly, properly dressed and equipped for study. In addition, they were to keep silent until addressed and then to respond deferentially. Law students disappointed these expectations. In class, they were disruptive. Many failed to present themselves in class at all, preparing for their exams through private study. Educational reforms in 1679 required that they sign the matriculation register four times a year, but complaints persisted that law students paid copyists to attend lectures in their places. Examiners were condemned as both indulgent and corrupt: prior to the educational reforms of the seventeenth century, there was an open traffic in diplomas.[19]

While the specific content of legal education varied from one university to another, all universities taught Roman and canon law in the first two years, and French law only in the last year of study. In this last year of study, civil law, civil and criminal procedure, commercial law, public law, and more were to be covered. Indeed, in Toulouse, an edict required that all the ordinances of the Bourbon kings be taught within a six-month period.[20] Professors were therefore required to teach succinct résumés of the law that were of necessity incomplete. The result was that *avocats* were forced to study jurisprudence on their own, after the acquisition of their degrees, in order to engage in the contemporary practice of the law.[21]

The question then arises: what books did they consult to meet this need for further education? Several attempts have been made to discover what French jurists read in an effort to determine their relationship to radical ideas and their subsequent role in the revolution. In an examination of the sociology of literature, Robert Darnton concludes that the most successful applications of the quantitative history of books occur within studies of a single social group.[22]

French jurists comprise just such a coherent social group with similar book-buying patterns, as studies based on estate inventories in the Midi illustrate. Lenard Berlanstein finds that the libraries of eighteenth-century Toulousain *avocats* were, in fact, composed primarily of legal works, including collections of decisions, treatises about specific questions, and commentaries on ordinances: as much as 85 percent of their libraries were taken up with law books. The twenty most common books were all juridical works; and the most frequently possessed works included the *Corpus juris civilis*, and the *arrêts* of Cambolas and Maynard. La Roche Flavin's *Treze livres des parlemens de France* was found in most jurists' libraries.[23] Bordelais jurists' libraries were likewise dominated by works on law, theology, and history, with collections of and commentaries on royal ordinances, legal dictionaries, and the customs of Bordeaux forming the core of these collections.[24]

Still other sources assist in reconstructing the professional libraries of jurists. During the course of their professional development, jurists were encouraged to create their own legal reference libraries. Guidance in doing so was provided by books like Pierre Biarnoy de Merville's *Règles pour former un avocat* and Armand-Gaston Camus's *Lettres sur la profession d'avocat*, each of which concluded with a list of essential volumes.[25] Merville provided a list of almost three hundred books, divided into eight categories: Roman law, French law, treatises, ordinances, pleadings, customs, practice, and canon law. Camus's bibliography was more detailed: over one thousand titles were arranged topically, most accompanied by annotations to guide the reader in selecting the appropriate work. Works found in each of these bibliographies include Claude Joseph de Ferrière's *Dictionnaire de droit et de pratique* and Guy du Rousseaud de la Combe's *Traité des matières criminelles*.

Publishers' and booksellers' lists, occasionally included in legal texts, also help to establish which works on criminal law were commonly available to men of the legal profession. The 1742 edition of Georges Louet's *Recueil de plusieurs arrêts notables du parlement de Paris*, for example, contains a list of law books that were available at his publisher's shop: ten of these books appear in Merville's bibliography, and three, in Camus's.[26] Among these titles are Philippe Bornier's *Conférences des nouvelles ordonnances de Louis XIV*, and Claude Joseph de Ferrière's *La science parfaite des notaires*. Publishers of necessity stressed the importance of particular legal works in circulars informing the public of forthcoming titles. One such advertisement heralded the publication of the five-volume *Grande Bibliothèque de Toulousaine*, which was to contain the works of Maynard, Puymisson, Lestang, Cambolas, La Roche Flavin, Duranty, Coras, de Segla, Dolive, Dalbert, and Descorbiac.[27]

This combination of estate inventories, prescriptive guides, and booksellers' lists does not provide a guide to the practice of torture, but it is a guide to the theory of torture as jurists must have encountered it, alone in their libraries, seeking guidance not obtained in formal studies. In examining the books that appear on these lists and in these libraries, we can examine the books that articulated the theory of torture, whatever its practice may have been and however that practice diverged from this theory. Indeed, one of reasons that these guides are so useful is precisely that the actual practice of torture can be reconstructed from other documents; for its theory, we must turn to books.

So it was to these books that jurists had recourse when weighing the rules of procedure and evidence, trying to determine if cases could rightfully be considered ones that might call for the *question*. Procedural manuals, style guides, collections of *arrêts, plaidoyers* (pleadings), causes célèbres—all could be consulted when seeking clarification of the laws and precedents governing torture.

Procedural manuals were organized either as legal dictionaries or as title-by-title explications of legal codes. Seeking information about torture, jurists could look up *question* in a dictionary-style manual or could consult the relevant title in a manual structured around the criminal ordinance. The former method permitted problem-oriented thinking, encouraging a kind of free association of ideas; the latter presumed familiarity with the structure of the legal code, an understanding of the "natural" place of torture between discussions of interrogations and of proof.

Style guides were intended to be used by notaries more than by judges. Nonetheless, these guides contained important information on the procedure governing torture. Specifically, they reminded the reader of the restraining effects of the language of sentencing and of the necessity of including the phrase "demeurant les preuves et indices" (reserving the proofs and evidence) in sentencing in cases in which full proof was lacking and in which the court was determined to impose a penalty even if that penalty fell short of capital punishment.[28]

Collections of *arrêts*, published by each of the *parlements*, together served as a body of precedent. These collections, arranged or indexed alphabetically, explained the circumstances under which the given *parlement* had issued a decision. These works were particularly valuable since there were few guides on the subject of jurisprudence. Although legal manuals laid out the rules of procedures according to royal ordinances, they provided little assistance in determining how a case should be decided. The collections of *arrêts*, which explained how and why a given case had been decided, provided just this help. On the other hand, these collections devoted the bulk of their attention to civil rather than to criminal cases.

Another type of source was *plaidoyers*, the texts of the oral arguments in cases heard before the *parlements*, which were published as the work of a single author. Cumbersome to consult, they were nonetheless a valued addition to a legal library because they provided models of eloquence. Finally, jurists occasionally published personal accounts of cases on which they had served, which explored puzzling or curious facets of these cases in detail. Jean de Coras's *Arrest memorable du parlement de Tholose,* for example, which examined his involvement in the case of Martin Guerre, was one such *mémoire;* Guillaume de Segla, like Coras a Toulousain jurist, published another in the 1610s entitled *Histoire tragique et arrests de la cour de parlement de Toulouse.*[29]

All of these professional texts can be distinguished from more popular works on the law, like collections of causes célèbres and issue-specific tracts by comparing their introductory materials. Professional legal works are usually dedicated to colleagues within the legal profession, and they tend to lack letters directed to the reader. Instead, these works contain laudatory poems dedicated to the author by colleagues in praise of his eloquence and erudition. Popular legal works, on the other hand, are typically dedicated to members of the nobility and usually contain directive letters to the reader, which focus on issues of style and which are highly critical of professional works.

In 1738, for example, François Gayot de Pitaval began publication of his *Causes célèbres et intéressantes,* a twenty-volume collection of causes célèbres directed to a professional legal audience. The expressed purpose of the work was to explore and to explain the reasoning behind sentences in celebrated cases in a narrative form that would permit readers to reach their own conclusions before discovering the resolution of the case, thereby testing their own legal skills against those of the nation's *parlements.* By the time of publication of the third volume of the series, Gayot de Pitaval acknowledged the growing number of non–legal specialists among his readers:

> Let me be permitted to pride myself on the fact that I have been read by people of high society, of which women are the loveliest ornaments. It is perhaps the first time that they have tamed themselves with a law book and that one finds a work of the courts on their *toilette.*[30]

The popular success of these volumes, as indicated by their female readership, suggests that these collections served a different purpose than did the professional legal manuals: the causes célèbres served as much to entertain as to instruct.

Gayot de Pitaval's work inspired many imitations. These rewritings and reworkings, as is indicated by their prefatory materials, were aimed at a much broader audience than was Gayot de Pitaval's seminal collection. F. A. P. Garsault offered the following explanation for his *Faits des causes célèbres et intéressantes* (1757):

> This book, I say, is for those who, not destined to be called to the bar, are interested only in a simple telling of the famous and interesting adventures

that caused the trials contained therein . . . People of society don't plead cases;
they hire lawyers when they have lawsuits: but they like to savor the essence
of everything.[31]

This suggests that by the mid-eighteenth century, the drama of the courts
had spilled beyond the confines of the courtroom and provided a staple of
popular literary entertainment.[32]

François Richer, likewise, introducing the first of the twenty-two volumes that composed his *Causes célèbres et intéressantes* (1772) noted that

Few works have been more in vogue than the interesting causes célèbres of
M. Gayot de Pitaval, and few works have been more censured. Everyone has
read them, and everyone has complained that the author followed no method,
that the facts are tossed in with no order, that they are drowned in a mass of
trivial reflections, that one is usually reduced to the trouble of guessing at
them, that the means are explained with a prolixity that causes them to lose
any intrinsic interest. I could not finish, if I wanted to make a list, of all the
reproaches that have been and still are made concerning this book.

I have dared to undertake to give them a new form. I have tried to abstract
the facts from the chaos in which it is said they are engulfed. I tried, as much
as things permitted, to arrange the narration in such a manner that the reader
cannot foresee the official judgment, so that his own remains uncertain until
the conclusion. I thought that this method would make each case more interesting, by keeping the reader in suspense and by exciting his curiosity to the
last by balancing motives, significance, and passions.[33]

Here, the very virtues of the professional legal text, the qualities that render
it of use to the legal profession, are condemned: the volume of detail, the
examination of subtle points of law, the lack of dramatic narrative order. In
their place appear the stylish marks of the new genre: the poignant detail,
the suspense created by a narrative structure, the mystery resolved by the
careful restructuring of facts.

There are manifest differences, therefore, between professional and popular legal works: the former attempt to instruct, the latter, to entertain; the
former claim the authenticity of fact, the latter, the drama of fiction. Legal
historians have tended to rely on professional legal works for the light they
shed on procedural issues, and on popular legal works, not at all. And while
I, too, will focus my attention on professional texts for the moment, I will
return to the popular texts and their growing importance in French culture
in the context of the "enlightened" debate that addressed judicial practice.

My own interest in professional texts goes beyond the light they shed on
procedural issues. Not what rules, but what premises underlay the legal
practice of torture? What was the theory that informed this practice?[34] Despite changes in the laws and procedures governing torture and despite intellectual and political differences among authors, legal manuals published

over the course of the seventeenth and eighteenth centuries presented a remarkably coherent, even static, vision of the theory of torture.

Although legal texts were in no way polemical works, their authors occasionally pondered the goals of justice and the appropriate relationship of law and society. La Roche Flavin addressed this question in an unusually metaphorical passage in his *Treze livres des parlemens de France* (1617): the magistrature, he writes, like music, is composed of distinct and different tones, some sweet, some harsh, which together create an agreeable harmony. The social harmony created by justice is the achievement of peace, union, and the public good. Just as the goal of the individual is his own preservation, achieved through his various members, so too the end of society is its preservation, achieved through the limbs of justice.[35] Torture, by implication, is one of those necessary discordant notes struck by justice in the harmonious composition of society, one of the measures that composes the social harmony. These harsh notes must be struck to maintain this balance. Judges and *exécuteurs de la haute justice* in the performance of their duties should thus be seen as neither inhuman nor unjust, because they carry out a necessary function of the law.

Judicial comportment, therefore, was to be governed by the standard of societal good and not by the common standards of humanity; the judge must behave in such a way as to benefit the community rather than the accused. La Roche Flavin compared the judge and a surgeon, whose healing work must be done mercilessly:

> The surgeon who [only] pities, and does not cut [his patient] makes the wound incurable; the indulgent father makes the son incorrigible: likewise, the merciful judge nourishes and enhances vices, and betrays the laws and the majesty of justice.[36]

The criminal is an infection of the social body. Mercy for a decayed limb can only imperil the whole. Determining the degree of corruption—and the corresponding method of purgation—is the task of the judge. In the context of this metaphor, torture must be understood not as a punitive procedure, but as an exploratory one.

In the performance of his task, during the course of an interrogation under torture, the judge was counseled to modify his bearing in response to the social status, physical constitution, and temperament of the accused, altering his language and approach appropriately.[37] In no circumstance, however, should the judge make promises or threats to the accused, nor should he physically involve himself in the torture: his role is more remote, more aloof.[38] Pain rather than fear should induce the accused to speak the truth. Other writers agreed: in interrogations conducted under torture, the judge must comport himself coldly, "froidement," not heeding to pleas for mercy.[39]

Yet the absence of mercy did not exclude all compassion. The judge was counseled to act with pity out of consideration for the condition of the accused:

> The judge who is present [at the interrogation] should order the torture of the accused, not to satisfy the appetite of the accuser, but moderately, such that the accused remains safe and sound, either for innocence or for punishment.[40]

In part, this attitude is assumed as a means to an end, the extortion of truth:

> In general, in order to extract the truth from the mouth of an accused, the judge must conduct himself toward the accused with great gentleness and affability; to see that the accused be treated in the prison with humanity, if he has just been made uncomfortable; and even procure for him some special foods.[41]

Yet there are other writers who more sincerely suggest a "Christian" attitude.[42] Nor, I would suggest, is this characterization as inconsistent with the ritual of torture as it might first appear.

As he puts his questions, the judge is advised by these manuals to examine the accused carefully, heeding not only the verbal but also the bodily responses of the accused:

> The judge must have his eyes fixed upon the accused, during the whole time that he interrogates him, and must observe all his movements with attention. If the accused trembles, if he weeps, or sighs, the judge will ask him the cause of these movements. Also, if he falters, or if he hesitates; if he is slow, and considers his responses; the judge will press him with reiterated questions, and will make mention of everything in the interrogation.[43]

This attentiveness to the whole response was integral to the practice of judicial torture.

Judges sought not only to catch out the accused with their own verbal responses, but also relied on their bodily responses, their tremblings, tears, and sighs, their pallors and faintnesses. Any one of these physical signs might speak of guilt; each movement might betray the knowledge of crime that the mouth refused to speak. Philippe Bornier notes that "the movements of the man are sometimes the greatest evidence."[44] These movements ranged from intentional to involuntary gestures, from deliberate gestures—like protection against the evil eye—to the spontaneous and expressive gestures that were believed to convey such basic emotions as joy, anger, and fear.[45]

The question that next arises is this: were the involuntary gestures of the accused routinely interpreted as intentional gestures, that is, as gestures containing a culturally agreed-upon content, or did they belong to that class of gestures that were considered to have a transparent and natural content? It was widely believed that the body had many ways to betray the criminal involuntarily, speaking the truth in signs for all to see while the will stopped the tongue. Pallor, for example, was well known to indicate guilty knowledge.[46] The belief that pallor reflects guilt was not specific to France. John Evelyn, illegally admitted to witness an interrogation conducted under torture in 1651, noted that "the fellows suspicious, pale lookes, before he knew he shold be rack'd, betraid some guilt."[47] Gestures, from blushes to silences, were carefully recorded as evidence in the trial transcripts pertaining to the Friulian witches.[48]

Nor was the body of the accused the only body scrutinized by the judges: bodies gave witness in many ways. The corpses of murder victims were used for the evidence they might bring against their assailants. In 1619, La Roche Flavin spoke critically of this sort of evidence:

> Among other proofs and evidence against murderers, accepted and approved by our Doctors, was the blood that ran from the wounds of the murder victim in the presence of the murderers. Even during my childhood they used to make the suspect or guilty parties go nine times around the bodies of the newly dead, even disinterring them if they had been buried. Each time the procedure gave no appearance of truth, nor of certainty; because among the dead, some bled not at all, others bled as much in the absence as in the presence of people; or as much in the presence of blood relatives, kin, and friends, as in that of strangers, enemies, or murderers.[49]

Yet some jurists continued to support the evidence of the accusing dead. La Brun de la Rochette noted that

> If the murdered body of the dead, being shown to the accused, bleeds from its wounds, its nose, or by another part, there is no doubt whatsoever that this is a strong *indica* [when] joined to public opinion: being reputed a miracle of nature, as if this blood sought vengeance against the one who dislodged its soul from its domicile by force and violence . . .[50]

Despite sporadic objections, this method of producing evidence against an accused was noted in legal texts published as late as 1750.[51] Faith in the evidence of the movement of blood toward the living heart, which produced guilty pallor; or away from the dead heart, which produced accusatory bleeding, bespoke an implicit belief in an intimate connection between the physical body and the moral conscience.

Even when this evidence was no longer regarded as entirely trustworthy, the bodies of the dead and of the living continued to be examined for the signs of the crime. Out of the sense that the spirit of the victim might accuse the murderer through bodily signs, speaking voicelessly, grew the beginnings of forensic medicine.[52] Even if bodies could not accuse their murderers directly by bleeding in their presence, they could be examined for the clues they offered as to the murderer's identity: doctors were called upon to examine the bodies of the dead for just these clues.[53] Was the blackness in the bowels natural or the result of poison? Was the blow struck by a left-handed or right-handed assailant?[54]

These were the various languages of the body: the silent self-betrayals of the accused, the voiceless accusations of the dead, the mute language of bruises and bleeding interpreted by the experts—and the confessions of guilt. Supporting the practice of torture involved a particular understanding of the body, its relationship to language, and its ability to produce language.

Historians have conflated three separate issues within the single phrase "language of the body," failing to distinguish them clearly from one another. The first language of the body is a sensual and silent language: the murdered body that names its attacker by bleeding in his or her presence; and the murderous body that pales at its crime, as if the body were itself revolted by the deed it committed. The second language of the body is a language *about* the body. It is the language of medicine, the voice of the expert speaking in the autopsy report and the case history. The third language of the body is language *from* the body, language coaxed or coerced from the body, the voice of the self brought to speaking by another, in scenes of mesmerism, hypnotism, and torture.[55]

As is apparent from the evidence of the legal manuals, each of these languages found its place in the courts. The language of the body itself constituted a form of trial evidence, as when pallor was interpreted as a sign of guilt, a bodily confession of crime. Language about the bodies of alleged criminals and their victims formed another kind of evidence, in the shape of surgeons' reports and autopsies. The coercion of language—of truth—from the body was itself the central purpose of the practice of early modern torture.

The language used to describe this process of coercion reveals the essential properties of the truth sought by the magistrates. In the world of the manuals, truth is static: it precedes the legal intervention, it does not arise from it. Torture is employed in order "to know" *(savoir)* or "to discover" *(découvrir)* the truth and, on occasion, "to extort" *(extorquer)* it. Like some strange new world, the truth awaits its discoverers, who must wrench it for themselves from its unlawful possessor. The truth is neither, therefore, created cooperatively through comparison of testimonies (the truth of the philosopher), nor is it recognized by an inner moral conviction (the truth of the jurist). It is a static reality awaiting perception. Torture does not create this truth; it merely reveals it.

This truth is lodged in the matter of the body: judges were required to draw it out *(tirer)* or extract it *(arracher)* from the body, just as tears and teeth are drawn. Truth resides in the flesh itself and must be torn out of that flesh piece by piece. It is a physical as much as a metaphysical property. As a result, any attempt to reach the truth must occur through a physical process of discovery. Because of its physical location, truth must be discovered by physical means. No amount of discussion will achieve it; although the truth has a language, it is the revealing and unwilled language of the body. Only torture can satisfy the demand for the real truth, hidden in the flesh, perhaps unknown even to its possessor. Pain is, then, the vehicle of truth-telling, a distillation of the pure substance lodged in the impure flesh. Pain betrays the truth in the sense of exposing it to view through the sounds and gestures it produces.

Anticipating that the body was susceptible to betrayal through involuntary bodily signs or through the pain that produced speech, victims sought to stop or to hide these responses through the use of charms. Again and again, legal writers caution their readers to be alert to the use of the charms. In 1611, Gabriel Cayron, the former *procureur* of the *parlement* of Toulouse, instructed magistrates that they must exhort the accused to tell the truth, and then the *exécuteur de la haute justice* must do his duty, "who in so doing customarily shaves the hair from the head of the accused with scissors: and sometimes passes his finger in the mouth of the accused, to know if there are any charms hidden there."[56] In a work published in 1671, Laurent Bouchel recounted witnessing persons being shaved and searched for charms—"any enchanted remedy against the force of the pain, in order to be without feeling during the pain and torture"—preparatory to torture.[57] Philippe Bornier, in his commentary on the ordinance of 1670, also warned against "some charms or drugs to render oneself less sensitive to the pains of the *question.*"[58]

More than a hundred years later, the belief persisted: Antoine Despeisses noted that torture could be repeated without the introduction of new evidence if there was reason to suspect that the accused had eaten or drunk something to protect him from the pain or used artifices that might prevent him from speaking the truth.[59] Preventing the use of such charms was preferable to repeating interrogations, and so, as late as the 1750s, writers recommended that the accused be shaved and searched for charms hidden on or in the body. In 1784, four years after the abolition of the *question préparatoire* and four years before the abolition of the *question préalable,* François Serpillon reprinted the story of a bandit who sought to protect himself from the pain of torture by eating soap, which was believed to render the nerves insensible. Upon administration of the necessary "antidote" to this induced painlessness—some wine—the bandit regained his bodily sensation and confessed.[60] Even at this late date, there remained a conviction—now medicalized—that individuals could employ magical or medical charms to protect themselves from pain.

The evidence of the manuals suggests that, despite customary regional differences in the actual practice of torture, there was a broad consensus about the practice. Legal writers, north and south, agreed for two hundred years that the experience of pain was central to the function of torture: eliminate the pain, and the truth would cease to issue forth. The fear and humiliation attendant upon the experience were not adequate to force the truth, nor should they be deliberately employed to coerce speech. So much was pain considered central to the truth of the confession that in 1750, Antoine Despeisses defended the necessity of the reiteration of confession twenty-four hours after torture by explaining that the repudiation of testimony was an indication that it was given out of fear and, as such, should not be trusted.[61] Pain was the primary channel of truth.[62]

These authors agreed that charms could stop this pain, obstructing justice while they numbed pain. And the charms employed were often the same ones across the country: a bullet concealed on the body, a scrap of paper with magical words hidden under the tongue, a soap solution drunk in the cell.[63]

The belief that pain would force truth from the guilty, provided that the proper measures were taken to deprive them of magical defenses, was joined to another belief about the body and the supernatural: that God would protect the innocent from unjust punishment.[64] Several authors reproduced a narrative from Saint Jerome to demonstrate this conviction.[65] In their retellings, Jerome relates that a man and a woman were accused of adultery and tortured for their confessions: the man, who preferred a quick death to long suffering, admitted his guilt; but the woman maintained her innocence, calling upon Jesus Christ to help her as witness to her innocence. Despite her refusal to confess her guilt, she was condemned to die. But when the time came to execute her, the executioner could not: four times he tried to plunge a dagger into her throat, without creating a wound. The crowd, believing they had witnessed a miracle, chased away the executioner in order to save the woman. But the official responsible for the execution was determined to carry out his duty and struck her three times more, and on the third stroke she fell as if dead. The religious charged with her care received her body for burial, and during that time she was revived. Hearing of her miraculous recovery, the judge again demanded fulfillment of the sentence, but the religious intervened on her behalf with the emperor to gain her life and liberty.

This story is in many ways at the core of jurists' view of torture. Without charms, the guilty will confess and be condemned; without charms, the innocent will suffer and be saved. The guilty will tell the truth; the innocent will as well. That the woman's accused partner apparently lied and thus wrongly incriminated himself, provoking his own death, is not admitted or examined by these writers. The guilty will be punished; the innocent will be spared. All of this is true because God will act in the world to save them: miracles happen. Guilty and innocent alike will receive their just rewards.

By means of such narratives, torture is connected to the sacred: it purports to be the scene of divine intervention, of divine truth, of innocent witnesses suffering for their merciful God. But the divine element of torture was also linked to its opposite, to the infernal. Etienne Pasquier devoted an article to the already archaic word *gehir* in his *Les recherches de la France*. The noun *géhenne* derived from this verb meant "une peine de mort éternelle" (an eternal suffering); the common noun derived from it, *gesne*, meant torture "in order to extort . . . the truth of the fact."[66] Guillaume de Segla identifies the word *géhenne* as derived from the Hebrew place name for a valley near Jerusalem "in which they threw refuse, and burned corpses," a word extended to mean Hell, "to show that it was a horrible and cruel thing."[67] Yet another etymology of the word was offered by Philippe Bornier:

> It is called *géhenne* because of the violence of the torment, from the Hebrew word *Gehinnon*, which was a valley near Jerusalem where they threw refuse, and burned corpses, and Hell is also called *géhenne* in the Holy Scriptures.[68]

The archaic word denoting torture, then, was identified by French legal writers as derived from a word meaning Hell, but a hell in which God might yet be present.

These connections between torture, Heaven, and Hell; these elaborate rituals of stripping and shaving and searching bodily cavities for magical aids; these counsels that judges behave in a Christian fashion: all identify torture as a ritualized activity. If rituals are understood to be repetitive and rule-governed, if they are understood to connect the visible and invisible realms through the performance of ceremonial activities, then torture must be considered to be a ritual.[69] The ritual aspects of torture will be fully explored in the following chapter; here, I want only to introduce the idea that the authors of these manuals implicitly viewed torture as such.

What identifies torture as an early modern ritual? Not only the articulated connections to the sacred that we find upon examination of the derivations of words, and in the use of classical narrative; not only the elaborate purifying rituals of shaving and searching; not only the ritual garb worn by all the participants and the ritual phrases employed throughout the procedure identify it as ritual, but so too do the rational and measured descriptions and definitions of torture frame it as ritual. Torture is a liminal experience because it cannot be pinned down in definitions: it is always "between" other experiences. It is worse than death but it is not death; more painful than any punishment, but it is not a true punishment in that it carries none of the infamy of a punishment.[70]

Furthermore, the physical practice of torture symbolically reinforces its liminal character. The *estrapade* literally takes the accused out of his element, hauling him from the earth into the air; the *question d'eau* acts as some strange reversal of baptism, expelling the accused from the community of citizens.

From that liminal space, that antisocial space, came the voice of the accused, speaking truth. Involuntarily, without the will or against the will of the accused, the truth spilled into the social space of the cell, recorded while it was manifest in the body and the voice. Truth came from outside the community, from inside the body of the one who has been thrust outside of the community. The accused spoke the truth not freely but under compulsion, and it was precisely this compulsion—the inability to lie, to speak anything but the truth that resides in the flesh—which made evidence acquired under torture so valuable.

But what about those instances mentioned in the manuals, when men and women lie and condemn others? There was an explanation, a partial explanation, for this. Some truths are not truths. Testimony about the self can be trusted: what you say about yourself in pain is true. What you say about others is not.

And yet there continued to be anxiety on this count. Many authors noted that not only are there cases in which people try to accuse others of crimes they themselves have committed but that there are even cases of people confessing to crimes they themselves have not committed. There was a deep concern in these laconic accounts about truth-telling and its consequences, about ultimate rewards, and about the presence of God in this world.

In place of the missing truth, these authors offered evidence to their readers. Many manuals reproduced manuscript material from the *parlements*, reprinting interrogations in their entirety. Verisimilitude, the appearance of truth, stood in for truth, as if it might substitute for the lies sometimes told in torture. Truth about torture might substitute for truth in torture.

Torture for these legal writers was a means to *savoir la vérité de sa bouche*, to know the truth from the mouth of the accused. But these authors exhibit profound uncertainty about the truth. They were themselves led into contradictions: torture achieves the truth, although only the truth about the self; but sometimes people lie even about themselves, even when it means their own death. Torture's ultimate defense, therefore, lay in its social utility, the "good results" it produced in the form of convictions. But this utilitarian defense of the practice bore little relation to its epistemological underpinning. If torture produced truth in situations of uncertainty, then certainty rather than utility was the only appropriate defense of the practice.

It is as if jurists had sought in torture for the one true language of truth and of humanity: in the sounds and signs of the body, in the words and gestures of the accused, the unavoidable truth would express itself independent of its immediate source. But in place of this epistemological certainty, jurists had only certain convictions.

Jurists found themselves confronted by evidence that made them doubt the certainty that it was truth that was being expressed through these means. As magistrates lost faith in traditional forms of evidence, which relied on the body and its ability to produce language, like bleeding corpses, so too did they lose faith in pain and its ability to produce truth. Indeed, the royal edict of 1788 that abolished the *question préalable* took up this problem directly:

> This proof almost always becomes questionable by the absurd confessions, the contradictions and the retractions of the criminals. It is embarrassing for the judges who cannot untangle the truth from the midst of the cries of pain. Finally, it is dangerous for the innocent, in that torture pushes the tortured to make false declarations, that they dare not retract for fear of seeing their torments renewed.[71]

That some truths were being spoken in pain was doubtless—but that there was a necessary relationship between pain and truth was less sure. Truths could no longer be distinguished from insignificant bodily expressions; lies seemed to be reinforced by pain.

French criminal procedure permitted the practice of torture as a legal procedure in specific cases when evidence was lacking, and this practice was supported by a perceived relationship between pain and truth, between the body and language. As the connections between these terms were weakened, however, the location of the truth was itself put in question. Should truth not have a bodily location, should it be a metaphysical rather than a physical property, or should it be the result of a process of agreement rather than the discovery of a unitary fact, then the entire process was called into question. Torture thus lay at the center of an epistemological crisis.

Likewise, should pain fail to produce the language of the body (despite its success in coercing language from the body), should the body fall silent or speak meaninglessly, as when bodies bled indiscriminately, before any and all witnesses, then torture lost its best tool in rooting out truth. When pain ceased to produce meaning, torture became a meaningless activity—cruel and inhuman because it was pointless.

These legal manuals sought to establish a clear and irrefutable connection between truth and the body, pain and language. Yet they failed to theorize a relationship between them, despite their biblical references, reprinted interrogations, and personal anecdotes, that was convincing even to themselves. Despite their attempts to represent cries of pain as the mediate language of truth, doubts remained. Torture was supported by a pair of interconnected relationships: between the body and language, and between truth and pain. Over time, each of these relationships was deconstructed and reconstituted, undermining the stability of the foundation of torture. Bodies no longer spoke a mediate and visual language, nor did they speak in blood; but the marks upon them were signs that could be interpreted like a language. Similarly, the relationship between pain and truth was broken down: charms were no longer feared because the pain they might or might not prevent bore no stable relationship to the truth. Without these solid relations, the theory of painful truths, which supported judicial torture, crumbled.

The *mordaches* or *brodequins*. From Jean Milles de Souvigny, *Praxis criminis persequendi* (Paris, 1541). Courtesy of New York Public Library, Spencer Collection.

3

"To know the truth from his mouth": The Practice

of Torture in the *Parlement* of Toulouse, 1600–1788

We have viewed early modern torture closely, through a single case and through the manuals that the *parlementaires* consulted when seeking guidance. Now let us step back for a broader view in ways that the judges could not. In this chapter, statistical analysis of sentences to torture, combined with close readings of interrogations conducted under torture, yield another view of the practice, one that demonstrates the slow changes at work in the courts. For if the theory of torture as expressed in legal manuals held a kernel of instability, what can be said of the practice of torture? Was it, too, essentially static despite internal contradictions, or did it change over time? Just as legal manuals reveal the theory of torture, how it was supposed to work, manuscript sources reveal its quotidian practice, how it did in fact work.

Examination of the sentences to torture pronounced by the *parlement* of Toulouse from 1600 to 1780 demonstrates that torture was deployed with diminishing frequency over the course of the period under study. Close readings of the same sentences hint at other changes. As the kinds of information presented and the turns of phrase employed in the sentences change, we can begin to sketch changes in the function and meaning of torture, most notably, the loss of its purgatory function in the 1620s. Such readings also point to the enduring belief in truth as a physical property lodged in the body.

Interrogations, on the other hand, reveal the gradual breakdown of the epistemology of torture. Growing uncertainty about the meaning of pain and its relationship to the truth is suggested in the loss of the language of pain, visible in the increasingly abstract and concise language of the interrogations and in the desacralization of truth in the 1720s. What remained after these changes were the oaths and questions associated with all early modern European justice systems, and the physical practice of torture itself, stripped of its rationale, stripped of the meaningful pain and sacred truth that justified its painful practice.

Examination of trial records, therefore, produces a different picture than the one derived from legal manuals. Where the manuals present a picture of surprising stasis as regards the theory of torture, the court documents offer an image of gradual change in the practice of torture. Weighted with formulaic language and ritualized procedures, the practice of torture did not change rapidly, but it did change. Likewise, the manner in which torture was recorded and represented underwent significant changes. Throughout the period under study, state authorities maintained careful records: the *dossiers*, the sentences, and the interrogations themselves. These records are what permit us to reconstitute the practice of torture.

In collecting data for this study, I began by examining all extant interrogations conducted under torture during the seventeenth and eighteenth centuries—sixty-three cases involving seventy-seven individuals—which were filed in a subseries during the nineteenth century.[1] These interrogations include procedural information concerning the legal history of each case. As a result, I was able to trace the interlocutory or definitive sentence in these cases in which the defendant was sentenced to torture. As I read the sentences in cases for which interrogations are extant, however, I noticed that in some instances there was no mention of torture whatsoever in the sentence.

In the case of Armans Grassie, for example, the interrogation clearly indicates that the court of first instance had ordered that Grassie be sentenced to torture.[2] However, the *arrêt* of the *parlement* that was pronounced when the case was reviewed on appeal fails to make either the death sentence or the sentence to torture explicit, noting only the traditional phrase, "the Court orders that the said sentence will have its full and entire effect and will be executed following its form and terms."[3] A survey of the registers of the criminal court would not identify this case as one involving torture because there is no explicit reference to torture in the sentence, only the confirmation of an unspecified sentence of the lower court. Given the relative silence of the *parlement* concerning details of sentences, any survey of its *arrêts* must of necessity undercount the number of cases involving torture.

Yet even a partial view of the relative frequency with which torture was employed by the *parlement* seemed essential. I therefore went on to sample the sentences in the volumes of *arrêts* produced by the *parlement* of Toulouse at ten-year intervals from 1600 to 1780, when the *question préparatoire* was abolished, and annually from 1780 to 1788, when the *question préalable* was in turn abolished. This sample produced a further seventy-seven cases involving eighty-five individuals, thus yielding a total of 140 cases in which sentences to torture were pronounced either by a court of first instance or by the *parlement*.[4] The goals of conducting this sample were both to determine the frequency with which torture was employed and to track any changes in its use.

When I discuss the quotidian practice of torture, therefore, I am drawing on information derived from two distinct groups. The first group includes those cases identified through the extant interrogations that are irregularly distributed across the period under study; the second, those cases identified through regular sampling of the registers of sentences, in the full knowledge that such a sample would necessarily miss an unknown number of cases involving torture. Because these groups are not easy to compare, in any discussion of changes reflected in statistics I will make reference to each group individually.

Together, these two groups of sentences name 162 persons to be tortured. Also, they note the presence of 106 additional codefendants who awaited the reports of interrogations under torture before judgment was pronounced in their cases. Because, as noted above, some sentences fail to mention explicitly the use of torture, this sample must be regarded as offering a minimum estimate of the use of torture, as there are undoubtedly still more sentences in which there is no explicit reference to torture but that nonetheless involved a sentence of torture pronounced by the court of first instance.

The number of cases located in the sample is inadequate for a developed statistical study of the practice. Indeed, so small a number of cases might suggest to the reader, as it has to some historians, the diminished importance of the practice of torture thanks to its restricted and declining use over the course of the seventeenth and eighteenth centuries.[5] Yet the infrequent practice of torture by no means suggests its insignificance. However few or many victims of torture there were in old regime France, the issue of torture was an important one throughout this period, as is demonstrated by the contemporary commentaries on the practice. In this way, the practice of torture in early modern France was not unlike the practice of capital punishment in the contemporary United States; to dismiss the issue as insignificant because of the relatively few individuals who are sentenced to death and executed is to misunderstand its place in law and in culture. The information drawn from these documents is important, therefore, not because of the volume of cases but because of their contemporary importance. In addition, what these documents lack in numbers they make up for in detail: they offer the opportunity to examine legal language and legal rituals at the same time as they provide the documentary evidence that lay behind the eighteenth-century debate about torture. But it is also true that, given

the small number of cases, the statistics these documents yield are suggestive at best.

There were two principal forms of torture, which differed according to the
legal status of the accused and to the intent of the procedure. The *question
préparatoire* was designed to elicit a confession from the accused before guilt
was determined, while the *question préalable* aimed to elicit the names of
accomplices after the guilt of the accused had been determined. The use of
both the *question préparatoire* and the *question préalable* was in steady decline throughout the period in question, when viewed through the sample
group, with use of the *question préparatoire* declining dramatically. The
parlement of Toulouse sentenced forty-six individuals to the *question préparatoire* from 1600 to 1659, and a further twelve individuals from 1660 to
1719, followed by only five individuals from 1720 to 1779. Use of the *question préalable*, never as frequent as that of the *question préparatoire*, declined
at ever-increasing rates. From a high of twelve individuals sentenced to the
question préalable from 1600 to 1659, the number dropped to six individuals
from 1660 to 1719, and then to only two individuals from 1720 to 1779.[6]
Should these numbers be inflated by a factor of, say, 10 to estimate the
numbers of sentences to torture? Simply inflating these numbers is deceiv-
ing in part because inventories of sentences—not found in Toulouse—help
to reconstruct the practice of torture differently than sampling the registers
of sentences, which underreport the numbers.

The numbers derived from the sample should not suggest, however, that
torture was not a regular procedure of the *parlement* in the last third of this
period. Examination of the extant interrogations provides a corrective to
this view. Although the sample reveals only five individuals sentenced to
the *question préparatoire* and only two individuals to the *question préalable*
from 1720 to 1779, the interrogation sentences find fourteen individuals
sentenced to the *question préparatoire* and thirty individuals sentenced to
the *question préalable* during the same period. An annual sample of sentences would in all probability support the conclusion that torture was ordered at least once annually in the *parlement* of Toulouse until the abolition
of the *question préparatoire* in 1780.[7] Studies of other courts estimate an
average of three sentences to the *question préparatoire* and twenty-one cases
of the *question préalable* during the seventeenth century.[8]

One of the most significant findings that derive from the examination
of these two groups of sentences concerns the timing of the decline in sentencing to torture. This study indicates that the dramatic decline in sentencing to torture occurred in the first third of the period from 1600 to
1659, specifically, during the period between 1640 and 1660, when sen-

tences to torture dropped by more than half. The criminal reform legislation of 1670, which permitted sentences to corporal and capital punishments without full confessions, did not, therefore, have a significant impact on the use of torture in the *parlement* of Toulouse.[9] The decline in sentencing to torture cannot be attributed solely to legislative changes that permitted greater ease in sentencing to punishment. And it must be noted at the same time that this legislation failed to eliminate the practice of torture. Although the judges of the *parlement* of Toulouse greatly diminished their use of torture before the criminal law reforms of 1670, they remained committed to the practice, despite its theoretical obsolescence.

The other noteworthy finding is the ratio of *question préparatoire* to *question préalable* sentences. In other *parlements*, sentences to the *question préalable* were far more frequent than sentences to the *question préparatoire*, in some courts by a factor of 7:1.[10] Yet my findings in Toulouse—which I would again stress are not definitive because of the failure of those sentences to be reliably explicit as regards the use of torture—show a preference for the use of the *question préparatoire* over the *question préalable*. Is this why the *parlement* of Toulouse acquired a reputation for judicial fanaticism—because it relied more heavily than did other *parlements* on the torture of individuals not yet convicted of crimes? Does it suggest a different epistemology of truth in that *parlement*? Only further research into patterns of sentences to torture in other *parlements* would fully answer these questions.

The pattern of the actual employment of torture, however, differs from the pattern of sentencing to torture. When the *parlement* reviewed the capital and corporal sentences of lower courts, it had the option to amend, overturn, or confirm those sentences. Despite political conflicts between the *parlement* and lower courts, it tended to support sentences to torture pronounced by lower courts: in fourteen cases, the *parlement* added a sentence of torture; in fifteen cases, it overturned a sentence to torture; and in all other cases, it confirmed the lower court sentence.[11]

Yet the general support of lower court sentences to torture displayed by the *parlement* did not prevent the court from tinkering with these sentences. The *parlement* intervened in lower court sentences not only by amending or overturning them, but also by limiting the performance of sentences to torture through the use of *retentums*. The *retentum* was a secret instruction added to the sentence. In the case of *retentums* added to sentences of torture, the purpose of this instruction was to reduce the rigor of the sentence or to require that the *question* be "presented" rather than performed, so that the accused be prepared in every way for torture but that the torture not be physically performed. The *retentum* was kept from the listening public, including the accused. It was never read aloud, although it was acted upon. In practice, *retentums* were never added to sentences to the *question préparatoire,* but only to sentences to the *question préalable,* in absolute defiance of the instructions of legal manuals.[12] This suggests that the *question préalable* was viewed by the *parlementaires* to some degree as a form of punishment from which the condemned might mercifully be spared. The *question préparatoire,* on the other hand, seems to have been regarded by the *parlement* as a purely evidentiary procedure that had to be completed in order to bring a trial to successful completion.

Retentums restricting the use of the *question* by reducing the sentence from the *question ordinaire et extraordinaire* to the *question ordinaire,* for example, or requiring that the *question* be presented rather than performed were added to sentences from 1620 on. The sample group yields three instances in which *retentums* were employed to restrict the use of torture, and only one instance requiring a diminution of the *question* from performance to presentation. The interrogations likewise yield a single case in which the *retentum* was employed to restrict the use of torture. But *retentums* were widely employed in the interrogation sentences to alter the sentence from performance to presentation of the *question:* twenty-three instances of such *retentums* exist, or one-third of the interrogation sentences.

Sentencing to torture, therefore, cannot be equated with use of torture. Sentencing to torture declined dramatically around 1650 while the use of restrictive *retentums* speeded the diminution of the use of torture. Diminished use of sentences to torture and increased use of restrictive *retentums* combined to lower the numbers of individuals who suffered the *question* in full.

Examination of sentences to torture thus yields a picture of relative clemency in contrast to the one painted by eighteenth-century abolitionists. Toulousain judges required the use of torture with ever-declining frequency and attached restrictive *retentums* to sentences of *question préalable* that would spare the condemned the pain of the torture they were instructed to endure, if not the terror. At the same time, judges remained committed to the *question préparatoire* as an evidentiary procedure, requesting it with consistently greater frequency than its counterpart and refusing to attach *retentums* to sentences in which it was called for.

The reforms of 1670 did not produce a dramatic decline in sentencing to torture, because that decline had occurred independently of legal reforms, two or three decades previously. And despite this voluntary retrenchment, judges remained committed to the use of torture, employing it with regularity over the next 120 years. The reforms of 1670 failed to bring about either a dramatic decline in or a complete halt to sentencing to torture. The epistemological power of torture was not addressed by those reforms. It remained a compelling evidentiary procedure employed with some regularity until its abolition, despite the questions and controversies it accumulated over time. For the rationale that governed torture was driven not simply by laws, but by cultural beliefs that legal reforms did not address.

Any and all statistics generated from the sentences of necessity reflect more information about the judges and judicial behavior than about the defendants. Nonetheless, these data can be used to derive some limited information about the accused. Some patterns emerge among these statistics: the vast majority of torture victims were adult men; and the women most likely to be tortured were older single women, especially widows.[13]

But what is truly striking is the lack of clear patterns. Torture victims were not members of particular social or ethnic groups, they neither espoused nor were alleged to espouse a particular religion or ideology, they were not marginal to the society in which they lived but rather, insofar as can be determined from the occupations of the men, were drawn from a great variety of circumstances. Early modern victims of torture came to the attention of judges solely on the basis of the crimes of which they were suspected. Judicial torture was not an ideological tool in the narrow sense of the word.

Jean Bourdil's sentence was, within this context, altogether typical. Sentenced to the *question préparatoire,* the form of torture that consistently predominated, he was granted no clemency in the form of a *retentum,* as was the case for all those sentenced to the *question préparatoire.* Only twenty-five, he was younger than the average man sentenced to torture but, like most of the other men, was married. Although the very proofs that were required to sentence him to torture were also adequate to sentence him to any penalty short of death—thanks to the reforms of 1670—his judges were nonetheless determined to employ the *question.*

Although the sentences fail to provide information that illuminates popular attitudes toward criminal activity, they offer unique insight into elite attitudes.[14] Rich in formulae and ritual phrases, close examination of the language of sentencing provides the basis for the study of changing elite attitudes toward crime, criminals, and appropriate official responses. Examination of the *arrêts* for their turns of phrase therefore offers the possibility of discerning some shifts of attitude as regards torture. Not only the occurrence of ritual phrases, but also the gradual incorporation of new pieces of information into the genre offers material for study.

An "ideal" sentence, compiled from the information presented in actual sentences, would contain a great deal of information, including the present status of the case; the legal history of the case; information concerning the accused; information concerning the crime; and the outcome of the case. Yet few, if any, sentences conform to this model.[15] Rather, sentences reflect a slowly shifting accretion of information. A few pieces of information were standard throughout the period: the name of the accused; the prison in which he or she was being held; the names of the judges hearing the case; the date of the hearing; the name of the court of first instance and the date of its sentence; and the sentence of the *parlement*. These bits of information provided the essence of the sentence: a sketch of the persons present in the court and the traces of the legal history that accompanied them. But more information than this was available, and was gradually included.

Information concerning the trial itself was and remained most complete. The legal history of the case was noted with great precision: the court of first instance was noted in 142 of 151 cases; and the date of its sentence, in 140 cases.[16] Despite this, the specifics of the sentence passed by the lower court was noted in only fourteen instances, or fewer than 10 percent of cases—which may give some hint as to how seriously sampling the registers of the *parlement* undercounts sentencing to torture. The date of the hearing was noted in every sentence; the location of the hearing, in 151 instances; the names of the judges, in 148 instances. When the court sat in special session that too was noted.

The location of the hearing was consistently noted and was alternately called the *chambre criminelle* or the *chambre tournelle*. The first term predominated until the 1680s, when some sentences noted hearings occurring in the *chambre tournelle*. These two terms were used interchangeably from 1680 to 1720, after which *tournelle* was employed exclusively. The *tournelle* was the name of the criminal court of the *parlement* of Paris, because the court sat in the *Petit Tour de Saint-Louis*, and the name was gradually transferred to the criminal courts of the provincial *parlements*.[17] Numerous manuals and subsequent histories of the court were forced to derive careful etymologies of the term. The reason for the name change was perhaps part of the *parlementaires'* desire to elaborate a history and a tradition for the court, perhaps part of the co-optation of the court by the crown.

Information concerning the accused altered most. Although the name of the accused was the single piece of information concerning the accused most frequently recorded in the sentences (98 percent of total extant sentences), little other information pertaining to the accused was included at the beginning of the period.[18] Nicknames were noted in a total of twenty-eight sentences. Among the sample sentences, this practice was focused in the period 1600–1659, when eleven sentences noted a nickname of the accused; this practice virtually disappeared after 1720.

The accused's marital status was infrequently noted in the sentences although it was a matter of routine inquiry during interrogations. Other familial relationships were more likely to be noted in the sentence: in twenty-four instances, the accused was defined in relation to someone other than a spouse (16 percent of total extant sentences). Information concerning the accused's familial relationships was included primarily after 1680. The accused's occupation and residence or birthplace were noted with less frequency.

The legal standing enjoyed by the accused received more attention than his or her social location: 126 total extant sentences (83.4 percent of total extant sentences) note the specific prison in which the accused was held pending trial. A further seventy-one sentences (46.4 percent of total extant sentences) noted whether the accused stood at the *barre* or sat on the *sellette* in requesting an appeal. This information, like that pertaining to the accused's familial location, was recorded only after 1680. After 1680, this information was contained in 78.8 percent of total extant sentences.

Oddly enough, information concerning the crime itself was sparse. Less than half of the sentences record the charge against the accused, whereas after 1680, all sentences except one included the charge. Likewise, the name of the victim and his or her relationship to the accused were recorded in only eight instances, primarily in the decade after 1770.

The *parlement's* sentence was recorded in every *arrêt*, though not always with a great degree of specificity. As noted above, some sentences merely confirmed the sentence of the lower court with the phrase, "the Court orders that the said sentence will have its full and entire effect and will be executed following its form and terms." Most sentences specified who should perform the sentence, and in almost two-thirds of the cases in which that information was provided, the *parlement* requested that the *capitouls* of Toulouse execute the sentence. In twenty cases, the officers of the *parlement* deputized to witness the interrogation itself were also named in the sentence. This information was most often recorded after 1720.

This examination suggests that sentences calling for torture began to record additional information in three distinct stages. After 1680, the charge against the accused and his or her likelihood of guilt in the eyes of the court as indicated by his or her presence on the *sellette* or behind the *barre*, as well as his or her place within a social world outside the court were noted. Around 1720, the court began to view itself and its procedure with a new seriousness, definitively renaming its criminal chamber and recording the names of those officers deputized to hear interrogations with some regularity. Then, after 1770, the name of the victim and his or her relationship to the accused was more often recorded.

Changes in the representation of crime can, therefore, be read in the accretion of information in the sentences. Their evidence suggests that the judges increasingly located crime within a social as well as a legal world, as indicated by notations of the accused's relationships, the name of the victim where pertinent, and the victim's relationship to the accused. At the same time, the legal world within which crime was defined and criminals were judged grew ever more concerned with the specifics of violations and the probabilities of guilt and with its own professional importance.

Not only do the sentences indicate changes in the perception of crime, criminals, and the courts, they also offer some insight into the cultural beliefs that supported the practice of torture. Almost one-fifth of the sentences offer no rationale whatsoever for the use of torture, but in the majority of cases, standard phrases were employed to offer a rationale for ordering a sentence to torture. In the case of the *question préparatoire*, torture could be ordered only to obtain a confession of or knowledge about an actual crime; in the case of the *question préalable*, information concerning alleged accomplices might also be sought. In each instance, the language of the sentence reflected not only the specific purpose of the sentence, but also traces of the beliefs that supported the practice of torture.

Belief in the bodily location of evidence is reflected in the formulaic phrases employed in the sentences that sought confessions of crimes. The phrase most often encountered in these sentences is some variant of "pour de sa bouche savoir la vérité" (to know the truth from his mouth). The wording of the phrase is arranged in three ways: "pour de sa bouche savoir la vérité des cas et crimes" (to know the truth of the case and crime from his mouth), "pour de sa bouche savoir la vérité du fait" (to know the truth of the event from his mouth), and "pour de sa bouche savoir la vérité du fait de sa prestation" (to know the truth of his oath from his mouth). Truth and the act of knowing are consistently connected with the physical body rather than with the act of speaking or telling. In fact, in the various formulaic phrases that appear as the rationales for torture, "savoir" (to know) appears only once without the concomitant "sa bouche" (his mouth). Truth and the body appear to be virtually inseparable through the lens of these sentences. The embodiedness of the truth, its physical reality and location, are not merely assumed but expressed in the sentences. Torture is thus the means of revealing the intimate connection of truth and the body and then severing that tie.

The physical rootedness of knowledge is further stressed in the single sentence that ordered torture without the use of the verb *savoir* and instead ordered the use of torture "pour tirer la vérité de sa bouche" (to draw the truth from his mouth). Here, the struggle to make body and truth part ways is demonstrated by the verb, "tirer": truth, like teeth, is drawn from the body. The discovery of truth is a physical operation.

On occasion it is a confession, truthful or not, that is sought, "pour tirer de lui l'aveu de son crime, complices et circonstances" (to draw the confession of his crime, accomplices, and circumstances from him). The location of confessional knowledge differs from that of truth. Truth, as we have seen, is located in the body; confession, on the other hand, is located more ambiguously in the self, the *lui*. Truth is located in the body; confession, with all its moral complexities, in the conscious self.

In sentences to the *question préalable*, which sought the names of accomplices, another formulaic phrase was employed. The accused was sentenced to torture "pour de sa bouche savoir ses complices" (to know his accomplices from his mouth) or "pour de sa bouche savoir le nom et qualité de ses complices" (to know the name and *qualité* of his accomplices from his mouth), phrases that again stress the connection between knowledge and the body. It should be noted, however, that it is knowledge concerning accomplices that is sought rather than the truth about oneself. An epistemological distinction is being drawn in these sentences between the evidence one can produce against oneself and against others. Torture was employed to produce truth concerning the self, and knowledge or information concerning others.

The range of verbs that describe the attempt to acquire information concerning accomplices is far more varied than the monotonous "savoir" (to know) the truth of the crime. Torture might be ordered "pour savoir" (to know) information concerning accomplices, but the phrases "pour découvrir ses complices" (to discover his accomplices), "pour déclarer ses complices" (to state [the names of] his accomplices), and "pour avoir révélation de ses complices" (to reveal his accomplices) also appear. Information concerning accomplices might be known, discovered, confessed, and simply possessed; in any case, it must be surrendered through the physical process of discovery that was torture.

The formulaic language of the sentences points to cultural beliefs that encouraged the legal practice of torture: a sincere belief in the physical location of knowledge, in embodied truth. Still obscure is the true nature of pain: was it the cause of the separation of truth and the body, the instrument that severed the two, or simply the effect of that severance? The refusal of judges to attach restrictive *retentums* to sentences to the *question préparatoire* suggests that pain was in fact viewed as the cause of the disjunction of body and truth. In cases in which evidentiary questions concerning the accused were at stake, pain was viewed as a reliable tool to extort personal truths.

There is still one other phrase found in the sentences that requires attention. To the *question préparatoire*, to which no restrictive *retentums* were added, another *retentum* was regularly added from 1600 through 1620: the phrase "demeurant les preuves et indices" (reserving the proofs and evidence). The effect of this *retentum* was to prevent the purgation of evidence in interrogations that sought to determine the guilt or innocence of the accused. Failure to add this *retentum* meant that in cases in which the accused confessed nothing the charges against the accused had to be dropped since, by his or her maintenance of innocence, the evidence against him or her was nullified. Legal manuals reminded the *greffier* of the power of the phrase. In seventeen sentences between 1600 and 1620, almost two-thirds of the sentences to the *question préparatoire*, this phrase was added in a *retentum*.

This same phrase began to appear in the body of sentences in the 1620s.[19] No longer appended to prevent the natural purgatory function of torture, the phrase "demeurant les preuves et indices" regularly appeared in the bodies of sentences, sixteen times from 1620 to 1659, seventeen times from 1660 to 1719, and nine times from 1720 to 1779. As this phrase became part of the formulaic language that sentenced an individual to torture, rather than an exceptional notion included after the specifics of sentencing, torture lost its purgatory function in practice if not in theory. As the language of the sentences ossified, the possibility that torture might or might not purge proofs diminished, as it was never permitted to do so; thus, by the eighteenth century, although the phrase was only irregularly included, proofs were not purged even in those cases in which the accused failed to confess. The regular inclusion of the phrase in the middle period from 1660 to 1719 implied the impossibility of purgation; so that by the last period, torture was assumed not to possess this power. To order the *question préparatoire* strongly implied a reserve of proofs. Beginning in the 1620s, when the phrase "demeurant les preuves et indices" was shifted from *retentums* to the bodies of sentences, torture was stripped of one of its original functions, that which permitted the accused to convict or acquit himself on the basis of his own truthful testimony.

In theory, the reforms of 1670 made the phrase obsolete. And, as indicated above, it appeared with greatly diminished frequency after that date. But still it appeared on occasion, an archaic reminder of a moment when, but for its inclusion, all evidence against the accused might be waived in the face of their insistence upon their innocence.

Examination of sentences to torture permits the construction of a chronology of torture during the period of its decline. Changes in the conceptualization and employment of torture can be noted as early as 1620, when judicial discretion in sentencing determined that the *question préparatoire* lost its ability to purge the proofs against the accused. From this point on, torture was an unambiguous evidentiary procedure of the courts, entirely different from earlier judicial procedures like the ordeal, which conflated the giving of evidence with indications of guilt or innocence.[20]

A generation later, around 1650, sentencing to torture experienced a dramatic decline. Although it was regularly employed by the *parlement* of Toulouse until its abolition, torture would never again be employed as frequently. Thus, the decrease in the use of torture seems unrelated to the legal reforms of 1670. Whether or not those reforms made torture obsolete, judges had already diminished their use of the procedure. That they continued to use it even after the reforms suggests that although the *question* may well have been obsolete from a strictly legal point of view in that torture was no longer necessary to obtain criminal convictions, the practice of torture had strong foundations that made its continued use compelling, if only on a minor scale.

Other changes, less directly related to the practice of torture, are evident. In the 1680s, questions of guilt and crime were foregrounded as the specifics of the violation, and the probabilities of innocence or guilt were noted with greater frequency by the court. In the 1720s, the court's view of its own importance was reflected in notations of the names of the officials required to attend interrogations and in its new archaic-sounding name for the criminal chamber. Finally, in the 1770s, crime was itself represented by the court as a violation not only of the legal order but also of the social order, as more details concerning the victim were included in sentences.

Throughout the period under study, however, the cultural beliefs that supported the practice of torture—that the truth was embodied and that pain might free it from its carnal location—were sustained. In one sentence after another, the phrase "pour savoir la vérité de sa bouche" was reiterated. Although the practice of torture underwent gradual change, its epistemological foundations, as represented in the sentences, remained solid. The interrogations tell another story.

Just as the sentences of the *parlement* reveal important changes in the employment and function of torture, so do the interrogations record shifts in the way in which torture was understood by the men who ordered its use. Interrogations conducted under torture were characterized by distant and hierarchical relations between judge and accused. In the seclusion of the torture chamber, no greetings or insults were exchanged. Admonitions addressed to the accused warned of divine consequences for the failure to tell the truth. Oaths were required of some, though not all, of the participants. Questions that presupposed a sequence of events prevailed over questions that sought to elicit new information. Questions put to the accused under torture were ritualized and formulaic, asking for no more than an acknowledgment or confession of guilt, rather than asking for the telling details that might demonstrate guilt or innocence. Although legal manuals required that every word and gesture be recorded, the *greffiers* did not, in fact, record every piece of information. Over time, abstracts of testimony of the accused were recorded in preference to the careful and literal transcriptions of an earlier period. Through it all, the physical practice of torture was unchanged.

On 25 May 1726, Jean Bourdil was taken from his cell in the *hôtel de ville* and transferred to the *chambre de la gesne et question*, the torture chamber, to face his interrogators. They were guided that morning both by legal manuals and by customary practice. Their actions were neither arbitrary nor spontaneous. Their questions were prepared in advance. For these three men, the interrogation was a fully anticipated and carefully orchestrated event, one of the many rituals of old regime justice. Their first words to the prisoner were to instruct him and to place the burden of the responsibility for the proceedings upon him:

> We exhorted him to tell the truth, and that in so doing he would avoid the torment that is prepared for him, asking him moreover to tell us if anyone had advised him to deny the truth to justice.[21]

For the rest of the morning, the interrogators would alternate between exhorting and questioning the prisoner.

Bourdil was urged to tell the truth as a means of avoiding physical pain. In earlier decades, these exhortations and admonitions also promised divine consequences, which ranged from direct intercession to ease the physical pain of torture for those who spoke the truth to spiritual damnation for the failure to confess. In 1685, Marie Lavaur was urged to tell the truth and was promised that in so doing "God will have pity on her soul, and will ease the torments of the *géhenne* and *question*."[22] Jeanne Bellegarde, likewise, was assured that if she told the truth "God will have pity on her soul and receive her into the realm of the blessed."[23] Truthfulness was represented to the accused as a charm that might protect them from pain. Truthfulness, if not innocence itself, might call God's protection upon them.

Secular and sacred confession were conflated in these admonitions. Truthfulness was thus represented as a religious duty to oneself: "He must consider his conscience, and in telling the truth God will have pity on him and he will avoid the torments of the *question*."[24] Likewise, the failure to tell the truth might condemn the accused to still greater eternal sufferings: "He must oblige by telling the truth in order to discharge his conscience and to avoid a still greater torment than the *question* that is prepared for him."[25] The failure to tell the truth was, therefore, constituted as itself a kind of sin for which there would be everlasting consequences. In the torture chamber, confession was represented as good for both body and soul.

Admonitions couched in religious terms were most common in the middle third of the period under study, from 1660 to 1719. In other words, just when sentences to torture dramatically declined between 1640 and 1660, the metaphysical consequences of truth-telling were stressed and redefined as spiritually meaningful. Once again, it appears that the decline in sentencing did not represent a loss of faith in the practice of torture. Although judges decided to employ torture with diminished frequency, they attributed a heightened importance to the practice, emphasizing through these admonitions their own conviction that the practice connected body and soul, human and divine, this world and the next, in an evidentiary procedure that had to yield truth or damnation.

After 1720, the admonitions rarely employed phrases connecting the truthfulness of the accused to his or her spiritual destiny. Rather, they placed the entire burden of subsequent events upon the accused. They imply that by telling the truth, the accused could avoid pain because the torture would not be employed or would be interrupted. In any case, God would not intervene to ease the pain of torture, nor would truthfulness bring spiritual reward. The admonition offered to Gabrielle Massotte in 1724 exemplifies this desacralized approach:

> . . . she could easily avoid the torments to which she will be exposed, and that to do so, she has only frankly to tell the truth of facts about which she will be questioned, that she owes this truth to justice, since in order to discover it, justice must employ such severe torments employed against those who refuse to state it [truth], after which she must think seriously, and then tell each and every fact concerning the truth of the said facts before the violence of the pain . . .[26]

In contrast to the earlier admonitions, there is a striking lack of religious language. Truth is a debt owed to justice, not to God or to the soul. In addition, Massotte was made responsible for any pain she might feel. Her refusal to speak the truth would create the pain she felt by forcing the interrogators to inflict it; her willingness would permit them to relieve it.

The diminution of religious threats and promises after 1720 thus constitutes one of the most important changes that occurred within the ritualized practice of torture. The loss of the Christian consequences of truth—in effect, a kind of desacralization of the truth—removed torture from a set of practices seen to engage the supernatural. With the loss of the association of torture, truth, and the divine, torture was deprived of a vital part of its intellectual foundation, and truth increasingly was constructed as a secular reality expressed through the limited notion of evidence.

Despite important differences between these two styles, the admonitions share one important feature. In each instance, the interrogators were absolved of any responsibility for the situation. Either God would intervene to relieve the pain suffered by the accused, or the accused would suffer justly for their own failure to comply. In no instance would the interrogators be morally responsible for the pain they inflicted. Jean Bourdil, like Gabrielle Massotte two years before him, was made responsible for his own suffering.

And in these circumstances, how many did confess? This question encompasses many problems of definition for us, problems philosophical and political, psychological and physical, problems of knowing and doing. It forces us to consider a host of questions. How do we know and identify the truth? To what degree are human beings mind and to what degree body? What is the difference between gathering information and punishment, between detention and punishment, between coercion and punishment? To what lengths may the state legitimately pursue its own security, as a corporate being, as against the security of its subjects? Is the state ever justified in laying hands on its subjects, or should bodily integrity always be inviolable?

Modern scholars have tried to answer these questions in a variety of ways. When historians and literary critics study the practice of torture and the victims of torture, a common feature emerges in their work. When referring to the practice of torture in either the early modern or the modern period, these scholars tend to dismiss the evidence given under torture as false. They do so for diametrically opposed reasons.

When historians write about early modern torture, they often represent the testimony of torture victims as composed of deliberate lies. To take a single example, Elizabeth Cohen, in her analysis of a case of slander heard by the Roman courts in the seventeenth century, asserts that the accused, an adolescent boy, lied under torture: "Despite his own testimony, which consisted largely of denials, and despite the absence of a record of the outcome of the trial, I will accept as true that this 'beardless youth' was the author of the love letter."[27] In this case, Cohen imputes guilt to the accused in precisely such situations as once required the application of torture in order to determine guilt or innocence and suggests that the accused acted deliberately and self-consciously to save himself from punishment and to cheat the system. She further implies that the accused, during torture, was possessed of sufficient presence of mind to compose a series of lies that covered up his true guilt. By contrast, literary critics tend to represent modern torture victims as profoundly passive persons, stripped of any agency whatsoever and incapable of articulating any truth whatsoever. This is the essence of Elaine Scarry's argument, that the very purpose of torture is to strip the victim of voice and of agency, to render the victim voiceless and so to destroy their humanity.[28] Literary critics thus represent the modern victims of torture as absolute victims, innocent of the actions of which they are accused, yet rendered so passive through pain that they cannot articulate this innocence.

Historians, in other words, tend to represent torture victims as if they were fully endowed with agency, volition, and rationality; literary critics, as if they were entirely stripped of such possessions. Likewise, there is lurking in this tendency an implication of the guilt or innocence of victims based on testimony that is always perceived to be lies: lies about innocence in regard to common crimes in the past, lies about guilt in regard to political crimes in the present. Perhaps these differences in the representation of the victims of torture reflect profound disciplinary differences, profoundly different understandings of human agency that are enshrined in disciplines of study.

But neither these historians nor these literary critics have adequately attended to the testimony of survivors of torture. In the early modern period, we have available a variety of documents, from interrogations themselves to letters composed by victims of torture to records of what these victims were reputed to have said; in the modern period we have a depressing wealth of prison memoirs. And these documents paint a very different picture from the black-and-white portrait sketched above of absolute guilt disguised by willing lies or absolute innocence silenced by pain or besmirched with helpless lies. At no time do these writers suggest that they were capable of constructing deliberate and intentional lies or of deliberately lapsing into inarticulate cries. Rather, they suggest that people talk or remain silent for reasons entirely opaque and mysterious. Often they point to heroic individuals—never themselves—who do remain silent, but always as the exception to the unstated rule that holds that people can be forced to talk but that the content of what they say is unpredictable.[29]

When historians attribute agency to victims of torture to the degree that they do, writing about the lies of the guilty, or literary critics, lack of agency, writing about the lies of the innocent, they speak out of a modern cultural consensus concerning torture rather than out of an informed sense guided by survivors and evidence. On the basis of modern memoirs written by survivors of torture, we need to take seriously that people can both be silent and speak under torture, and that when they speak they can both lie and tell the truth. What we need to examine, therefore, is not so much the truth of what victims of torture have said but rather what they have said has been taken to be true. As a result, we need to be prepared to accept that, just as modern scholars take it as axiomatic that people lie under torture, early modern Europeans took it as axiomatic that people told the truth under torture, however odd that belief may appear to us. It was a belief carefully constructed out of a cultural consensus concerning the meanings of pain, truth, and the body.

For at the same time as modern memoirs are useful in illuminating scholarly prejudice and disciplinary constructions of truth and agency, they cannot speak to the experiences of the past. Their words cannot substitute for the words of other centuries. The experiences of these modern survivors are not the same as the experiences of early modern victims for a number of reasons. First, there is little clarity in the modern world as to what constitutes torture. The distinction between extralegal torture, cruel and unusual punishment, and treatment that violates international conventions is unclear, if it exists at all. In the modern world, there is often an air of uncertainty to all prison proceedings. Are the withholding of food, the disruption of sleep, the lack of privacy for use of toilets and bathing facilities, the regulation of detainees' movements within their cells such that they cannot sit or lie on their beds until a specified hour, or that their hands be visible while they sleep—are all of these torture, punishment, or prison business as usual?[30] The modern situation is therefore quite unlike that of early modern France. In France in the seventeenth and eighteenth centuries, defendants knew with certainty when they were being tortured and when they were being punished. Torture was clearly and carefully delineated such that there could be no confusion between the use of torture and the imposition of punishment. Yet such confusions are particular to and endemic in the modern world.[31]

Second, there is diminished belief in the modern world that torture can consistently produce truth because there is diminished belief in the modern world that body and self are connected in such a way that physical interventions can touch the self. Quite the contrary: one of the axioms of modernity is a belief in the duality of the person. Modern survivors of torture sometimes see the practice of torture as one that reinforces this duality of mind and body, or as one which eliminates mind entirely. In the modern world, torture reinforces a contempt for the body on the part of both torturer and victim. It reinforces a conviction that the person resides somewhere other than the flesh at the same time as it demonstrates the weakness of the flesh and thus the vulnerability of the person.[32] But it can also suggest a total destruction of the completeness that is the person. Jean Améry, recalling his own torture at the hands of the Gestapo, writes: "The tortured person never ceases to be amazed that all those things one may, according to inclination, call his soul, or his mind, or his consciousness, or his identity, are destroyed when there is that cracking and splintering in the shoulder joints."[33] Likewise, there is diminished belief in the modern world that pain serves any useful function.

Finally, the truth status of testimony derived under torture differs dramatically over time. In the modern world, torture is secret because of the contemporary conviction that it is only testimony that is given voluntarily that is true. Therefore, even in regimes that regularly employ torture, the fact of its employment must be kept secret, or else all the testimony gathered through its use would be invalidated. In the early modern period, by contrast, the fact of torture was not secret because of the conviction that torture yields essential truths precisely because the evidence given under torture was not given freely. The truth-value of what was said by the early modern torture victim was not under question. The issue in early modern courts was how to square the evidence given under torture with evidence already in the *dossier*. Therefore, the assumption of modern scholars that such evidence must always be false misrepresents what we seem to know about modern torture victims as well as to misrepresent the understandings of early modern jurists.

The employment by historians of confession rates derived from death sentences implies that the purpose and therefore the efficacy of torture lay in its ability to achieve death sentences. But it is possible that judges simply wanted to hear what was constituted as legal truth through the medium of the interrogation. Of ninety interlocutory sentences to the *question prépara-toire,* twenty-eight of the ensuing definitive sentences could be found. Among these twenty-eight cases, there were four in which the accused was sentenced to death rather than to lesser penalties.[34] These four cases resulted in a minimum of six executions, as there were several persons accused in each of these cases. In Toulouse during the seventeenth and eighteenth centuries, therefore, a very tentative figure of some 14.2 percent of cases seem to have culminated in confession.[35] This figure can be compared with those gathered for other regions of the country. In the jurisdiction of

the *parlement* of Paris in the sixteenth century, 8.5 percent of those sentenced to the *question préparatoire* confessed; in the seventeenth century,
confessions dropped to 2.3 percent. Between 1735 and 1749, the Chatêlet
de Paris achieved a confession rate of between 3 percent and 7 percent. In
Brittany in the seventeenth century, confessions were acquired in 8.3 percent of cases, and in the eighteenth century, in 9 percent of cases. In Roussillon, the figure was comparable, around 10 percent in cases of the *question
préparatoire* and 13 percent in cases of the *question préalable.*[36]

What are we to make of these few confessions? Historians have proposed several interpretations of this relative silence, all of which take up
the problem of pain. Some state explicitly that early modern torture was
not successful in achieving confessions because it was not painful, though
my evidence and that of others strongly suggests the contrary.[37] Some suggest that in denying their guilt, whatever pain they may have suffered in so
doing, accused persons rejected the legal definition of their acts as criminal.[38] Others argue that those who were subject to torture understood the
importance of their silence because they understood the convoluted legal
system of this period and were as a consequence able to resist their suffering, though we have yet to demonstrate how thorough and specific public
knowledge was in fact.[39] To understand the few confessions yielded under
torture, I would suggest that we take seriously the admonitions of the interrogators and the responses of the interrogated, both of which suggest the
importance of truth-telling given its divine consequences.

Seated in the *chambre de la gesne,* sworn to tell the truth, and warned of
the pain he must soon endure, Bourdil awaited questioning. The interrogators began, as they always did:

> Asked his name, surname, age, *qualité,* if he is married, and if he has children.
>
> Answers that he is called Jean Bourdil, aged 25, *archer* by profession, exercising
> also the office of the *arche de leveille* for the confinement of the poor, married to
> Jeanne de Monsegon, and has two children.[40]

Interrogations were fundamentally occasions of questioning. Questions
prior to torture permitted interrogators to construct a narrative of events
that the accused was encouraged to confirm. Questions during torture were
highly ritualized, asking only for confirmation of guilt.

Questioning is regarded intuitively as a means of securing information.
Yet the meaning of questions depends upon the social context within which
they are posed: the same words may represent a request, a command, a
compliment, or an insult, all couched in interrogatory form. Status constraints also shape the meaning of questions. Questioning may be a means
of control, confirming the dominant role of the questioner, or it may be a

means of disclaiming power, confirming the subordinate role of the questioner. Between status equals, questions may be genuine requests for information. In every case, questions demand response; they tend to carry a command message by their very form. The exchange of question and answer, like the exchange of gifts, binds speakers into relationships of immediate reciprocity. These relationships are shaped by the social context of speech and by the relative status of the speakers.

There are two main forms of the question. The open question is an incomplete proposition whose missing clause is provided by the answer, as when the interrogators asked Bourdil to identify himself. The closed question is a complete proposition requiring only confirmation or denial.[41] The interrogators' first substantive question was of the latter sort:

> Asked if it isn't true that the respondent and his comrade-colleagues were attacked on the Pont-Neuf last April 17, and forced by a mutinous mob to release a beggar whom they were escorting to the Hôpital de la Grave.
>
> Answers and affirms.[42]

Judicial interrogations represent one instance of institutionalized questioning. Other such occasions include religious confessions and medical examinations. In each case, the questioner is cast in a dominant role. The supply of new information in response to open questions fails to equalize the status imbalance between the speakers. In the institutionalized setting of the interrogation, the questioner is always dominant, despite his or her apparent ignorance. The ability to ask questions, to command information through questions, and to expose private matters without reciprocal exposure supports the dominant status of the questioner. The interrogation, then, is an occasion of questioning that binds the speakers into a relationship of immediate reciprocity in which the respondent must exchange words with the questioner, yet in which there is no reciprocity of personal disclosure.

The interrogators built up their questions carefully, creating a narrative of events through a series of closed questions designed to elicit agreement rather than new information. Wasn't it true, they asked, that the mutinous mob that attacked Bourdil in the performance of his duty that afternoon on the Pont Neuf included a number of soldiers, and didn't he recognize any of them? And on the evening following the scuffle on the Pont Neuf, didn't Bourdil met his colleagues around half past eight in the evening at Chez Perruque, in Saint Cyprien, a suburb of Toulouse?

Open questions were employed as a means of confusing the accused by pointing out flaws and inconsistencies in his or her narrative, as the following exchange suggests:

> Asked if it was night.
>
> Answers that it was beginning to be night.
>
> Asked if they drank by candlelight.
>
> Answers that there was a candle in the said tavern.
>
> We pointed out to him that he is not telling the truth, since if there was a candle in the said tavern and it was night outdoors, those who were in the tavern could not have seen those who were in the street.[43]

Open questions thus functioned in one of two ways: to draw out new information or a narrative of events that departed from the interrogators' own, or to confront the accused with inconsistencies in his or her evidence. When questions failed to elicit a narrative that corresponded in its significant details with the narrative proposed by the interrogators or which failed to include an admission of guilt, it was time to execute the sentence of torture.

At this point in Bourdil's interrogation, the *exécuteur de la haute justice* and his assistants were called in. Like the accused, they were required to take an oath upon entering the room:

> And seeing that the said Jean Bourdil persisted in his negations, we ordered the *exécuteur de la haute justice*, his valet, and his guards to enter, to apply the said Bourdil to the *question;* they having entered, we received their oaths in the ordinary form and had them promise never to reveal the secrets of justice.[44]

Examination of other interrogations indicates that "the ordinary form" required these officers of justice, like the accused before them, to swear a sacred oath. They took the oath with their hands raised to a crucifix, "la main levée à la passion figurer [de] nostre seigneur."[45] They promised one of three things: "to exercise the sentence of the court and to do their duty," "to well and faithfully execute the said sentence of the court, and not to reveal the secret," or "to engage their functions in conformity with the said sentence, and not to reveal the secret."[46]

The two oaths sworn during the course of an interrogation—the one by the accused and the other by the *exécuteur de la haute justice*—make manifest a connection among gesture, language, and meaning. In each case, the hand placed or pledged against the sacred object—the Bible or the crucifix—is combined with the spoken oath; the action of the body is combined with speech. In each case, this combination means something about secrets. In the case of the accused, the oath-gesture means a promise to tell secrets; in the case of the *exécuteur de la haute justice*, a promise to keep secrets. The oath-gesture thus has opposing meanings, which are dependent upon the status of the person employing it. It means alternately forced speech or forced silence.

The oath raises the question of the relationship of torture to secrecy, privacy, and publicity. The rituals of torture, unlike those of execution, were not exposed to public view.[47] But were they therefore private? The language of the oaths employed as part of the ritual practice of torture suggests that as a ritual practice, torture was at once a secret and a private practice, while as an administrative and judicial practice, it was a public practice.[48]

The employment of the oath constructs two distinct sources of privileged information. As seekers of knowledge, the judges investigate secret matters through the imposition of an oath that demands speech from the accused. As keepers of knowledge, the judges prohibit further investigation of secret matters through the imposition of an oath that demands silence from the *exécuteur de la haute justice*. The judges thus construct the occasion of the telling of secrets as itself secret in requiring the oath of the *exécuteur de la haute justice* not to reveal what he has seen and heard. His speech must guarantee his silence. The accused is the first source of secrets; the interrogation itself, the second. These secrets were further protected by the private surroundings within which torture was conducted and by limitations imposed on the number of officials permitted to be present.

The *procès-verbaux* of these interrogations named the officials involved. In Toulouse, a traditional arrangement between the *parlement* and the *capitoulat* held that the *capitouls* would oversee or assist in the execution of sentences to torture pronounced by the *parlementaires*.[49] This arrangement provided that at each interrogation in the *chambre de la gesne*, there would be present the two *parlementaires* named by their fellow judges to hear the interrogation, one of whom was the *rapporteur* in the case; two or more *capitouls;* one or more of the *gens du roi*, usually the *procureur-général* or his proxy; the *greffier;* the accused; and the *exécuteur de la haute justice* and his assistants, called in only when the judges were ready to put or present the accused to the *question*—as many as seventeen people on occasion.[50] A doctor or surgeon might be standing by, ready to examine the accused, to determine if the interrogation might proceed without permanent harm to the accused, and to provide assistance if necessary. A priest, too, stood ready when it was a case of the *question préalable*, because between the interrogation and the execution the accused had to make a last confession. Apart from these officials, no one else might legally be present.

Although the oath required secrecy, and the practice guaranteed a certain level of privacy, the public reading of sentences at executions and the evident knowledge of contemporaries indicate that torture occupied a public position as well. Their evidence suggests that while the fact of torture as a judicial and administrative practice was well known, thanks to the public reading of sentences, and while some details of torture as a ritual practice could be gleaned from anecdotal accounts of eyewitnesses, the practice retained much of its mystery within the public eye, mystery that stimulated curiosity. Despite individual violations of procedure, the specific information revealed under torture tended to remain secret, the employment of torture to be private, and the fact of torture to be public. The early modern practice of torture thus stands in complete opposition to the practice of torture in our own time. Today, the fact of torture is secret, the actual performance of torture is private in that it is conducted under secure conditions, and the details of the confession extracted under torture public, and publicly used as trial evidence.

Why did the oath enjoin silence upon the *exécuteur de la haute justice?* The telling and keeping of secrets, the many layers of secrecy and revelation, make no sense if torture is regarded as a punitive and expulsive ritual like execution. In that case, torture, like execution, should have been public and exemplary. If, on the other hand, it is viewed as an incorporative ritual, the emphasis on secrecy makes sense. Torture can then be understood as the reincorporation of antisocial secrets—narratives of antisocial acts—and thus, the reincorporation of antisocial persons. The act of telling secrets transforms suspects from antisocial persons to persons who have committed antisocial acts. Ironically, torture is a ritual of inclusion. The price of inclusion is spontaneous self-accusation, a spontaneity achieved through bodily pain.

The *exécuteur de la haute justice* and his assistants, having taken the oath and pledged their silence, were ordered to proceed with the interrogation, "after which the *exécuteur de la haute justice* prepared the said Bourdil to be applied to the *question*."[51] How did the *exécuteur de la haute justice* prepare the accused for torture? Stripping the accused was certainly part of the preparation for torture, a procedure noted in many interrogations: in 1684, Vital Saltel was "stripped nude to the waist by the *exécuteur de la haute justice* and his valets."[52] Sexual modesty between the sexes was not preserved: in 1696, the *exécuteur de la haute justice,* swearing the oath, "and having stripped the said [Anne] Verches, prepared her to be applied to the first *bouton* of the *question*"; and in 1710, François Allemand, too, "having been stripped in the customary form, was applied to the first *bouton* of the question, and raised, the guards at the [wheel], and the wife of the *exécuteur de la haute justice* holding the ropes."[53] The practice of stripping the accused persisted throughout the period under study: in 1774, Blaise Theron, like many before him, "was stripped in the customary form."[54] The evidence drawn from the Toulousain interrogations, as well as from firsthand witness accounts of torture, suggests that the accused was stripped only to the waist, though contemporary illustrations show the accused sometimes completely clothed, sometimes completely naked.[55]

In addition to stripping the accused, legal manuals advised both shaving the accused and searching bodily cavities for concealed charms that might protect the accused from the pain of torture.[56] While none of the Toulousain interrogations yield direct evidence of these practices, printed sources including legal manuals, judicial *mémoires*, and causes célèbres confirm their use.[57]

Incidents of shaving the accused are found in interrogations cited in legal manuals. What purpose did this practice serve? Anthropologists assert that human hair is particularly laden with cultural meaning: because hair grows constantly, it is associated with human vitality and as such is regarded as an extension of the person. Cutting of the hair is therefore symbolic of submission to social authority. It is a ritual of social control.[58] While anthropological analyses focus on the meaning of haircutting for men, historians examine the meaning of hair and its uncovering for women. In early modern France from 1650 on, the covered female head was associated with female purity and chastity. Uncovering a woman's head therefore unleashed a chain of associations concerning her sexual honor.[59]

That hair was of special importance to the French is suggested by travelers' accounts, including this one by Tobias Smollet:

> A Frenchman will sooner part with his religion rather than with his hair, which, indeed, no consideration will induce him to forgo. . . . [E]very soldier in this country wears a long *queue* (ponytail), which makes a delicate mark on his white clothing; and this ridiculous foppery has descended even to the lowest class of people. The *décrotteur* who cleans your shoes at the corner of the Pont Neuf, has a tail of this kind hanging down to his rump, and even the peasant who drives an ass loaded with dung, wears his hair *en queue*, though, perhaps, he has neither shirt nor breeches. This is the ornament upon which he bestows much time and pains and in the exhibition of which he finds full gratification for his vanity.[60]

Therefore, the suggestion of the legal manuals that the accused's head be shaved suggests that an important part of the ritual of torture was the shaming and degrading of the accused, the more so as this preparation seems to have possessed no other clear purpose, nor to have performed any concrete function.

Not all preparations for torture lacked concrete function. Searching the accused had a very specific purpose: to deprive the accused of any charms, which might diminish the experience of pain. Nor were these searches based solely in magisterial paranoia. In 1613, Guillaume de Segla testified to the use of charms in his memoir concerning a celebrated murder case.

Prior to his execution, one of the condemned asked his confessor to tell the *premier président* of the *parlement* of Toulouse, "that he had a charm in his body in the form of a lead bullet that he had taken to more easily endure the question."[61] Whether the condemned man swallowed the bullet or concealed it within his body is not apparent. The use of the "magic" bullet suggests that one who has absorbed the instrument of harm will henceforth be impervious to harm. De Segla fails to note if the condemned man exhibited behavior different from that of his codefendants during his interrogation.

Thus stripped, shaven, and searched, Bourdil was ready to be put to the *question*. The physical practice of torture in the *parlement* of Toulouse was constituted by three different forms of torture: the *estrapade*, the *question d'eau*, and the *brodequins*. The *question ordinaire*, suffered by both men and women, was inflicted through the *estrapade*, or strappado. Tobias Smollet provided a detailed description of its use, although he discussed it as a form of civilian punishment:

> The punishments inflicted upon malefactors and delinquents at Nice, are, hanging for capital crimes; slavery on board the galleys for a limited term, or for life, according to the nature of the transgression; flagellation, and the corda or strappado. This last is performed by hoisting up the criminal by his hands tied behind his back, on a pulley, about two stories high; from whence the rope being suddenly slackened, he falls to within a yard or two of the ground, where he is stopped with a violent shock, arising from the weight of his body, and the velocity of his descent, which generally dislocates his shoulders, with incredible pain. This dreadful execution is sometimes repeated in a few minutes on the same delinquent; so that the very ligaments are torn from his joints, and his arms are rendered useless for life.[62]

The strappado was, in fact, used both as a form of torture and as a form of military punishment.[63]

In the parlement of Toulouse, the *question d'eau* constituted the customary *question extraordinaire* for men.[64] It was this torture that John Evelyn reported witnessing in Paris in 1651:

> This morning I went to the Chastlett or prison, where a Malefactor was to have the Question or Torture given to him, which was thus: They first bound his wrists with a strong roope or smalle Cable, & one end of it to an iron ring made fast to the wall about 4 foote from the floore, & then his feete, with another cable, fastned about 6 foote farther than his utmost length, to another ringe on the floore of the roome, thus suspended, & yet lying but a slant; they slid an horse of wood under the rope which bound his feet, which so exceedingly stiffned it, as severd the fellows joynts in miserable sort, drawing him out at length in an extraordinary manner, he having onely a paire of linnen drawers on his naked body: Then they question'd him of a robery, (the Lieu-

tennant Criminal being present, & a clearke that wrot) which not Confessing, they put an higher horse under the rope, to increase the torture & extension: In this Agonie, confessing nothing, the Executioner with a horne (such as they drench horses with) struck the end of it into his mouth, and pour'd the quantity of 2 boaketts of Water downe his throat, which so prodigiously swell'd him, face, Eyes ready to start, brest & all his limbs, as would have pittied & almost affrited one to see it; for all this he denied all was charged to him: Then they let him downe, & carried him before a warme fire to bring him to himselfe, being now to all appearances dead with paine . . .[65]

Evelyn's account not only clarifies the specifics of the water torture, but also confirms other details. As was the case in Toulouse, the accused was stripped preparatory to the interrogation. The *lieutenant criminel,* who directed the interrogation, was present, along with the *greffier* and the *exécuteur de la haute justice.* Despite the terrible pain that was manifest to Evelyn, the accused failed to confess.

The agonies endured by the accused persistently recalled for Evelyn the event to which they pledged that pain. His observation continues:

> . . . the spectacle was so uncomfortable, that I was not able to stay the sight of another: It represented yet to me, the intollerable suffering which our B:S: must needes undergo, when his blessed body was hanging with all its weight upon the nailes on the Crosse.[66]

And some did in fact offer up their pain as a sacrifice. Jean Julien Boucage, after suffering the first part of the *question,* was warned "that next Monday at the same time, the execution of the sentence of the Court will proceed, and that the continued question is more painful than the one he just suffered, which should require him to tell the truth to avoid the torment," to which he responded "that he would suffer everything for the love of God and the holy Virgin."[67] Not all of the accused, however, submitted so meekly to their fate. Some challenged their interrogators, saying "that it is useless to torment him more since he has nothing else to confess"; others mockingly noted that they "would have nothing to say when they were torn in pieces."[68]

The *question extraordinaire* for women was the *brodequins* or *mordaches.* It was described in detail by the Toulousain diarist Pierre Barthès because of the curious circumstances that arose in the torture of Claire Reynaud in 1778. As Barthès noted, no woman had been tortured in the *parlement* of Toulouse for over thirty-five years, and so it required a certain amount of research to recover the appropriate technique, which he duly noted in his journal:[69]

> NOTE. The ordinary *question* was the same that they give to men, but the extraordinary, which is the *question d'eau* for men, is different for women;

they were at pains to know what this sort of *question* was, because it had been forty-three years since they gave the *question* to a woman, but after some researching, they found an instrument called the *mordaches,* with which to make her submit to this last *question.* They make the woman sit down, then they make her bend her calf back toward her thigh as close as she can, after which they encircle the thigh and the leg near the knee with the *mordache;* the vice which grasps the leg rests on the bone, such that in the turning the screw, the bones of the leg flatten, and it is thus that the torment makes itself most felt. The part of the *mordache* that clasps the thigh above the knee does nothing more than mark itself in the flesh.[70]

No contemporary rationale exists for these gender-specific tortures, which in fact varied from *parlement* to *parlement.* Although only men received the *question d'eau* and only women received the *question des mordaches* in the jurisdiction of the *parlement* of Toulouse, Urbain Grandier suffered the *question des mordaches* in 1634, and the marquise de Brinvilliers, the *question d'eau* in 1676, both given in the jurisdiction of the *parlement* of Paris. Psychoanalytic readings of these gender-specific tortures, which within the Toulousain context would suggest a carnivalesque kind of reversal of sex roles, therefore seem inadequate when seen within the national context. Nor do interpretations which suggest that these tortures sought to preserve feminine modesty seem entirely convincing, in view of the fact that both men and women were made to strip before both male officials and their female companions.[71] If, however, we choose to understand male and female bodies as inversions of each other, then these tortures, too, can be read as inversions of the same physical operation. This is the thesis/ model proposed by Thomas Laqueur, who argues that until the eighteenth century, male and female bodies were understood to exist along a physical continuum, each being the literal inversion of the other. If the one-sex body was the model of the human body supported by jurists, then it is possible that the *question d'eau* and the *question des mordaches* were seen as the same practice turned inside out, to be employed interchangeably on the one-sex body, itself turned inside out.[72]

These, then, were the tortures endured by Jean Bourdil: the *question ordinaire* in the form of the *estrapade* three times on 25 May and once again on 27 May, followed by the *question extraordinaire* in the form of the *question d'eau* five times. Raised for the first time,

The same questions and remonstrances as above were put to him, and we exhorted him to tell the truth and say if he is guilty of the murder of the said two soldiers who were killed, or if he is an accomplice of the murderers, or if he knows the guilty murderers or accomplices.

Answered [that] he told the truth and that he is innocent of the murder of the
said two soldiers, and that he knows neither the murderers nor the accomplices.[73]

The questions put to him during the physical infliction of his torture continued in this ritualized and repetitive way. Again and again, he was asked
nothing more than to confess his guilt in the matter of these murders. This
was typical of the questioning of the accused under torture. Although the
questions that preceded the infliction of physical pain often sought detailed
information concerning the crime that only the perpetrator could know,
questions during the infliction of pain asked only for a statement of guilt
or innocence.

But did Jean Bourdil really maintain his innocence in the words of the
interrogation? It is unlikely that he did so, and the failure of the *greffier* to
note his exact words marks another of the important changes in the practice of torture. Until around 1720, interrogations note the precise utterances of the tortured. Then, throughout the decade of the 1720s, they note
the fact that the accused was unable to answer articulately because of the
pain that they suffered. But from around 1730, all language of pain, either
as spoken verbatim by the accused or as noted generally by the *greffier*, was
omitted from the interrogations. Henceforth, the accused would seem to
speak with the same measured voices as did their interrogators, with the
same calm, the same containment.

The earliest interrogations contain explicit discussions about pain between the accused and the interrogators. In 1633, Pierre Faure, a notary
accused of falsifying documents "most humbly begged the court to please
itself in not tormenting him, which he fears more than death itself."[74] On
later occasions, the accused might make direct reference to the pain they
endured in addressing their interrogators as did Gabriel Larrivere: "it is
useless to torment him more since he has nothing else to confess."[75] Interrogators would continue to exhort the accused to confess in the face of the
pain they must soon endure, but these exchanges faded away.

Other records of pain persisted. Of the nineteen extant interrogations
from 1600 to 1719 in which the sentence of torture was performed rather
than presented, eight include detailed notations not only of each fact of
testimony, but of the precise words with which those facts were expressed.
Cries, pleas, beseechments, all were recorded until the 1720s. That these
are faithful and complete records, unlike those after 1730, is suggested by
the fact that the responses of the accused under torture were recorded in
the dialect of the *pays* d'oc, rather than in the French with which their
answers prior to torture were recorded.

In 1662, for example, Jean Barbet was accused with two codefendants of counterfeit. One of his interrogators, the Sieur Dutil, was trying to determine if Barbet was a recidivist, and therefore urged him "de dire la vérité de ses crimes & accorder ses complices à la justice, et s'il a eu le fouet cy devant pour larrassin ou autre crime . . ." (to tell the truth concerning his crimes, and confess his accomplices to justice, and if he had been whipped before for theft or any other crime). In the same French as he was questioned, Barbet appeared to respond, "A dict avoir dict la vérité & n'avoir eu jamais le fouet pour aucun crime n'y autrement" (that he had spoken the truth and had never been whipped for any crime or any other reason).[76]

Immediately following this response, Barbet was prepared for the *estrapade*. Raised for the first time and questioned concerning conversations he had had in connection to the charges, he responded in dialect: "Jou lai ditte à la damnation de mon âme" (I said so, to the damnation of my soul).[77] Raised for the second time, he cried out in dialect: "A dit me tuas a tort, ay ditte la bertat jamas de ma vito nau ai fait" (You're killing me wrongly; I told the truth; never in my life did I do so).[78]

Other early interrogations record this same shift from French to dialect and from indirect to direct discourse when the torture begins, and the same faithful reproduction of each word, each cry. Antoine Delbosc under torture cried, "A dict Lay dito soun innoussent nou sabi res Jesus Lay dito nou sabi res Jesus" (I said I'm innocent, I don't know anything, Jesus, I said I don't know anything, Jesus), and again, "A dict Mondieu Santo Vierges assistatsmé se vous plai Mondieu assistatsmé aÿ aÿ assistatsmé Santo Vierges Mondieu La voulounte de dieu sio faito soun innoussent" (My God, Holy Virgin, help me, please My God help me, oh, oh, help me Holy Virgin, My God, the will of God be done, I am innocent).[79] Even when responses by the accused provided no substantive information whatsoever, the *greffier* recorded each utterance with precision. Jean Seaubert, raised for the third time and unable to endure any more, begged "A dit mon dieu ajacte pietat de Jou missericordio un coutessou sy vous play" (My God, have pity on me, mercy, a knife please).[80]

This precision was lost by the 1720s. Of the nine interrogations in which the question was performed during the 1720s, four contain notations of the utterances of the accused under torture without transcribing them directly. In the interrogations of Marc Bermon, Gabrielle Massotte, Louise Bonaille, and Arnaud Carguecol, the *greffier* noted only that during questioning under torture, the accused did not respond "sans qu'elle ait proféré que les cris et gémissements que la douleur peut produire en cettes occasions" (except to utter the cries and moans that pain can produce on these occasions).[81] Beginning in this decade, the *greffier* abstracted the response of the accused so that only the legally relevant response of the accused was preserved. Thus it was that Jean Bourdil, even at the very last, appeared to speak so rationally in the French foreign to the pays d'oc: "A repondu être innocent" (Answered that he is innocent).[82]

What answers remained seem to have been recorded intact. That the *greffier* failed to alter the substantive responses of the accused is suggested by the accused themselves. In 1697, Simone Gilibert alleged that during her first trial, the *greffier* was forced to destroy the record of her first interrogation and to substitute another set of responses, responses that were extorted from her in some way:

> Asked if she had said in her first hearing before the *consuls* of Lectoure what she says now.
>
> Answered that she had said the same thing then as now, that Dagasson made her say what she said before the *consuls,* and that the *greffier* who wrote for M. Guilhon had torn up and thrown into the fire her first hearing.[83]

This excerpt suggests that the *greffier* faithfully recorded her first responses only to destroy them later, rather than falsify her statement. In other words, the written record produced by the *greffiers* adhered closely to oral testimony, reproducing only the spoken word—even when that speech was coerced. Untruth was not produced by the *greffiers.*

In these early interrogations, truth is seen to possess two essential qualities: it is at once spontaneous and interactive. The truth lies in spontaneity rather than in composition: it is what emerges first. That is why it must be immediately and precisely recorded. Time for reflection only provides the accused an opportunity for invention. Likewise, the truth is obtained interactively, through engagement, not in isolation, in written or otherwise prepared confessions. The interplay of question and answer creates the conditions in which the truth can emerge.

But it is not only the nature of the truth that is seen to change in these interrogations, but the meaning of pain. Pain is an increasingly unstable tool: what do the responses of the accused mean when they say nothing about the case at hand? The effects of pain are therefore recorded with diminished frequency.

Changes in the recording of the interrogations—from including to excluding the specific language of the accused—parallel changes in the wording of judicial sentences in the 1720s. Just as the phrase "demuerant les preuves et indices" was moved from the *retentum* to the body of the sentence during the 1620s, a shift which reflected changing notions of the purgatorial power of torture, so too did the banishment of the language of pain during the 1720s represent changing definitions of the truth. In the later interrogations, the definition of the truth was increasingly limited to mean legal evidence. Over time, truth was what the *greffier* found to be relevant within the legal context. The role of pain in the practice of torture also underwent changes, from providing evidence in the very cries of the accused to simply extracting evidence in the condensed responses noted by the *greffier.* Pain per se was of diminished importance by 1730.

Spontaneous and involuntary speech was seen to provide an essential and immediate truth. But not all involuntary utterances were equally valued. As noted above, involuntary expressions of pain that had no immediate bearing upon the evidence of a case were gradually excluded from the transcripts of interrogations. In fact, some manuals urged interrogators to deafen themselves to these expressions.[84] Only those sounds and words that contained meaning were to be attended. None of the manuals suggested how such meaning might be discerned.

Through the use of torture, interrogators sought evidence that included language and gesture, evidence that ranged from verbal confession (the spoken) to intentional gesture (the unspoken) to unintentional gesture (the unspeakable). Each of these kinds of evidence was to be considered within the context of the sex, age, status, and constitution of the accused. The practice of torture, therefore, employed and examined bodily evidence as a crucial component of testimony.

Bodily evidence included comportment and gesture, whether intentional or unintentional, planned or spontaneous, produced by both the living and the dead. Some gestures or behaviors that we now tend to see as unintentional and spontaneous were not always perceived as such. Let us take the example of tears. In sixteenth-century Spain, tears were seen as a gift from God and were interpreted as an indication of one's openheartedness or tenderheartedness toward God.[85] Deliberate provocation of weeping was a feature of many public religious demonstrations. These events gave the community an opportunity both to demonstrate its attachment to God and to cultivate that attachment through provoked weeping. That this weeping was deliberate did not diminish its sincerity. Tears were not and did not need to be unintentional or spontaneous in order to be authentic.

In seventeenth-century France, tears were likewise taken to be a mark of sincerity in a variety of contexts from conversion to confession.[86] In cases of witchcraft, French judges were encouraged to conjure such marks of sincerity from accused witches by referring to the tears of the blessed. Weeping on the part of the accused at the mention of holy tears would therefore constitute evidence of the sincerity of protestations of innocence as well as demonstrating a continued posture of openheartedness toward God. Attachment to God as demonstrated by weeping was destroyed by the Devil, who was known literally to harden the hearts and to dry up the tears of his minions.[87] I would argue, therefore, that tears were seen as one of several bodily manifestations of the human connection to the supernatural: those who could shed tears demonstrated not only their sincerity but also demonstrated their affinity to God, while those who could not shed tears showed by this very failure that they were under demonic influence. Weeping had a specific meaning and was understood as a gesture that could be willed if the subject existed within a certain relationship to God and the Devil. It was, therefore, a gesture that could be employed as evidence for or against the accused. And it was one of the many gestures for which judges were instructed to search during interrogations under torture.

These gestures were given meaning not only in the judicial context but within the popular context as well. As demonstrated by the evidence of Daniel Jousse and John Evelyn, pallor was seen to provide direct evidence of guilt both by judges and by the populace.[88] Like pallor, trembling was taken by all to be evidence of guilt. In 1755, interrogators asked Paul Marty to confirm a conversation in which a witness reported saying to Marty, "your hands are trembling because you are guilty of murder, and mine don't tremble because I am innocent."[89] Here, judges asked for confirmation of testimony that addressed the moral implications of gesture.

Only the living could weep, pale, and tremble. But the dead, too, could testify through their bodies as to the events of their lives. The most celebrated form of bodily evidence yielded by the dead was spontaneous bleeding in the presence of their murderers.[90] But the dead could testify in other ways as well. In Germany, a dead child pointed at its mother when asked to indicate its murderer.[91] The gestures of the dead, the testimony that emanated from the body itself when the soul no longer animated it, had to be accorded careful consideration. From beyond the grave and beyond consciousness, the dead still had the power to communicate through the medium of their bodies.

Tears and blood, pallor and trembling, the evidence from living and dead bodies was not the only bodily evidence of concern to judges. Evidence *about* bodies was also employed in the interrogations. Surgeons' reports, for example, provided information about the appearance of dead bodies, which provided the interrogators the information they needed to challenge the accused. In the case of Jeanne Destampes, for example, interrogators were able to challenge her account of her daughter-in-law's death on the basis of the surgeon's report that suggested that the young woman had been strangled rather than suffocated in her own blood, as Destampes had testified.[92] Not only the appearance of the dead, but the treatment of the bodies of the dead formed part of the evidence against the accused. Inappropriate behavior in the handling of the dead provided serious grounds for suspicion. Arnaud Ruilhes's failure to visit the home of his neighbor upon learning of the latter's sudden death, Blaise Theron's immediate acts of possession of his dead father's belongings and of stripping the corpse of its *sabots* to place them upon his own feet, and Gabrielle Massotte's too rapid preparation of her sister's corpse, all threw suspicion on these accused.[93] The failure to demonstrate appropriate grief, too, was noted as suspicious.[94] Likewise, the furtive employment of one's own body or the destruction of physical evidence was suspect.[95]

As this analysis of court records suggests, a variety of bodily gestures and behaviors were under scrutiny during interrogations, ranging from the voluntary actions of the accused after the crime in question, to the deliberate ritual gestures required of the accused during the oath, to the involuntary gestures of pain under torture, to the mystical gestures of the dead. Some gestures the interrogators were required to notice, and others, to ignore. Voluntary gestures required little attention unless the accused failed to perform them: the refusal to swear an oath or the failure to weep themselves constituted damning evidence. Involuntary gestures, on the other hand, were regularly taken to be especially revealing. They were understood to reveal truths precisely because they escaped the conscious will of the accused. Through gesture, the body betrayed itself.

As we have seen, interrogations are characterized by the presence of formulaic language, particularly by the use of admonitions and oaths. Other formulae are as remarkable for their absence. Insults, greeting, and parting phrases were notably absent.

Insult was itself a form of assault in early modern Europe, and its use was highly formalized. In early modern France, insults were typically exchanged by social equals who were well known to each other, in a public place, and often before an audience of sorts. For a person of superior social status to recognize the insult of his or her inferior was itself an act degrading of personal honor, lowering the one to the level of the other. Likewise, the verbal abuse of social inferiors by their superiors was not consonant with the social role of superiority. The absence of the exchange of insult within the torture chamber is therefore unsurprising: there, the participants in the social exchange were of unequal status, speaking to one another in private. In addition, the use of names that might in some other setting be considered libelous was here precisely the subject at issue, whether the accused might legally or libelously be called a pimp, a thief, or a murderer. Alternatively, the alleged crime under investigation might itself be one involving insult.[96] Therefore, though they were not exchanged by judges or the accused, insults were reported during the course of interrogations. During his interrogation, Jean Bourdil reported that one of his companions surprised a soldier in the street at night by turning on him with the words, "Is that you, you B*****, who look for me in front of my house to kill me? We'll see about that now!"[97] Here, the accused introduced the insult into evidence. The judges later reintroduced it in the course of questioning, asking for confirmation of the fact that his companion had "abused the said Pintous, soldier, in saying to him, 'B*****, it's you who want to kill me.'"[98] On other occasions, however, it was judges themselves who introduced evidence of insult. In 1714, judges asked Jeanne Destampes if it wasn't true that she had "several times verbally abused the said Lacroix," her daughter-in-law, evidence which she denied.[99]

While it is likely that judges addressed the accused in the second person singular, as "tu," without this in itself being regarded as insulting, it is impossible to be certain. The interrogations couch all questions and most answers in the third person. The nuances of the use of the second person are lost to us.[100] On rare occasions, the *greffier* notes the accused's use of "vous," but because the accused may well have been addressing the group of interrogators, these slips of the pen offer no further insight.[101]

The normal functioning of social life depends upon formulaic language, suppressed as in the case of insult, and expressed as in the case of greetings. Greetings and other politeness formulae, typically empty of content, are nonetheless crucial to daily interaction. Their presence creates a social relationship where once existed only physical proximity; their omission within extant social relationships is experienced as insult.[102] Yet the interrogations fail to provide any exchange of greetings between judges and accused or between judges and other officials of justice. Thus it was that Jean Bourdil, removed from the instruments of his torture, heard the transcription of his interrogation read back to him and was returned to his prison without an exchange of greeting or parting phrase:

> . . . we ordered the said Bourdil to be returned to the prisons in the care of the
> concierge, which done we retired and prepared and signed this transcript.[103]

This failure to exchange formulaic recognition implies a deliberate failure to create a social relationship within which the interrogators might feel a personal sense of responsibility for the accused and thus hesitate to perform their appointed task.

Changes in the recording of sentences and interrogations suggest profound epistemological changes. As early as the 1620s, judges began to rework the traditional structure of sentences to torture, moving the phrase "demeurant les preuves et indices" from the *retentum* to the body of the sentence, a shift that undermined the purgatorial function of torture. Between 1640 and 1660, sentencing to torture dropped dramatically. But as the number of sentences decreased, the gravity of those sentences increased. As fewer individuals were sentenced to torture, judges sought to impress upon them the divine consequences of their testimony through the use of admonitions that threatened spiritual consequences for temporal actions.

The omission of threatened divine consequences in admonitions addressed to the accused after 1720 suggests a desacralization of the truth. The devaluation of the language of pain at the same moment suggests a diminution of its meaning. These changes together point to the gradual substitution of empty ceremony for meaningful ritual in the practice of torture. Yet throughout the eighteenth century, judges remained convinced of the utility of torture in the search for truth—and they continued to call for its use. Judges remained convinced—or tried to remain convinced—that the accused told the truth under torture. Throughout the seventeenth and eighteenth centuries, confessions under torture were accorded the legal, moral, and epistemological status of truth.

The judges who ordered Jean Bourdil's torture did so in order to hear authentic testimony. They did not prepare his confession in advance. They did not know what they would hear. And when Jean Bourdil persisted in declaiming his innocence—in French or Occitan, in screams or whispers— his judges attended to his testimony. And they sentenced him accordingly.

PART TWO

Pain, Truth, and the Body

Historians—including myself—have found that torture in early modern France was infrequently employed, that it rarely achieved full confessions, and that it was not, in fact, necessary in order to punish individuals charged with serious crimes. At the same time, everything we know about the laws governing torture and about the practice of torture suggests that French judges were deeply committed to employing the practice in a strictly legal fashion long after most historians have argued it was obsolete. My aim in this book is not to undermine the legal historical interpretation but to expand on it by exploring the meanings of torture in the hopes of explaining the persistent reliance on torture.

Torture existed in a cultural context that was crucial to its meaning. In order to understand the causes of its demise, it is essential that we investigate that cultural context. If we are to understand these judges as reasonable beings, therefore, governed not only by logic and law but also by belief and custom, we need to look outside the world of law to explain their actions. The task of relocating torture is a highly interpretive one since few if any judges left records that might indicate their thoughts and feelings concerning the practice of torture: there are no extant court debates, no memoirs, no caches of books in libraries, no private letters to illuminate their thoughts directly. There is only the evidence of a persistent and diminishing practice of torture and of a culture increasingly conflicted about its meanings.

Beliefs about the body and bodily experience had a central role to play in determining what constituted legal and ethical behavior in the courts. These beliefs did not exist in a legal vacuum, but were formulated in the context of a culture that evaluated pain from a variety of perspectives, each of which was in the process of change. There were profound disagreements about the value of pain; the conflicting understandings of pain in early modern France created room for the reassessment of painful practices.

How was pain defined in the early modern period? Did it mean the same thing in every context? Was it experienced in the same way? What purpose, if any, did it serve? Should it be sought out or avoided, inflicted or relieved?

These were the questions explored in a variety of cultural contexts. Specific constructions of pain and truth were proposed in the practice of torture.

Judges were not alone in seeking answers to these questions. And legal manuals were not the only texts that provided judges with intellectual support for the practice of torture, nor was participation in its practice the only activity that provided them with experience of pain. There were still other models of bodily understanding that offered judges the means with which to explicate their employment of torture, still other institutional settings within which pain was valorized. Chapter 4 examines judicial involvement in lay confraternities and offers suggestive evidence of extralegal influences on judicial thought. Without seeking to imply that lay confraternities were limited to such concerns, this chapter explores the implications of confraternal practices as they related to the problems of pain and suffering and as they served to guide judges in the employment of torture.

It is apparent that people of the seventeenth and eighteenth centuries suffered extremes of pain both voluntarily and involuntarily. But pain was differently experienced, just as it was differently understood, in different contexts. In the context of medicine, the subject of chapter 5, reports of pain were richly detailed. Rather than living with suffering that in the religious context might be characterized as ennobling, patients sought to procure relief from pain. Reports of pain drew complex responses from healers, some dismissive, some empathetic. But in the medical context, there was a general consensus that pain was a negative experience that posed real dangers not only for patients but for their attendants as well.

The implicit conflict between these two visions pointed to a growing tension in the culture. If there was no agreement about the meaning and the purpose of pain, then painful practices like torture that relied on narrowly constructed definitions of pain became more difficult to support. And indeed, in the late eighteenth century, criticisms of torture began to emerge. Chapter 6 examines the writings of philosophes who attacked the practice of torture by negating the sacramental value of pain, by redefining the nature of truth, and by rejecting the epistemology of the living body.

נכח

L'INSTITVTION, REGLES ET EXERCI-es des cõfrairies des penitens, où il se trai-te de plusieurs exer-cices de deuotion, propres à tous les Chrestiens.

Av Roy,

Par E. Molinier Tolosain, Prestre et Docteur

A THOLOSE, Par R. Colomier, Imp. ord. du Roy et de l'Vniuersité. 1625.

auec priuilege du Roy.

L. Gaultier incidit

Sana me Domine

Frontispiece from Étienne Molinier, *Des confraires pénitents* (Toulouse, 1625).

4

"The executioner of his own life": Lay Piety and the Valorization of Pain

Lay confraternities, voluntary associations of the faithful that gathered to perform a variety of social, political, cultural, and devotional functions, have been studied largely to elucidate lay piety.[1] In these associations, members of the laity had the power to control membership, draw up statutes, and devise devotions. Confraternities can be used to explore still other cultural preoccupations, in particular, the preoccupation with meaningful suffering.

Analysis of the statutes of lay confraternities and the records of confraternal meetings, as well as records of published works detailing confraternal practices, reveals both clerical and lay understandings of pain and the body. Because judges were members of confraternities, analysis of these sources allows us to explore the varieties of discourses about the body to which judges were exposed and helps us to explain the varieties of ways they had to think through the practice of torture. Judicial behavior was influenced by the religious milieu, and in some instances it was specifically influenced by judges' membership in penitential confraternities. Judges found themselves in a cultural environment within which pain was endorsed as a valuable experience both by the Roman Catholic Church and by penitential confraternities.

The religious reformations of the sixteenth century prompted the Roman Catholic Church to reformulate its theology, most notably at the Council of Trent. In France, meaningful adoption of Tridentine reforms was delayed by the wars of religion. But when the wars were concluded and peace finally negotiated, reform flowered.[2]

Support for doctrines that articulated the relationship between sacred and profane bodies and for devotions that explored the boundaries between them was but one of the consequences of Trent.[3] In its promotion of devotions that focused on the body of Christ, including attachment to the cults of the Sacred Heart, the Five Wounds, and the Stations of the Cross, the theology behind Roman Catholic reform placed new emphasis on suffering both in the experience of suffering as a gift from God and in the relief of suffering as an act of Christian charity. The Church implied that it was the body that helped individuals to establish a connection to the divine, given that one of the primary connections between man and God was established through suffering.[4] The suffering of Christ was represented as an experience above and outside of time, an experience at once frozen in time and so forever present in time, an experience without ending or beginning. The faithful participate in this experience either by providing comfort without ever being able to diminish that suffering or by adding still more suffering through sin. Divine suffering was the price of human redemption; human suffering, payment for sin. Human suffering was a shadow of divine suffering and a reminder of the promise of redemption. The Roman Catholic tradition thereby glorified suffering, transforming it from a mundane and earthly reality to a sublime and transcendent element of spiritual redemption.[5] It offered a means of recovering and interpreting bodily experiences, and promised a meaning for the most debased and unpleasant of them.

The proliferation of new orders for men and women was another consequence of Roman Catholic reform. Many of these new orders were dedicated to service in the world; the new religious and newly devout served the sick and the poor, foundlings, and galley convicts. In Toulouse, enthusiasm for new religious professions was widespread and translated into an accompanying building program so sweeping that in 1698 the intendant Lamoignon de Basville estimated that religious houses occupied half of the city.[6] Some of these orders sent missionaries into the French countryside; some, much further afield.

The laic response to this reform was not always what the Church anticipated. One unexpected response was the effort to appropriate the experience of suffering. Women were most successful in this enterprise in the context of mysticism; men, in the context of confraternal life.[7] In each case, the privilege of suffering was jealously guarded. In the midst of reform, laic devotional practices flourished without the encouragement of the Church, at times even against the orders of the Church.

As pious or impious Roman Catholics, as *pénitents* or pilgrims, as members of devotional confraternities or simply as urban residents who witnessed the great religious processions of Toulouse, the *parlementaires* had access to this religious tradition. In their churches, in their catechisms, in their confessions, judges were regularly exposed to the Church's teachings. Although judges did not shape doctrine as they shaped jurisprudence, as members of the Church they were in a position to resist official doctrine and to offer their own interpretations of religiosity. As Roman Catholics committed to charitable activity and as members of lay confraternities, they did just that.

Three times each year—at Christmas, Easter, and Pentecost—the *parlement* of Toulouse observed a tradition known as the *Reddes*, when the magistrates of the court visited the prisons of the city to offer temporary releases to detainees.[8] Bound to deliver justice in the courts, they chose to offer charity in the prisons. Within the constraints of early modern law, this ritual offered them a singular opportunity to temper justice with mercy.

Two or three days before the performance of the *Reddes*, the *gens du roi* visited the prisons of the city to inquire into the situations of detainees, speaking with both jailers and prisoners. They prepared written reports of their findings. On the eve of each holiday, judges participating in the observation of the *Reddes* assembled in the *parlement* to consider the reports on the cases of all those currently detained and awaiting trial. If the offense with which a given detainee was charged was not deemed serious, then the *premier président* of the court wrote the words "à la redde" in the margin of the report; if it were too serious to permit release, then the word "maneat" was written in the margin. This charitable release was not a pardon, but required of detainees that they return to the court to have their cases heard.[9] After this hearing, the *gens du roi* and the *premier président* of the *parlement* in turn delivered harangues on the proper duty of judges. The *premier président* then chose ten or twelve judges to accompany him in visiting the prisons of the *conciergerie* and selected others to visit the remaining prisons of the city: the Hauts Murats Prison, those of the *sénéchaussée*, the *viguierie*, the *hôtel de ville*, and the *écarlate*.

The judges marched in procession to the prisons in the company of the *huissiers* and were received there by jailers who had taken pains to prepare the most comfortable room for their coming, strewing the floor with sweet-smelling herbs and preparing bouquets of flowers for the entryway. The detainees were then called into their presence one by one to explain the circumstances of their cases and to be informed of the decision of the court as to their release. After each prisoner was heard in turn, the jailers were dismissed from the room, and all the prisoners assembled together before the judges so that if they had complaints concerning their treatment while in detention they could voice them. The jailers were informed of the results of this interview and were duly fined or arrested if dereliction of their duties made such action necessary. The judges next made a little speech to those prisoners who could not be released "to console them in their disgrace, to exhort them to place their trust in God and to pray to him to inspire the judges to give them grace and mercy if they were guilty, or to give them justice against their accusers if they were innocent, to take communion and [to perform] other Christian works during the holidays."[10] Finally, the judges departed, leaving alms in a bowl presented to them by the prisoners at the door.

The purpose of the *Reddes*, according to an eighteenth-century observer, was "to renew the memory of the goodness of the Son of God who, according to Jewish custom, could have been released, [but] wished that a rogue be preferred in his place in order to achieve the redemption of men."[11] In the eighteenth century, in other words, the *Reddes* was understood as an essentially religious ritual that evoked the sacrificial compassion of Christ. Parlementary involvement in the *Reddes*, which blended elements of the sacred and the secular, offered judges a means of making sense of their judicial responsibilities. It allowed them to confront their responsibilities in a charitable context, to meet with the men and women on whom they were bound to deliver sentence, and to seek pardon by offering mercy to the compatriots of those they condemned in the courts. The *Reddes* allowed judges an opportunity to make restitution for the suffering they were required to inflict. Other rituals, more directly connected to religious practice, allowed them to justify that suffering.

Religious life in France from the sixteenth century was a charged affair.[12] Over the first half of the sixteenth century, as late medieval manifestations of devotion declined, as confraternities, religious processions, and mystery plays lost adherents or were officially prohibited, the growth of religious reform troubled what remained of communal observances.[13] Religion became less and less a means of uniting people through ritual, and more and more a means of division.[14] The wars of religion, fought with particular ferocity in the Huguenot strongholds in the south of France, put an end to hopes for religious unanimity and locked each party into a particular style of devotion.

At the same time as late medieval devotions dwindled of their own accord in the north of France, they were fanned into flames by the dual forces of church and state.[15] In the mid-sixteenth century, at just the moment when medieval devotional confraternities began to lose membership, the Church itself began to create new confraternities devoted to objects of worship that met with Tridentine approval.[16] Through the creation of parish-based confraternities, the Church sought to suppress popular communal observances, to diminish the outrageous festivities, the all-night processions with their potential for sexual license, and the excessive devotions of *pénitents* who observed their ascetic practices with an uncomfortable fervor unsupervised by any priest.

Lay confraternities had been established first in Provence in the early sixteenth century, and there they gained their strongest foothold.[17] Modeled on Italian confraternities, they arrived earliest and survived latest in the south of France.[18] During the wars of religion, these voluntary associations began to spread throughout France. There was, in particular, a dramatic increase in the number of penitential confraternities. These groups made explicit religious duty, spelling out spiritual obligations in confraternal statutes. Daily prayers, weekly fasts and self-flagellation, regular confession and communion, regular attendance at services and processions, mourning for the dead, and payment of dues tended to equate behavior with piety, rather than stressing the relationship between belief and piety. The *pénitents* further distinguished themselves from other confraternities by their adoption of distinctive costumes that consisted of robes and hoods that covered them from head to foot, costumes that both obscured individual identity during processions and stressed the common identity of the *pénitents*.

As confraternal groups grew and spread, they served not to foster peace among warring factions as they had once done in Italy—quite the contrary.[19] In France, penitential confraternities served to make manifest essential aspects of Roman Catholic doctrine under attack by the Huguenots. They served to demonstrate and to defend the sacrament of penance and the doctrine of Purgatory. And they often did so in deliberately provocative fashion.[20]

It has been argued, therefore, that the wars of religion created a unique opportunity for the laity.[21] At this moment of crisis, in the absence of priests to guide them, members of the laity were free to create their own devotions and to express their own interpretations of official doctrine. And indeed, the wars saw the foundation of many lay religious organizations, including penitential confraternities.

These confraternities made themselves useful to the Church during the wars of religion, as they offered visible proof of the strength and devotion of the Roman Catholic laity.[22] But their unwillingness to submit to clerical control after the wars was troubling. No less enthusiastic about lay piety than it had once been, the Church sought to control that piety on the authority of the papal bull *Quaecumque,* issued in 1604. The bull required that confraternities submit themselves to clerical supervision. French clerics went beyond the requirements of the bull by insisting that lay confraternities submit their statutes for clerical review. Across the realm, the Church created parish-based confraternities to rival those established by lay founders and to promote the theology of the Counter-Reformation. They were popular and successful among women and adolescents.[23] In fact, the French confraternal movement as a whole was so successful that as late as the beginning of the eighteenth century, one in twelve persons was a member of a confraternity.[24] Despite clerical efforts at control, rural lay confraternities continued to flourish without clerical support or direction through much of the seventeenth century.[25] And adult men in the Midi, if not throughout France, remained committed to the old confraternities, most particularly to the *pénitents*.

In the wake of *Quaecumque,* many urban lay confraternities faced a great struggle to preserve their autonomy. In Lyon and Grenoble, the Counter-Reformation program of obedience to clerics, Christocentric devotions, and parish-based worship was largely successful, thanks to the general enthusiasm of urban lay elites—except for the persistent refusal of *pénitents* to submit themselves to Church authority.[26] Well into the eighteenth century, there was an ongoing struggle between the Roman Catholic Church and penitential confraternities, who continued to insist upon writing their own statutes and choosing their own members.[27] In the south of France, as was the case elsewhere, it was the *pénitents* who most strongly resisted clerical intervention, who were most likely to retain their autonomy and to direct their own devotions.[28] And so, despite the official opposition of church and state, the *pénitents* survived.[29] Throughout the early modern period, they managed to express their distinctive vision of religiosity and their devotion to meaningful suffering.

In the Languedoc, throughout the diocese of Toulouse, the wars created tremendous disruption of Roman Catholic religious life. Under the guidance of Cardinal François de Joyeuse, archbishop of Toulouse from 1588 to 1605, a series of diocesan pastoral visits in 1596 and 1597 established the gravity of the situation.[30] Of 330 places of worship, 141 were damaged to some degree. The number of clerics had been almost halved: in 1538, there had been 834 priests; in 1596, there were only 440 priests. Of those that remained, many were unable to fulfill their offices either for lack of education or for lack of liturgical objects. The survival of the Church had in many ways become the responsibility of the urban laity, of individuals who demonstrated their faith through new organizations and new devotions with extraordinary militancy.

The wars of religion had a different effect on the city of Toulouse, transforming it from a mixed community of Huguenots and Roman Catholics to a Roman Catholic bastion at the cost of its Protestant community, murdered and driven out in the riots of 1562.[31] As members of religious orders were in turn threatened in the largely Huguenot countryside, they sought refuge in Toulouse. Expelled from Pamiers, the Jesuits arrived in 1563. The Benedictine Feuillants arrived the same year. In 1576, the religious of the Chartreuse of Saix sought refuge first in Carcassonne and then in Toulouse. Four years later, in 1580, they were followed by the Cordeliers of the Order of Saint Francis of Isle-Jourdain. The city became a center of Roman Catholic devotion for both clergy and laity. At the same time, foundations of confraternal associations were spurred by the joint influences of the wars of religion and the sponsorship of the Church such that, by 1789, the diocese of Toulouse claimed 228 confraternities scattered across its 215 parishes.[32] The four penitential confraternities of the city were founded in the 1570s and enjoyed an enduring life, persisting into the nineteenth century. As was the case with all penitential confraternities, they sought to combat Protestantism through the visible manifestation of faith, reclaiming urban space for Roman Catholicism. Penitential piety was held to spring from love and fear and demanded "blood and tears," mortification and repentance.[33]

It should be stressed that both the continued activity on the part of these Toulousain confraternities and the ongoing participation of local elites after the wars of religion were in themselves unusual.[34] In many other cities in southern France, lay confraternities had become small groups of artisans who struggled unsuccessfully against clerical attempts at control of their organizations. In those cities, the clergy was opposed to these groups, whose activities it deemed impious, immoral, and disobedient. But in Toulouse, the local clergy had no such complaint. Indeed, clerics themselves continued to enroll as members in the confraternities into the eighteenth century. Participation in penitential piety was not seen to be at odds with orthodox devotion.

Who belonged to the penitential confraternities of Toulouse? Membership in the penitential confraternities is difficult to establish definitively for the seventeenth and eighteenth centuries because of the paucity of documentation. Although membership lists were carefully maintained by these groups, the majority of these documents have been lost.[35] There remain incomplete lists of officers of the confraternities, minutes of confraternal meetings with partial listings of the officers present, undated membership lists, and printed histories of the confraternities. What they reveal is the surprising engagement of *parlementaires* with the elite confraternities of Toulouse, in particular, with the *Pénitents Bleus*.[36] For the continuing success and independence of the *pénitents* and the preponderance of nobles in Toulousain confraternities—26 percent of the total membership of the four lay penitential confraternities, a number disproportionate with their representation in the population at large—was simply not to be found in other cities. The penitential confraternities of Toulouse enrolled the elite and the nonelite, offering to all an opportunity to direct their own devotions.

All of the Toulousain penitential confraternities recruited citywide, but the membership of different confraternities tended to be concentrated in specific quarters of the city. The *Pénitents Bleus,* for example, drew more than half of their members from the aristocratic quarters of Saint-Etienne, Saint-Barthélémy, and La Dalbade—the same neighborhoods in which the *gens de loi* lived and worked.[37] These geographical patterns of recruitment reflected the social exclusivity of the confraternities, for the social composition of the *pénitents* differed from one company to another. Almost 40 percent of the membership of the *Pénitents Bleus* was drawn from the second estate. One quarter of these nobles, or almost 10 percent of the confraternity's membership, were *magistrats parlementaires*—almost the entire *parlement,* according to some estimates.[38] The *Pénitents Noirs* included among its members yet more members of the nobility, some of the wealthy bourgeoisie, and some members of the liberal professions. This was the confraternity most favored by *avocats* and *procureurs,* though they joined the *Pénitents Bleus* and the *Pénitents Blancs* as well. Among the latter, they found themselves in company with a preponderance of middling *bourgeoisie* and low clerics. The *Pénitents Gris* were the least socially distinguished of these companies: over 40 percent of their members were artisans.[39] The Italian ideal of fraternal equality within the confraternity was poorly expressed in Toulouse. And so the old tag concerning the *pénitents* was borne out in fact: "Noblesse des bleus, richesse des noirs, antiquité des gris, pauvreté des blancs."[40]

The *Pénitents Bleus,* the confraternity with the greatest numbers of judges, was founded in 1576.[41] Confraternal histories of the *Pénitents Bleus* boasted of the elevated origins of the order. Jean-François Thouron, the official historian of the order in the seventeenth century, included on his list of the founding members of the order three cardinals, one bishop, two abbots, three *premiers présidents* of the *parlement,* a *conseiller,* and five *avocats.*[42] Modern archival research suggests a different and much more humble history of foundation.[43] The order was dedicated to the Virgin Mary, though their robes bore the image of the penitent Saint Jerome. Their official name was "Company of Messieurs the *Pénitents Bleus* of Toulouse, erected to the glory of God and the honor of Jesus, crucified, resurrected, immolated sacramentally in the adorable Eucharist, placed under the protection of the Sacred Virgin, his mother assompte, and under the invocation of the glorious Saint Hierosme, of the great Saint Louis, king of

France, and of the illustrious *pénitent* Saint Magdalaine, perfect lover of the crucified Jesus Christ." Two years after their foundation, they had 111 members.[44]

By the early seventeenth century, the *Pénitents Bleus* were the largest of the city's confraternities with over 1,000 members.[45] Indeed, membership was highest in the early seventeenth century. Published works like the *Annales de Toulouse* and histories of the confraternity jointly confirm a decline in membership after the mid-seventeenth century, a decline that came later than in other French cities but that mimicked them. The *Pénitents Bleus,* who still had as many as 900 members in 1622, had only 534 members on their lists in 1778, 150 years later.[46]

How much more extraordinary, then, that at the end of the eighteenth century as many as 200 nobles were still members of the *Pénitents Bleus*— more than one-third of the membership of the confraternity at the end of the eighteenth century.[47] In addition, an extant membership list whose internal dating suggests its compilation post-1766 demonstrates that of the fifty-eight members of the *parlement* who heard cases that culminated in sentences to torture in 1770, at least eighteen—nearly one-third of these men—were members of the *Pénitents Bleus.*[48] Judicial involvement in the penitential confraternity remained at unusually high levels until and through the period of the French Revolution. Until the end of the old regime, members of the local elite remained involved in these groups, often serving as officers, directing the activities of the confraternity.[49] In those roles, they continued to support many of the traditional practices of the confraternity, among them, the practice of self-flagellation, which served to distinguish the *pénitents* from other confraternities.[50] Despite the diminished number of confraternal brothers, or *confrères,* the membership of the penitential confraternities remained active until the end of the eighteenth century, staging prayer meetings and processions, visiting prisoners and the sick, and providing dowries and apprenticeships to the worthy poor.

This is not to suggest that the practices of the confraternities were unchanged from the moment of their foundation in the sixteenth century to their decline in the revolutionary period. Examination of the names of the officers of the *Pénitents Bleus* indicates that while the confraternity began as the local expression of Roman Catholic militancy in the absence of effective Church leadership at the end of the wars of religion, it soon became an organization that linked the local elite to the national political elite through joint membership and activity.

Published lists of priors and subpriors of the confraternity are available for the period from 1600 to 1688.[51] From 1600 to 1628, these officers were selected from the Toulousain elite and typically included one cleric and one member of the laity. The *gens de loi* took prominence among the lay officers: fourteen *conseillers du parlement* held the office of prior from 1600 to 1621; and from 1622 to 1625, one man, Pierre Desplats, *président* of the *parlement*, served continuously as prior of the confraternity.[52] This period of local dominance and intense piety correlates with the explosion of new orders and new professions in the city.

Yet local dominance of the *Pénitents Bleus* was soon ended. In 1629, Monsieur le Prince, Henri de Bourbon, was installed as the prior of the confraternity, despite the fact that his nonresidence in Toulouse made performance of the prior's duties impossible. In the five years that followed, still other nonresident members of the high nobility were installed in this office, a pattern that continued intermittently throughout the rest of the seventeenth century: in 1660 the Prince de Conti served as prior; and, in 1675, the Prince de Condé. Special processions ordered by the officers of the confraternity also suggest a special link to the monarchy and further indicate the increasingly social rather than devout nature of the confraternity—a linkage stressed by the informal name of the company as the *pénitents royales*. In addition to the regular processions staged by the *Pénitents Bleus*, confraternal officers ordered general processions for the birth of Louis XIV in 1638 and for the death of his father in 1643. Yielding local control of confraternal offices and celebrating national events transformed the *Pénitents Bleus* from a group that stressed piety to one that stressed political sociability.[53]

In 1727, the anonymous author of *L'esprit de l'institut de la congrégation royale de messieurs les pénitens bleus* deplored what he perceived as a diminution in piety:

> It is sad to see that those who profess to practice most strictly the works of piety and penitence, like those who engage themselves in the penitent confraternities, lead a life that little conforms to the state that they have embraced; they only wear the costume and the name of *Pénitent*, [and] they render useless the indulgences that the sovereign pontiffs have conceded them in failing to observe the rules prescribed by their statutes; it must be hoped that reading this simple little work will produce in them the effect of its pious purpose.[54]

By the end of the eighteenth century, changes in understanding of what constituted appropriate and pious practice had accelerated: in 1777, members of the *Pénitents Bleus* requested the right to walk shod in their processions, and considered abandoning their distinctive costume.[55] In addition, they no longer participated directly in charitable works, but delegated twelve commissioners to assist the poor and the sick. At the same time, donations and bequests offered by members throughout the seventeenth century suggest an ongoing faith in the spiritual efficacy of participation in and action by the confraternity.[56] Significant changes in practice were manifest over the two centuries and more of the confraternities' existence, but these changes came quite late.

But the rhetoric of the *Pénitents Bleus* changed remarkably little over this period of time. In his early and extravagant defense of the ascetic practices of the *pénitents,* Étienne Molinier offered a vision of the perfect *pénitent,* "his eyes open to tears, his heart to sighs, his mouth to moans, and the pain that possesses him that does not allow him to draw breath."[57] On the evidence of their confraternal statutes, the members of the confraternity remained as committed to prayer, procession, and penitence. Although official practices of the penitential confraternities began to change toward the end of the eighteenth century, members of confraternities were exposed on a regular basis to a rhetoric that continued to espouse pious practices that ranged from almsgiving to self-flagellation and that endorsed pain as a legitimate means of achieving spiritual enlightenment.

How did *confrères* come to understand their spiritual opportunities and responsibilities? They were first exposed to the philosophy of the confraternity in the ceremony of admission. Admission to these companies was not open. Each man who desired to join was required to be presented by two sponsors. After the censors informed the company as to the moral state of the petitioner, the prior or subprior formally admitted him.[58] New members received their costumes during the ceremony of admission from a superior officer in the presence of the entire company. Among the *Pénitents Bleus,* this costume consisted of coarse robes of dark-blue canvas, the left side of which was embroidered with an image of the *pénitent* Saint Jerome, his body wasted by fasts, his breast torn by blows, his face drowned in tears.[59]

Confraternal statutes required many things of them. Membership was a serious responsibility. The *Processionnaire* of 1675 explained that "persons that the officers and *confrères* receive into this confraternity, on the advice and consent of the censors after an exact report concerning their morals and estate, contract a special obligation."[60] The statutes governing this "special obligation" were known to the *confrères* because they were read on the last Sunday of every month. For members of the laity, confraternal statutes were therefore among the most familiar of all religious texts.[61]

These statutes urged the *Pénitents Bleus* "to observe the laws of God and the Church; to instruct their servants, families, and friends on Christian doctrine";[62] "to avoid every sort of dissolution, dangerous conversation and oaths, and to abstain from the pomp of the world and the Devil, which they renounced at their baptism";[63] and "to visit, instruct, console and generously assist the poor and sick in the hospitals, prisons, and private homes, and with alms to apprentice orphan boys, or to dower poor girls, or at least contribute to the visits of the almoners, and sometimes to accompany them in a spirit of charity and mortification."[64] These charitable obligations—to clothe the naked, comfort the sick, and feed the hungry— were among the most basic of all confraternal obligations.[65]

Confraternal statutes helped to construct a private devotional calendar for their members.[66] Every morning, the *Pénitents Bleus* were required to say five Our Fathers and five Hail Marys on their knees "to honor the passion of Jesus Christ and his divine mother, the amiable advocate of the *pénitents*";[67] and every evening to conduct an examination of conscience followed by the De Profundis for dead *confrères*. They were also encouraged to engage in mental prayer, and to attend mass daily. *Confrères* were also advised "to have set apart somewhere in their residence a hair shirt to wear in secret," in accord with the requirement that members engage in ascetic practices.[68]

Public devotions were just as carefully regulated. Every Friday, *confrères* were to meet in their chapel to pray. Flagellation was also permitted each Friday in the confraternal chapel. This practice was to be done in private "in the shadows, in the view only of the angels and God."[69] It was urged on *confrères* as an exercise "that is very salutary for *pénitents* who practice it in memory of the Passion of the Savior and for those who join them through prayer."[70] They were to fast each Friday, except those Fridays from Christmas to the Purification and from Easter to Pentecost and to participate in penitential exercises in their chapel. On the first Friday of each month, they were "to approach the sacrament of penitence, to participate in the mass of the confraternity carrying a burning white candle (mark of the purity and love with which they must receive the Holy Eucharist), at the office of the Holy Cross, at the Exhortation, and at the rest of the exercises of the company, [and] to participate all together at the mass and the Friday offices of Lent and Holy Week, times specially devoted to penitence."[71] In addition, they were "to receive the sacraments and to appear at the exercises of the company on the feasts of the Holy Cross, and the patron saints, on the days of Holy Thursday and the Octave of the very holy sacrament, and at ordinary and extraordinary processions."[72] Just as statutes helped to construct the private rhythms of the day, so too did they help to impose the public rhythms of the year.

In their duties toward others, *confrères* were again reminded by confraternal statutes of the special significance of penance to their chosen style of devotion. They were obliged by their statutes to visit their sick *confrères* and to serve them with fraternal charity, to inspire in them grounds for penitence and to exhort them to receive the sacraments; and when God allows one of them to die, to participate in the offices for the souls of the dead in their chapel, to accompany their bodies to the tomb and each to give money out of devotion to the treasurer for masses for the dead, so that a mass can be sung in their chapel on the following Monday and several other low masses celebrated for the repose of these same souls, and those of all the dead *confrères*.[73]

And when suffering sickness themselves, they were urged "to confess when they are ill, and to abandon themselves entirely into the merciful hands of God, who punishes their bodies in this world by infirmities in order to preserve their souls from an eternal punishment."[74] The obligations imposed by these statutes imply first, that suffering in sickness comes from God; second, that bodily suffering is a gift from God, whose effect is to spare the individual further spiritual suffering; third, that God-given bodily suffering has spiritual effects; and fourth, that confession at moments of suffering has special merit. Within the confraternal context, temporal suffering was a spiritual opportunity.

The most public of the *pénitents'* devotions were their processions. In the early years, *confrères* processed twice each year: on the night of Holy Thursday, to accompany Christ in his suffering to the tomb, and on Corpus Christi, with the Holy Sacrament.[75] The number of public processions was doubled in the seventeenth century when the company added Sexagesime and the little procession of the Octave. The purpose of these processions was explained in the *Processionnaire* of 1675:

> [to] mark to the faithful the different voyages that Jesus Christ made for their health, and [to] represent to them that their life is only a pilgrimage, during which they must walk continually in the steps of the Savior until they arrive in the country of their birth, that is to say, in the breast of God from whom they take their origin, just as in the processions they walk under the banner of the crucified Jesus Christ until they return to the church from which they left.[76]

Processions, therefore, gave *confrères* an opportunity both to reenact the travels of Christ and so to identify with Christ, and to follow the path of Christ.

In public processions, *confrères* donned their robes and hoods and walked two by two, barefoot through the streets of the city. Veiled faces were required to demonstrate the shame of sin; exposed feet, the pain of repentance. These costumes reduced the members of the confraternity to an anonymous equality. No longer identifiable as individuals, hundreds of *confrères* marched the streets, carrying with them burning candles, heavy crosses, and scourges. They walked in silence or in song, but ordinary speech was prohibited. These processions, the visible manifestation of lay Roman Catholic piety, were believed by members of the confraternity to be of profound importance in winning over heretics and Huguenots. Jean-François Thouron cited the following story as proof of the efficaciousness of processions. In 1621, a procession of the *Pénitents Bleus* stopped at the Church of the Religious of the Order of Saint Clare, where the procession itself became the instrument for the conversion of one Monsieur de Fontarailles, "one of the most blatant and unyielding heretics of his day":

> This lord, coming to Toulouse with eight gentlemen friends, was no sooner at the end of the Pont du Bois, where is the Church of the Dalbade of the Maltaises, when he saw appear at the other end of the bridge this troop of *pénitents*, the cross raised [above them], all barefoot, in very great number, marching two by two, each with a white candle in his hand, in such modesty as to inspire a holy admiration in all those who encountered them.
>
> He was so shaken by this unexpected encounter that he reflected on the piety and zeal of this company that he saw pass before him and that he knew was composed of persons of the first quality; this matter impressed itself so much in the forefront of his heart that it appeared incessantly before his eyes, in whatever company he was and wherever he found himself; he sighed from the bottom of his heart; he felt remorseful and troubled in his conscience, and was never in repose until he abjured his heresy.[77]

In the interpretation of the confraternity, the simple sight of *pénitents* in procession was sufficient to convert this Huguenot. In the context of this story, conversion is more than a spiritual turning—it is actually a physical turning to God: Monsieur de Fontarailles had the sight of these *pénitents* so deeply seared into his heart that the vision reappeared before his eyes in every circumstance in which he found himself, while the feeling in his heart troubled his rest until only recantation could soothe this physical hurt.

Penitential processions did indeed impress themselves on witnesses. Traveling through the south of France in the late seventeenth century, John Locke witnessed a joint procession of parish and penitential confraternities, which he noted in his diary:

> Sund. Apr.19. [1676] Aix, whilst we were there, was fild those 2 days with processions of the villages round about, the Archbishop, Cardinal Grimaldi, having obtaind of the Pope the benefit of the last year's Jubilee to his diocesse, which they are to receive upon processions, soe that the whole towns come in these processions, scarce leaving people anough to look to their houses. From Brignole there will come 4,000. Some parishes come ten leagues, & severall of them in the processions walke bare foot with banners fild with pictures of Our Saviour, the Virgin & other saints, statues of saints & heads in silver,

etc., & soe march through the streets with lighted tapers in their hands, 2 &
2, great numbers of them clad as *Pénitents* Noirs, Blancs & Gris, etc.[78]

His careful observation notes the public elements of penitential piety, both
the distinctive costumes and the bare feet. These sorts of processions were
performed across the south of France throughout the seventeenth and
eighteenth centuries.

Not only did Toulouse enjoy secular processions, therefore, ranging from
the processions that accompanied the opening of the *parlement* on Saint
Martin's Day to the celebration of Roman Catholic victory over Protestant
heresy staged each year on 17 May, but it also enjoyed penitential processions throughout the year: on Holy Thursday, the *Pénitents Bleus, Pénitents
Blancs,* and *Pénitents Gris* processed at night; the *Pénitents Gris* on the feast
of Saint John the Baptist; the *Pénitents Bleus* and *Pénitents Blancs* on Corpus Christi; and the *Pénitents Bleus* on Sexagesime and on the Octave. On
several of these occasions, *confrères* carried the Eucharist in their processions. Processions were therefore a meeting of bodily devotions, in their
symbolic imitation of Christ in penitential procession and in the visible
reminder of the symbolic union with others through Christ in the Eucharist. Participation in these events won indulgences for members. Far from
suppressing the activities of the *pénitents,* as did clerics in other regions,
Toulousain clerics used indulgences as a means of creating and reinforcing
confraternal piety—and, of course, as a means of controlling and directing
the *pénitents* themselves.[79]

These processions were intended for the benefit not only of *confrères* but
also of passersby, who had to salute the sacrament appropriately.[80] As the
Processionnaire of 1675 noted:

> While Christians of this century think only of following the mad delights
> that the Devil offers them, the Church their good Mother occupies herself
> shedding tears for them and seeking the means to remove them from their
> madness: and it is as much in order to bemoan with this Dove the hardness
> of her unnatural Children as to withdraw themselves from these criminal
> paths that the *pénitents* of this congregation assemble on this day [of the
> Quinquagesima]. They leave their chapel arranged like an army corps in order
> to oppose themselves to the [moral] slackening of the world by these public
> exercises of penitence [and] in order to repair the offenses that Our Lord
> receives in these unhappy days.[81]

Despite the rigor of this rhetoric, it would appear that these processions
ended in feasts or the consumption of sweets. Grocers' bills sent to the
Pénitents Bleus that include "yellow torches for the procession," also make
mention of quince jelly, jars of jam, candied citrus peels, sweets and sugar,
lemon syrup, and hippocras.[82]

What truly distinguished the *pénitents* from other confraternities? Their continued and successful control over their statutes and membership and their particular style of devotion—including their adoption of distinctive costumes and their devotion to the sacrament of penance—set them apart from other confraternities. In particular, their pursuit of pain as a legitimate means of approaching divinity set them apart.

Whether the practice of flagellation among penitential confraternities was real or symbolic is debated. In Italy, silk flails were sometimes used to symbolize penitence, though cords covered in paper and barbed at the ends with small metal spikes were listed in confraternal inventories.[83] In Spain, members of confraternities flagellated themselves with scourges tipped with wax in order to draw blood.[84] In France, well into the eighteenth century, the *Pénitents Blancs* in Nice whipped themselves in public processions until they bled, sobbing all the while.[85]

While flagellation was intended to remit the sins of *pénitents* and to procure spiritual merit only for the members of the confraternity, it is probable that on occasions of public flagellation, witnesses to these devotions understood the practice as one that contributed to a common fund of merit from which all participants—witnesses as well as actors—might draw. Whether they flagellated themselves in public or not, *pénitent* processions were filled with signs of bodily mortification: *confrères* walked barefoot, clad in the garments that obscured their individuality and bound them together in fraternal equality and anonymity, crowned with thorns and weighed down with the heavy crosses they carried, or the chains they wore.[86]

The French *pénitents* were socially exclusive groups.[87] They sought not to create fellowship among persons of all classes, but to celebrate and to ritualize social distinctions. In this, the *pénitents* were distinguished from the church-sponsored parish confraternities of the seventeenth and eighteenth centuries, which were socially heterogeneous and which encouraged men and women, children and adults, members of the clergy and members of the laity, to participate jointly.[88]

The dramatization of social difference by the confraternities was not restricted to issues of class and locality. The predominance of men among their membership was another of the distinguishing characteristics of the *pénitents*. It is true that in Nice, women were not excluded from penitential companies, but marched in processions with their *confrères*. Maurice Bordes cites evidence from 1671 that demonstrates that women, dressed in the traditional *sacs* and *cagoules* of these companies, walked barefoot through the streets, crowned with thorns, with ropes around their necks, flagellating themselves with leather thongs.[89] But the Niçoise example is an unusual one. Far more commonly, French women were excluded from membership in penitential confraternities or were permitted only limited participation.[90] In this, the French *pénitents* resembled their Italian and Spanish counterparts.[91] Yet few scholars have explored the profound sexual segregation of the confraternities.[92]

Of the four penitential confraternities in Toulouse, the *Pénitents Blancs, Pénitents Gris,* and *Pénitents Bleus* all admitted women as members.[93] Female participation was hedged with restrictions. Female members of the *Pénitents Blancs* could not wear the hair shirt of the company except on the day of their own funerals. They were permitted to participate in processions and public devotions, but they could not convene at the same time as their *confrères.* Women could and did flagellate themselves in private, but never in public processions or in the confraternal chapel.[94] What was the practice of flagellation about that women could not publicly participate?

Ascetic practices of all kinds were central to the identity of the *pénitents,* none more so than flagellation.[95] Indeed, many companies were informally known as *battus,* the ones who flagellate themselves.[96] As can be seen from the Toulousain evidence, the prohibition on its practice by their female members was equally central. The *pénitents* chose this act of positive mortification to symbolize the depth of their devotion but denied their female members the right to participate in this defining ritual.

This look at penitential confraternities and the role of women in them raises interesting questions. Why were women largely excluded from membership? Why, when admitted, was their active participation restricted to specific forms of devotion? And why were women forbidden from the public practice of flagellation?

John Henderson has suggested that in Italy women did not publicly flagellate themselves for reasons of sexual modesty. However, most contemporary descriptions of flagellants suggest that men remained fully clothed, and that the garments they wore were specially designed such that they could flagellate themselves without disrobing.[97] James Banker, by contrast, suggests women were excluded from confraternal membership and its attendant practices because their male contemporaries deemed them incapable of the necessary self-examination and self-discipline.[98] And yet according to his own analysis this rationale was beside the point, as he goes on to suggest that from the fourteenth century, the ritual of flagellation was intended to purify men immured in the moral ambiguities of market economies.[99] In his analysis, as women were excluded from these economies, they were equally excluded from the ritual purification of flagellation because they had no need for it.[100] In the Italian context, other authors have argued that men's participation in confraternities was stimulated as they were excluded from political participation, that the confraternities provided these men with an alternative arena within which to hold office and administer authority.[101] In other words, when discussing male participation in confraternities, exclusion from one realm is seen to encourage participation in another, while in discussing female participation, exclusion from one realm is seen to support exclusion in another.

The act of flagellation, whether performed in public during a procession or in private in the confraternal chapel, stood at the liturgical center of confraternal worship.[102] It was intended to perform a multiplicity of functions. Flagellation dramatized the doctrine of Purgatory and the sacrament of penance because it implied that there was divine forgiveness for visible contrition, that self-punishment for sin might mitigate divine punishment. But flagellation was also a self-conscious imitation of Christ. Most commentators on the practice, both early modern contemporaries and modern historians, have discussed this *imitatio* as one whose essential quality lies in shared suffering—that in suffering bodily pain as Christ did, *confrères* shared his suffering and through intimate knowledge of the experience of God drew closer to God, perfecting themselves spiritually while they attacked themselves physically.[103]

But this *imitatio* had another key feature not often discussed by these commentators—its voluntariness. While part of the mystery of the Passion is the human suffering of Christ, the other part of the mystery is his volition. What is mysterious is not only that God *can* suffer in the human body with which he is garbed, but also that he *chooses* to endure this suffering out of his divine love. And just as Christ chose to suffer and die for the redemption of humanity, so too did the *pénitents* choose to suffer for their own sins. They imitated Christ not only in his suffering but also in his choosing to suffer. The voluntary aspect of penitential suffering was of enormous importance to Molinier, who struggled to defend the practice of self-flagellation from those who recoiled from it in horror or found room in it for mockery, and who stressed the fact that *pénitents* chose this practice as one which allowed them spiritual purity: "he who reprimands, mortifies, distresses his flesh, who seems to exercise a hatred against himself, and acts the executioner of his own life before the eyes of those rendered effeminate by delights wisely preserves himself for Heaven."[104] The rigor of the practice is here cast as an explicitly masculine endeavor.

This ability to choose suffering required a freedom of choice that women were not seen to possess. Women had been cursed with pain as the burden they must bear for the fault of Eve. Pain was their lot. It could not be chosen because it was already ordained. Self-mortification on the part of men was therefore at once an act of great humility and great hubris. It both demonstrated the recognition of sin and suggested a fellowship between

Christ and the literal man, each of whom could choose to suffer for redemption, as women could not.

This reading of flagellation suggests that there had been an extraordinary shift in the understanding of pain from the twelfth to the sixteenth
century within the context of religious observation. Georges Duby has suggested that during the High Middle Ages, just as work *(labor)* was seen as
the property of the poor, so pain *(dolor)* was seen as the property of women,
in each case because of the Biblical injunction upon the expulsion from
Eden. The injunction implicitly established the principle that not all persons could voluntarily elect pain, since some—women and those who must
labor—were already condemned to suffer pain.[105] In other words, Duby
identifies the eleventh and twelfth centuries as a period during which
bodily experience was equated with social status, when to work meant to
be poor and to suffer pain meant to be female, when elite men were literally
unmanned by expressions of pain.[106] It was during this same period that
monks adopted manual labor as a positive mortification. They chose to
labor not only because it was good for monastic brothers to support themselves, but also because to suffer the pains of *labor,* and to be seen to suffer
them, was not only a physical mortification but also a spiritual one.
Through voluntary labor and its attendant pains, the monk was unmanned,
unsexed as he was through voluntary chastity. But I would argue that unlike
the curses of *labor* and *dolor,* voluntary suffering was seen to be redemptive,
redeeming the sins of the sinful self.

Over time, this monastic ideal of voluntary suffering as an avenue to
redemption was taken up by the laity.[107] Choosing to suffer became a high-
status activity, a mark of elite masculinity. Suffering was transformed. In
this transformation, ritual flagellation helped to manifest the hierarchy of
grace, in which different kinds of suffering were assigned different spiritual
merit: *dolor* was a debt owed to God, mortification a gift given voluntarily.
The religious understanding of pain as expressed through confraternal
flagellation was therefore a profoundly hierarchical one. The spiritual value
of pain derived from the person who suffered it because the physical nature
of the person—man or woman—helped to determine the chosenness of
the pain. So while it was true that the Church and confraternities endorsed
the experience of voluntary suffering as one that permitted members of the
laity to approach the divine and to grasp essential spiritual truths, it was also
true that it was an experience restricted to particular members of the laity.

Did membership in penitential confraternities exert a direct influence on
judicial behavior in the courts? Did participation in confraternal life predis-
pose judges to a greater willingness to inflict pain on others, as they did on

themselves? I suspect that judges sat on courts that became increasingly contentious over the course of the period, as they argued among themselves over the meanings and purposes of pain. But that suspicion cannot be proved, as the *parlement* of Toulouse kept no records of judicial debates and largely failed to record the opinions of individual judges as to sentencing. Surely engagement in confraternal life gave judges a way to understand and to value the pain they inflicted at the same time as it gave them a way to beg forgiveness by taking suffering on themselves or by offering charitable assistance to those on whom they sat in judgment, inspired by the theology that suffering was a meaningful experience. I am suggesting here what cannot be demonstrated absolutely: that judicial involvement in confraternal life lent epistemological support to the practice of torture and that as judges gradually abandoned painful practices in their religious observation—as textual defenses of flagellation from the 1650s and petitions for the right to process shod from the 1770s both suggest—so did they gradually abandon painful practices in their legal work.

The role of confraternal participation in the readiness of judges to employ torture should not be overemphasized.[108] Whether particular judges were active in these groups, all judges inhabited a deeply, even fanatically Roman Catholic city and were, therefore, surrounded by images and icons that reinforced belief in the efficacy of pain. This cultural milieu itself had a profound influence on a sincere belief in the efficacy of torture. There is every reason to imagine that these men *believed* in the sacramentality of suffering and in the ability of physical pain to connect the sacred to the profane. This belief, enshrined in their religious practices, surely found its way into their professional lives, authorizing their employment of judicial torture, encouraging them to inflict pain on the bodies of the accused before them deliberately, perhaps with a sense of wonder at what they were empowered to do by the king, the church, and the law.

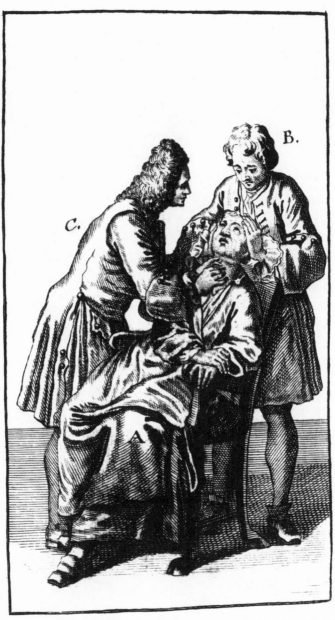

A surgical procedure. From René Garengeot, *Traité des operations de chirurgie,* third edition, volume 2 (Paris, 1748), facing page 449.

5

"The tortur'd patient": Pain, Surgery, and Suffering

Was there only one vision of pain in early modern France? Was the judicial belief in the efficacy of pain, bolstered by the religious devotion to pain, the only way in which pain was understood in this period? The evidence suggests that throughout the seventeenth century, the elite of France were remarkably dedicated to a sacramental vision of pain, one that they carried into the realm of health and illness. Pascal was perhaps the best known and most public exponent of the spiritual opportunities inherent in physical suffering, but he was by no means the only one. The memoirs of Mme. de Motteville, in which she offers accounts of the illnesses of Anne of Austria, constructed illness as a spiritual and moral opportunity. In Toulouse, Jean-George Gargaud, one of the *présidents à mortiers* of the *parlement,* thanked God for the opportunity "to do penance in the pains of a long illness." And in the early eighteenth century, an abbot confided in his surgeon that "his approaching death gave him no displeasure, because he hoped that his long sufferings would contribute to the expiation of his sins."[1] In a variety of public and private contexts, the elite represented illness and its attendant sufferings as gifts from God. But in each case, this spiritual resignation was an attitude achieved only after the sufferers had exhausted the resources of medicine. And in the medical context, pain meant something quite different than what has thus far been described.

This chapter sketches both how pain was described by medical practitioners and by their patients, and how those descriptions shaped the meaning of pain, how pain was understood, and even how it was experienced within the context of medicine, as opposed to the contexts of law and religion. I am less interested here in medical theories of the physiology of pain than I am in what were considered appropriate responses to pain on the part of practitioners, less concerned with supposed sources of pain than with whether pain was considered a meaningful experience.[2] The evidence of case histories and surgical texts suggests that levels of reported pain varied tremendously, that surgeons took those reports seriously, and that they sought to relieve pain by a variety of means when they thought it safe to do so. The growing complexity of their understanding of pain led

them to revise their understanding of its meanings; most significantly, in
the eighteenth century, surgeons understood pain to be at once an individual and a social experience, a complex phenomenon that began in one body
but that spread inexorably to others.

All early modern healers worked with people in pain. But it was the peculiar role of surgeons alone to inflict pain on their patients in the hopes of
bringing relief to them—just as judges might inflict pain on those accused
of capital crimes, and *pénitents*, on themselves. For that reason, we shall
turn primarily to their writings to elucidate the problem of pain in the
context of medicine, rather than those of the host of other healers who
abounded.

The practices of healing in early modern France were divided among
trained and untrained practitioners.[3] Trained practitioners were divided
into three groups: physicians, surgeons, and apothecaries. In theory, each
type of practitioner had a specific training and a defined area of practice.
Physicians were university-trained and treated internal diseases; surgeons
were apprenticed and specialized in external diseases; and apothecaries
were apprentice-trained but schooled in Latin and prepared and administered drugs.[4] French surgeons were therefore possessed of rigorous craft
training.[5] Their exposure to formal university studies was minimal; their
knowledge was gained instead through experience. But their reputations
were unparalleled. They pioneered new surgical techniques, including the
resolution of cataract by extraction and the performance of cesarean section
on a live woman; and they perfected procedures for the removal of bladder
stones and the resolution of harelips.[6] It was universally acknowledged that
French surgeons far surpassed their foreign counterparts in skill and understanding. Students arrived from all over Europe to study with them. Paris
remained the center of European surgery well after the close of the eighteenth century.[7] The most esteemed surgeons of the eighteenth century
included Jean-Louis Petit, Henri-François Le Dran, and Sauveur-François
Morand and their students, Antoine Louis and Jacques Tenon, all of whom
were indebted in turn to renowned surgeons of the past, including Ambroise Paré and Pierre Dionis.

By the eighteenth century, the prestige of surgery and of surgeons was
on the rise as the epistemology of medicine was reshaped and the roles of
clinical observation and experimentation were revalued. Despite the new
emphasis on techniques long employed in the practice of surgery, surgeons
were never part of the theoretical elite. It remained physicians and scientists who contributed to the most widely received theories of medicine.
Despite this theoretical preeminence, surgeons were consulted more fre-

quently than physicians were both because they were more numerous than physicians and because their expertise took in many of the most common complaints. And as a result, surgical understandings of health and illness were the ones most available to those seeking relief from illness and injury.

Instead, surgeons continued to devote themselves to patient care in all its mundane realities. The bulk of surgical practice was taken up with letting blood, lancing boils, pulling teeth, setting bones, dressing wounds, treating fractures and dislocations resulting from work accidents, trussing hernias, and treating skin disorders, including those arising from sexually transmitted diseases. Invasive surgeries were undertaken only when deemed an essential last resort, and included amputation of limbs, lithotomy for removal of bladder stones, surgical repairs of fistulas, and excision of breast tumors. Surgical consultations were generally performed in the surgeon's office or in the patient's home and, unlike physician's consultations, might well incorporate visual or manual examination of the patient in addition to discussion of the patient's medical history.[8] Surgical procedures took place in a mutually agreeable location. Phlebotomies, for example, were generally performed in the patient's home, but surgeons worked in rented rooms and in hospitals as well, sometimes relying on their patients to gather together some of the items necessary for their surgeries.[9] Although surgeons employed invasive procedures infrequently, they regularly dealt with patients who were frightened or in pain.[10]

Despite people's fear of pain, surgeons did not lack for patients. This fear was deserved; physical suffering dramatically altered patients' lives. Case histories demonstrate that the symptoms of illness were overwhelming and came to intrude on every aspect of patients' lives. Pain had the power to alter patients' quality of life. Barthélemy Saviard wrote of patients whose livelihoods were disrupted by their illnesses and of those whose very lives had become a torment: the sixteen-year-old water carrier who could no longer perform her work; the hernia patient whose pains daily redoubled until he was forced to take to his bed; the woman suffering from a headache so violent that for the four years of her illness she had not had a moment without complaint; or the woman forced to take to her bed with violent pains all over her body that prevented her from walking freely and who at the merest touch suffered broken bones and pains that continued to grow.[11] Speaking of one of his venereal patients, Jacques Daran noted that "he was reduced to so deplorable a state that he could neither act nor live like the rest of men."[12] And Pierre Dionis, speaking of his cancer patients, noted that they suffered "such pains as make them every day wish for death."[13]

To read surgical texts is to read a catalog of human misery. Patients hurried to surgeons with illnesses of short duration that included animal bites, broken bones, and concussions. And they came reluctantly to surgeons after having endured terrible suffering over long periods of time: months of fever and pain resulting from wound abscesses, uterine prolapses of long duration "that reduced [the patient] to a state in which she could not walk without inconceivable pain," and the complications of sexually transmitted diseases that dragged on for years.[14] Some patients were incurable, like the man who fell from the second story of a building onto the pavement below and who for six weeks survived the dislocation of his eleventh vertebra and the paralysis of the lower half of his body "such that he could urinate only with a catheter and could perform his evacuations only by means of enemas."[15] Others held out hopes of recovery.

Those who hoped for a return to health included a Mademoiselle Chabot, who in 1727 at the age of 27 sought relief for "very violent pains in all the teeth on the left side, the temple and ear of the same side, the palate, chin, and throat."[16] She visited a doctor and a surgeon in Orléans who treated her for rheumatism by ordering bleedings, enemas, emetics, and poultices, none of which brought her any relief. She then met with an apprentice surgeon who drew a tooth that was rotted, but an hour after the procedure the pain returned and remained for several months, after which it subsided of its own accord. In February 1728, in Paris, she consulted the surgeon Jean-Louis Petit, who referred her to the dentist-surgeon Pierre Fauchard. After examining her, Fauchard pulled another tooth: "this tooth was no sooner pulled than the sharp and extreme pains that had tormented this person dissipated entirely and without any return."[17]

The surgeon Jacques Daran, among his many case histories, cited the case of a Monsieur G***, who contracted a second case of gonorrhea in 1728, which, after six months of treatment with copahu balm, came to an end.[18] Three years later, a bubo appeared, which opened and then closed on its own, but from that point on, he suffered a slight drainage from this site. Then his urine stream began to diminish, but without any accompanying pain. In 1733, he contracted a new case of gonorrhea, which, after curative treatment, left him in the same state. In 1743, he contracted the illness for a fourth time, which caused an inflammation of both testicles and pain all along his penis to his anus, such that he could neither sit nor walk. He was treated by a surgeon with mercurial frictions, which permitted him again to walk, though with continuing pain. During this treatment, he again suffered from slight retention of urine, though this was a less severe episode than he had suffered on two previous occasions. After treatment, he had no more pain, but his urine stream was reduced to drops, and he suffered from incontinence. Since that time, Daran reported, the patient had a sensation of heaviness along his penis, much pain in the glans, great pains in his kidneys, incontinence, pain on erection, and an inability to ejaculate. After two years in this state, his kidney pains were greatly increased, and his urine came to contain a lot of purulent, thick and viscous matter, with such cruel pains that he lost sleep and appetite, and had visibly lost weight. Finally, in 1746, after eighteen years of recurrent illness—almost half his life—he sought Daran's help, who claimed to have effected a cure by early 1747.

Surgeons' case histories suggest that the majority of patients did not view their pain as ennobling, nor did they willingly endure it. They believed that doctors could help them relieve their pain, and they actively sought them out. Only with the failure of treatment did patients seem to treasure their sufferings as spiritual opportunities. And surgeons themselves rarely expressed the view that suffering might be ennobling; instead, they sought to relieve pain with every means available. In the context of medicine, quite unlike the religious context, suffering was deeply negative, something to be avoided whenever possible.

How did surgeons describe the phenomenon of pain? Robert James, in his *A Medicinal Dictionary* (1743–45), noted the difficulty of providing an exact definition of pain:

> Of pain there are various kinds: one is attended with pulsation; another with a sense of incumbent weight; another with a tension. There is a pain which attends erosion, incision, punction, and perforation, comprehended, with these and the like differences, under the name of acute. And, lastly, there is a pain attended with torpor or numbness. . . . Besides the before-mentioned, there are other distinctions of pain: thus some pains are fixed; others are moveable and wandering, as it often happens in a redundance of humors; some pains are continual, and others intermittent; some intense, others remiss; some again afflict the patient in the beginning of a disease, others afterwards; and sometimes they arise on the critical day, sometimes not; and, to mention no more, some pains are seated in the external parts, some in the internal; some in the noble, some in the ignoble parts.[19]

As they sought to provide themselves with an adequate understanding of pain, surgeons drew on the rich and expressive descriptions employed by patients, in case histories that reported patients' language in indirect discourse, as well as employing characterizations of their own.

Pain was described in terms that referred to its temporal duration, its perceived intensity, its emotional quality, and its effects on consciousness, as well as in terms that described its pulsating, weighing, piercing, wrenching, and shooting qualities. Pain could be intermittent or continual, and ranged along a scale of intensity from feeble and slight to extreme, excessive, and violent.[20] Pain was fixed or wandering; beating, throbbing, or pulsating; heavy and dull; sharp and shooting; tense and tender; pricking, piercing, or poignant.[21] It had the ability to transform the consciousness of the patient, in its stupefying effects; it had the capacity to transform the experience of time.[22] And it had profound emotional resonance: pain was troublesome and disquieting, grievous, cruel, and in the end, unbearable.[23] Pain evoked feelings of anxiety, horror, and grief and was experienced as a cruel assault that could not be endured, not even imagined.[24] Implicit in these characterizations of pain was a continuum of physical and emotional feeling.

This richness of language suggests a pressing need to categorize pain not found in other cultural arenas. *Pénitents* did not detail their sufferings any more than did victims of torture, as no amount of description would render their sufferings less—and of course, in the case of the *pénitents,* was entirely beside the point. But pain in the medical context could be put to use. In the medical context the specific quality of pain was more important than the mere fact of pain. It was of diagnostic value to surgeons, who relied on exact descriptions to confirm their suspicions about injuries and illnesses. The ability to communicate the specificity of pain was therefore the first step in relieving it.

At the same time, it is true that surgeons always viewed pain somewhat differently than did their patients. Patients sought medical advice until they had found both relief for pain and an underlying cause of their pain. Surgeons, by contrast, tended to recognize pain as a symptom of injury and disease, as a secondary condition that would resolve of its own accord once the primary condition had been addressed. Pain was useful in diagnosing disease, and surgeons were therefore reluctant to treat pain, since treatment could mask symptoms essential to diagnosis. As long as surgeons understood pain as symptomatic of disease rather than as a problem in and of itself, then their understanding—rather than inadequate pharmacopoeia or lower pain thresholds—itself helps to account for the apparent failure to treat pain noted by modern historians.

Pain was sometimes understood by surgeons as an independent problem demanding therapeutic attention. Some pains that are today associated with normal developmental processes were singled out for treatment. Teething pains, for example, attracted a great deal of attention, because they were seen to presage a variety of potential illnesses. Surgeons therefore advised a variety of remedies, from topical ointments to soporifics, to ease the teething pains of infants and young children. Teethers were suggested by some authors both to relieve pain and to distract the child:

When the teeth are ready to cut, a silver coral furnish'd with small bells, is ordinarily made use of, to divert the child from the pain it then feels, and to cool its gums, which are then inflamed, and to facilitate the cutting of the teeth.[25]

When they proved insufficient, other remedies were suggested, from gentle massage to change the direction of the humors to herbs and stones hung around the neck to the simple expedient of rubbing the gums with substances thought to bring relief:

the nurse must often rub the child's gums with her finger alone, thereby to open the pores of them, & make them soft, that the moisture may breathe out the better: and sometimes let her annoint her finger either with honey, fresh butter, the brains of a hare, or such like (either toasted or raw) or else with oil of lilies or hen's grease. Some hold it for a great secret to rub the child's gums with the milk of a bitch, either of itself, or mingled with the brains of a pig. Avicen prescribes that they should hold a slice of fat meat between their gums, and chaw it often. And it is to be noted, that all the foresaid medicines ought to be applied more than lukewarm.[26]

Though soporifics were sometimes employed, most surgeons cautioned against them.

Teething pains thus stood in marked contrasted to labor pains. Labor pains were also understood to be part of normal health processes, but they were not seen to require any pharmacological relief, not only because that pain was seen by some as a necessary spiritual component of the process, but also because it was seen to provide positive assistance to physical processes that speed labor. And this idea existed despite the fact that women themselves actively sought to achieve painless labors through the use of charms and rituals, by sitting rather than standing during mass in the last weeks of their pregnancies, for example, and by wearing eaglestone amulets. During labor, they prayed to Saint Mamart, they wore charms made of scraps of paper with bits of writing on them (or ate them), and girdles believed to have belonged to the Virgin Mary, they slipped knives under their beds, and they screamed.[27] At the same time, both surgeons and midwives offered other means to ease the laboring woman's suffering, including her anxiety regarding her pain, and freely offered remedies for pains that persisted after delivery.

Throughout the period, some pains associated with disease processes not only merited therapeutic attention but were the very definition of the disease. Earache, for example, was regarded as an illness that consisted of nothing more than pain and was treated in a variety of ways. Bleeding, the universal remedy, was suggested for earache. Books of remedies also suggested that a variety of warm liquids be dropped into the ear, from oils infused with specific herbal remedies to alcohol mixed with vegetable juices to milk infused with opium and saffron.[28] By the mid- to late-eighteenth century, pain had come to be defined as the very essence of still other diseases: a medical dictionary of 1747 defined rheumatism, for example, as "pain that is felt in the muscles, the membranes, and often in the periosteum," and sciatica as "pain that occupies not only the joint, but also the hip, the loins, the sacrum, the thigh, the back of the knee, the leg, and that sometimes spreads as far as the end of the foot."[29]

There were scattered references to pains that neither reflected underlying diseases nor constituted diseases in themselves. In the sixteenth century, Ambroise Paré made note of phantom limb pain. In the eighteenth century, Pierre Dionis made reference to the same phenomenon:

> Almost all patients who have had an arm or a leg cut off complain of feeling a pain in the part that they have lost; sometimes they tell us 'tis their great, and at other times their little toe, which prevents their sleeping. And I have met with some patients who have told me that those sorts of pains were more insupportable than those of the wounds.[30]

It would appear that these pains were particularly baffling to early modern medical practitioners, as no treatments of any kind were proposed for them.

Although the surgical texts of the early modern period did not characterize or categorize pain quite as we do, it is clear that different kinds of pain were under discussion: the acute pains of injuries and the chronic pains of degenerative diseases, the uninflicted pains of developmental processes like teething and the inflicted pains of surgery. And in all cases, the surgeons who authored these texts acknowledged that there was a great variety of responses to these varied pains. As reported in summary discussions and in case histories, early modern patients were seen to respond to these pains as individuals, with different pain thresholds and different personal histories of pain. What they shared was a common culture that helped them make sense of that pain and that helped surgeons determine how best to respond to that pain.

The evidence presented thus far suggests that it is difficult to make generalizations about the way in which pain was experienced and expressed. What we do know is that both patients and surgeons recognized pain as a problem that needed to be addressed. And once again, the fact that patients and surgeons possessed different interpretations of pain meant that they pursued different avenues of pain relief.

The remedies that patients sought for pain ranged from spiritual intercession to surgical intervention and included everything in between.[31] For

medical relief of pain during illness, patients employed bleedings and cup-
pings, enemas and emetics, sudorifics, anodynes, and changes of diet.
When these remedies failed either to cure illness or to relieve pain, patients
sought more drastic measures.

The nagging sense that something was not quite right was sufficient for
some patients to request surgery. Writing of hernias, the English surgeon
Samuel Sharp noted the following:

> There are a great many people who are so uneasy with ruptures, though they
> are not painful, that a little encouragement from surgeons of character will
> make them submit to any means of cure; but as I have seen two or three
> patients, who were in every respect hale and strong, die in a very few days
> after the operation, the event, though surprising, should be a lesson never to
> recommend this method of treating an epiplocele, unless it is attended with
> inflammation, &c.[32]

Indeed, Pierre Dionis noted that after Louis XIV's surgery for anal fistula
in 1687, the desire for surgery became a positive fad. This was, of course,
an atypical event, but worth noting nonetheless. The willingness to endure
pain arose from many sources, vanity and status-seeking among them. It is
clear, therefore, that despite the knowledge that surgery in this period before anesthesia was intensely painful, some patients sought it out. Most
often, patients sought surgery as a last resort, a cure for both illness and the
pain it caused. Intense and chronic pain, and not merely the fear of death,
could itself drive patients to endure the pains of surgery.

Illness alone could produce terrible suffering, as noted above. Surgery
also produced suffering. Yet in full knowledge of the pain of surgery without anesthesia, patients insisted on their surgeries. Some begged for help
in moments of extremity. Garengeot recounted a case history involving the
renowned surgeon Jean-Louis Petit:

> Monsieur Petit saw an officer who, having received a sword thrust, com-
> plained only of the enormous pains that he felt at the end of his penis. As we
> wanted to undress him to discover the cause of his pains, he kept displaying
> his penis, crying with all his might: Here is my problem, why are you looking
> elsewhere? And he kept tugging his penis, saying, cut it off.[33]

Further examination of this patient suggested that his pain was the result
of the sword thrust and that the pain he felt was referred pain that required
no direct treatment. Nor were these the only patients to demand surgery
for the relief of pain.

Other patients came to surgeons after having endured months of pain,
determined to attain relief at last. In an extraordinary case, Saviard reported that another of his patients, a young woman of nineteen, had come

to him in July 1692 complaining of a great pain in her breast that had lasted for more than eighteen months, a pain that she believed to have been caused by a pin that was lodged there, though Saviard himself found no sign of it. She insisted that he operate. He allowed himself to be won over by her and made an incision in her breast whose juncture was situated directly over the site of her pain:

> I introduced my finger into this opening, where I searched in vain for the foreign body in question; after which the patient, who had suffered this much-desired incision without making the slightest complaint, surprised that we found no foreign body, had enough fortitude to raise herself from her seat and herself to search the opening of her wound without feeling anything, about which I tried to console her, saying that the foreign body could appear in the days of supuration.[34]

During her recovery from surgery, this patient no longer felt the stabbing pain that had troubled her, but Saviard and his colleagues noted that her pain returned proportionate with her recovery, until by the time she was healed, her pain was as great as it had been before the surgery. She continued to consult with one of the surgeons, who after performing the same surgery a second time, noted in the ensuing suppuration an encysted object as big as the head of a pin, after which her pain ceased, and she was completely cured.[35]

There were still others; indeed, patients eager for surgery appear often in surgeons' case histories. Oftentimes, it is true, this eagerness was motivated only by the fear of death, but that fear was a real motivation that helped patients to endure surgery. Pierre Dionis remarked on this phenomenon:

> When a chirurgeon has without hesitation acquainted the patient that he must of necessity resolve to die, there are none but will choose the operation. We are not willing to die; and tho' we are certain of suffering great pains, we always prefer them to death. I have seen some press the proceeding of it so hard, that they would not allow time for the preparation of the apparatus, and I have found others suffer it with an angelic patience, which shews that there is nothing that men will not endure to protract that last hour.[36]

So eager were some to avoid death that they defied the advice of their surgeons. Saviard noted the case of an abbot who sought treatment for a carcinoma against his original surgeons' suggestion. His treatments worsened his state and brought him to the verge of death. This case of iatrogenic illness is a good example of the way in which surgery could produce suffering. The recovery from surgery could itself be very painful, and in some cases, like this one, surgery caused greater problems.

Just as some patients insisted on surgery while others refused it, some demonstrated remarkable endurance in surgery while others were overwhelmed by pain. Saviard noted of a surgery performed in 1691 that "the patient suffered this long and painful operation with great fortitude, and he said to us several times that the tourniquet gave him more pain than the rest of the operation."[37] Others were devastated by the pain of surgery. Among Saviard's case histories is that of a woman who, seven months after a therapeutic bleeding, had developed a tumor the size of a goose egg in the crook of her arm that needed to be removed.[38] He began to perform the necessary surgery:

> after the first incision was made, she lost the fortitude that she had at first demonstrated to suffer all for her healing; such that she could suffer none and we were obliged to complete the operation by violence, which obliged me to do everything more precipitously than desirable.[39]

This woman was not the only patient to be overwhelmed by fear and pain during surgery. In a discussion of mastectomy, Robert James provided the most concise statement of this variety of response in surgery:

> There are indeed some women, who bear this operation with uncommon fortitude, and more than heroic bravery of mind; whereas others of their sex, lose their courage so far, as to shriek and cry in a manner so terrible, as is sufficient to shock and confuse the most intrepid surgeon, and disconcert him in his operation. 'Tis therefore absolutely necessary in this case, that the surgeon, as Celsus directs, be intrepid, and acquit himself in all the steps of his operation, in such a manner, as if he was deaf to the moving groans, and piercing shrieks, of the tortur'd patient.[40]

Patients all had intensely personal responses to pain. But all suffered in a specific cultural context that helped surgeons determine how best to respond.

These texts make clear that in most cases, far from leaving their patients in agony, surgeons made efforts to minimize pain.[41] They did so first by trying to avoid the infliction of pain. Many surgical texts included introductory materials that urged surgeons to cause no unnecessary pain. Pierre Dionis, for example, spoke eloquently to this issue:

> Nor can I more approve, that at an operation, all the chirurgeons present should probe, or poke their fingers into the wound: these are so many fresh pains which they put the patient to, and only prolong the time of his torment. The operator ought to examine what he has to do, and not to admit any more to do it at most, than one of the consulting chirurgeons who are there to assist him with their advice.[42]

Not only did he urge surgeons to spare their patients physical pain by spending as little time as possible in surgery, but he also requested that surgeons empathize with their patients' pain in his direction that surgeons learn to tolerate the expressions of pain made by those patients.

But after this basic injunction, surgeons were divided in their assessments of the safety of treating pain. As noted above, pain was understood to perform an essential function, that of assisting in diagnosis, and for that reason alone surgeons were sometimes hesitant to relieve it. Some physicians went further and sought to argue that pain served an active and useful function. In 1753, the French physician Alexandre Dienert suggested that pain should not be treated because it was an essential aspect of the curative process. And he made this claim in the context of a discussion of the use of opium. In other words, well aware of the analgesic effects of opium, Dienert cautioned against its use precisely because it might disrupt the healing experience of pain. In his view, pain had physical utility for the patient, despite the distress it caused.[43] More common among surgeons was the argument that whatever functions pain might serve, treating pain directly was inadequate and potentially dangerous.[44]

While patients and practitioners did not always agree on the function of pain in illness, both were concerned that pain and the cause of pain be addressed in the course of treatments whenever it was safe to do so. Jacques Daran made note of a patient who had been treated for gonorrhea by a variety of methods, including bitter drops that caused vertigo, astringent injections, and candles, none of which succeeded either in removing the infection or in relieving the pain. Mercurial frictions in the hands of an expert practitioner removed the pain. "But the patient, feeling that this remedy did not attack the cause of the problem put himself into my hands. . . ."[45] This patient wanted more than symptomatic relief, although this was certainly one of his goals. Others were content with the simple relief of pain.

When pain relief alone was the goal, what could surgeons offer their patients in the period before anesthesia? Here we need to distinguish between pain relief offered during illness and during surgery. Pain relief during illness could be procured by use of calming and refreshing drugs, some of which shared the properties of anodynes. A look at remedy books of the seventeenth and eighteenth centuries demonstrates the wide variety of preparations employed for analgesic purposes at the same time as it confirms the recognition of pain as a common medical problem that was both deserving of and amenable to treatment.

The most celebrated of the remedy books was Madame Fouquet's *Re-*

mèdes charitables, published in 1681. It lists over thirty separate instances of pain that could be treated, including the pains of headache and migraine, gout and sciatica, earache and toothache, kidney and stomach pains, hemorrhoids and dysentery, leg pains and pinpricks (best treated with ear wax). The principles underlying these remedies were informed by different philosophies of medicine. To take the cure of headache and migraine as an example, remedies that attempt cure by chemical means, by means of distraction, and by sympathetic magic were all proposed.[46] There is no explanation here of how pain remedies work, only instructions on how to make them and how to use them.

Without providing a fully realized theory of medicine, some books of remedies did make a distinction between anodynes that removed the cause of pain, and those that simply remedied pain. Paul Dubé's *Le médecin et le chirurgien des pauvres* (1674) notes that while bleeding and purgation alone have the power to remove the causes of pain, there are three classes of remedy that can relieve pain: anodynes, *somnifères* or hypnotics, and narcotics. Where Fouquet remains silent on how the proposed remedies work, Dubé explains the action of these analgesics. According to his text, anodynes have a warming quality that eases pain. They are employed by external application to the afflicted part and include marsh mallow root, egg yolk, and the bodies of animals applied warm. *Somnifères* provoke sleep and are taken as a decoction at bedtime. Narcotics ease pain by exciting sleep and by removing the lively feeling of the affected part, and include opium, henbane, mandrake, white poppy, and solanum. For the most part, however, the manner in which drugs operated was of remarkably little interest to these authors.

The most potent analgesics employed by surgeons and physicians of the period were rarely mentioned in remedy books.[47] The infrequent use of opium is typical of the remedy books but by no means universal. *Le medecin des pauvres* encourages what is in this context an extremely free use of opium, recommending its use for almost every ill after other remedies have been exhausted, including headache, earache, toothache, stomachache, colic, and hemorrhoids. In Fouquet's remedy book, opium is employed in only three topical preparations, two of which are for pain, the third of which is a depilatory.[48] While many of the remedies suggested sound outlandish to modern readers, some employ substances increasingly believed to have a curative effect, as in the use of eyedrops containing breast-milk.[49]

The most powerful drugs employed by surgeons for pain relief during illness included mandrake, henbane, solanum, wild lettuce, and opium. In general, these drugs were approved for use by medieval authors and then cautioned against by early modern authors, often with the support of ancient texts. Mandrake, for example, was recognized as of narcotic value by Dioscorides. In the sixteenth century, Ambroise Paré discouraged its use, a position echoed by Symphorien Champier, who noted that mandrake could cause lethargy and sleep without waking.[50] Pierre Pomet rejected it as an unsafe and ineffective drug.

There were few remedies for pain during surgery. Medieval surgical texts had recommended the use of soporific sponges during surgery. These sponges were impregnated with a variety of drugs, most often including opium, mandrake, henbane, and solanum. Held over the nose or in the mouth, they allegedly caused the patient to sleep.[51] By the sixteenth century, French surgeons recommended these sponges primarily for the relief of insomnia.[52] Yet it was at just this point, in the mid-sixteenth century, when surgical therapies entered an active phase—at the very moment when the analgesic and anesthetic drugs most often employed in the medieval surgeries were being discouraged by surgeons.[53] Indeed, although the Dutch surgeon Jerome Brunschwig mentioned a sleeping potion for use during surgery composed of opium, mandrake, and poppies, his colleague Hans von Gersdorff asserted that he had neither used such a potion himself nor heard of its use by any other surgeon.[54] Opiates, though well known, were not employed during surgery, probably because of their many dangerous side effects, including the depression of respiration. Surgeons relied instead on alcohol.[55]

Surgeons had good reason to hesitate when it came to pain relief. Opiates were seen as poisons that could be useful in specific circumstances, but that required a careful hand. As was true of soporific sponges, opiates had been employed for amputative surgeries during the medieval period. But the great French surgeon Guy de Chauliac warned against the use of opium on the grounds that it caused addiction.[56] Other accounts also caution against the internal use of opiates.[57] It would appear, then, that by the seventeenth and eighteenth centuries, opium was most often employed externally after surgical procedures, in plasters and cataplasms.

There was a rich pharmacopoeia available to surgeons and other healers for the relief of pain. Remedies that were employed internally and externally and that operated according to various principles could be pressed into service. If and when surgeons did not employ this pharmacopoeia, it was because they thought it was unsafe to do so, not because they did not recognize pain as a problem. When pain could be safely treated, surgeons did so, drawing on a pharmacopoeia that changed but little during this period.

Patients feared the pain of illness and the threat of death enough that they were willing, sometimes insistent, to undergo painful therapeutic procedures. They described their pains before and after surgical procedures with descriptive language that demonstrates the epistemological existence of pain in the period. And surgeons employed a rich pharmacopoeia to treat this pain. But what did pain mean to the surgeons who witnessed, inflicted, and treated it? Surgeons' understandings of pain changed over the course of the early modern period.

Outside published case histories, discussions of pain inflicted during surgery were relatively rare. Indeed, in the surgical texts that detail the necessary preparations for surgery, the kinds of tools to employ, and the specific techniques for the performance of surgical procedures, the relative silence around the question of pain in surgery is eerily disturbing. Early modern surgeons of necessity operated on patients who moved convulsively and fainted repeatedly, who screamed and begged and moaned and cursed. The pain they suffered in surgery sent many into shock, provoking their deaths within hours. Yet surprisingly few mentions were made of the patient's response during pain. This laconic approach has suggested to many modern historians that patients in premodern periods and cultures, in the absence of analgesics, seemed to suffer little pain.[58]

Surgeons were sometimes reluctant to devote explicit and extended attention to the problem of pain. Le Dran and Saviard noted only in passing that patients often fainted or cried out during surgery.[59] And there is no question that surgeons spoke approvingly of those patients who refrained from expressions of pain. Dionis, for example, remarked:

> I have, in the army, seen soldiers who not only never once cried, "Oh!" but never moved their eyebrows, what pain soever we have put them to, in order to get out a bullet or splinter of a granado, or by making incisions on them: the chirurgeon is to take advantage of this favorable disposition, because it frequently happens that on the morrow, or another day, he does not find the patient much inclined to resign himself up to his will.[60]

Dionis's soldiers who neither cried out nor moved their eyebrows and Saviard's abbot resigned to his death spared their surgeons suffering.

This reluctance to acknowledge pain openly as a problem was deeply rooted in the tradition of surgical writings. Close reading of surgical texts suggests that surgeons' attitudes toward pain changed significantly over the course of the early modern period, from the sixteenth century, when pain was viewed as symptomatic of disease, to the early nineteenth century, when it was described as causative of disease.[61] Not only were the causes and effects of pain reassessed during these years, so too were the appro-

priate attitudes toward those suffering pain and the understandings of the
effects of pain on witnesses to pain.

In several early works, little sympathy was expressed for those who suffer
pain. In his *Popular Errors* (1578), Laurent Joubert recounted an anecdote
concerning a patient who was unconcerned with painless illnesses, believing that medicines had no effect on the course of illness and who, by
implication, was interested only in pain relief. Joubert had this to say about
pain relief:

> As for painful illnesses, it must be understood that pain is not the main con-
> sideration (even though an important one), and that pain must be removed
> at the source if one wishes to give proper treatment.
>
> If one spends time merely alleviating pain and neglects its cause (which is
> the illness, source, root, and matrix of the pain), there are but two methods:
> soothing drugs, which alleviate the pain somewhat and make the person able
> to put up with what remains, and stupefacient drugs, that is, benumbing ones
> that put the limb to sleep by arresting natural heat. The latter should only be
> used in dire necessity and with prudence.
>
> But both of these only lighten the pain or make it disappear for a while.
> One must always come back to treating the essential. Otherwise, one must
> begin all over again.[62]

Joubert reveals the disjunction in expectations and understandings that
existed between doctors and patients in the sixteenth century. Doctors believed that pain was a secondary effect of illness and that treating it was at
best a temporary measure that could never address the real problem. Patients, on the other hand, were articulate in their desire for pain relief above
all. Joubert, in other words, saw a certain inevitability in the experience of
pain, not because pain could not be treated—indeed, this passage suggests
its amenability to treatment—but because it was a secondary effect of an
underlying illness. Pain relief was useless in his view because it failed to
address the central problem. And he expresses little sympathy for patients
who sought this relief.

Surgeons saw pain as a secondary issue until the end of the sixteenth
century, and were therefore reluctant to treat it. As pain came to be seen
as a problem in and of itself, one that had serious consequences not only
for the patient but also for witnesses to pain, they began to treat pain
more aggressively whenever it was safe to do so. Some surgeons hinted that
identification with patients' pain served to mobilize their surgeons. Pierre
Dionis, for example, gave voice to the empathy evoked by the sight of
suffering:

> But how are you to resist the persecutions of a poor suffering patient, which
> implores your help? Are you to abandon her to the rigour of her distemper,

which torments her day and night? No, a chirurgeon must not be so cruel: he must search out means to cure her: and if that is not in his power, he must at least endeavor to soften the disease, and render it more supportable.[63]

Here the sight of suffering urges the surgeon into necessary action, even when the immediate effect of that action might be to augment the patient's suffering. Dionis came to express pity for patients suffering during surgery:

> There are surgeons who are offended at the cries of their patients, and who scold at and chide them, as though they ought to be insensible to the tortures which they make them endure: these ways of acting are too cruel; a surgeon must have humanity, and exhort those under his hands to patience: he must share their pain; which, though he cannot help putting them to, he must, at least, leave them the liberty of crying and complaining.[64]

Dionis implies that the failure to empathize increases the suffering of the patient; more than that, he hints that the experience of suffering is not and should not be the patient's alone.

Some authors made note of the pain of witnesses to surgery. Recounting an operation for anal fistula, Saviard noted the distress it caused all the witnesses: "[I performed these operations] as quickly as possible . . . without allowing myself to be moved by the cries of the patient, nor those of the woman who was present, nor of the servant who held the light for me."[65] Dionis remarked on the emotion inspired by anticipated pain not only in the patient but in all those witness to surgery: "we separate from [surgery] whatever is rough and barbarous, we retrench those burning irons and horrible instruments, which not only the patients, but the bystanders, could not see without trembling."[66] When pain was understood as a social phenomenon that affected more people than the patient, then injunctions not only to spare the patient pain but to share that pain as a means of diminishing it make sense.

The spectacle of suffering could evoke more than pity and empathy. Surgeons expressed their own distress on witnessing suffering. The experience of inflicted pain was one that was wrenching for the surgeon as well as his subject. Ambroise Paré made mention of a patient who came to him requesting that his rotting leg be amputated: "[A]fter his body was prepared I caused his leg to be cut off, four fingers below the rotula of the knee, by Daniel Poullet one of my servants, to teach him and to embolden him in such works."[67] Surgeons came to express not only pity but also horror at the spectacle of suffering. Pierre Dionis remarked explicitly that surgeries range in their difficulty of performance and danger to the patient, and that grave surgeries "are ordinarily accompanied with great pains, and strike horror in the spectators, as the amputation of an arm or a leg."[68] In a discussion of amputation of the leg, Sauveur-François Morand noted possible obstacles to the surgery. The first of them was the terror of the enterprise. He responded: "This is a slight difficulty. All major operations are more or less terrible, and I very much doubt that the spectacle of this one is more difficult to bear than that of the cesarean operation on a living woman, which I once saw."[69] Morand's statement, at first glance a remarkably callous one, here must be placed within a specific surgical context. Cesarean sections had been performed in fewer than one hundred cases in France between 1750 and 1800, and the maternal death rate following the surgery stood at 66 percent. Morand's comparison of major invasive surgeries with cesarean sections must therefore convey the real terrors and dangers of such procedures for all concerned even while he seeks to encourage surgeons to practice invasive procedures.

What is significant about these representations of suffering is the way in which they suggest that pain ceases to be the sole property of the sufferer. Indeed, from the modern perspective, pain is radically redefined in these texts: it is no longer merely nocioception, a physical response to negative stimulus. In these texts, pain is more even than the emotional and intellectual response of the suffering patient to nocioception. It is a profoundly social experience that provokes negative affect in all those involved as witnesses to pain, be they medical practitioners or not. If by the eighteenth century pain was understood as a social phenomenon, then deciding to treat it had to do with the health of observers as well as with the health of patients. It was in part the communicability of pain that rendered it so dangerous, so disturbing; in part, the fear that repeated exposure to the sight of suffering was itself damaging.

Decades before Hallerian theories of sensibility and irritability were taken up by the philosophes, surgeons were exploring the effects of pain not only on the individual sufferer but also on witnesses to suffering. As noted above, surgeons were largely excluded from theoretical discussions. But pain was a practical problem they dealt with every day. Physicians might speculate about the therapeutic effects of pain; surgeons knew its ravages and were regularly confronted with its effects in their patients, their assistants, and themselves.[70] In their examinations of these effects, surgeons evoked their own sensibility and made explicit their anxieties that frequent exposure to pain might be damaging and disabling to the witnesses to pain—including themselves. In so doing, they foreshadowed the arguments of those who argued both that people of sensibility felt exquisitely and that excessive feeling might coarsen the very sensibility that rendered sensible persons such acute emotional barometers. In the surgical context, pain was represented as profoundly negative, an experience that demanded the empathetic care of practitioners at the same time as it threatened to overtake all witnesses to itself. In the secular context of medicine, pain had to be extirpated—and its potentially painful extirpation was enormously dangerous. These surgical discussions provided a model of sorts for all those concerned with the potentially damaging effects of pain.

Calas's good-byes to his family, by Chodowiecki, no. 1.459. Courtesy of Musée Paul-Dupuy, Toulouse, Cliché S.T.C.

6

". . . as if pain could draw the truth from a suffering wretch": Pain as Politics

While pain was differently constructed in different arenas of cultural activity, the fact remains that the legal infliction of pain through the institution of judicial torture remained virtually unchallenged until the middle of the eighteenth century. Given the negative assessment of pain in the context of medicine, it seems unlikely that the silence around torture implied approval for the experience of pain, broadly speaking. Was this silence due to the fact that torture was unknown to the public? Did reform lag because the practice was so secret as to arouse no protest? Or was there no outcry because the French did indeed know and approve of the use of torture?

The French public was well aware of the existence and employment of torture in capital cases, for while the employment of torture was at once secret and private, the practice per se of torture was not. That torture occurred was common knowledge in early modern France. From the sixteenth century on, torture was made mention of in print. Montaigne, Paré, Racine, Molière, and La Bruyère—all published references to the fact of torture, some fleeting, some more deeply exploratory.[1] Dictionaries provided straightforward definitions of "géhenne," "question," and "torture"; collections of causes célèbres contained far more sensational and sympathetic accounts of cases that constituted implicit criticisms of the practice. François Richer, for example, made mention of several celebrated cases in which the true culprit confessed to crimes only after an innocent had been tortured, each time with terrible physical effects.[2] In one such case, he exclaimed:

> The tears of a mother who weeps for her murdered son should without doubt touch the hearts of judges; but should they be less sensitive to the moans of an innocent whom they made to suffer the torments of the most rigorous torture and who remains so crippled in all his limbs that it is impossible for him to earn a living for himself, his wife, and five children?[3]

He also provided evidence to suggest that the reading public was well acquainted with the laws governing torture.[4]

Numerous writers, both French and foreign, from diarists to essayists, commented more privately on the fact of torture. Because it was not performed in public, few individuals not connected to the court had the opportunity to observe its use.[5] John Evelyn, illegally admitted to an interrogation in the Chatêlet of Paris in 1651, was one of only a handful of contemporary observers who had the opportunity to pen a firsthand account in his journal.[6]

While few natives had the chance to observe interrogations, they were well aware of them. In 1676, the trial and execution of Mme. de Brinvilliers, the celebrated poisoner, gripped Paris. Mme. de Sévigné wrote about the case in letters to her daughter from April to September of that year. The question of Mme. de Brinvilliers's torture was of persistent interest to her: was the *question* performed or presented? On the day of the execution itself, Mme. de Sévigné wrote to her daughter:

> She was judged yesterday; this morning they read her her sentence, which was to make an *amende honorable* at Notre-Dame, and to have her head cut off, her corpse burned, her ashes thrown to the wind. They presented her to the *question:* she said there was no need to, and that she would tell all.[7]

Almost two weeks later, she noted, "never have so many crimes been treated so gently, she did not have the *question*."[8] Her observations on the case were not restricted to these legalistic questions but extended to more anecdotal evidence. In a letter to her daughter after Mme. de Brinvilliers's execution, she wrote:

> Another little word about *la Brinvilliers:* she died as she lived, that is to say, resolutely. She went into the place where they were to give her the *question;* and seeing three buckets of water: "That is surely to drown me," she said; "since given my size, no one can claim that I could drink all that."[9]

Sévigné's knowledge of the event included not only the fact of de Brinvilliers's torture but also detailed knowledge of the actual course of the interrogation. The secrecy of the torture chamber enjoined by the oath had somehow been breached.

Nor was public awareness of the practice of torture restricted to Paris. Toulouse, too, had its observers. Pierre Barthès, a private tutor in Toulouse, kept a journal from 1737 until 1780, the year of his presumed death.[10] Religious processions and criminal executions were his peculiar fascinations.

In July 1772, he attended the execution of Jean Begue.[11] Barthès's account of the case, like Mme. de Sévigné's, was extraordinarily detailed and roughly accurate. Jean Begue, nineteen years old, was accused with fourteen codefendants of stealing livestock on several occasions, of numerous thefts of property, including robbing a church three times, and of the murder of a hermit. Begue alone among the accused was sentenced to the *question préalable ordinaire et extraordinaire*. Throughout the *question ordinaire*, the *estrapade*, which was applied four times, he denied the charges against him. But after suffering the first application of the *question extraordinaire*, the *question d'eau*, he began to confess.

Some of the details that Barthès provides in his journal are absent from the interrogation: there is no record in the court documents that Begue requested a change of clothes, nor did he provide in the interrogation any of the details concerning the murder of the hermit recounted by Barthès, confessing only "that he did the murder with his father, and does not recall the circumstances."[12] His father, when confronted with his son, did not confess to striking the first blow, but rather denied any complicity: "he said that he wasn't present at the said murder, that his son entered the hermitage, and that he himself stayed outside."[13] Nonetheless, the overall outline of the case, including details of the interrogation that should have remained secret, were known to Barthès. From what source this detailed and specific knowledge derived is unclear.

On another occasion, that of the execution of Joseph Martiniac in July 1774, the language that Barthès used to report this execution suggests that the sentence was read aloud, as many of the legal phrases were echoed in his description. The details of the case, including the name of the court of first instance and the date it pronounced sentence, the names of Martiniac's codefendants and their relationships to him, Martiniac's many crimes, the name of the man he murdered, and his sentence, including the condemnation to the *question préalable ordinaire et extraordinaire*, were all correct in Barthès's summary of the execution. And Barthès noted that "son cadavre fut exposé aux fourches patibulaires, pour y servir d'exemple, et donner de la terreur aux méchants" (his corpse was exposed in the *fourches patibulaires* to serve there as an example and to terrify the wicked), an almost word-for-word replication of the sentence, which stated that "son corps mort sera exposé aux fourches patibulaires pour y servir d'exemple pour y servir d'exemple [*sic*] et donner de la terreur aux méchants" (his dead body will be exposed in the *fourches patibulaires* to serve there as an example and to terrify the wicked).[14]

But the accompanying *retentum* in the Martiniac case seems not to have been read. For while Joseph Martiniac was indeed sentenced to be tortured, a *retentum* was added to his sentence, specifying that "the said Martiniac will only be presented to the *question*."[15] Barthès's account, however, vaguely implies that the *question* was performed in Martiniac's case, rather than presented:

> he left the prisons mounted on the wagon, his *confesseur* close by, the *exécuteurs* following, in the same state that they are taken to executions, to go to the *maison de ville* to suffer there the two *questions* to which he had been condemned.[16]

This haziness around the distinction of presentation versus performance is as typical of Barthès as it appears to be of Sévigné. Of a total of twenty-five cases in which the *question préalable* was employed between 1737 and 1780, Barthès made note of three cases in which he said that torture was performed when in fact the accused was presented to the *question* (those of Jean Tournier in 1768, Jean Martiniac in 1773, and François Vialettes in 1774), and in a further four cases he failed to make mention of any use of torture, although the accused were again presented to the *question* (those of Dominique Geze in 1753, Paul Marty in 1755, François Verge in 1762, and Jean Oudet in 1764).

Yet overall, his accounts were roughly accurate. He correctly notes that in nine cases from 1751 to 1780, the condemned was tortured before execution. In three cases he fails to mention the use of torture, though it was performed (those of Jean Calas in 1762, Pierre Fourtese in 1772, and Louis Bertron in 1773). He also makes no mention of the use of torture in the six cases in which the sentence to torture was overturned, either explicitly or in the *retentum* (those of Jean Rey in 1761, Jean Berge in 1766, Francoise Guichon in 1766, Jean Valentin in 1768, Marie Dejean in 1770, and Raymond Frechon in 1773). He omits any mention of only a single case of the *question préalable*, that of Réné Soubeyran in 1751. Cases of the *question préparatoire* are not mentioned by Barthès.

Some of Barthès's information derived from personal observation, some from hearing court sentences read aloud at executions, and some from sources unspecified. But in no instance did Barthès write with disapproval or discomfort. To the contrary, like Mme. de Sévigné, his writings suggest a deep interest in judicial torture, as in his account of the "rediscovery" of the *question des brodequins* in the case of Claire Reynaud.[17]

Judges themselves were plainly aware of the fact of torture, but few chose to comment on the practice either in public or in private. Montaigne and Montesquieu, each of whom served as *parlementaires* in southern courts, did so in passing; Pierre de Fermat, who served in the *parlement* of Toulouse, did not. The only significant judicial writings on torture are those of Muyart de Vouglans, who provided a remarkably late public defense of the practice when it was in the process of being dismantled. Judges were, on the whole, remarkably silent. Nor can their opinions easily be reconstructed from indirect evidence: no court records of debates concerning the use of torture in specific cases were preserved; judicial libraries reveal little, consisting as they do largely of purely professional works; no memoirs or private letters hint at judges' private perceptions, at their evaluations of the utility of pain in eliciting truth. So it is not to the judges to whom we must turn in seeking contemporary accounts of torture and its epistemology; it is rather to the philosophes, many of whom possessed legal training but who did not practice in the courts.

As these sources and silences suggest, torture was tolerated, if not actually approved of, by the literate public and by legal professionals throughout much of the seventeenth and eighteenth centuries.[18] Public awareness of torture failed to lead to public condemnation of torture. But all this was to change in the 1760s.

On the evening of 13 October 1761, in the Grand Rue des Filatiers in Toulouse, the body of Marc Antoine Calas was discovered by his family. It was hanging by a rope from a cloth dowel balanced over the open French doors that divided the shop from the storeroom. His clothing was neatly folded beside his body. His family, presuming suicide, agreed to conceal the manner of his death, hoping to spare themselves the indignity of the punishment inflicted upon suicides: the body dragged naked and face down through the streets, then exhibited in a gibbet. They told the investigating *capitoul* that Marc Antoine had been murdered.[19]

But the *capitoul* believed that they were lying and arrested Jean Calas, Marc Antoine's father; Anne Rose Cabibel, his mother; Pierre Calas, his brother; Jeanne Viguier, their servant; Gaubert Lavaysse, a visitor from Bordeaux and the son of an *avocat* of the *parlement* of Toulouse; and M. Cazeing, the neighbor with whom Lavaysse was staying. With the exception of the servant Jeanne Viguier, all were Huguenots. Public rumor had it that the six had been involved in a conspiracy to murder Marc Antoine, who was allegedly on the verge of converting to Roman Catholicism.

The investigation was an involved one: 193 witnesses were called in all. The *capitouls* pronounced sentence on 18 November 1761: Jean Calas, Anne Rose Cabibel, and Pierre Calas were sentenced to the *question préparatoire;* and Jeanne Viguier and Gaubert de Lavaysse were sentenced to be presented to the *question préparatoire.* The case was of necessity automatically appealed to the *parlement.*

The *parlement* ruled on the case on 9 March 1762. It found adequate evidence to sentence Jean Calas alone to death by breaking on the wheel and to the *question préalable.*[20] Under torture, Calas failed to confess to the crime himself and failed to implicate others, maintaining what many contemporary observers saw as a heroic silence. He was executed by breaking on the wheel on 12 March 1762 in the Place St. George in Toulouse.

His son, Pierre, was sentenced to banishment, while his wife, Anne Rose Cabibel, together with her daughters—who had been staying with friends in the country on the night of the alleged murder—left Toulouse to stay with friends in the predominantly Huguenot city of Montauban. Ultimately, *lettres de cache*, royal orders, forced the daughters into detention in convents. The youngest son of the family, Donat, who had been in Nîmes serving an apprenticeship to a merchant throughout the affair, fled to Geneva.

Voltaire had already heard about the case from a Huguenot merchant from Marseilles, and with the arrival of Donat in Geneva, he resolved to explore it more fully. He interviewed Donat, sent for more information from Toulouse, and began writing *mémoires* on the family's behalf. Convinced of the unjustness of the case, he began to raise money for the support of the family. By late 1762, he had obtained the release of the Calas daughters, Nanette and Rosine. In the meantime, Pierre had left the monastery in which he was housed—theoretically outside the jurisdiction of the *parlement* and therefore in accordance with his sentence of banishment. It remained only to convince Anne Rose Cabibel and Gaubert de Lavaysse to move to Paris before launching the campaign to rehabilitate the Calas name and to reverse the sentence.

Numerous *mémoires* were published on behalf of the family by Mariette, Elie de Beaumont, and Loyseau de Mauléon, all of whom sought to open an investigation into the conduct of the trial itself. At the same time, Voltaire began work on two essays inspired by the case, *Histoire d'Elisabeth Canning et de Jean Calas* and the *Traité sur la tolerance*.[21] In each, he formulated a different argument related to the case: *Histoire d'Elisabeth Canning et de Jean Calas* sought to establish the necessity of appeals procedures, while the *Traité sur la tolerance* attacked religious intolerance, which represented the primary source of the injustice of the case to Voltaire.

The case was examined by the *Conseil Royal* in March 1763 and June 1764, which set aside the verdicts in the case on technical grounds, and on 9 March 1765, three years to the day after Calas's execution, the *maîtres des requêtes* voted for acquittal.

Even before the case was heard by the Paris courts, it was the subject of intense public scrutiny. The surgeon Antoine Louis published an essay in forensics prompted by the case, *Mémoire sur une question relative à la jurisprudence; dans lequel on établit les principes pour distinguer à l'inspection d'un corps trouvé pendu, les signes du suicide d'avec ceux de l'assassinat*, which sought medically to distinguish the bodies of suicides from those of murder victims.[22] Several accounts of the case were published within the ten years following the rehabilitation, including three poems, an essay, and a group of sermons, to which were attached letters purportedly written by Marc Antoine Calas.[23] The case was revisited during the revolution, when numerous plays concerning its central events were staged.[24] In addition, the *Journal des Dames* referred to the case on several occasions, and of course, Voltaire himself kept the case alive in his letters.[25] Nor was this publicity limited to France. Numerous English translations of Voltaire's *Commentaire sur le livre des délits et des peines, Histoire d'Elisabeth Canning et de Jean Calas,* and *Traité sur la tolérance* were published in England, Scotland, Ireland, and the United States.[26] German translations of French plays dramatizing the case were published after 1774.[27]

The multiple representations of the case permitted multiple interpretations of its meaning. For Voltaire, the case was as much about the rigidity of the judicial system as it was about religious intolerance. While the legal campaign to rehabilitate the memory of Jean Calas therefore focused on the problem of toleration, the case as a whole opened up a host of legal issues for consideration, among them, the employment of judicial torture. The general critique of French criminal law that the case launched permitted a critical reexamination of torture despite the fact that torture was not initially considered by contemporaries to have been a central issue in the case.

The Calas case, then, provided the first significant occasion for public criticism of torture. Abolitionists employed the case explicitly to critique the structure of the legal system, and implicitly, to articulate new ideas about the relationships among truth and pain, language and the body. The practice of torture excited their attention not because of the large numbers of victims involved, but because it represented an epistemology and a politics that these activists sought to overturn. From this perspective, the practice of torture must be understood not only as a legal procedure but as a practice embedded in cultural traditions and political institutions. The campaign for abolition of necessity, therefore, engaged not only questions internal to the law, but also cultural and political questions as well.

It is also true that the many publications attacking the practice of judicial torture that appeared in the wake of the Calas case were not the first ones to condemn its use in France. But these criticisms did not have sufficient power in the culture of law or in the culture at large to create change. Even before the crown revised the laws governing criminal procedure, the *avocats* of the *parlement* of Toulouse independently examined the appropriate employment of judicial torture. The *mémoires* of Etienne Malenfant, chief civil clerk of the *parlement*, document a remarkable debate among the officers of the court:

> On 17 November 1620 a joint report authored by M. Catel and M. Masnau was judged, by which it was determined that condemnation to the galleys for six years was harsher than condemnation to torture with proofs reserved. . . . M. Catel maintained that torture with proofs reserved was harsher; M. Masnau was of the opposite opinion; nevertheless by the [reduction] of M. le Doyen Assezat and M. Melet, who were first of the opinion of M. Catel and then looking to the opinion of M. Masnau, the thesis noted above was judged, and handed down the decision that condemnation to the galleys for six years was harsher.[28]

In a system in which legal deliberations went unrecorded, scraps of evidence that document the rationale behind judicial decision-making are priceless.[29] While this entry by no means suggests that officers of the court questioned the moral or legal utility of torture, it does demonstrate that the precise position of torture within the criminal system and system of proofs was formally contested.

The questions with which the *parlement* of Toulouse struggled were not theirs alone. When the criminal code was rewritten in 1670, others were required to examine these practices and to pronounce upon their utility. The revision of the criminal code required the most elite officers of the law to determine, among other things, the place of torture in criminal procedure. When the deliberations of this counsel were complete, the crown sent copies of its deliberations to the *parlements*. This *procès-verbal* documented a debate about the use of torture:

> M. le *premier président* [Lamoignon] said that he wished that the manner in which torture was inflicted was uniform throughout the realm because in certain places it was given so harshly that those who suffered it were rendered unable to work and often crippled the rest of their days. However the *question* was not a punishment and did not render infamous those who were applied to it.
> Monsieur Pussort replied that it was difficult to render torture uniform, that the description of it that one would need to make would be indecent in an ordinance, but that it would be understood that judges would take care that when they tortured those condemned not to cripple them.
> That, moreover, the *question préparatoire* had always seemed useless to him and that if one wanted the estimation of a former judge, one would find that it was rare that it drew the truth from the mouth of the condemned.
> Monsieur le *premier président* said that he saw significant reasons to remove it but that that was only his personal opinion.[30]

When judges considered whether to retain torture as a part of criminal procedure, they expressed two specific objections. The long-lasting physical harm caused to those who suffered torture was one of them. The concern that torture did not succeed in its stated aim of achieving the truth was the other. But because these objections were qualified as personal opinion, they had no compelling weight. Although the rules governing the use of torture were altered in the new criminal ordinance of 1670, the practice was itself retained. And, as the evidence suggests, it was regularly employed after this date despite the growing concerns of judges on these counts.

It was only in 1682, then, that the first work openly critical of the practice of torture appeared.[31] Entitled *Si la torture est un moyen seur à vérifier les crimes secrets,* it was written by Augustin Nicolas, *président* of the *parlement* of Dijon. He wrote principally to discourage the use of torture in cases of witchcraft, but in the process thoroughly condemned the practice of torture in all instances. He was prompted by a deep sense of shame at the violation of modesty required by the practice of torture. That his was a minority opinion is suggested by the hesitations expressed in the opening lines of the work:

> For a long time I swung between the desire to succor the innocence of those who might suffer unjust punishments in trials in which both their lives and their honor were concerned, and the fear of giving the public something that might seem contrary to common opinions.[32]

In what followed, Nicolas offered every major criticism of torture that was to be expressed during the early modern period. After providing a clear and noncontroversial definition of torture, Nicolas went on to argue that while it was certainly a method of seeking truth, it was by no means a guaranteed method of finding it; that quite to the contrary, torture evoked lies rather than truth. Like other writers, he represented two extreme cases: the delicate innocent who confesses guilt falsely and the robust criminal who denies guilt falsely.[33] He was able to point to instances in which torture had been demonstrated to have produced false confessions.[34] Not only did it fail to achieve the truth, torture was a punishment still worse than death, Nicolas argued.[35] For pain was itself punishment, not an experience that drove the accused beyond the limits of ego to testify directly to the truth.

Nicolas also examined the nature of confession. He rejected the evidence of confessions made under duress as illegitimate.[36] And he conflated confession with contrition: "It is not the pain of the human body that pushes a criminal to the confession of his crime, but contrition and the pain of the soul."[37] It was true that the infliction of pain could force speech, but not truth.[38] In other words, physical pain had no effect on the act of truthful confession. Truth-telling depended on the exercise of the will. The bodily signs employed as evidence by judges on the advice of legal manuals testified to nothing but the fainting horror of the victim of torture.[39] Because the preservation of the public good lay more in protecting the innocent than in punishing the guilty, torture must be abolished.[40] For all these reasons, Nicolas concluded, torture was repugnant to common sense.[41] But because he wrote in response to witchcraft trials rather than secular trials, his critique was rarely referred to by later writers. And so there was silence for decades.

By the mid-eighteenth century, the *Encyclopédie* had made mention of torture in at least three groups of articles: "Douleur," "Question," and "Torture." In the fifth volume of the *Encyclopédie*, published in 1755, three articles appeared addressing *douleur:* the first, by d'Alembert, addressed "the pains of the mind or of the heart"; the second and longest, by d'Aumont, took up the problem of physical pain; and the third, unsigned, provided an account of the genealogy of pain in Greek mythology.[42] While there is no direct evidence in the form of lecture notes or attendance registers to prove that the philosophes were influenced by medical writings on pain, we do know that many of them were well-read in medicine and that they, with other elites, attended dissections, surgical demonstrations, and lectures at surgical colleges in Paris and elsewhere. Given this fact, and the remarkable echoes of the surgical perspective in their writings, I suggest that the attack on torture that began in earnest in the mid-eighteenth century owed a great deal to the surgical delineation of pain as dangerous in both physical and psychological terms.

D'Aumont's article defined pain from a medical perspective. He described pain as a disagreeable physical experience that has real and specific physical causes whose effects vary according to intensity and circumstances, and that can be mitigated with appropriate treatment. Pain could also be classified according to its cause and the differing sensations that it produced. Specifically, d'Aumont noted four categories of pain: the tensile, associated with feelings of distention; the gravative, associated with feelings of weightiness; the pulsative, associated with feelings of flickering pain; and the pungative, associated with feelings of sharp penetration. He offered examples of each of these kinds of pain, turning his attention to tensile pain first:

> Such is the effect of the torture that one causes malefactors to suffer to make them confess their crimes, when they are suspended by the arms and weights

are attached to their feet, which are increased little by little, which lengthens all the fleshy parts by degrees, and augments the pain until it is extreme, putting the nerves in a state of near rupture, from which results a pain yet stronger, there being more nerves put in this state at once.[43]

Evidently, torture came quickly to mind when thinking about pain in the eighteenth century, providing an excellent and accessible example of a certain sort of pain. What is striking about this passage, however, is not only the fact that torture serves as a matter-of-fact example of pain, but also the nature of the language employed: torture is not described in any but physical terms. It is not described in metaphysical terms, with an explanation of its purpose, nor in political terms, with an account of its failings. Torture is presented as a purely physical fact.

Pain was defined in this article as an essentially animal experience, one that deprived human beings of the ability to exercise their will:

This feeling is distinguished from every other, because it is human nature to have so much aversion for it that whoever is affected by it is led, even despite themselves, to remove, to cause to cease what he thinks to be the cause of the disagreeable perception that constitutes pain because everything that can excite it tends to the destruction of the machine, and because every animal has an innate inclination to preserve itself.[44]

There is no discussion in this article of the moral or spiritual qualities of pain, no discussion of the ethics of pain infliction or pain relief. According to this article, experiences of pain are purely physical. The implications of the physicality and the animality of pain were worked out by other authors.

The thirteenth volume of the *Encyclopédie*, published in 1765 after the many delays suffered by its editors, took up the definition of torture in two articles entitled "Question," by Boucher d'Argis, which straightforwardly explained the place of torture in criminal procedure, the other by the Chevalier Jaucourt, which provided a critique of the practice.[45] Jaucourt employed three arguments against the practice of torture: that it violated the law of nature, that it failed to accomplish its stated goal of finding truth, and that confessions extorted under duress should not serve as evidence in capital cases, in which case, by implication, the use of torture would be obviated. Like many others, he noted that the success of the practice rested on the physical capacities of the accused:

it is a certain invention to condemn an innocent man who has a weak and delicate constitution, and to save a guilty one who was born robust. Those who can bear this punishment, and those who don't have enough strength to sustain it lie equally. The torment that is suffered in the question is certain, and the crime of the man who suffers it is not; the wretch whom you torture reflects less on confessing what he did than on being delivered from what he feels.[46]

This is not a humanitarian indictment of the practice of torture as we might now understand humanitarianism. There is remarkably little compassion expressed for those who endure torture, and what little there is, is directed toward the problem of truth: if those who are tortured think only of delivering themselves from the pain they feel, then they will lie to save themselves their immediate agony. In this text and in others, truth—not the human being—was the primary victim of torture.

This concern with the loss of truth pervades writings on torture from the early seventeenth to the late eighteenth centuries. Over and over, authors repeated this scenario. Montaigne was perhaps the first:

> The invention of tortures is a dangerous invention; they seem to be a test of endurance rather than of truth. He who can endure them conceals the truth as well as he who cannot. For why should pain rather make me confess what is, than force me to say what is not? And, on the other hand, if the man who has not done what he is accused of has the patience to suffer these tortures, why should not the guilty man have that patience, being offered so fair a reward as life?[47]

But he was by no means the last. La Bruyère, Beccaria, Voltaire, Letrosne, and Brissot de Warville, among others, employing much the same language, articulated the same concern.[48] At one level, this concern with truth should come as no surprise: given that the rationale for the use of torture was that it gave judges direct access to the truth, attacks on the successful achievement of this goal were one of the most effective tools employed in defeat of the practice.

But there is more in these passages than an effort to point out the futility of torture in achieving truth. First, there is an implicit rejection of the notion that truth is lodged in the body, an insistence that truth is not a property of the body but one of the mind. Jaucourt, for example, suggests that the victim of torture is engaged in constant thought, struggling to find the words the judges want to hear—and lying to do so. Second, these passages frame the problem of truth-telling in a highly particular setting, suggesting that in the torture chamber there can be only one of two persons, each of whom will ultimately behave in the same way: either the frail innocent who must lie or the hardy criminal who will lie. The frail innocents and hardy criminals of these texts lied together, twisted truth, and left it behind. But what about the robust innocent who confessed to nothing? or, more provocatively, the weak criminal who readily confessed his or her crimes?

These passages imply that it was offensive only to achieve false testimony through torture. Was it less outrageous to achieve true confessions through torture? In fact, the failure to discuss weak criminals suggests that these authors did not disapprove of the infliction of pain on those who were found to be guilty, even when that pain was inflicted on them before the formal determination of guilt was made. In the eyes of the philosophes, pain was always punitive—and there were occasions on which its use was entirely justified. For that reason, torture failed not only because it falsely condemned the innocent but because it failed to provide adequate grounds on which to punish the guilty. What was intolerable about torture was that it caused people to lie, not that it caused people to suffer.

In fact, Jaucourt, again like other authors writing on this matter, concerns himself far more deeply with the moral state of the judges than with that of torture victims:

> The innocent man whose confession is torn from him by torture is in a truly lamentable state; but the state of the judge who, believing himself authorized by the law to torture this innocent man, must be, in my opinion, a frightful one. Has he the means to compensate him for his sufferings?[49]

It is the agency of judges that is at stake, not the agency of torture victims. It is the judges who require the reader's deepest feelings of compassion. A tragic error of the law requires them to enter into a moral abyss from which there is no exit. Was Jaucourt alone in this analysis?

Historians of the Enlightenment have debated whether members of radical salons and the Encyclopedists are best understood as individuals who disagreed with one another on many matters, or as collaborators in a great intellectual project who were in general agreement with one another.[50] Two things, at least, seem certain: their contemporaries did tend to view them as members of intellectual cabals, whatever careful examination of the evidence might today suggest; and there were strong animosities among them. The significance of the movement to reform penal codes and to abolish torture should therefore not be understated. It drew together philosophes who were in deep disagreement with one another on many issues and who bore one another great personal animosity.[51] Men who disagreed on many issues were in agreement on this one. And though the number of tracts criticizing the practice of legal torture may today appear small, from the perspective of their eighteenth-century contemporaries, writings about torture represented a dangerous radicalism.

It is true that at midcentury, relatively few voices were raised in protest. Voltaire and Beccaria were the most celebrated among them.[52] Voltaire's entry into the fray corresponded with his entry into the Calas case. As noted above, he first conceptualized the case as one that revealed the injustices of religion. Over the years, however, Voltaire had the opportunity to reconsider the meaning of the case. In the *Commentaire sur le livre des délits et des peines* and in the "Prix de la justice et de l'humanité" he engaged questions of penal reform directly.

It was no more than coincidence that Cesare Beccaria published *On Crimes and Punishments* while the Calas appeal went forward. At the urging of his friends and mentors, the Verri brothers, and with the assistance of evidence gathered by them, he wrote a draft of the book that was published anonymously in 1764. Two years later, at the suggestion of d'Alembert, it was translated into French in 1766 by the abbot André Morellet. Morellet was a member of the baron d'Holbach's *salon*, a contributor to the *Encyclopédie*, and had already provided the French reading public with a translation that sought to illuminate the history of law and punishment, *Le manuel des inquisiteurs*. Beccaria's work was enthusiastically endorsed by the French— at least nine editions of the *Traité des délits et des peines* appeared between 1766 and 1797.[53]

While Voltaire's genius lay in exploiting individual cases for maximum effect, Beccaria's gift was to provide a broad conceptual framework that was grounded in a few basic principles. He argued that penal laws needed to be rationalized so that they could conform to utilitarian principles and posed explicit questions of the law in a way that was entirely new: "Is the death penalty really *useful* and *necessary* for the security and good order of society? Are torture and torments *just*, and do they attain the *end* for which laws are instituted?"[54] He was deeply critical of the practice of torture and rejected out of hand any potential claims to legitimacy it might have had— in the discovery and confession of crimes, and the purgation of evidence— at the same time as he rejected its claims to achieve the truth: "it tends to confound all relations to require that a man be at the same time accuser and accused, that pain be made the crucible of truth, as if its criterion lay in the muscles and sinews of a miserable wretch."[55] He insisted on redefining the very meaning of torture, speaking of it as a form of punishment rather than as a form of discovery. And he argued that torture failed in the essential purpose of punishment, the instillation of fear, because it was a secret procedure.

Like d'Aumont in the *Encyclopédie*, Beccaria saw torture as a purely physical practice that produced no meaningful connection to the metaphysical realm of the truth. Quite the contrary; he argued that the experience of pain in torture was so overwhelming as to make it impossible for the victim of torture to provide anything like a truthful response:

One is as much free to tell the truth in the midst of convulsions and torments, as one was free then to impede without fraud the effects of fire and boiling water. Every act of our will is invariably proportioned to the force of the sensory impression which is its source; and the sensory capacity of every man is limited. Thus the impression of pain may become so great that, filling the entire sensory capacity of the tortured person, it leaves him free to choose only what for the moment is the shortest way of escape from pain.[56]

This passage suggests that what Beccaria and other philosophes understood by truth was quite different than what jurists had understood. Where the jurists sought the spontaneous utterances of people in pain, the philosophes insisted that truth was cultivated in moments of self-control and that people in pain were incapable of the kind of thoughtful reflection necessary to create that truth.[57]

Voltaire was much impressed by Beccaria's book, and determined to write a commentary on it, the *Commentaire sur le livre des délits et des peines*.[58] Unlike his earlier works, the *Commentaire* attempted to provide a critique of the legal system as a whole and called for the laws of France to be rationalized through the creation of a single code of law that would hold sway throughout the realm and over all persons. In his discussion of torture, like Beccaria before him, Voltaire conflated torture and punishment. Because he represented torture as a form of punishment, he was able to put forward the suggestion that an examination of the experience of countries that had abolished torture would assist in determining whether torture was a successful deterrent of crime, a role never imagined for it by the *parlements*.

But this was not his final word on the subject. In 1777, Voltaire became a sponsor of the contest initiated by the Economic Society of Berne, which had requested entries to provide a plan for the reform of criminal legislation. Voltaire himself composed an essay on the subject that addressed a variety of crimes and then turned to questions of proof and procedure, including the use of torture.[59] In this essay, he stressed the horror of torture, arguing that the sufferings imposed by torture surpassed those of execution.[60] He granted that in isolated instances torture might be legitimately employed, as in the case of Ravaillac, Henri IV's assassin—but here, too, he conflated torture with punishment, detailing the specifics of the gruesome death sentence rather than the evidentiary procedures that preceded his conviction or those that sought to discover his accomplices.[61] He paid closer attention to the celebrated cases of Le Brun and Anglade, who had been executed after confessing under torture, only to have others come forward after their deaths to confess to the same crimes. Other authors also endorsed the continued employment of the *question préalable,* often because they understood it as a form of punishment legitimately exercised on the body of the criminal:

> No doubt a man condemned to death is no longer a citizen; he becomes a slave to punishment: the society that he has offended has the right to demand that he repair this offense in discovering its enemies through him, and torture plays a part in his punishment.[62]

But this endorsement continued to represent torture as a form of punishment rather than as an evidentiary procedure.

Philosophes took up the problem of torture at midcentury not because it was newly discovered—as noted above, the fact of torture had been common knowledge in France for more than two centuries—nor because it was on the rise. They did so because it represented an epistemology they did not support, what we might call an epistemology of pain. They entirely rejected the notion that pain had truth value. They were therefore in a position to make two primary criticisms of the practice of torture, both of which were centrally concerned with the problem of pain. First, these writers recast the evidentiary procedure of torture as a form of punishment. They did so because they understood pain to be a punishing experience in and of itself. That is what the entries in the *Encyclopédie* and in surgical texts suggest: that pain was understood to possess no redeeming value and no connection to metaphysical truths, that it was an experience to be relieved as quickly as possible. This position represents at once a rejection of the religious vision of pain, in which suffering serves as redemption, and an acceptance of the medical vision of pain, in which suffering requires relief for the benefit of both sufferer and witnesses to suffering. Second, these writers argued that torture could never lead to the truth because it failed to create the necessary conditions of truth-telling. By implication, these conditions included a situation of calm in which the accused might compose him- or herself long enough to contemplate and to create the truth. These writers rejected the notion of spontaneous truths screamed in moments of suffering. Because they chose to represent pain in ways hinted at in the language of medicine, the philosophes constructed a newly antipathetic experience of pain that had ramifications far beyond those imagined by surgeons.

In the hands of the philosophes, pain came to represent not merely an unpleasant experience endured by an individual but an assault on society, and an assault on the rights of individuals. In their hands, pain was transformed. Far from an experience of the divine, it was an animalistic experience that threatened the very existence of human society. To support the practice of torture was to support this descent into animality. In Voltaire's words: "Do the people who pride themselves on being polite not pride themselves on being human(e)?"[63] Through their writings, suffering entered into the public sphere as a political problem that threatened to engulf not only those in pain, but also those who caused that pain.

It is important to note here that many of the critics of torture had had some legal training. Their reframing of torture as a painful punishment that culminated in the proliferation of untruths was deliberate, not accidental. They did not misunderstand the law. They understood it and its limits quite well, and sought to reform it. And they saw in the law the expression of cultural values that they sought to challenge. In their discussions of torture, they asked and answered a series of questions about pain and truth. What is the meaning of human pain? Can it serve a purpose? Who should be made to suffer, and how? Whose suffering should be relieved? And what is the effect of inflicted suffering on those who suffer no pain but who are witnesses to it?

Did any of these works have an effect on the practice of judicial torture? In 1780, the *question préparatoire* was abolished by royal edict. But the criticism of the practice of torture did not stop. If anything, the tempo of protest quickened.

In that same year, Brissot de Warville began publication of his *Bibliothèque philosophique du législateur,* a compendium of writings on penal reform. From the beginning, Brissot de Warville conceptualized this publishing project as one which would make apparent the connection between penal law and political freedom.[64] It was to be an extension of his own *Théorie des lois criminelles,* written for entry into the competition sponsored by the Economic Society of Berne and rushed into print:

> Still too young and in too much of a hurry to publish my ideas, I yielded to impatience to debut with a great work and to draw attention to myself striking in my turn the political tyranny that had always revolted me. I have since that time sworn to consecrate all my life to its destruction. Religious tyranny succumbed to the blows of Voltaire, of Rousseau, of Diderot; I wanted to attack political tyranny and to shatter the idol of governments that, under the name of monarchy, practiced despotism.[65]

Through Brissot de Warville's work as writer and editor, the critique of torture was to develop in a new direction. No longer content simply to attack the epistemological foundations of torture, writers of the late-eighteenth century sought to develop the political consequences of that critique. They associated penal reform with political reform.

Some of the works collected for the *Bibliothèque* were written as early as the 1760s, some even earlier. Among them was François Seigneux de Correvon's *Essai sur l'usage, les abus et les inconvéniens de la torture dans la procédure criminelle* (1768), best discussed in the context of these later works. Brissot de Warville's notes on this work suggest that it was not in wide circulation immediately after its publication and for that reason may have had less impact than others published around the same time.[66] Brissot de Warville offered only a summary of this work, with which he was most unimpressed: "I found nothing new in this essay: when one has read the few lines written by Beccaria and Servan, and some pages in Sonnenfels, one has read everything."[67] And indeed, Brissot de Warville's analysis is of more significance than Seigneux de Correvon's work itself, for in the course of it he broadens the definition of torture:

> M. le Seigneux de Correvon instructs us in the method employed in place of torture for confession of the crime [in Switzerland]: irons, a more austere diet, a rigor tempered with pathetic representations. It is still torture disguised under other names. You starve this wretch for a confession: do you think that, when his mind is deranged from the effects of a continuous fast, he will be able to defend himself? Is this the equality that the law requires between the judge who interrogates and the accused who defends himself? Irons, force, rigor, for an accused who has not been convicted! Are these then proofs? Aren't they punishments before conviction?[68]

In the space of this short paragraph, Brissot de Warville redefined the practice of torture and offered some implicit standards for the justice system. He insisted that the judge and the accused be equals in the processes of justice. He suggested that torture, as part of the investigation of the crime, was equally part of the accused's self-defense, and that the accused must therefore be offered conditions that promote the clear thinking necessary to create such a defense. In other words, he entirely rejected the hierarchical principles of early modern law at the same time as he rejected the definition of torture, which had been developed over the centuries, as a procedure that sought to achieve spontaneous truths rather than considered ones. And he went yet further, suggesting first that torture was not a carefully bounded set of practices defined in law, but any painful practice leading to confession, and second that any painful practice, including torture, must be understood to be punishment.[69] In Brissot de Warville's eyes, pain was never an avenue of discovery but only a form of retribution.

Joseph-Michel-Antoine Servan's *Discours sur les moeurs* (1769) made only passing references to torture in the original text. But after 1780 Servan added an appendix that was devoted to the question of torture. It began with a nod in the direction of Louis XVI and his abolition of the *question préparatoire* and went on to address the nation of Switzerland. Brave, virtuous, and wise, Servan called on the nation to redeem its essential qualities by abolishing the practice that threatened its integrity and the liberty not only of its own citizens, but of people around the world:

> Doubt it no longer; when you deliver a citizen to the torture, be it at the other end of the universe, despotism will be heard to cry and to speak with derision to the men whom it oppresses: "There then is Switzerland, there is that free government, which employs the *question* in the name of the laws," and it will add, "Happy slaves! You dare to complain now that I scorn both laws and liberty. You can still hope to bend your despot; but who will bend the law when the very virtue of the magistrates renders it inflexible?"[70]

Here torture has been recast as a tool of despotism and, therefore, as a weapon in the arsenal of political oppression. Servan suggested by his rhetoric that torture violates the integrity of republicanism:

> O citizens! Wise and free men! Ah! Respect yourselves more; remember that you are the greatest store of human liberty on the continent of Europe; conserve this wise, noble, and proud attitude without relaxation, which is suited to the model that brave virtue will set out on the peak of the Alps, in order to be seen by all the princes, to encourage the good and to cause the tyrants to tremble. If you do not correct this barbarous law for yourselves, correct it for us, for all men. Don't you know that all the faults of free men are spied out and tallied up by those who don't want men to be free? Don't you know that each abuse of equality is a pretext to oppress it elsewhere, and that the greatest evils of servitude are cemented by the slightest drawbacks of liberty?[71]

Servan called for the abolition of torture because he understood it to be a violation of political freedom. In passages like this one, philosophes recast torture, transforming it from an integral part of criminal procedure to a violation of the rights of citizens and republics that must be combated in the name of liberty and equality.

Other authors saw in the practice of torture a test of political liberty; its presence or absence suggested the moral health of a nation:

> Among modern societies torture has been adopted and carried to the last degree of atrocity in the countries where humanity is most debased, the most tyrannized, that is to say, in some countries of the Orient and in those of the Inquisition. It has been, on the contrary, abolished or moderated in those in which the human spirit [*esprit*] has regained its liberty, in England, in Geneva, in France under Louis XVI.[72]

Again and again, authors pointed to examples of states in which torture was not employed, with no ill effects in the form of elevated crime rates.[73]

That torture had the potential to corrupt political society by depriving citizens of their rights was a radical suggestion, and one that had dangerous implications. These implications were fully developed by Brissot de Warville himself: "The object of this memoir is not so much to reform all branches of our criminal legislation as *to give the means to render crimes less common in reconciling social interest with the rights of citizens.*"[74] If torture posed a threat to enlightened civil society, then subjects might legitimately combat the practice and all it stood for. But Brissot de Warville went further still, speaking not of subjects but of citizens. In this way, torture was caught up in the critique of despotism and the demand for greater political liberty. And because in monarchies the law was the expression of the will of the monarch, there was no way not to see in torture an expression of despotism issuing directly from the monarch. Other writers expressed this interpretation yet more forcefully.[75] As was true at midcentury, what lay behind these arguments was a profound conviction that torture was a form of punishment because the infliction of pain was itself punishing:

> It is the excess of pain, it is the length of the punishment that stops me . . .
> But it is not a punishment, it is nothing other than an inquisition! . . . Eh!
> that the sharpest pains were dulled by these subtle distinctions! that such a
> game of words could deaden the sensitivity of the nerves![76]

In all these works, there is an absolute rejection of pain as an enlightening experience, either for the sufferer or for the witnesses, marking a dramatic departure from the legal manuals that espoused a faith in the power of pain to extract truth from the body.

At the core of these protests lay a radical redefinition of the three terms on which the practice of torture was based: truth, pain, and the body. What the abolitionists understood by each of these terms was profoundly different than what was understood by the jurists. The consequence of that differing understanding was a rejection of the meaningfulness and the legitimacy of torture.

For the abolitionists, truth was not a physical property housed in the body to be extracted through the medium of pain. To the contrary, they understood truth to be opposed to the conditions of torture, of constraint and force.[77] The jurists believed that truth emerged spontaneously from its fleshly home, without consideration or deliberation on the part of the accused; the abolitionists believed that truth depended utterly on the will of the accused.[78] To speak the truth required a presence of mind that pain obscured, and an ability to think rationally rather than testify spontaneously. Truth depended upon the exercise of free will, which could not operate under conditions of bodily duress.

The effect of pain was therefore seen to obscure the workings of the will and thus, the acquisition of truth. In the words of Letrosne, "Which is the man who can surrender himself and promise himself to resist pain, when carried to an excess it impairs all his faculties, such that it absorbs every other feeling and occupies all the power of his soul?"[79] The pain that once encouraged the loss of self necessary for the bodily release of truth now prevented the authenticity of self required to produce the truth.[80] The infliction of pain, in this assessment, would therefore ensure the falsity of the confession by confusing the accused, depriving him of the crucial ability to reason.[81] Interior spiritual pain might prompt valid confession; but external physical pain could not.[82] Pain might well produce verbal evidence, but was it the evidence sought?

> In the critical instant in which sensibility is pushed to the extreme, pain triumphs over the accused: but what is the cry that it tears from him? That of truth? What error! . . . It is really that of weakness, that speaks in a man tormented in this way.[83]

These cries, the product of bodily distress, were clearly distinguished from truth. The principal effect of pain, then, was a destruction of the circumstances necessary for truth telling.

The philosophes also argued that the body could never produce the truth the judges sought. The physical signs that they insisted on interpreting as signs of guilt were no more than expressions of an interior emotional state, not signs of an existential moral state: "A man can be timid and modest by nature, or inclined toward anger, and can pale, blush, tremble at the imputation of a crime, without being guilty."[84] Indeed, the insistence that truth and the body were connected implied, in the eyes of the abolitionists, a profound misunderstanding of human nature. The will could produce the truth but the body could not, because the will constructed the truth and the body did not, given that the truth was not a static physical property but an active metaphysical creation.

There was, however, an important connection between will and the body, whose middle term was pain. The abolitionists did not believe that truth and body existed in close relation, but they did believe that will and the body did. Pain could disrupt the relationship between will and the body, just as surely as the jurists knew that pain could expose the relationship between truth and the body. The overwhelming sensory experience of pain demanded immediate relief in the form of speech—but not truthful speech nor contrite confession, both of which required the free exercise of will and reason.

The philosophes were fascinated with the problem of pain as a physical and as a metaphysical problem at the same time as they perceived pain as deeply negative. The philosophic concern with pain predated the Calas case, but the case gave them a new avenue for contemplation of the meaning, purpose, and ramifications of pain in and for the state. The philosophes expressed a discomfort with pain reminiscent of the surgeons, a discomfort that suggests that the social component of pain was key for them, seeing in pain a contagion that spread visually to spectators. In their hands, pain was rendered a profoundly dangerous social experience, one that had the capacity to destroy human society as it separated individuals from one another, sunk in the immediacy of their own suffering. They therefore characterized pain as dangerous to human community. Pain was endlessly circulating, endlessly damaging. Pain had the capacity to bring people together in the grip of a powerful sensual experience and to tear them apart by sinking each of them into a sensory state so overwhelming as to render social communication impossible. It was precisely this interpretation that the philosophes drew on in their critique of torture, claiming that judges were damaged by repetitious viewings of pain.

The attacks of the philosophes on torture were couched in a new kind of narrative which sought at once to reveal the emotions of the author and to evoke the emotions of the reader. Narrative itself became a means of marshaling sympathy and political support.[85] Abolitionists sought to invoke the sensibility of both author and reader. In discussing the case of an innocent man who confessed under torture, "through pure despair, as if weary of life," Paul Risi exclaimed, "but I am too moved by this grievous scene. . . ."[86] Many authors evoked their sensitivity implicitly, through the accretion of adjectives, or through reiterated rhetorical questions. More often, authors sought to inspire emotion in the reader.

When abolitionists employed paired phrases to heighten intensity, when they posed reiterated questions as a method of argumentation, when they relied on the dramatic appearance of the page, filled with exclamations and italics, they were invoking at once the popular literary style of sensibility and the host of ideas associated with that style; predominantly, the belief in the essential benevolence of humanity and the uncertainness of the possibility for action grounded in benevolence.[87] The belief not merely in the ability, but in the compulsion to sympathize encouraged these writers to posit the naturalness of the humanitarian movement.[88]

Within the context of the doctrine of sensibility, torture should have provoked judicial sympathies because the sight of suffering should evoke sympathetic feeling. That it did not may have suggested judicial insensibility and, by extension, judicial insufficiency and immorality, for when bodily feeling and moral feeling were associated, to be unmoved was to be immoral. This was an attack on torture that had less to do with the victims of torture than with those who employed it. Unfeeling judges were represented as a greater threat to society than the institution of torture and the victims it created. At the same time, the victims themselves offered enlightened readers the opportunity to experience themselves as sensible beings. So the victims of torture were doubly useful: they let readers feel their own sympathetic virtue while revealing the unfeeling cruelty of the judges, as lack of feeling was associated with cruelty when kindness was sympathetic identification.

We need to ask if these philosophical tracts, which displayed the marks of the genres of the cause célèbre and the novel of sentiment, were themselves attempts to educate sentiment, to evoke the sentimental and sensible response of the reader, provoking tears and sighs from the reader who reads of moans and cries? Or were they attempts to demonstrate the authors' sensibilities, their tender feelings? Did torture serve the function of allowing eighteenth-century authors and readers an opportunity to cultivate and demonstrate their sensibility, to indulge themselves in the delicious feelings of pity rather than those of compassion?[89] To what degree was pain understood as fundamentally more dangerous to its observers than to its sufferers, to what degree an opportunity to cultivate the self through observation?

Pain was clearly condemned by the philosophes as a negative physical experience that had no redeeming value for the sufferer and that threatened, under certain circumstances, to overwhelm even the witnesses to that suffering. At the same time, they enthusiastically endorsed painful punishments for criminals condemned on the strength of physical evidence and witness testimony. For in the eyes of the philosophes, pain was an animalistic experience that could not lead to the creation of human truths and human community; for that reason, once someone was condemned of a crime and cast out of the community, then they might be employed as painful examples of what their violation meant—but never before judgment was rendered.

What is striking about the campaign against torture is that while the writers who criticized the employment of torture represented a wide spectrum of political beliefs, they were united on this issue. They marshaled arguments that reached essentially the same conclusions: that torture extorted confessions under extreme physical duress and that that duress itself rendered the confessions suspect. In other words, those concerned with the abolition of torture, though they had different political goals, were in agreement on one thing: that pain was not the means to the truth.

The institution of torture, which had experienced little change and little criticism over the course of the old regime, and which was supported by judges who believed in the ritualized meaningfulness of pain, was profoundly challenged by events of the mid-eighteenth century. The growing debate about torture represented, among other things, a dramatic conflict in understandings of the meaningfulness of pain. Judges believed not only in the efficacy of pain but also in the meaningfulness of pain—and the philosophes did not. Prompted by specific causes célèbres, the philosophes reworked the very meaning of torture as they redefined the meanings of pain, truth, and the body. In their hands, torture was recast: no longer a tool in the creation of a more harmonious society, it was represented as a violation of the rights of citizens and as a danger to civil society.

Legal manuals had advanced a theory of torture that was grounded in specific meanings of truth, pain, and the body. The use of torture implied a particular vision of truth; legal torture constructed truth as a static property that awaited discovery, rather than requiring construction or consensus. It was seen to be as much a physical as a metaphysical property, which lodged in the body and required extraction from the body through the infliction of pain. The pain of torture would liberate truth from its fleshly location and render it available as evidence. And the body, location of metaphysical truths, was itself seen to be capable of communication, whatever the will of the individual.

The abolitionist literature reflected a profound and dramatic paradigm shift in which the three primary terms that had long defined judicial torture were understood differently than they once had been. The spontaneous and static truth of the jurists became a conscious and created truth; the revealing pain of the jurists became an obscuring pain; and the subjective and expressive body of the jurists became an object whose ownership was contested. Whatever the explicit arguments of the abolitionists, the great significance of their arguments lay in their redefinitions of truth, pain, and the body: in the new conviction that pain is in and of itself punishing; that truth is a human construction dependent upon the will, not an existential fact; and that the body is a mechanical device, without meaningful connection to the divine.

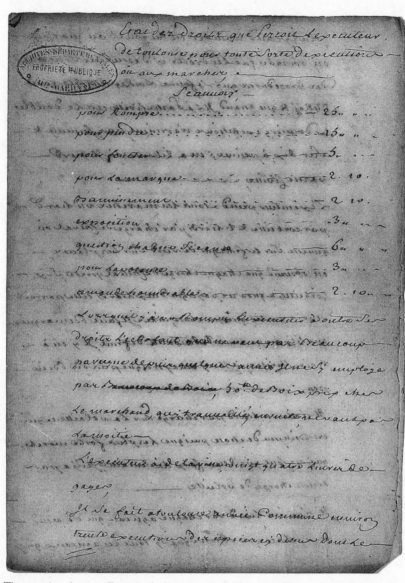

The executioner's wages. From the Archives Départementales de la Haute-Garonne, MS C 92.

EPILOGUE

In 1766, Muyart de Vouglans published his *Réfutation du traité des délits et peines*. He sneered at the sensible style adopted by the philosophes:

> I don't know if you felt that lively sentiment that the translator obligingly made strong for everyone in reading this work. I like to think I know as much about sensibility as anyone; but no doubt I lack as fine an organization of fibers as our modern criminalists, since I didn't feel the *sweet thrill* of which they speak. The sentiment I most felt, after reading some pages of this work, was surprise, to say the least: I didn't expect to find under the name of a *Treatise on Crimes* an apology for humanity, or rather a pleading in favor of that unhappy portion of humankind that is its scourge, dishonors it, and sometimes is even its destroyer.[1]

At the end of the eighteenth century, *parlementaires* and philosophes remained locked into rhetorical positions. *Parlementaires* continued publicly to insist on the legitimacy of torture as a means of acquiring the truth; philosophes, to reject the very notion of truth as constructed in the courts. But they did agree on one point: they agreed that pain was an essentially social experience, not one that was confined to the individual. And it was the sociality of pain that drove this debate, as the relative merits of pain were contested. Ultimately, it was the monarch who ended the impasse by legislating torture out of existence.

Despite the contempt expressed by the judicial establishment for the philosophical critique of torture, judges were plainly engaged in reconsidering the role of pain in justice. Always prepared to employ torture until expressly forbidden to do so, they did temper their use of it. They were increasingly ready to sentence individuals to punishments less final than death with less than full proofs and were therefore less reliant on torture. Their growing rejection of the meaningfulness of sacramental pain was reflected not only in their behavior in the courts in their gradual turning away from torture, but in the confraternities, too, requesting the right as *confrères* to process shod through the cobbled streets of the city.

The philosophic attack was fundamentally irrelevant to the practice of torture per se, because much of it came too late. And in the hands of the philosophes, torture was a tool in a larger political struggle. But they successfully redefined the public meaning of pain. And while their under-standing of pain as antisocial and antipolitical helped to encourage the rejec-tion of the employment of pain in public life, their understanding of pain as weakness rendered the plight of torture victims perhaps yet more perilous, as those who survived and talked were condemned by their fellows.

The legal institution of judicial torture disappeared from France in 1788. Yet the practice of torture was illegally employed by the French in the 1950s, during the Algerian wars of decolonization, and with such ferocity that the French were emulated and sought after as experts by other repres-sive regimes. Should this interrupted history suggest, as it has to some, that torture is natural to human beings?[2] My account should make plain that torture is a practice specific to certain places and moments, that its legal status, its specific methods, its alleged purposes, its unspoken values, all are crafted to meet the perceived needs of those who employ it. The institution of torture is, therefore, profoundly historical, and as such it is amenable to challenge and to change. In the modern West, the language of the philo-sophes has been one of the primary tools available to us in our efforts to contain our violence.

The philosophes were artisans who crafted a new language, who swept away a world we can try to explain but never excuse. But in their passionate and sentimental concern for the truth and for themselves, they failed to remember the peasants and artisans, the millers and goldsmiths and cow-herds taken from their families, removed from their villages, who faced their torturers alone, with an ill understanding of what was about to happen to them. And in that space of forgetting, the philosophes established the foundation of the culture in which we live, where we are urged to "save a life for the price of a stamp"—as my local public radio station regularly urges me to do, exhorting me to send letters on behalf of prisoners of con-science whose cases are supported by Amnesty International—as if lives could be redeemed so cheaply, as if suffering ends when torture stops; they built a world in which "compassion fatigue," that ennui that envelops the witnesses to suffering, receives as much attention as does suffering itself. Like the philosophes, we are mired in our own feelings, fascinated by our own emotions, and terribly lacking in a compassionate public language with which to talk about pain and suffering.

And the survivors of torture? What did they make of their experiences? How did they reassemble the pieces of their lives? Here the archives fall silent. I cannot reconstruct their inner lives or follow them out of the pris-ons that once held them. I can only try to evoke the meaning of their expe-rience in the context of their culture and perhaps, in some small measure, bear witness to their suffering.

APPENDIX

It is difficult to compare the use of torture among the French courts, as scholars have both employed different sampling methods and sought different statistics. That said, I have gathered here some basic figures— some grounded in very slender evidence—that provide perspective on the relative frequency of the practice. It should also be added that torture was last employed in the following courts in these years: in Toulouse, the *question préparatoire* was last employed in 1774, and the *question préalable*, in 1785; in Rousillon, the *question préparatoire* was last employed in 1737, and the *question préalable*, in 1743; in the *parlement* of Flanders, the *question préalable* was last employed in 1753; in the *parlement* of Burgundy, the *question préparatoire* was last employed in 1766, and the *question préalable*, in 1783; and in the Châtelet of Paris, the *question préalable* was last employed in 1788.

Comparison of the Use of Torture in French Courts

	Bordeaux (1510–1565)	Paris (1539–1542)	Paris (1535–1545)	Brittany (1600–1699)	Toulouse (1600–1788)	Rousillon (1660–1790)	Burgundy (1715–1783)	Paris (1735–1749)
Number of cases of *question* under discussion	...	125	152	272	77 sample cases involving 85 persons	69	41	41
Number of cases of *question préparatoire* under discussion	...	...	...	36	63	30	19	...
Number of cases of *question préalable* under discussion	...	...	...	236	20	39	22	...
Percent of cases of torture among *grand criminel*	22.9	...	17	13	...	...	...	3.5
Percent of cases culminating in confession	...	8.5	...	8.3	14.2	10 of *préparatoire*; 13 of *préalable*	33 of *préalable*	3–7

Sources: These figures are drawn from the following: for Bordeaux, see Schnapper, "La répression pénale au XVIe siècle"; for Paris during the years 1535–1545, see Schnapper, "La justice criminelle"; for Paris during the years 1539–1542, see Soman, "Criminal jurisprudence in Ancien-Régime France"; for Brittany, see Pinson-Ramet, "La torture judiciaire"; for Toulouse, this work; for Rousillon, see Durand, "Arbitraire du juge et droit de la torture"; for Burgundy, see Ulrich, "La répression en Bourgogne"; and for Paris during the years 1735–1749, see Andrews, *Law, Magistracy, and Crime.*

Introduction

1. There is a large literature on the Calas case. Useful bibliographies can be found in David Bien, *The Calas Affair: Persecution, Toleration and Heresy in Eighteenth-century Toulouse* (Princeton, N.J.: Princeton University Press, 1960) and in *La réforme à Toulouse de 1562 à 1762* (Toulouse: n.p., 1962).

Primary sources in Toulouse include the *dossier* compiled in the case (Archives Départementales de la Haute-Garonne [ADHG] 101 B 2 and 101 B 3, the sentences of the *parlement* of Toulouse (ADHG B 3850, 9, 12, and 18 March 1762), and a copy of the interrogation (ADHG 51 B 25). Primary printed sources include the many *mémoires* published during the course of the case; the decrees of the *Convention Nationale;* scientific works inspired by the case, most notably Antoine Louis, *Mémoire sur une question relative à la jurisprudence; dans lequel on établit les principes pour distinguer, à l'inspection d'un corps trouvé pendu, les signes du suicide d'avec ceux de l'assassinat,* reprinted in Jacques-Pierre Brissot de Warville, *Bibliothèque philosophique de législateur* (Berlin, 1763); and a variety of fictional works, including poems and plays.

2. The primary sources in the Bourdil case include the *dossier* (ADHG 101 B 159), sentences (ADHG B 3814, 10 May and 6 June 1726), and the interrogation (ADHG 51 B 23, folios 284–295).

3. On the use of arbitration in the medieval Languedoc, see Jan Rogozinski, *Power, Caste, and Law: Social Conflict in Fourteenth-Century Montpellier* (Cambridge, Mass.: Medieval Academy of America, 1982), especially 84–114. Two studies of the south of France in the early modern period suggest the continued importance of private justice. Malcolm Greenshields, *An Economy of Violence in Early Modern France: Crime and Justice in the Haute Auvergne, 1587–1664* (University Park: Pennsylvania State University Press, 1994), argues that vengeance served as a form of justice; Steven G. Reinhardt, *Justice in the Sarladais, 1770–1790* (Baton Rouge: Louisiana State University Press, 1991), examines the early modern employment of dispute settlement through arbitration.

4. On the gradual separation of popular and elite cultures, see Peter Burke, *Popular Culture in Early Modern Europe* (New York: Harper & Row, 1978).

5. For the development of the debate over the problems of embodiment in the medieval period, see, among many others, the works of Caroline Walker Bynum, especially *The Resurrection of the Body in Western Christianity, 200–1336* (New York: Columbia University Press, 1995). For the early modern period, see Natalie Zemon Davis, "Ghosts, Kin, and Progeny: Some Features of Family Life in Early Modern France," *Daedalus* 106 (spring 1977): 87–114. The enormous symbolic significance of bodies for the public negotiation of honor and identity is explored by William H. Beik, *Urban*

Protest in Seventeenth-Century France: The Culture of Retribution (Cambridge: Cambridge University Press, 1997), 57–60, 66, 68–70, 120–21, 149–50, 162; Natalie Zemon Davis, "The Rites of Violence," in *Society and Culture in Early Modern France: Eight Essays* (Stanford, Calif.: Stanford University Press, 1974); and Barbara B. Diefendorf, *Beneath the Cross: Catholics and Huguenots in Sixteenth-Century Paris* (New York: Oxford University Press, 1991), 50, 53, 58–59, 63–67, 71.

6. See *Voltaire's Correspondence*, 107 vols., ed. Theodore Besterman (Geneva: Institut et Musée Voltaire, 1953–67), letter D10860, vol. 54, 105.

7. On the early employment of torture in the Languedoc, see John Hine Mundy, *Liberty and Political Power in Toulouse, 1050–1230* (New York: Columbia University Press, 1954), 107, 63, 320 n40; and James B. Given, *State and Society in Medieval Europe: Gwynedd and Languedoc under Outside Rule* (Ithaca, N.Y.: Cornell University Press, 1990), 81–82. Walter Wakefield suggests that torture was employed first in the Languedoc by secular authorities in trials of heretics and that its use remained relatively rare until the fourteenth century. See Walter L. Wakefield, *Heresy, Crusade, and Inquisition in Southern France, 1100–1250* (Berkeley: University of California Press, 1974), 174, 192–93 n7.

8. Torture played a similar role in conflict between the municipal consuls and counts of Ghent. See Edward Peters, *Torture* (New York: Basil Blackwell, 1985), 49.

9. See J. H. Shennan, *The Parlement of Paris* (Ithaca, N.Y.: Cornell University Press, 1968), especially chapter 2.

10. The inquisitions associated with the Albigensian Crusades have generated a large literature of their own. Useful bibliographic guidance can be found in James B. Given, "The Inquisitors of Languedoc and the Medieval Technology of Power," *American Historical Review* 94, no. 2 (April 1989): 336–59.

11. Ecclesiastical inquisitors were believed to have used liberal amounts of torture to force untrue confessions from those accused of heresy. See Given, *State and Society*, 230–32. See also Wakefield, *Heresy, Crusade, and Inquisition*, 179, and Given, "Inquisitors of Languedoc," 351.

12. On clerical debates about the use of torture, see Peters, *Torture*, 40–67.

13. On the cultural consequences of this crisis, see R. Howard Bloch, *Medieval French Literature and Law* (Berkeley and Los Angeles: University of California Press, 1977).

14. Rogozinski, *Power, Caste, and Law*, 107, speaks of an "undivided spectrum of custom."

15. See Bynum, *Resurrection of the Body*, on the resurrection as the promise of literal physical salvation.

16. On the assertion by medieval flagellants that their pain is Christ's pain, and their blood, Christ's blood, see Norman R. C. Cohn, *The Pursuit of the Millennium: Revolutionary Millenarians and Mystical Anarchists of the Middle Ages*, rev. and exp. ed. (New York: Oxford University Press, 1970).

17. On suffering as the destruction of self, see Elizabeth Rapley, "Her Body the Enemy: Self-Mortification in Seventeenth-Century Convents," *Proceedings of the Annual Meeting of the Western Society for French History* 21 (1994): 25–35. Patricia Curran, *Grace before Meals: Food Ritual and Body Discipline in Convent Culture* (Urbana: University of Illinois Press, 1989), argues that this understanding continues to inform the experience of the Roman Catholic religious.

18. Elaine Scarry, *The Body in Pain: The Making and Unmaking of the World* (New

York: Oxford University Press, 1985), concurs that pain and personal agency cannot co-exist.

19. On the early modern assessment of the pursuit of pain as a form of mental illness, see Michael MacDonald, *Mystical Bedlam: Madness, Anxiety, and Healing in Seventeenth-Century England* (Cambridge: Cambridge University Press, 1981), 130–32. Maureen Flynn looks at the relationship of human and divine suffering as expressed in the Holy Thursday processions of flagellants in sixteenth-century Spain and finds a lay devotion to the healing properties of the human body and blood. See Maureen Flynn, "The Spectacle of Suffering in Spanish Streets," in *City and Spectacle in Medieval Europe,* ed. Barbara A. Hanawalt and Kathryn L. Reyerson (Minneapolis: University of Minnesota Press, 1993), 153–70; and Robert A. Schneider, "Mortification on Parade: Penitential Processions in Sixteenth- and Seventeenth-Century France," *Renaissance and Reformation* 10, no. 1 (February 1986): 123–46.

20. On sensibility in the English and French contexts, see G. J. Barker-Benfield, *The Culture of Sensibility: Sex and Society in Eighteenth-Century Britain* (Chicago: University of Chicago Press, 1992) and Anne C. Vila, *Enlightenment and Pathology: Sensibility in the Literature and Medicine of Eighteenth-Century France* (Baltimore, Md.: Johns Hopkins University Press, 1998), respectively.

21. Anthropologists are engaged in an attempt to reexamine the nature of suffering and to render the experience of pain meaningful once again. See Mary-Jo DelVecchio Good, et al., eds., *Pain as Human Experience: An Anthropological Perspective* (Berkeley and Los Angeles: University of California Press, 1992). Authors of patient memoirs are likewise engaged in this endeavor. See, for example, Anatole Broyard, *Intoxicated by My Illness, and Other Writings on Life and Death* (New York: Fawcett Columbine, 1992); Andre Dubus, *Broken Vessels* (Boston: David R. Godine, 1991); Lucy Grealy, *Autobiography of a Face* (Boston: Houghton Mifflin Co., 1994); Nancy Mairs, *Plaintext: Essays* (Tucson: University of Arizona Press, 1986); and Reynolds Price, *A Whole New Life* (New York: Atheneum, 1994). These memoirs, and others like them, have begun to attract scholarly attention. The lengthiest study to date is Anne Hunsaker Hawkins's *Reconstructing Illness: Studies in Pathography* (West Lafayette, Ind.: Purdue University Press, 1993). See also Nancy Mairs, "The Literature of Personal Disaster," in *Voice Lessons,* ed. Nancy Mairs (Boston: Beacon Press, 1994), 123–35, and Rosemarie Garland Thomson, "Redrawing the Boundaries of Feminist Disability Studies," *Feminist Studies* 20, no. 3 (fall 1994): 583–95.

22. In fact, this embrace of suffering was never entirely eradicated in France—to say nothing of Roman Catholic theology and hagiography more broadly—as the presence and popularity of figures like Thérèse de Lisieux and Simone Weil make abundantly clear.

23. On marriage contracts, see Julie Hardwick, *The Practice of Patriarchy: Gender and the Politics of Household Authority in Early Modern France* (University Park: Pennsylvania State University Press, 1998); on minutes of guild meetings, see Laurie Nussdorfer, "Writing and the Power of Speech: Notaries and Artisans in Baroque Rome," in Diefendorf and Hesse, *Culture and Identity in Early Modern Europe (1500–1800)* (Ann Arbor: University of Michigan Press, 1993), 103–18; on criminal court records, see Elizabeth Cohen, "Between Written and Oral Culture: The Social Meaning of an Illustrated Love Letter," in Diefendorf and Hesse, *Culture and Identity in Early Modern Europe,* 181–202; on ecclesiastical court records, specifically, the records of the Venetian Inquisition, see Brian Pullan, *The Jews of Europe and the Inquisition of Venice, 1550–1670*

(Totowa, N.J.: Barnes & Noble, 1983), chapter 8. Historians of medieval and early modern Europe exploring what constituted proper oral evidence, what constituted the conventions of producing and preserving such evidence, and how faith in writing was constructed include M. T. Clanchy, *From Memory to Written Record: England, 1066–1307* (Cambridge, Mass.: Harvard University Press, 1979); Frances Yates, *The Art of Memory* (London: Routledge & Kegan Paul, 1966); Brian Stock, *Listening for the Text: On the Uses of the Past* (Baltimore, Md.: Johns Hopkins University Press, 1990); and Walter J. Ong, *Orality and Literacy: The Technologizing of the Word* (London: Methuen, 1982).

24. On the accuracy of notarial records, see Pullan, *The Jews of Europe*, chapter 8; Nussdorfer, "Writing and the Power of Speech," and Cohen, "Between Written and Oral Culture." Without challenging the fundamental accuracy of notarial records, Julie Hardwick has suggested that some notarial documents were not records of oral events at which all parties were present but were in fact records of a series of events that were represented as if they had occurred on a single occasion. See Hardwick, *The Practice of Patriarchy*, 34–49. Clanchy, *From Memory to Written Record*, examines the problem of forgery in regions not governed by Roman law.

25. See, for example, Cohen, "Between Written and Oral Culture," 197 n7.

26. Cohen, "Between Written and Oral Culture," 184; Richard Mowery Andrews, *Law, Magistracy, and Crime in Old Regime Paris, 1735–1789* (Cambridge: Cambridge University Press, 1994), 463.

27. Gayle Brunelle, "Policing the Unruly Women of Nantes," paper presented to the Early Modern French Studies Group of Los Angeles, 9 April 1995.

28. See, respectively, Andrews, *Law, Magistracy, and Crime*, 455; Joseph Klaits, *Servants of Satan: The Age of the Witch Hunts* (Bloomington: Indiana University Press, 1985), 128–31; and Etienne Delcambre, "The Psychology of Lorraine Witchcraft Suspects," in *European Witchcraft*, ed. E. William Monter (New York: John Wiley & Sons, Inc., 1969).

29. Thanks to the relatively restrained physical practice of torture in France during this period, I have chosen not to rely on the actual instruments of torture as a source of documentation. For a survey of instruments of torture and punishment, see Robert Held, *Inquisition: A Bilingual Guide to the Exhibition of Torture Instruments from the Middle Ages to the Industrial Era, Presented in Various European Cities in 1983–87* (in English and Spanish) (Florence: Qua d'Arno, 1985).

30. Clanchy, *From Memory to Written Record*, has explored the various purposes which documents were made to serve. While state institutions like the *parlement* did not need to produce documents to verify their activities at law, private individuals and corporations did employ notaries to produce documents that lent legal weight to their proceedings. On guild employment of notaries in early modern Italy to create group action and group awareness made permanent and legally binding through writing, see Nussdorfer, "Writing and the Power of Speech."

31. It has been suggested that interrogations were prepared first in note form during the interrogation itself and were later written up in final form. I have found no documentary evidence—no such notes and no copies of interrogations—that would suggest that this was the case. Furthermore, the fact that the interrogations had to be countersigned by the accused immediately after the interrogation was completed tends to suggest that these documents are original copies.

32. A brief biography of Barthès can be found in Edmond Lamouzele, *Toulouse au*

dix-huitième siècle, d'après les heures perdues de Pierre Barthès (Toulouse: J. Marqueste, 1914); for a more recent study based on the diary see Robert A. Schneider, *The Ceremonial City: Toulouse Observed, 1738–1780* (Princeton: Princeton University Press, 1995).

33. Bibliothèque Municipale de Toulouse [BMT], MS 706, Pierre Barthès, "Les heures perdus de Pierre Barthès," 7: 147–48 (March 1778).

34. See, for example, Georges Vigarello, *Concepts of Cleanliness: Changing Attitudes in France since the Middle Ages* (Cambridge: Cambridge University Press, 1988), on the permeability of the skin; Jacques Gélis, *History of Childbirth: Fertility, Pregnancy, and Birth in Early Modern Europe*, trans. Rosemary Morris (Boston: Northeastern University Press, 1991), on the heightened permeability of women's bodies during pregnancy; Barbara Duden, *The Woman beneath the Skin: A Doctor's Patients in Eighteenth-Century Germany* (Cambridge, Mass.: Harvard University Press, 1991), on the fluidity of the body and the ways in which it is subjected to external forces; and Mikhail M. Bahktin, *Rabelais and His World* (Bloomington: Indiana University Press, 1984), on the grotesqueness of this open and permeable body.

35. On the nature of the Eucharist, see Sarah Beckwith, *Christ's Body: Identity, Culture, and Society in Late Medieval Writings* (New York: Routledge, 1993); and Miri Rubin, *Corpus Christi: The Eucharist in Late Medieval Culture* (Cambridge: Cambridge University Press, 1991). On the princely body as the site of power, see Marc Bloch, *The Royal Touch: Sacred Monarchy and Scrofula in France and England*, trans. J. E. Anderson (London: Routledge & Kegan Paul, 1973); Ralph E. Giesey, *The Royal Funeral Ceremony in Renaissance France* (Geneva: E. Droz, 1960); and Ernst H. Kantorowicz, *The King's Two Bodies: A Study in Mediaeval Political Theology* (Princeton, N.J.: Princeton University Press, 1957).

36. Many other historians are engaged in a similar effort. See, for example, Edward Muir and Guido Ruggiero, introduction to *History from Crime*, ed. Edward Muir and Guido Ruggiero (Baltimore, Md.: Johns Hopkins University Press, 1994), vii–xviii.

37. Historical studies of torture in early modern France include Henry Charles Lea, *Torture*, vol. 4 of *Superstition and Force: Essays on the Wager of Law, the Wager of Battle, the Ordeal, Torture*, ed. Edward Peters (1866; reprint, Philadelphia: University of Pennsylvania Press, 1973); Paul Bondois, "La torture dans le ressort du parlement de Paris aux XVIIIe siècle," *Annales historiques de la révolution française* 5 (1928): 322–37; Walter Ullmann, "Reflections on Medieval Torture," *Juridical Review* 56 (1944): 123–37; Etienne Delcambre, "Witchcraft Trials in Lorraine: Psychology of the Judges," and "The Psychology of Lorraine Witchcraft Suspects," in *European Witchcraft*, ed. E. William Monter (New York: John Wiley & Sons, Inc., 1969), 88–94, 95–110; D. Ulrich, "La répression en Bourgogne au XVIIIe siècle," *Revue historique de droit français et étranger* 50 (1972): 398–437; Bernard Schnapper, "La justice criminelle rendue par le parlement de Paris sous le règne de François I," *Revue historique de droit français et étranger* 52 (1974): 252–84; Joanne Kaufmann, "The Critique of Criminal Justice in Eighteenth-Century France: A Study in the Changing Social Ethics of Crime and Punishment" (Ph.D. diss., Harvard University, 1976); John H. Langbein, *Torture and the Law of Proof: Europe and England in the Ancien Régime* (Chicago: University of Chicago Press, 1977); Mirjan Damaska, "The Death of Legal Torture," *Yale Law Journal* 87 (1978): 860–90; Bernard Durand, "Arbitraire du juge et le droit de la torture: L'exemple du conseil souverain de Roussillon," *Recueil des mémoires et travaux publié par la Société d'Histoire du Droit et des Institutions des Anciens Pays de Droit Ecrit*, fasc. 10 (1979): 141–79; L. B. Mer, "La procédure criminelle au XVIIIe siècle: L'énseignement

des archives bretonnes," *Revue historique* 555 (July–September 1985): 9–42; Alfred Soman, *Sorcellerie et justice criminelle: Le parlement de Paris, 16e–18e siècles* (Hampshire:
Variorum, 1992); Andrews, *Law, Magistracy, and Crime;* and Véronique Pinson-
Ramin, "La torture judiciaire en Bretagne au XVIIe siècle," *Revue historique de droit
français et étranger* 72 (1994): 549–68.

Studies of torture and punishment that focus on visual evidence in largely non-
French contexts include Tabatha Catte, Tobia Delmolino, and Robert Held, eds., *Catalogo della mostra di strumenti di tortura, 1400–1800* (Florence: Qua d'Arno, 1983); Held,
ed., *Inquisition;* Samuel Y. Edgerton, Jr., *Pictures and Punishment: Art and Criminal
Prosecution during the Florentine Renaissance* (Ithaca, N.Y.: Cornell University Press,
1985); Lionello Puppi, *Torment in Art: Pain, Violence, and Martyrdom* (New York: Rizzoli, 1990); and Mitchell B. Merback, *The Thief, the Cross, and the Wheel: Pain and
the Spectacle of Punishment in Medieval and Renaissance Europe* (Chicago: University of
Chicago Press, 1998).

Classicists, literary critics, philosophers, theologians, political scientists, and anthropologists have also considered the problem of torture. For those works that cast the
most light on the historical development of torture in the West, see Page DuBois, *Torture and Truth* (New York: Routledge, 1990); Scarry, *The Body in Pain,* especially part
1; Elizabeth Hanson, "Torture and Truth in Renaissance England," *Representations* 34
(spring 1991): 53–84; Henry Shue, "Torture," *Philosophy and Public Affairs* 7 (1978):
124–43; Franz Böckle and Jacques Pohier, eds., *The Death Penalty and Torture* (New
York: Seabury Press, 1979); Judith Shklar, "Putting Cruelty First," *Daedalus* 111 (summer 1982): 17–27; Talal Asad, "Notes on Body Pain and Truth in Medieval Christian
Ritual," *Economy and Society* 12 (1983): 287–327; and Peggy Reeves Sanday, *Divine
Hunger: Cannibalism as a Cultural System* (Cambridge: Cambridge University Press,
1986).

There is also a distinguished journalistic tradition of writing about torture. Journalists
have directed their attention primarily to abuses that have occurred in contemporary
contexts, including the Algerian war of independence and the Latin American military
dictatorships of the 1970s. See, for example, Henri Alleg, *The Question,* intro. by Jean
Paul Sarte, trans. John Calder (New York: George Braziller, 1958); Jacobo Timerman,
Prisoner without a Name, Cell without a Number, trans. Toby Talbot (New York: Vintage
Books, 1981); Michael Ignatieff, "Torture's Dead Simplicity," *New Statesman* 110 (20
September 1985): 24–26; and Lawrence Weschler, *A Miracle, a Universe: Settling Ac-
counts with Torturers* (New York: Pantheon, 1990).

38. See, most notoriously, Michel Foucault, *Discipline and Punish: The Birth of the
Prison,* trans. Alan Sheridan (New York: Vintage Books, 1979).

39. See Iain Cameron, *Crime and Repression in the Auvergne and the Guyenne, 1720–
1790* (Cambridge: Cambridge University Press, 1981); and Julius R. Ruff, *Crime, Justice
and Public Order in Old Regime France: The Sénéchaussées of Libourne and Bazas, 1696–
1789* (London: Croom Helm, 1984).

40. See Adhemar Esmein, *A History of Continental Criminal Procedure, with Special
Reference to France,* trans. John Simpson (Boston: Little, Brown and Company, 1913);
Marcel Marion, *Dictionnaire des institutions de la France aux dix-septième et dix-huitième
siècles* (1923; reprint, Paris: Picard, 1984); and Roland E. Mousnier, *The Institutions of
France under the Absolute Monarchy, 1598–1789,* 2 vols. (Chicago: University of Chicago
Press, 1979–84).

41. David Yale Jacobson, "The Politics of Criminal Law Reform in Pre-

Revolutionary France," Ph.D. diss., Brown University, 1976; Esmein, *History of Continental Criminal Procedure.*

42. Nicole Castan, "Crime and Justice in Languedoc: The Critical Years, 1750–1790," *Criminal Justice History* 1 (1980): 175–84; Antoinette Wills, *Crime and Punishment in Revolutionary Paris* (Westport, Conn.: Greenwood Press, 1981).

43. Asad, "Notes on Body Pain and Truth," critiques this progressive interpretation; he suggests that the emergence of torture as a judicial ritual is chronologically and epistemologically linked to the emergence of personal confession as an ecclesiastical ritual as both rituals required the verbalization of the truth about oneself. Torture inflicted pain prior to verbalization to elicit that truth; confession inflicted pain following verbalization to purge those truths.

44. Langbein, *Torture and the Law of Proof.* For a thoughtful critique of Langbein's work, see Damaska, "Death of Legal Torture."

45. Andrews, *Law, Magistracy, and Crime,* 436–72; Mer, "La procédure criminelle"; Pinson-Ramin, "La torture judiciaire en Bretagne"; Alfred Soman, "Criminal Jurisprudence in *Ancien-régime* France: The *Parlement* of Paris in the Sixteenth and Seventeenth Centuries," in *Crime and Criminal Justice in Europe and Canada,* ed. Louis A. Knafla (Waterloo, Ontario: Wilfred Laurier University Press, 1981); Ulrich, "La répression en Bourgogne."

46. There were two principal forms of torture: the *question préparatoire,* designed to elicit information from the accused before judgment, and the *question préalable,* designed to elicit the names of accomplices of the accused after judgment of guilt. The significance of this distinction will be explored below.

47. See Soman, *Sorcellerie et justice criminelle,* 33, 51. In these collected essays, Soman refutes the findings of Robert Mandrou concerning the administration of justice in the Paris *parlement* developed in *Magistrats et sorciers en France aux XVIIe siècle: Une analyse de psychologie historique* (Paris: Plon, 1968). Torture was employed far more frequently in German courts and achieved much higher rates of confession, perhaps because German judges and executioners failed to observe the legal limits on the use of torture. In Munich, torture was employed in 44 percent of cases in 1650 and in 16 percent of cases in 1690. See Richard J. Evans, *Rituals of Retribution: Capital punishment in Germany, 1600–1987* (Oxford: Oxford University Press, 1996), 39, 114–15.

48. See Soman, *Sorcellerie et justice criminelle,* 17, 29, 48, for the suggestion that witchcraft trials were indicative of political instability.

49. See Pinson-Ramin, "La torture judiciaire en Bretagne," 536.

50. On the illogic of torture, see, for example, Andrews, *Law, Magistracy, and Crime,* 453, 471.

51. Foucault, *Discipline and Punish, passim.*

52. DuBois, *Torture and Truth, passim.* For another recent study of torture within a specific historical context, see Hanson, "Torture and Truth." Like DuBois, Hanson focuses her attention on the problem of competing truths.

53. Scarry, *The Body in Pain,* especially 3–59.

54. Scarry, *The Body in Pain,* 22.

55. Scarry, *The Body in Pain,* 18.

56. For another critique of Scarry's work, see Ñacuñán Sáez, "Torture: A Discourse on Practice," in *Tattoo, Torture, Mutilation, and Adornment: The Denaturalization of the Body in Culture and Text,* ed. Frances E. Mascia-Lees and Patricia Sharpe (Albany: State University of New York Press, 1992), 126–44.

57. Scarry, *The Body in Pain*, 28, 40, and 44. For another account of the euphemisms employed in the modern practice of torture, see Marguerite Feitlowitz, *A Lexicon of Terror: Argentina and the Legacies of Torture* (New York: Oxford University Press, 1998), 51–60.

58. Scarry, *The Body in Pain*, 21.

59. For an investigation of the consent of victims to torture in early modern France, see Delcambre, "The Psychology of Lorraine Witchcraft Suspects," 95–110.

60. See David Morris's exploration of the meanings of pain in the modern Western world, *The Culture of Pain* (Berkeley: University of California Press, 1991). His work focuses primarily on uninflicted chronic pain, unlike Scarry's study, which focuses primarily on inflicted acute pain. On the cross-cultural dimension of the expression of pain, see Mark Zborowski, *People in Pain*, foreword by Margaret Mead (San Francisco: Jossey-Bass, 1969). Zborowski maintains that there is a universal pain threshold at which pain is physiologically sensed but that the perception and expression of pain as negative affect differs cross-culturally. On the consequences of the belief that a human's threshold itself varies according to race, sex, and class, see Martin S. Pernick, *A Calculus of Suffering: Pain, Professionalism, and Anesthesia in Nineteenth-Century America* (New York: Columbia University Press, 1985). Other historical and anthropological investigations support Zborowski's findings concerning cross-cultural differences in the experience and expression of pain. On the appropriate expression of pain during childbirth, for example, see Mireille Laget, "Childbirth in Seventeenth- and Eighteenth-Century France: Obstetrical Practices and Collective Attitudes," in *Medicine and Society in France*, ed. Robert Forster and Orest Ranum (Baltimore, Md.: Johns Hopkins University Press, 1980), 137–76, and Marjorie Shostak, *Nisa: The Life and Words of a !Kung Woman* (New York: Vintage Books, 1981). For several thoughtful examinations of the expression and experience of pain in the modern world, see the special spring 1989 issue of *Soundings* entitled "Metaphors, Language and Medicine."

61. Scarry, *The Body in Pain*, 34.

Chapter 1

1. On the history of Toulouse, see Jules Chalande, *Histoire des rues de Toulouse: Monuments, institutions, habitants* (1919–29; reprint, Marseille: Laffitte, 1982); Georges Frêche, *Toulouse et la région Midi-Pyrénées au siècle des lumières vers 1670–1789* (Paris: Cujas, 1974); Robert Mesuret, *Évocation du vieux Toulouse* (Paris: Éditions de Minuit, 1960); Robert A. Schneider, *Public Life in Toulouse, 1463–1789: From Municipal Republic to Cosmopolitan City* (Ithaca, N.Y.: Cornell University Press, 1989) and *The Ceremonial City: Toulouse Observed, 1738–1780* (Princeton, N.J.: Princeton University Press, 1995); and Philippe Wolff, *Histoire de Toulouse*, 2d ed. (Toulouse: Privat, 1970). In the early eighteenth century, the population stood between 43,000 and 48,000; the city had therefore diminished in size since the middle of the sixteenth century. See Philip Benedict, ed., *Cities and Social Change in Early Modern France* (London: Unwin Hyman, 1989), 24.

2. Geographic mobility in France has been examined by James Collins, "Geographic and Social Mobility in Early Modern France," *Journal of Social History* 24, no. 3 (spring 1991): 563–77, and Olwen H. Hufton, *The Poor of Eighteenth-Century France* (Oxford: Clarendon Press, 1974), 69–106. For residential choices and residential mobility in Toulouse, see Lenard Berlanstein, *The Barristers of Toulouse in the Eighteenth Century, 1740–1793* (Baltimore, Md.: Johns Hopkins University Press, 1975), 29–30; Cissie

Fairchilds, *Domestic Enemies: Masters and Servants in Old Regime France* (Baltimore, Md.: Johns Hopkins University Press, 1984), 61–66; and Schneider, *Public Life in Toulouse,* 21–27.

On the conventions of dress, see Aileen Ribeiro, *Dress in Eighteenth-Century Europe, 1715–1789* (New York: Holmes & Meier, 1984). Leah Otis, *Prostitution in Medieval Society: The History of an Urban Institution in Languedoc* (Chicago: University of Chicago Press, 1985), 79–80, notes that in 1369, Toulousain prostitutes petitioned for the right to abandon such identifying gowns for more discreet insignia sewn to their sleeves.

On the bodily effects of occupation, see Arlette Farge, "Les artisans malade de leur travail," *Annales Economie, Sociétés, Civilizations* 32, no. 5 (September–October 1977): 993–1006; John Rule, *The Experience of Labour in Eighteenth-Century English Industry* (New York: St. Martin's Press, 1981), chapter 3; and Michael Sonenscher, *The Hatters of Eighteenth-Century France* (Berkeley and Los Angeles: University of California Press, 1987), chapter 9.

3. On the importance of dress as regards the expression of gender, regardless of sex, see Lorraine Daston and Katherine Park, "Hermaphrodites in Renaissance France," *Critical Matrix* 1, no. 5 (1985): 1–15. On dress, etiquette, and honor, see Norbert Elias, *The History of Manners* (New York: Pantheon Books, 1978), 143–52, 160–68; James R. Farr, *Hands of Honor: Artisans and Their World in Dijon, 1550–1650* (Ithaca, N.Y.: Cornell University Press, 1988), 183, 248–49; and Sonenscher, *Hatters of Eighteenth-Century France,* chapter 2.

The history of gesture is being written by two groups of historians. The principal discussions by art historians and literary critics include Moshe Barasch, *Gestures of Despair in Medieval and Early Renaissance Art* (New York: New York University Press, 1976); Jan Bremmer and Herman Roodenburg, eds., *A Cultural History of Gesture from Antiquity to the Present* (Ithaca, N.Y.: Cornell University Press, 1992); Laurinda S. Dixon, *Perilous Chastity: Women and Illness in Pre-Enlightenment Art and Medicine* (Ithaca, N.Y.: Cornell University Press, 1995), 59–70; and Stephen Greenblatt, "Toward a Universal Language of Motion: Reflections on a Seventeenth-Century Muscle Man," in *Choreographing History,* ed. Susan Leigh Foster (Bloomington: Indiana University Press, 1995), 25–31. Social historians and historians of crime have contributed the following studies, which in many instances overlap studies of insult: Yves Castan, *Honnêteté et relations sociales en Languedoc, 1715–1780* (Paris: Plon, 1974); Farr, *Hands of Honor,* 177–95; Gregory Hanlon, "Les rituels d'aggression en Aquitaine au XVIIe siècle," *Annales Economie, Sociétés, Civilizations* 40, no. 2 (1985): 244–68; and Robert Muchembled, "Pour une histoire des gestes (XVe–XVIIIe siècle)," *Revue d'histoire moderne et contemporaine* 34 (1987): 87–101.

The association of undress with intimate favor, as suggested by the voluntary removal of gloves, was also played out in European courts: the *lever* and *coucher* of Louis XIV and his successors, like the undress sported by Elizabeth I of England, were ritualized moments of nakedness, privilege, and power. On Elizabeth I, see Louis A. Montrose, "*A Midsummer Night's Dream* and the Shaping Fantasies of Elizabethan Culture: Gender, Power, Form," in *Rewriting the Renaissance: The Discourses of Sexual Difference in Early Modern Europe,* ed. Margaret Ferguson, Maureen Quilligan, and Nancy Vickers (Chicago: University of Chicago Press, 1986), especially 66–67.

4. For a powerful evocation of the appearance of the French in the eighteenth century, see John McManners, *Death and the Enlightenment* (Oxford: Oxford University Press, 1981), chapter 1. On the particular importance of the nose in the construction

of honor in late medieval Europe, see Valentin Groebner, "Losing Face, Saving Face: Noses and Honour in the Late Medieval Town," *History Workshop Journal* 40 (1995): 1–15. For a continuation of this discussion into the early modern and modern periods, see Sander Gilman, *Making the Body Beautiful: A Cultural History of Aesthetic Surgery* (Princeton, N.J.: Princeton University Press, 1999).

5. "Kill, kill!" ADHG 101 B 159, *dossier* of Jean Bourdil, document DD (27 April 1726), second cahier.

6. ADHG 101 B 159, *dossier* of Jean Bourdil, document DD (27 April 1726), second cahier.

7. ADHG 101 B 159, *dossier* of Jean Bourdil, document DD (27 April 1726), second cahier.

8. ADHG 101 B 159, *dossier* of Jean Bourdil, untitled report of François de Turle de Labrespin (April 1726).

9. ADHG 101 B 159, *dossier* of Jean Bourdil, document A (18 April 1726), "Verbal dressé par Monsieur de Turle de Labrespin."

10. The role of the *archers* has been examined by Robert Schwartz, *Policing the Poor in Eighteenth-Century France* (Chapel Hill: University of North Carolina Press, 1988). Note that this case falls within the period 1724–1733, which Schwartz designates as "the great confinement." Conflicts that arose between the *archers* as petty government officials and the populace form the material of Arlette Farge and Jacques Revel, *The Vanishing Children of Paris: Rumor and Politics before the French Revolution*, trans. Claudia Miéville (Cambridge, Mass.: Harvard University Press, 1991).

11. On the *archers*, see Schwartz, *Policing the Poor*, 90–92. On the popular violence that erupted around urban officials, see Beik, *Urban Protest in Seventeenth-Century France*.

12. ADHG 101 B 159, *dossier* of Jean Bourdil, unlettered document (17 April 1726), "Verbal dressé par le sieur Duclos."

13. ADHG 101 B 159, *dossier* of Jean Bourdil, document B (18 April 1726), "Requette en plainte pour M. le procureur du Roy."

14. The *capitouls* were in charge of the preliminary investigation because their jurisdiction extended over crimes committed within the city. For the documents in the case, see ADHG 101 B 159, *dossier* of Jean Bourdil, documents C–H (18–19 April 1726), *auditions* of Jean Bourdil, Louis Prieur, Anthoine Bajou, Bernard Lauzere, Pierre Bagneres, and Jean Puntis; document J (20 April 1726), subpoenas to be served by Jean Abadie, *huissier*; and unlettered document (20 April 1726), "Verbal de perquisition."

15. ADHG 101 B 159, *dossier* of Jean Bourdil, document E (18 April 1726), "Audition d'Anthoine Bajou."

16. ADHG 101 B 159, *dossier* of Jean Bourdil, document F (18 April 1726), "Audition de Bernard Lauzere." On the employment of insult in early modern France, see Robert Darnton, "The Great Cat Massacre," in *The Great Cat Massacre and Other Episodes in French Cultural History* (New York: Basic Books, 1984); David Garrioch, "Verbal Insults in Eighteenth-Century Paris," in *The Social History of Language*, ed. Peter Burke and Roy Porter (Cambridge: Cambridge University Press, 1987), 104–19; and Hanlon, "Les rituels de l'agression"; in New France, see Peter N. Moogk, "'Thieving Buggers' and 'Stupid Sluts': Insults and Popular Culture in New France," *William and Mary Quarterly* 36 (1979): 524–47; in Italy, see Peter Burke, "Insult and Blasphemy in Early Modern Italy," in *The Historical Anthropology of Early Modern Italy: Essays on Perception and Communication* (Cambridge: Cambridge University Press, 1987), 95–

109; and in England, see Miranda Chaytor, "Household and Kinship: Ryton in the Late Sixteenth and Early Seventeenth Centuries," *History Workshop Journal* (1980): 24–60; and Laura Gowing, "Gender and the Language of Insult in Early Modern London," *History Workshop Journal* 35 (1993): 1–21. On the formal properties of insult, see William Labov, "Rules for Ritual Insults," in *Studies in Social Interaction,* ed. David Sudnow (New York: The Free Press, 1972), 120–69.

17. ADHG 101 B 159, *dossier* of Jean Bourdil, documents K and L (19–20 April 1726), "Inquisition."

18. ADHG 101 B 159, *dossier* of Jean Bourdil, document N (19, 20, and 24 April 1726), "Expédié de décret d'ordonnance d'écroue."

19. ADHG 101 B 159, *dossier* of Jean Bourdil, document N (19, 20, and 24 April 1726), "Expédié de décret d'ordonnance d'écroue."

20. ADHG 101 B 159, *dossier* of Jean Bourdil, document P (23 April 1726), "Audition de Louis Prieur."

21. ADHG 101 B 159, *dossier* of Jean Bourdil, document Q (24 April 1726), "Conclusions sur la forme de procédure." *Recollement* required witnesses to confirm previous depositions under oath. Any deviation from the deposition made those witnesses liable to perjury charges.

22. ADHG 101 B 159, *dossier* of Jean Bourdil, document R (24 April 1726), "Sentence de confrontation."

23. ADHG 101 B 159, *dossier* of Jean Bourdil, document R (24 April 1726), "Sentence de confrontation."

24. ADHG 101 B 159, *dossier* of Jean Bourdil, document U (24, 27, 29, and 30 April 1726), "Recollements de témoins."

25. ADHG 101 B 159, *dossier* of Jean Bourdil, document DD (27 April 1726), second cahier.

26. ADHG 101 B 159, *dossier* of Jean Bourdil, documents AA and BB (24, 27, 29, and 30 April 1726), "Confrontements faits à Prieur et Bourdil."

27. ADHG 101 B 159, *dossier* of Jean Bourdil, document EE (29 April 1726), "Troisième audition de Jean Bourdil."

28. ADHG 101 B 159, *dossier* of Jean Bourdil, document FF (1 May 1726), "Conclusions du procureur du Roy."

29. ADHG 101 B 159, *dossier* of Jean Bourdil, documents GG, HH, and JJ (4 May 1726), "Audition derrière la barre de Prieur," "Audition sur la sellette de Bourdil," and "Confrontements respectifs de Jean Bourdil et Louis Prieur."

30. ADHG 101 B 159, *dossier* of Jean Bourdil, document KK (4 May 1726), "Délibération de consuls."

31. ADHG 101 B 159, *dossier* of Jean Bourdil, document LL (4 May 1726), "Sentence dont est l'appel de suite."

32. Implicit in this definition is the suggestion that legal systems are systems of meaning and that it is through study of such systems that we can elucidate the particular and local meanings of concepts like justice. For further examination of the methodologies of legal anthropology, see June Starr and Jane F. Collier, eds., *History and Power in the Study of Law* (Ithaca, N.Y.: Cornell University Press, 1989).

33. The *parlement* followed these same procedures when judging cases in the first instance. When cases were heard on appeal, judges reviewed the dossiers and interviewed the accused; only very rarely would they seek new evidence in the case. Information on criminal procedures is drawn from François-André Isambert, ed., *Recueil général*

des anciennes lois françaises depuis l'an 420 jusqu'à la révolution de 1789 (Paris, 1827), Ordinance of Blois, articles 112–114, 11: 365–366; Ordinance of Villers-Cotterets, articles 163–164, 12: 633–634; and the criminal ordinance of 1670, title 19, articles 1–12, 18: 412–413; from the legal manuals under discussion in chapter 2; and from discussions in Andrews, *Law, Magistracy, and Crime*, chapters 11–15; Edmond Detourbet, *La procédure criminelle au XVIIe siècle* (Paris: Arthur Rousseau, 1881); Esmein, *Continental Criminal Procedure*, 183–286, 351–82, 609–31; Jean Imbert, *Quelques procès criminels des XVIIe et XVIIIe siècles* (Paris: Presses Universitaires de France, 1964), 1–12; Marion, *Dictionnaire des institutions, passim;* Mousnier, *Organs of State and Society*, 375–422; Reinhardt, *Justice in the Sarladais*, 56–94; Ruff, *Crime, Justice, and Public Order*, 24–44; and Shennan, *The Parlement of Paris*, 67–74.

34. Isambert, *Recueil général des anciennes lois françaises*, Ordinance of Blois (1498), article 108, 11: 364–365.

35. On the structure of the criminal system, see Andrews, *Law, Magistracy, and Crime*, chapters 1–2; Marion, *Dictionnaire des institutions, passim;* Mousnier, *Organs of State and Society*, 251–302; Ruff, *Crime, Justice, and Public Order*, 24–44; and Shennan, *The Parlement of Paris*, 30–49.

36. The courts were also distinguished by the kinds of sentences that they produced: courts pronounced *arrêts*, or final decrees; jurisdictions pronounced *sentences*, which were subject to appeal. The *parlement* was an ordinary court, and the *présidiaux, sénéchaussées*, and *prévôtés* were ordinary jurisdictions, whereas the *prévôtés des maréchaux* were extraordinary courts whose sentences were not subject to appeal. In criminal matters, the *sentences* of the *présidiaux* were likewise not subject to appeal. I will refer to all these judicial bodies as courts, however, since it is understood that all of the decisions of the ordinary courts, except those of the *parlements*, were subject to appeal. See Mousnier, *Organs of State and Society*, 253.

37. The *parlement* of Toulouse covered an area almost one-seventh of the country, including the *sénéchaussées* and *présidiaux* of Auch, Béziers, Cahors, Carcassonne, Castelnaudry, Lectoure, Limoux, Montauban, Montpellier, Nîmes, Pamiers, Puy-en-Velay, Rodez, Toulouse, and Villefranche-en-Rouergue, as well as ten other *sénéchaussées* without *présidiaux*. The jurisdiction of the *parlement* included the present *départements* of Haute-Garonne, Ariege, Aude, Haute-Pyrénées, Gers, Herault, Tarn, Tarn-et-Garonne, Lot, Aveyron, Gard, Lozère, Ardeche, and Haute-Loire. See Eugene Lapierre, *Le parlement de Toulouse: son ressort, ses attributions, et ses archives* (Toulouse: Typographie de Bonnal et Gibrac, 1860).

38. In fact, it appears that the members of the *tournelle* in the *parlement* of Toulouse were not selected by rota but served as semipermanent members of a standing chamber. The evidence of Pierre de Fermat, the mathematician and *parlementaire* of Toulouse, suggests that the chambers of the court existed in a formal hierarchy and that the *gens de loi* passed through each of these chambers in turn in their rise to prominence. See Michael Sean Mahoney, *The Mathematical Career of Pierre de Fermat, 1601–1665*, 2d ed. (Princeton, N.J.: Princeton University Press, 1994), 19–20. Sources that discuss the composition of the *parlement* include ADHG MS 147–149, "Collections et remarques du Palais faites par moi Etienne de Malenfant, depuis le 2 jour de mars 1602 auquel jour je fus reçu en l'office de Greffier civil" (1602–1647); and BMT MS 693, Pierre Lacombe, "Traité de l'audience du Parlement de Toulouse" (1654); BMT MS 1564, "Mémoire sur l'état du parlement de Toulouse en l'année 1678" (1678).

The *chambre des requêtes* was the lowest in this hierarchy and was composed of eleven members. The two *chambre des enquêtes* with twenty-eight members each were the next step on the way to the *tournelle*, which was a permanent chamber of three *présidents à mortier* and thirteen *conseillers*, three of whom were sent each year to serve in the *chambre de l'edit*, the court that heard cases involving Protestants, and two in the *grand' chambre*. See BMT MS 1564. No clerics could serve in the *tournelle*, despite the fact that the *parlement* of Toulouse, unlike other provincial *parlements*, considered the *tournelle* to be part of the same body as the *grand' chambre*, which possessed nineteen members. This shared quality was demonstrated by the fact that members of the *tournelle* and *grand' chambre* were regularly circulated between these chambers: each Saint Martin's Day, they exchanged two men, excepting only the two eldest members of the *grand' chambre* from the exchange.

The *tournelle* and *grand' chambre* therefore contained the thirty-two eldest and longest-serving members of the *parlements*. Young men moving up from the *chambre des enquêtes* had to move first to the *tournelle* before finally being promoted to the *grand' chambre*. If, however, a member of the *chambre des requêtes* had served in that chamber longer than anyone in the *tournelle*, he could be promoted directly to the *grand' chambre*. In other words, mechanisms existed to ensure regular promotion to the highest chamber, either through a system of regular and progressive promotion or through one of exceptional promotion in overcrowded times.

39. These two possibilities symbolized the court's opinion of the accused's innocence or guilt. The *sellette*, a low wooden bench, was reserved for those whom the court believed guilty of the charges against them; the *barre*, at which the accused stood, reflected the court's belief in the probability of their innocence.

40. ADHG B 3814 (10 May 1726).

41. Isambert, *Recueil général des anciennes lois*, Ordinance of Blois (1498), articles 112–114, 11: 365–366; Ordinance of Villers-Cotterets (1539), articles 163–164, 12: 633–634; and the criminal ordinance of 1670, title 19, articles 1–12, 18: 412–413.

42. Daniel Jousse, *Traité de la justice criminelle de France*, 4 vols. (Paris, 1771), 2: 480.

43. Jousse, *Traité de la justice criminelle*, 2: 483–84.

44. Jousse, *Traité de la justice criminelle*, 2: 492.

45. ADHG MS 46, "Procès-verbal de la conférence tenue entre les commissaires du Roi et les commissaires du Parlement, députés pour l'examen des articles de l'ordonnance de 1670, sur la procédure et instruction criminelle." Published editions include *Procès-verbal de la conférence tenue entre les commissaires du Roi et les commissaires du Parlement, députés pour l'examen des articles de l'ordonnance de 1670, sur la procédure et instruction criminelle* (Paris, 1757). See also Jousse, *Traité de la justice criminelle*, 2: 161.

46. On proof in criminal cases, see Andrews, *Law, Magistracy, and Crime*, 441–73, 579–83; Esmein, *Continental Criminal Procedure*, 251–71, 617–31; Langbein, *Torture and the Law of Proof*, chapters 1 and 3; Shennan, *The Parlement of Paris*, 69.

47. They did so by virtue of a royal edict of December 1554 that required that the *capitouls* execute sentence for cases heard on appeal by the *parlement*. See Raymond A. Mentzer, *Heresy Proceedings in Languedoc, 1500–1560* (Philadelphia: American Philosophical Society, 1984), 63.

48. ADHG B 3814 (10 May 1726).

49. For an analysis of the term *patient* to designate the torture victim, see Castan, *Honnêteté et relations sociales en Languedoc*, 97.

50. See Raymond A. Mentzer, "The Self-Image of the Magistrate in Sixteenth-Century France," *Criminal Justice History* 5 (1984): 23–43.

51. Marion indicates that the *question ordinaire* employed four, and the *question extra-ordinaire*, eight *pintes* (*Dictionnaire des institutions*, 469). Did he mean the modern pint, in which case the total amount of water employed could have been two gallons, or the early modern *pinte*, a measure equal to two liters, in which case the total could have been sixteen liters? On the *pinte*, see Mousnier, *The Organs of State and Society*, 395. Andrews, *Law, Magistracy, and Crime*, 448, implies that the measure was equivalent to the modern pint.

52. See Jousse, *Traité de la justice criminelle*, 2: 488–89; and François Serpillon, *Code criminel, ou Commentaire sur l'ordonnance de 1670*, new ed., 2 vols. (Lyon, 1780).

53. The Paris *parlement* forbade the use of the *estrapade* after 1697. See Robert Anchel, *Crimes et châtiments au XVIIe siècle* (Paris: Perrin, 1933), 121–42; Andrews, *Law, Magistracy, and Crime*, 447–48; and Marion, *Dictionnaire des instituitions*, 469. The survey of methods of torture in the jurisdiction of the *parlement* of Paris prepared by d'Aguesseau in 1729 has been published by Bondois, "La torture dans le ressort du parlement de Paris," 322–37.

54. As noted above, the accused could be tortured more than once only if new evidence was introduced. This was not the case in the trial of Jean Bourdil. Did his judges loosely interpret the law so as to torture him for the full amount of time permissible, ignoring the requirement that torture be performed in a single interrogation? Were they simply in violation of the law? If so, why didn't they continue to torture Bourdil until he said what they wanted to hear?

55. ADHG 51 B 23, "Procès-verbal de Jean Bourdil" (25 May 1726), 289v.

56. ADHG B 3814 (6 June 1726).

57. On the galleys, see Paul Bamford, *Fighting Ships and Prisons: The Mediterranean Galleys of France in the Age of Louis XIV* (Minneapolis: University of Minnesota Press, 1973), particularly 173–99.

58. See ADHG 101 B 159, *dossier* of Jean Bourdil.

Chapter 2

1. As many as 6,000 individuals, or more than 10 percent of the population, were constituted by the *gens de loi* and their families. See Micheline Thoumas-Scapira, "La bourgeoisie toulousaine à la fin du dix-septième siècle," *Annales du Midi* 67 (1955): 314, 319; Berlanstein, *Barristers of Toulouse*, 3; Daniel Roche, *Le siècle des lumières en province: Académies et académiciens provinciaux, 1680–1789*, 2 vols. (Paris: Mouton, 1978), 2: 359, 371; and Schneider, *Public Life in Toulouse*, 29–30.

2. On the influence of the *parlement* elites on the urban life of Toulouse, see Schneider, *Public Life in Toulouse, passim*.

3. For details concerning the *Reddes*, see BMT MS 693, Lacombe, "Traité de l'audience du Parlement de Toulouse" (1654); BMT MS 1789, Resseguier, "Mémoires chronologiques pour servir à l'histoire du parlement de Toulouse" (1732). Only one document produced by the annual visit has survived: see ADHG 51 B 76 (1700).

4. See BMT MS 1564, "Mémoire sur l'état du parlement de Toulouse en l'année 1678" (1678), 33r.

5. On the role of processions in the creation of early modern urban identity, see Darnton, "A Bourgeois Puts His World in Order," in *Great Cat Massacre*, 107–43. On the relative importance of such processions for Toulousain urban identity, see Schneider, *Public Life in Toulouse*, 302–303. For further discussion of Toulousain processional

life, see Henri Bruno Bastard-d'Etang, *Les parlements de France: Essai historique sur leurs usages, leur organisation et leur autorité*, 2 vols. (Paris: Didier, 1857).

6. For details on the calendar and rituals of the Toulousain *parlement*, see Bastard-d'Estang, *Les parlements de France*, 631–32.

7. On legal dress, see W. N. Hargreaves-Mawdsley, *A History of Legal Dress in Europe until the End of the Eighteenth Century* (Oxford: Clarendon Press, 1963), and BMT MS 693, Lacombe, "Traité de l'audience du Parlement de Toulouse" (1654).

8. For the numbers of *officiers* attached to the *parlement*, see Berlanstein, *Barristers of Toulouse*, 2; and Mousnier, *Organs of State and Society*, 308.

9. William Bouwsma suggests that, by virtue of their shared occupational experiences, the role of these *officiers* was "to man the frontiers between the safe and familiar on the one hand, the dangerous and new on the other; between the tolerable and intolerable; between the conventional world and the chaos beyond it." See William Bouwsma, "Lawyers and Early Modern Culture," *American Historical Review* 78 (April 1973): 314. Bouwsma defines the legal profession to include all those who provided legal or quasi-legal services, from judges and lawyers to *procureurs* and notaries.

10. Berlanstein notes that *magistrats, avocats, hussiers, greffiers*, clerks, and law students tended to live not only in the same parishes of Toulouse, but in the same streets, and that coresidence served to further professional loyalties. See Berlanstein, *Barristers of Toulouse*, 29. L. W. B. Brockliss, on the other hand, locates law students within the social world of the university, see *French Higher Education in the Seventeenth and Eighteenth Centuries: A Cultural History* (Oxford: Clarendon Press, 1987), 52.

11. This is the argument advanced in Jonathan Dewald, "'The Perfect Magistrate': *Parlementaires* and Crime in Sixteenth-Century Rouen," *Archive for Reformation History* 67 (1976): 284–300. For more information on the relations between *magistrats* and *avocats*, see Francis Delbèke, *L'action politique et sociale des avocats au XVIIIe siècle* (Paris and Louvain: Librairie Universitaire, 1927), 92–108.

12. In his examination of the *parlement* of Toulouse in the early seventeenth century, William Beik concurs: the lack of an effective police force created a style of rule embedded in ritual, the proclamation of regulations, the serving of warrants, and the staging of processions. See William H. Beik, "Magistrates and Popular Uprisings in France before the Fronde: The Case of Toulouse," *Journal of Modern History* 46 (December 1974): 585–608; and Beik, *Urban Protest in Seventeenth-Century France*, chapters 4 and 5.

13. See William Church, "The Decline of French Jurists as Political Theorists, 1660–1789," *French Historical Studies* 5 (1967): 1–40.

14. William Doyle, *The Parlement of Bordeaux and the End of the Old Regime, 1771–1790* (New York: St. Martin's Press, 1974), 24.

15. Berlanstein, *Barristers of Toulouse*, 5; and Marion, *Dictionnaire des institutions*, 460.

16. Berlanstein, *Barristers of Toulouse*, 8. See also Anne Vincent-Buffault, *The History of Tears: Sensibility and Sentimentality in France*, trans. Teresa Bridgeman (New York: St. Martin's Press, 1991), 32; and Keith P. Luria, "Rituals of Conversion: Catholics and Protestants in Seventeenth-Century Poitou," in *Culture and Identity in Early Modern Europe (1500–1800): Essays in Honor of Natalie Zemon Davis*, ed. Barbara B. Diefendorf and Carla Hesse (Ann Arbor: University of Michigan Press, 1993), 80 n36, on the meaning of tears in the context of witchcraft cases.

17. The information in this paragraph is drawn from Brockliss, *French Higher Educa-*

tion, chapter 2. More information on legal education is contained in Andrews, *Law, Magistracy, and Crime,* 247–49; and Delbèke, *L'action politique et sociale des avocats,* 45–65.

18. Alfred de Curzon states that in the final year of study devoted to French law, there were only five classes a week, half the number estimated by Brockliss. See Alfred de Curzon, "L'énseignement du droit français dans les universités de France aux XVIIe et XVIIIe siècles," *Nouvelle revue historique du droit français et étranger* 44 (1919): 253.

19. De Curzon, "L'énseignement du droit français," 213. Darnton presents evidence that suggests that, despite the educational reforms of 1679, individuals continued to purchase judicial offices without appropriate training, "A Bourgeois Puts His World in Order," in *Great Cat Massacre,* 120.

20. De Curzon, "L'énseignement du droit français," 255.

21. Brockliss cites several eighteenth-century jurists who claimed that legal studies began in earnest upon graduation from legal faculties. He suggests that the failure of the universities to address relevant issues in the law itself provoked much of the hostility of law students, who found their classes "professionally useless." See Brockliss, *French Higher Education,* 65, 70; and de Curzon, "L'énseignement du droit français," 214. Delbèke also notes the disjuncture between legal education and contemporary issues. Delbèke, *L'action politique et sociale des avocats,* 65.

22. Robert Darnton, "Reading, Writing and Publishing," in *The Literary Underground of the Old Regime* (Cambridge, Mass.: Harvard University Press, 1982).

23. Berlanstein, *Barristers of Toulouse,* 96–97, 112. As Jean Meyer points out, however, this large percentage of legal works within jurists' libraries may be due primarily to the small size of these libraries, which averaged 181 titles, or 250 volumes. See Jean Meyer, *La noblesse bretonne au XVIIIe siècle* (Paris: S.E.V.P.E.N., 1966), 1163.

24. Doyle, *Parlement of Bordeaux,* 137.

25. See Pierre Biarnoy de Merville, *Règles pour former un avocat . . . avec un index des livres de jurisprudence les plus nécessaires à un avocat,* new ed. (Paris, 1753) and Armand-Gaston Camus, *Lettre sur la profession d'avocat* (Paris, 1777). The *parlement* also provided such guidance in works like the *Calendrier de la cour de Parlement pour l'année 1749* (Toulouse, 1749), 88–94, listing the law books it considered essential.

26. Georges Louet, *Recueil de plusieurs arrêts notables du parlement de Paris,* 2 vols. (Paris, 1742).

27. ADHG 3 E 12450, undated printed advertisement that begins with "Avis touchant l'impression des Arretistes du Parlement de Toulouse, sous le titre de Grande Bibliotheque de Toulousaine."

28. For example, see Gabriel Cayron, *Stil et forme de proceder, tant en la cour de parlement de Toulouse, et chambre des requêtes d'icelle, qu'en toutes les courtes inférieures du ressort* (Toulouse, 1611), 629–30. For an analysis of the use of the phrase *"demeurant les preuves et indices,"* see chapter 3 below.

29. The case of Martin Guerre is well known to modern scholars thanks to Natalie Zemon Davis's *The Return of Martin Guerre* (Cambridge, Mass.: Harvard University Press, 1983).

30. François Gayot de Pitaval, *Causes célèbres et intéressantes, avec les jugements qui les ont décidées,* 20 vols., new ed. (Paris, 1738), 3: ii: "Qu'on me permette de tirer quelque vanité de ce que je me suis fait lire des gens du grand monde, dont les Dames sont le plus bel ornement. C'est peut-être la premiere fois qu'elles se sont apprivoiseés avec un Livre de Droit, & qu'on a trouvé un Ouvrage du Palais sur leur toilette."

31. F. A. P. Garsault, *Faits des causes célèbres et intéressantes, augmentées de quelques causes* (Amsterdam, 1757), i.

32. On causes célèbres as an eighteenth-century genre, see Jean Sgard, "La littérature des causes célèbres," in *Approches des lumières: Mélanges offerts à Jean Fabre* (Paris: Klincksieck, 1974), 459–70; and Sarah Maza, *Private Lives and Public Affairs: The Causes Célèbres of Prerevolutionary France* (Berkeley and Los Angeles: University of California Press, 1993).

33. François Richer, *Causes célèbres et intéressantes, avec les jugements qui les ont décidées: Rédigées de nouveau par M. Richer, ancien avocat au parlement,* 22 vols. (Amsterdam, 1772–88), 1: iii–vii.

34. In the section that follows, I draw primarily upon twelve seventeenth- and eighteenth-century legal manuals, many of which were found in legal libraries or recommended in guides for lawyers. The majority of them were written by *avocats*. Citations are to the following editions: Gabriel Cayron, *Stil et forme de procéder, tant en la cour de parlement de Toulouse, et chambre des requêtes d'icelle, qu'en toutes les courtes inférieures du ressort* (Toulouse, 1611); Guillaume de Segla, *Histoire tragique et arrests de la cour de parlement de Toulouse* (Paris, 1613); Bernard de la Roche Flavin, *Treze livres des parlements de France* (Bordeaux, 1617); Etienne Pasquier, *Les recherches de la France* (Paris, 1633); Claude Le Brun de la Rochette, *Les procez civil et criminel* (Lyon, 1643); Laurent Bouchel, *La bibliothèque, ou Trésor du droit français,* 3 vols. (Paris, 1671); Pierre Jacques Brillon, *Dictionnaire des arrêsts; ou, Jurisprudence universelle des parlements de France et autres tribunaux,* 6 vols. (Paris, 1727); Guy du Rousseaud de la Combe, *Traité des matières criminelles suivant l'ordonnance de 1670* (Paris, 1740); Antoine Despeisses, *Oeuvres de M. Antoine d'Espeisse* (Lyon, 1750); Claude-Joseph de Ferrière, *Dictionnaire de droit et de pratique,* 2 vols. (Paris, 1758); Daniel Jousse, *Traité de la justice criminelle de France,* 4 vols. (Paris, 1771); and François Serpillon, *Code criminel, ou commentaire sur l'ordonnance de 1670,* 2 vols., new ed. (Lyon, 1784).

35. La Roche Flavin, *Treze livres,* 535–36.

36. La Roche Flavin, *Treze livres,* 851: "Le Chirurgien, qui a pitié, et ne tranche pas, rend la playe incurable; le pere indulgent rend le fils incorrigible: aussi le juge misericordieux nourrit & accroist les vices, & trahit les loix & la Majesté de la justice."

37. See, for example, Jousse, *Traité de la justice criminelle,* 2: 270–71:

The first thing that judges must consider is the quality of the accused whom they interrogate. For example, if the accused is a common man, or if he is a respectable person by rank or by birth. For those who have some dignity, who are elevated above others, must be interrogated with more consideration and circumspection.

Likewise, if the accused seems firm and bold, he must be interrogated differently than one who is timid and trembling. To those who appear bold, the judge must appear severe; whereas with the others, he must employ soft and ingratiating words in order to encourage them to tell the truth.

For the same reason, the judge must behave differently with regards to an accused who is known to be a learned man, or a distinguished wit, than with regard to an unrefined and unenlightened man; and he will observe the same distinction between a silent and severe accused, and one who is simple and without disguise. For if the accused is a man of wit and learning, the judge must examine him with much care, employing convincing arguments drawn from the court proceedings. If he is silent and stubborn, the judge must wear him out with a great number of questions, taking his own answers and turning them around, and interrogating him even about those circumstances of the crime that seem inessential, for example, if at the time that the crime was committed the sky was clear or light, what clothes he was wearing that day, and other comparable things that will reveal the good or bad faith of the accused according to his responses. But if the accused is simple and coarse, the judge will interrogate him simply and consistently on all the facts.

38. On the self-control required of the judge, Jousse, *Traité de la justice criminelle*, 2: 280, notes: "The judge must also take care not to encourage the accused who is awaiting torture to confess by threats or cajoles." Note that the nouns employed here—"menaces" and "caresses"—do not clearly distinguish between the physical and the metaphorical. It is judicial physical control, or the lack thereof, that most concerns Jousse, *Traité de la justice criminelle*, 2: 493: "But one thing that judges must avoid above all, that would be unworthy of their nature: to add to the torments of the accused with their own hands, by lending their assistance to the torturer, or in any other way." Le Brun de la Rochette, *Les procez civil et criminel*, 2: 163, concurs that the judge must not threaten the accused.

39. Bouchel, *La bibliothèque*, 173. Bouchel continues: "The judge must have no regard or consideration for his cries, tears, sighs, moans, and pains: and all this with such moderation and temperance that the body of the *patient* is not stricken, strained, injured, or too crippled."

40. Despeisses, *Oeuvres*, 711.

41. Jousse, *Traité de la justice criminelle*, 2: 272.

42. Le Brun de la Rochette, *Les procez civil et criminel*, 2: 163: "But with a purely Christian soul, he must pacifically and without emotion, which alters the tranquility of a reasoned judgment, cause the torment to continue, until he recognizes that the questionee can no longer endure more." It is also the case that, in theory, judges were themselves liable for criminal prosecution leading to capital sentences if the accused died under torture. See Jousse, *Traité de la justice criminelle*, 2: 493.

43. Jousse, *Traité de la justice criminelle*, 2: 278.

44. Bornier, *Conférences*, 171.

45. On gesture as a natural language, see John Knowlson, "The Idea of Gesture as a Universal Language in the Seventeenth and Eighteenth Centuries," *Journal of the History of Ideas* 26 (1965): 495–508. Nicholas Mirzoeff connects the search for a universal language, the development of sign, and neo-classicalism in "Body Talk: Deafness, Sign and Visual Language in the Ancien Régime," *Eighteenth-Century Studies* 25 (summer 1992): 561–85. It is important to note that even "natural" gestures are socially constructed: most Americans today interpret pallor not as a sign of guilt but as a sign of fear but are as convinced as were the French that this telling gesture arises spontaneously.

46. See Jousse, *Traité de la justice criminelle*, 3: 552–53.

47. John Evelyn, *The Diary of John Evelyn*, 6 vols., ed. E. S. de Beer (Oxford: Clarendon Press, 1955), 3: 28. Evelyn's observation is particularly interesting because it reveals a cultural reliance on bodily evidence in England as well as in France, despite important differences between the Anglo-American and continental legal traditions, particularly with reference to the nature of evidence. On evidence in the Anglo-American tradition, see Barbara J. Shapiro, *Probability and Certainty in Seventeenth-Century England: A Study of the Relationships between Natural Science, Religion, History, Law and Literature* (Princeton, N.J.: Princeton University Press, 1983) and *Beyond Rea-*

sonable Doubt and Probable Cause: Historical Perspectives on the Anglo-American Law of Evidence (Berkeley and Los Angeles: University of California Press, 1991).

48. On the Italian reliance on gesture as evidence, see Carlo Ginzburg, "The Inquisitor as Anthropologist," in *Clues, Myths and the Historical Method*, trans. John and Anne C. Tedeschi (Baltimore, Md.: Johns Hopkins University Press, 1989), 160; and Thomas V. and Elizabeth S. Cohen, *Words and Deeds in Renaissance Rome: Trials before the Papal Magistrates* (Toronto: University of Toronto Press, 1993), 17.

49. La Roche Flavin, *Arrests notables du parlement de Toulouse*, 573. Anecdotal evidence indicates that this procedure was in fact employed at least as late as the 1550s. In his journal, Felix Platter mentions the trial of a servant for the murder of his master, a canon: "Although buried three years, the canon was disinterred, so that the murderer could be confronted with his victim. However, there were none of the signs they expected to see on such an occasion—as for example the opening of the wound and the gushing forth of blood; although it should be added that the corpse was very wasted." *Beloved Son Felix: The Journal of Felix Platter, a Medical Student in Montpellier in the Sixteenth Century*, trans. Seán Jennett (London: Frederick Muller Ltd., 1961), 127.

50. Le Brun de la Rochette, *Les procez civil et criminel*, 2: 118; see also 2: 156.

51. See Bornier, *Conférences*, 164; Brillon, *Dictionnaire des arrêsts*, 3: 607; and Despeisses, *Oeuvres*, 710. Whether this method was actually employed by the *parlement* of Toulouse is not apparent from my evidence.

Blood would seem to be the linguistic medium of the soul. Although the belief that the dead can name their murderers by bleeding in their presence was eventually discredited, the dead continue to indicate the number of masses they require by leaving bloody handprints on walls or drops of blood on linen. See Arnold van Gennep, *Manuel de folklore français contemporain*, 7 vols. (Paris: Picard, 1946), 2: 793. Barbara Duden finds a similar connection of the soul to the blood in eighteenth-century Germany: "Whatever was said metaphorically and physiologically about the blood's efforts toward expulsion spoke implicitly also of the soul, which was linked to the blood and mediated by it. . . . The language of the humors was the language of the soul," in *The Woman beneath the Skin*, 129. For an analysis of the way in which blood encoded gender, see Gail Kern Paster, *The Body Embarrassed: Drama and the Disciplines of Shame in Early Modern England* (Ithaca, N.Y.: Cornell University Press, 1993), especially chapter 2.

52. On the rise of forensic medicine in France in the eighteenth century, see McManners, *Death and the Enlightenment*, 24–58. On the meanings of the corpse in late-eighteenth- and early-nineteenth-century Britain, see Ruth Richardson, *Death, Dissection and the Destitute* (New York: Penguin Books, 1988), 3–74. On the development of the genre of the autopsy report, see Thomas Laqueur, "Bodies, Details, and the Humanitarian Narrative," in *The New Cultural History*, ed. Lynn Hunt (Berkeley: University of California Press, 1989), 176–204.

53. Ferriere, *Dictionnaire de droit et de pratique*, 206, notes: "It is the duty of the judge to order the surgeons to discover if [the deceased] died by accident, or if he killed himself with arms, or otherwise; if he was pushed or poisoned, or if he was caused to die in any manner whatsoever." See also Le Brun de la Rochette, *Les procez civil et criminel*, 2: 110.

54. While doctors looked for the traces of the gestures of assailants on the bodies of victims, judges examined the accused directly for involuntary gestures that might betray them. Thus, Brillon cites the example of a judge who tricks an accused into revealing himself through an involuntary gesture: "A magistrate should not employ trickery; but

he can use shrewdness to discover the author of a crime. Here are some examples. A man had been killed by a pistol shot fired by a left-handed person; in order to discover if the accused was left-handed, the judge let fall his glove; the accused immediately picked it up with his left hand." See Brillon, *Dictionnaire des arrêsts*, 5: 508.

55. On the development of the autopsy report, see Laqueur, "Bodies, Details, and the Humanitarian Narrative," 176–204. On mesmerism, see Robert Darnton, *Mesmerism and the End of the Enlightenment in France* (Cambridge, Mass.: Harvard University Press, 1968).

56. Cayron, *Stil et forme de procéder*, 630.

57. Bouchel, *La bibliothèque*, 2: 174.

58. Bornier, *Conférences*, 174.

59. Despeisses, *Oeuvres*, 713: "One can reapply to the *question* the accused who has confessed nothing, if there is a suspicion that during the first [interrogation under] torture he had taken some potion or eaten some drugs in order not to feel the pains of the *question*. . . . The accused is thus rendered suspect when he employs artifices in order not to be constrained to tell the truth. You can tell that there was a charm when the torture victim was unaware of the torment: some have said that the accused who, before the *question*, has swallowed soap mixed with water will not feel the pains of the *question*."

60. Serpillon, *Code criminel*, 188.

61. Despeisses, *Oeuvres*, 2: 712.

62. McManners likewise finds that pain was regarded as "a sort of truth drug." See McManners, *Death and the Enlightenment*, 378.

63. Segla, *Histoire tragique*, 64; Gayot de Pitaval, *Causes célèbres et intéressantes*, 18: 315–16; Despeisses, *Oeuvres*, 713; Serpillon, *Code criminel*, 188.

64. Satan was believed to possess the power to protect his servants from pain; indeed, the insensible witch's mark was one of the hallmarks of the demonic pact. See Joseph Klaits, *Servants of Satan: The Age of the Witch Hunts* (Bloomington: Indiana University Press, 1985), 56, 156. Klaits also presents evidence that suggests that accused witches may have expected divine protection from pain as proof of their innocence, protection that, when not forthcoming, convinced them of their own guilt. In the context of the witch trials, then, insensibility to pain acquired multiple meanings. In my own examinations of legal manuals, however, I find no comparable belief that the innocent can expect divine nor the guilty satanic protection from pain; only magical charms can stand in the way of pain.

65. See, for example, Brillon, *Dictionnaire des arrêsts*, 5: 640–41.

66. Pasquier, *Les recherches de la France*, 1020.

67. Segla, *Histoire tragique*, 177.

68. Bornier, *Conférences*, 173.

69. On these various definitions of ritual, see Max Gluckman, *Custom and Conflict in Africa* (Oxford: Basil Blackwell, 1966); Gilbert Lewis, *Day of Shining Red: An Essay on Understanding Ritual* (Cambridge: Cambridge University Press, 1980); and Victor Turner, *The Ritual Process: Structure and Anti-Structure* (Ithaca, N.Y.: Cornell University Press, 1977). On torture as a ritual, see Asad, "Notes on Body Pain and Truth."

70. See, for example, Jousse, *Traité de la justice criminelle*, 474.

71. Louis XVI, *Déclaration du roi concernant la procédure criminelle* (Auch: 1788), 5.

Chapter 3

1. All of these interrogations can be found in ADHG 51 B 21–27, "Procès-verbaux d'exécution et de torture, 1633–1788."

2. The interrogation notes that "the said Armans was condemned to be broken alive after being applied to the *question préalable*, and on appeal to the *parlement*, sentence was rendered today, which in confirming the said sentence orders that the said execution will take place outside the St. Etienne gate, first having made an *amende honorable*, then his dead body will be exposed in the *fourches patibulaires*." ADHG 51 B 26, "Procès-verbal d'Armans Grassie" (30 July 1771), 269r.

3. ADHG B 3857 (30 July 1771).

4. Pinson-Ramin finds that sentences to torture represent 13 percent of *grand criminel* cases in the *parlement* of Brittany. See Pinson-Ramin, "La torture judiciaire en Bretagne," 554. She is working with a total of 272 sentences to torture.

5. See, for example, the assessment of the place of torture in the early modern legal system in Langbein, *Torture and the Law of Proof,* especially chapter 1.

6. Another two sentences to the *question préalable* were ordered and executed against Paul Bila (1780) and Jean Planes (1785), after the *question préparatoire* had been outlawed. I have not included these two cases in the following calculations, because the different dates of abolition of the two forms of the *question*—1780 for the *question préparatoire* and 1788 for the *question préalable*—create an asymmetry in comparisons. See also Mentzer, *Heresy Proceedings in Languedoc*, 98. Mentzer finds seventeen persons sentenced to the *question préparatoire* and eleven persons sentenced to the *question préalable* in cases of heresy in Toulouse from 1543 to 1560, again indicative of the decline in the use of torture in the seventeenth and eighteenth centuries.

7. Compare these statistics with those offered by Pinson-Ramin, "La torture judiciaire en Bretagne," 556. She estimates an annual use of three sentences to the *question préparatoire* and twenty-one sentences to the *question préalable*. My estimate of one case per year during the period 1600–1780 is in all probability quite low. Pinson-Ramin also notes a dramatic decline in the use of torture during the seventeenth century: during the period 1600–1650, she proposes an annual mean of 4.8 sentences to the *question préparatoire* and 27.6 sentences to the *question préalable*, as opposed to the period 1651–1700, with an annual mean of 0.72 sentences to the *question préparatoire* and 12.7 sentences to the *question préalable*.

8. See Pinson-Ramin, "La torture judiciaire en Bretagne," 55.

9. This is, of course, the theory advanced by Langbein, *Torture and the Law of Proof.*

10. Pinson-Ramin, "La torture judiciaire en Bretagne," 55.

11. On the complex relationship among crown, *parlement*, and *capitoulat*, see Robert A. Schneider, "Crown and Capitoulat: Municipal Government in Toulouse, 1500–1789," in *Cities and Social Change in Early Modern France*, ed. Philip Benedict (London: Unwin Hyman, 1991), 195–220. The implications of adding a sentence of torture varied widely with the circumstances of the case. From the perspective of the accused, the worst possible outcome of adding a sentence to torture was that in a case in which the lower court had sentenced the accused to a noncapital sentence, the *parlement* demanded both a death sentence and the *question préalable:* this actually occurred in four cases. In eight cases, the *question préalable* was simply added to an extant death sentence, although in three of these eight cases, a *retentum* was also added to the sentence specifying that the *question* be presented only. On two occasions, the *parlement* employed this right of review to strike down capital sentences and to require the *question préparatoire* in

their place before reaching a judgment. Pinson-Ramin finds that the *parlement* of Brittany confirmed lower court sentences to the *question préparatoire* in 40 percent of cases, to the *question préalable* in 80 percent of cases; and that it added a sentence of *question préparatoire* to 47 percent of cases on appeal, the vast majority of which replaced death sentences, and which she suggests must be understood as acts of clemency, in that they gave the accused a chance of escaping capital punishment, "La torture judiciaire en Bretagne," 558–59.

12. See Jousse, *Traité de la justice criminelle,* 2: 487: "It is ordered by a *retentum* which is placed at the bottom of the sentence, and which is not read to the accused; it should appear only in sentences to the *question préparatoire,* and never in sentences to the *question préalable.*"

13. Almost 75 percent of the victims in the sample group were men, as were 84 percent of the victims in the interrogation group. It is impossible to discern from this evidence, however, whether men were sentenced to or subject to torture more frequently than women, as this evidence does not reflect the frequency with which men and women were charged with criminal offenses. Personal information about the accused, including age, marital status, and occupation, was generally omitted from sentences and is, therefore, available primarily in those cases in which interrogations are extant. In these latter cases, the sixty-five men sentenced to torture were on average 36.68 years old, and the twelve women, 42.28 years old. The ages of fifty men and seven women are included in their respective interrogations. The men ranged in age from 18 to 66; the women, from 23 to 64. No occupations were given for the women, but the men form a remarkably diverse group, including professionals, craftsmen, merchants, rural agricultural workers, and military men. Forty men stated their occupations as follows: two notaries; one surgeon; two smiths; one goldsmith; one locksmith; two carpenters; two weavers; one silk winder; two tailors; one cloth merchant; one grain dealer; one shepherd; one cowherd; one peasant; two sharecroppers; fourteen laborers; one soldier; one sailor; one hunter; one butcher's apprentice; and one man who declared that he had no occupation. A proportionally greater number of women than men were widowed: 41.6 percent of the women for whom interrogations are extant versus 4.6 percent of these men. Single women were sentenced to torture more often than married women (25 percent of single women versus 16 percent of married women) whereas married men were sentenced more often.

14. In an early and influential article, François Billaçois proposed using the *arrêts* of the *parlements* to write the social history of crime and punishment. See François Billaçois, "Pour une enquête sur la criminalité dans la France d'ancien régime," *Annales Economie, Sociétés, Civilizations* 22 (March–April 1967): 340–49. His proposal was intended to expand the field of data available to scholars, to permit the study of criminal activity rather than of criminal legislation, of criminals rather than prosecutors. But the very nature of these documents, their composition by officials of the court, frustrates this goal, as the criminal court sentences continue to yield less information about criminal activity per se than they do about definitions of crime.

15. The following represents a complete list of the kinds of information that might be included in sentences: (1) the present status of the case: the day and date of the hearing; the location of the hearing; whether it was a special session; and which judges were hearing the case; (2) the legal history of the case: the court of first instance, the date and specifics of its sentence; the name, marital status, occupation, residence and, if a public official, office of the person bringing suit; (3) information concerning the

accused: his or her name, nickname, marital status or other familial relationships, occupation, birthplace, residence; the prison in which he or she was being held, and whether he or she was heard on the *sellette* or behind the *barre;* (4) information concerning the crime: the nature of the crime; the name of the victim and his or her relation to the accused, where relevant; (5) the outcome of the case: the sentence per se, and any accompanying *retentum;* which officials were to perform and oversee the sentence; and the status of the court costs.

16. Although this chapter as a whole includes the sentences of 162 individuals, this section draws on the sentences of only 151 individuals. The sentences of Paul Bila (1780) and Jean Planes (1785) are excluded for reasons discussed above (see note 5). In nine other cases for which interrogations are extant, the sentences could not be located. Information drawn from these nine interrogations is examined elsewhere in this chapter.

17. See Mentzer, *Heresy Proceedings in Languedoc,* 47 n13.

18. The remaining 2 percent of sentences are incomplete. In these cases, only the second half of the sentence is extant. Information concerning the accused was located in the first half of the sentence.

19. Pinson-Ramin, "La torture judiciaire en Bretagne," 561, finds the same phenomenon in Brittany from the 1610s.

20. On the judicial ordeal see Asad, "Notes on Body Pain and Truth"; Robert Bartlett, *Trial by Fire and Water: The Medieval Judicial Ordeal* (Oxford: Clarendon Press, 1986), chapters 1–5; Margaret H. Kerr, Richard D. Forsyth, and Michael J. Plyley, "Cold Water and Hot Iron: Trial by Ordeal in England," *Journal of Interdisciplinary History* 22, no. 4 (spring 1992): 573–95; and Esther Cohen, *The Crossroads of Justice: Law and Culture in Late Medieval France* (Leiden: E. J. Brill, 1993), especially chapter 4.

21. ADHG 51 B 23, "Procès-verbal de Jean Bourdil" (25 May 1726), 284r.

22. ADHG 51 B 21, "Procès-verbal de Marie Lavaur" (9 August 1685), 274r.

23. ADHG 51 B 21, "Procès-verbal de Jeanne Bellegarde" (8 May 1686), 287v.

24. ADHG 51 B 21, "Procès-verbal de Charles Quesnel" (12 April 1692), 259r.

25. ADHG 51 B 23, "Procès-verbal de Gabriel Larrivere" (15 April 1717), 163v. Robin Briggs, "Witchcraft and the Community in France and French-Speaking Europe," in *Communities of Belief: Cultural and Social Tension in Early Modern France* (Oxford: Clarendon Press, 1989), 7–8, finds comparable admonitions in the late sixteenth century.

26. ADHG 51 B 23, "Procès-verbal de Gabrielle Massotte" (27 January 1724), 260r, 260v.

27. Cohen, *Crossroads of Justice,* 184. See Andrews, *Law, Magistracy, and Crime,* 452–57.

28. Scarry, *The Body in Pain,* part 1. This argument is echoed by Kate Millett, *The Politics of Cruelty* (New York: W. W. Norton, 1994). Millett employs memoirs, novels, and films to describe a variety of state-sponsored practices, among them torture, illegal detention, and genocide, practices that she conflates under the rubric of a "politics of cruelty." Her narrative stresses the passivity of the victim of torture, for example, 31–32: "Volition is gone entirely, will is useless. You are a creature now, their creature. . . . You will do exactly as they say; not only will you have no option to do otherwise, you will do it willingly, trembling, hoping to appease, propitiate, avoid further hurt and humiliation. Cowed animal that you are, you appreciate that defiance is useless, pride something you must save for yourself, conscious of it leaking away before the reality of your

predicament as your comprehension of it builds moment to moment." Laura Tanner, *Intimate Violence: Reading Rape and Torture in Twentieth-Century Fiction* (Bloomington: Indiana University Press, 1994), is more concerned with representations of violence than with its perpetration.

29. Jean Améry, *At the Mind's Limits* (Bloomington: Indiana University Press, 1980), 37, notes the unpredictability of who does and does not talk, citing the heroism of those who remain silent.

30. All of these forms of treatment are detailed by Lena Constante, *The Silent Escape* (Berkeley: University of California Press, 1995).

31. For an exposition of the meaning of modern torture see Darius M. Rejali, *Torture and Modernity: Self, Society, and State in Modern Iran* (Boulder, Colo.: Westview Press, 1994).

32. Constante speaks directly to the question in her memoir:

In this dungeon of a cell for unending hours I became aware of my duality. I was two. For I was here and I saw myself here. I was two. For I couldn't go through this bolted door and yet I could be elsewhere. The interrogator had ordered me to reflect and remember what I feigned—he said—not to know. On the contrary, I had to forget, forget everything, starting with him. No longer would I hear the click of the judas. Nor see the guard's eye. Nor "realize" the cold. Nor feel the hunger. I had to escape. Flee. Unable to get to the other side of the wall, escape from myself. To leave this body, now only a torment, behind. This miserable, hungry flesh. Repudiate my body's "me." No longer endure its pain. Nor tremble with its fear. My body could only be here. Me, I could be elsewhere. My body didn't have space to move its aching feet. But, *I* would grow wings. The wings of a bird. The wings of the wind. The wings of a star. And I would get away.

The Silent Escape, 9. And, "As the basis of my existence I had taken pride in the mind and had contempt for the body. I concentrated all my will on this lone goal. Respect for, in a person of flesh, what is least fleshly," 159.

33. Améry, *At the Mind's Limits*, 33, 40.

34. The four cases in question are those of François Grion (ADHG B 3619 [22, 30 January 1630]); Paul Norat and François Espry (ADHG B 3679 [5, 22 July 1650]); Louis Sudré and Jean Delmar (ADHG B 3761 [10 June 1682] and ADHG B 3762 [4 July 1682]); and Mathieu LaPlace, François Martel, and Arnaud Carguecol (ADHG B 3815 [23 August 1727 and 4 September 1727]). Grion was sentenced first to the *question préparatoire* and then to the *question préalable*. Note that in several cases, the *question* allowed the *parlement* to confirm the unspecified sentence of the court of first instance. In the case of Simone Gilibert (ADHG B 3785 [28 March and 3 December 1697]), for example, the court ordered the *question préparatoire* while her codefendants awaited the report of the interrogation. Once the report was returned, her original unspecified sentence was confirmed and one of her codefendants in turn sentenced to the *question préparatoire*, suggesting that she may have originally been sentenced to death. Here again, death sentences may be masked by the language of the court. In most of the remaining cases, the accused were sentenced to banishment or the galleys, but in at least two cases, codefendants were themselves sentenced to the *question*.

35. This figure should, of course, be employed with great caution, given the disproportionate number of definitive sentences relative to interlocutory ones—a problem inherent in sampling the registers of the *parlement*. In the remaining cases, individuals

were sentenced to terms in the galleys or terms of banishment. It should also be noted that only two definitive sentences following interlocutory sentences to the *question pré-paratoire* prior to 1650 could be found. Determining "confession" in cases of the *question préalable* is yet more complex as there is rarely a simple demonstration from the sentences that meaningful information was derived in the course of the interrogation. I can point to only one case with confidence, that of Claire Reynaud and Pierre Coulet, who were accused of poisoning her husband in 1778. Reynaud was sentenced to the *question préalable*, and after the report of her interrogation, Coulet was sentenced to death by burning.

36. For the Paris *parlement*, Soman, *Sorcellerie et justice criminelle*, 45–46; for the Chatêlet, Andrews, *Law, Magistracy, and Crime*, 455, 462; for seventeenth-century Brittany, Pinson-Ramet, "La torture judiciaire en Bretagne," 559; for eighteenth-century Brittany, Mer, "La procèdure criminelle," 28; and for Roussillon, Durand, "Arbitraire de juge et le droit de la torture," 148. Ulrich, "La répression en Bourgogne," 414, offers a confession rate of 32.7 percent in cases of the *question préalable*. Further comparisons are offered in the appendix.

37. Andrews, *Law, Magistracy, and Crime*, 448, 451, 455, 457; Pinson-Ramin, "La torture judiciaire en Bretagne," 564. In some celebrated cases, the excessive and illegal violence of interrogators became public knowledge. Richer, *Causes célèbres et intéressantes*, 4: 280–82, reporting the case of Urbain Grandier, sentenced to the *question des brodequins*, noted that he fainted several times during his interrogation and that his legs were so badly crushed that the marrow of his bones was visible. Evans, *Rituals of Retribution*, 111, also notes the tendency of historians to assert that people of the early modern period suffered pain less than do people of the modern moment.

38. Andrews, *Law, Magistracy, and Crime*, 463. This sensitive observation needs to be considered along with two pieces of conflicting evidence: the first, from Delcambre, "The Psychology of Lorraine Witchcraft Suspects," 97, and Klaits, *Servants of Satan*, 56, 156, which suggests that in some circumstances, individuals subject to torture may have come to believe their own confessions; and the second, also from Klaits, *Servants of Satan*, 128–31, which suggests that in some circumstances, individuals subject to torture disbelieved their own confessions. And if individuals believed in their innocence, did they undergo torture in a trancelike state that minimized pain and injury? This is one suggestion made as regards the judicial ordeal by Kerr et al., "Cold Water and Hot Iron," 590, 592.

39. Andrews, *Law, Magistracy, and Crime*, 449, 450–51, 452; Pinson-Ramin, "La torture judiciaire en Bretagne," 564. Andrews, *Law, Magistracy, and Crime*, 446, also states, "Denial of guilt under torture or retraction of confession immediately after torture made the death penalty inapplicable, whether the *question* was administered with or without reserve of evidence." If the legal rules governing the use of torture were as well known as he suggests elsewhere, and if torture was not regarded as a ritual genuinely connecting pain, truth, and body, surely individuals who suffered the *question* would have routinely retracted their confessions. In France, the causes célèbres published in the eighteenth century provided the most detailed accounts of torture, but they did not provide thoroughgoing exegesis of procedural rules. Evans, *Rituals of Retribution*, 159–67, provides compelling evidence that the people living in the German lands had sophisticated understandings of legal procedures.

40. ADHG 51 B 23, "Procès-verbal de Jean Bourdil" (25 May 1726), 284v.

41. These categories of openness and closedness are drawn from material in Esther

N. Goody, "Towards a Theory of Questions," in *Questions and Politeness: Strategies in Social Interaction* (Cambridge: Cambridge University Press, 1978), 17–43.

42. ADHG 51 B 23, "Procès-verbal de Jean Bourdil" (25 May 1726), 284v.

43. ADHG 51 B 23, "Procès-verbal de Jean Bourdil" (27 May 1726), 293r, 293v.

44. ADHG 51 B 23, "Procès-verbal de Jean Bourdil" (25 May 1726), 289r.

45. ADHG 51 B 21, "Procès-verbal de Vital Saltel" (22 September 1684), 268v.

46. ADHG 51 B 21, "Procès-verbal de Vital Saltel" (22 September 1684), 268v; ADHG 51 B 23, "Procès-verbal de François Allemand" (28 June 1710), 118r; and ADHG 51 B 24, "Procès-verbal de Georges Lafaille" (3 April 1751), 39v.

47. For analyses of execution as a public ritual of punishment, see Foucault, *Discipline and Punish;* and Pieter Spierenburg, *The Spectacle of Suffering: Executions and the Evolution of Repression from a Preindustrial Metropolis to the European Experience* (Cambridge: Cambridge University Press, 1984).

48. On the distinction between secrecy and privacy, see Sissela Bok, *Secrets: On the Ethics of Concealment and Revelation* (New York: Vintage Books, 1983).

49. What is curious about this arrangement in regards to the use of torture is that the *capitouls* were among the only individuals in the realm who were themselves exempt from torture. Legal manuals noted that this special exemption was one of the honors attendant upon that office. The *parlementaires,* themselves subject to torture under the appropriate conditions, thus required the participation in interrogations of those officials least likely to have any empathy for the accused. See Marion, *Dictionnaire des institutions,* 71.

50. There were seventeen people present at the interrogation of Jean Tacquie. See ADHG 51 B 22, "Procès-verbal de Jean Tacquie" (24 November 1699).

51. ADHG 51 B 23, "Procès-verbal de Jean Bourdil" (25 May 1726), 289r.

52. ADHG 51 B 21, "Procès-verbal de Vital Saltel" (22 September 1684), 268v.

53. ADHG 51 B 22, "Procès-verbal d'Anne Verches" (6 June 1696), 225v; ADHG 51 B 23, "Procès-verbal de François Allemand" (28 June 1710), 118r.

54. ADHG 51 B 27, "Procès-verbal de Blaise Theron" (24 March 1774), 219r.

55. See, for example, the illustrations in Jean Milles de Souvigny, *Pratique criminelle,* trans. Arlette Lebigre (1541; reprint, Moulins: Les Marmousets, 1983), and reproduced in this book, and the illustration of the torture of Mme. de Brinvilliers by Brouet, reprinted in Held, *Inquisition,* 57.

56. See Cayron, *Stil et forme de procéder,* 630; Bouchel, *La bibliothèque,* 2: 174; Bornier, *Conférences,* 174; Despeisses, *Oeuvres,* 713; Serpillon, *Code criminel,* 188. For a contemporary critique of this practice, see Augustin Nicolas, *Si la torture est un moyen seur à vérifier les crimes secrets: Dissertation morale et juridique* (1682; reprint, Marseilles: Laffitte, 1982), 145. Nicolas objects to stripping and searching the accused because it offends sexual propriety, and is the only source to suggest that defendants were subject to full body searches: "It is astonishing that Bodin, who had such zeal for his cabal, and so many clerics who profess modesty and a horror of blood and cruelty, exempt themselves from humanity in the name of magic unto violating the laws of modesty and decency in a sex that can have nothing more dear, and [deliver] them into the hands, the probes and the razors of the executioners unto the most tender and the most secret places of that sex, which is a kind of torment that they don't consider, and which alone is capable of driving many women and girls to false confessions in order to redeem themselves from this infamous spectacle and these vile touchings."

57. See, for example, Bouchel, *La bibliothèque*, 2: 174; Bornier, *Conférences*, 174; Despeisses, *Oeuvres*, 713; Segla, *Histoire tragique*, 64.

58. For an anthropological analysis of the cultural meanings of human hair, see C. R. Hallpike, "Social Hair," *Man* 4 (1969): 259–61.

59. See James R. Farr, "The Pure and Disciplined Body: Hierarchy, Morality, and Symbolism in France during the Catholic Reformation," *Journal of Interdisciplinary History* 21 (winter 1991): 391–414.

60. Tobias Smollett, *Travels through France and Italy* (1766; reprint, New York: Praeger, 1970), 80.

61. Segla, *Histoire tragique*, 64.

62. Smollett, *Travels*, 216–17.

63. "ESTRAPADE . . . the punishment that is given to a soldier, by raising him the height of a long piece of wood, his hands tied behind his back with a rope that supports the whole weight of his body, and letting him rudely fall to two or three feet from the ground." Académie Française, *Dictionnaire de l'Académie Française*, 2 vols., 3d ed. (Paris, 1740), 1: 625.

64. Customary differences in the practice of torture prescribed different forms of torture for men and women in different *parlements*. Although the *question d'eau* was applied only to men in Toulouse, it was applied to both men and women in Paris.

65. Evelyn, *Diary*, 3: 28–29.

66. Evelyn, *Diary*, 3: 29.

67. ADHG 51 B 22, "Procès-verbal de Jean Julien Boucage" (17 September 1695), 209v.

68. ADHG 51 B 23, "Procès-verbal de Gabriel Larrivere" (15 April 1717), 169v; ADHG 51 B 22, "Procès-verbal de Jacques Tacquie" (25 November 1699), 271v.

69. In fact, two women had been sentenced recently to torture. In 1770, Marie Dejean was sentenced by the court of first instance to the *question préparatoire* for poisoning her husband and her mother. In 1767, Françoise Guichon was sentenced by the court of first instance to the *question préparatoire*, also in a case of poisoning. In each of these cases, the *parlement* of Toulouse overturned the sentence to torture, deeming that there was adequate evidence to sentence each woman to death. The most recent instance of a woman's sentence to torture being sustained by the *parlement* seems to have occurred in 1740, thirty-eight years before Claire Reynaud's case. Gabrielle Bounelaybac, accused of murdering her husband, received an interlocutory sentence to the *question préparatoire*. No *retentum* was appended to the sentence. The interrogation, however, is not extant; nor could the definitive sentence be located. Therefore, the most recent case located in which a woman was certainly tortured occurred in 1724, when Gabrielle Massotte and her daughter-in-law Louise Bonaille were sentenced to the *question préparatoire* in the investigation of the murder of Massotte's sister. Neither woman confessed to the murder. Both were banished, Massotte from the realm in perpetuity, Bonaille from the *sénéchaussée* of Nîmes for five years. See ADHG B 3812 (17 January, 26 February 1724), and ADHG 51 B 23 (27, 29 January 1724), 260–71.

70. BMT MS 706, Barthès, "Les heures perdues de Pierre Barthès," (March 1778), 7: 147–48.

71. For the suggestion that such practices sought to preserve sexual modesty, see Gilbert Floutard and Marc Miguet, *La justice à Toulouse au XVIIIème siècle* (Toulouse: Service d'Action Culturelle et Educative, 1986), chapter 8. Cohen, *Crossroads of Justice*,

chapter 10, concurs that judicial rituals were unconcerned with the preservation of modesty and honor, but rather deliberately sought to shame the accused, and makes special note of the shamefulness of nakedness. In sixteenth-century Italy, public nudity was construed as an assault on one's honor. See Cohen and Cohen, *Words and Deeds in Renaissance Rome,* 8–12.

72. On the one-sex body, see Thomas Laqueur, *Making Sex: The Body and Sex from the Greeks to Freud* (Cambridge: Harvard University Press, 1990).

73. ADHG 51 B 23, "Procès-verbal de Jean Bourdil" (25 May 1726), 289v.

74. ADHG 51 B 21, "Procès-verbal de Pierre Faure" (12 February 1633), 2r.

75. ADHG 51 B 23, "Procès-verbal de Gabriel Larrivere" (15 April 1717), 169v.

76. ADHG 51 B 21, "Procès-verbal de Jean Barbet" (28 June 1662), 74v. In some early interrogations, interrogators are named, but this is infrequently the case.

77. ADHG 51 B 21, "Procès-verbal de Jean Barbet" (28 June 1662), 75v.

78. ADHG 51 B 21, "Procès-verbal de Jean Barbet" (28 June 1662), 76r.

79. ADHG 51 B 21, "Procès-verbal d'Antoine Delbosc" (20 March 1668), 159r, 164v.

80. ADHG 51 B 22, "Procès-verbal de Jean Seaubert" (12 March 1694), 144r.

81. The quotation is from ADHG 51 B 23, "Procès-verbal de Louise Bonaille" (27 January 1724), 267r. See also ADHG 51 B 23, "Procès-verbal de Marc Bermon" (14 May 1717); ADHG 51 B 23, "Procès-verbal de Gabrielle Massotte" (27 January 1724), 264v; and ADHG 51 B 23, "Procès-verbal d'Arnaud Carguecol" (26 August 1727), 307v.

82. ADHG 51 B 23, "Procès-verbal de Jean Bourdil" (27 May 1726), 295v.

83. ADHG 51 B 22, "Procès-verbal de Simone Gilibert" (14 May 1697), 243v.

84. Bouchel, *La bibliothèque,* 173.

85. On Spain, see William A. Christian, Jr., "Provoked Religious Weeping in Early Modern Spain," in *Religious Organization and Religious Experience,* ed. John Davis (London: Academic Press, 1982), 97–114.

86. On the use of tears in witchcraft interrogations in France, see Luria, "Rituals of Conversion," 80 n36. The connection between tears and tenderheartedness in France is demonstrated by Sheila Bayne, "Le rôle des larmes dans le discours sur la conversion," in *La conversion au XVIIe siècle: Actes du XIIe colloque de Marseille,* ed. Roger Duchêne (Marseilles: CMR, 1983), 417–27.

87. See, for example, Lyndal Roper, *Oedipus and the Devil: Witchcraft, Sexuality and Religion in Early Modern Europe* (New York: Routledge, 1994), 208.

88. Jousse, *Traité de la justice criminelle,* 3: 543–44; and Evelyn, *Diary,* 3: 28.

89. ADHG 51 B 24, "Procès-verbal de Paul Marty" (21 July 1755), 150r. The association of guilt with trembling is also found in the causes célèbres; see, for example, Gayot de Pitaval, *Causes célèbres et intéressantes,* 1: 547.

90. The origin of this form of proof is traced by Cohen, *Crossroads of Justice,* 139–41. The belief in bleeding corpses was one shared by Christians and Jews. See Joshua Trachtenberg, *Jewish Magic and Superstition: A Study in Folk Religion* (New York: Behrman's Jewish Book House, 1939), 227. Support for this form of evidence can be found in several legal manuals of the seventeenth and eighteenth centuries. See Bornier, *Conférences,* 164; Brillon, *Dictionnaire des arrêts,* 3: 607; and Despeisses, *Oeuvres,* 710. La Roche Flavin, *Arrests notables,* 573, speaks critically of this proof and in such a way as to suggest that it had fallen into disuse or become discredited.

91. See Merry Weisner, *Working Women in Renaissance Germany* (New Brunswick, N.J.: Rutgers University Press, 1986), 71.

92. ADHG 51 B 23, "Procès-verbal de Jeanne Destampes" (1, 3 December 1714), 136v, 140r.

93. See ADHG 51 B 23, "Procès-verbal de Gabrielle Massotte" (27 January 1714), 264r; ADHG 51 B 23, "Procès-verbal d'Arnaud Ruilhes" (13 July 1728), 351r, 251v; ADHG 51 B 27, "Procès-verbal de Blaise Theron" (24 March 1774), 222v.

94. Both Jean Seaubert and Gabrielle Massotte were asked about their lack of evident grief and anger upon the deaths of their near relatives. See ADHG 51 B 22, "Procès-verbal de Jean Seaubert" (10 March 1694), 140v; and ADHG 51 B 23, "Procès-verbal de Gabrielle Massotte" (27 January 1724), 264r.

95. François Vialettes had to explain why he hid his hands beneath his jerkin after the murder of a neighbor, ADHG 51 B 27, "Procès-verbal de François Vialettes" (28 December 1774), 250v. Jeanne Destampes was questioned concerning the destruction of the clothing she wore while attending her daughter-in-law's labor and death, ADHG 51 B 23, "Procès-verbal de Jeanne Destampes" (1, 3 December 1714), 140r.

96. When Arnaud Ruilhes was charged with murdering his neighbor, Pierre Guitard, one of the pieces of evidence brought against Ruilhes was the fact that he had insulted Guitard, calling him "un gras et un fripon," a fat rogue, indicative of their strained relations. See ADHG 51 B 23, "Procès-verbal d'Arnaud Ruilhes" (13 July 1728), 348r.

97. ADHG 51 B 23, "Procès-verbal de Jean Bourdil" (25 May 1726), 286r.

98. ADHG 51 B 23, "Procès-verbal de Jean Bourdil" (25 May 1726), 289r.

99. ADHG 51 B 23, "Procès-verbal de Jeanne Destampes" (1 December 1714), 135r.

100. On the uses of the second person in French, Italian, and German see Roger Brown and Albert Gilman, "The Pronouns of Power and Solidarity," in *Style in Language*, ed. Thomas A. Sebeok (Cambridge, Mass.: MIT Press, 1960), 253–76.

101. See ADHG 51 B 21, "Procès-verbal de Jean Barbet" (30 June 1662), 91v.

102. On the creation of social bonds through politeness formulae, see Raymond Firth, "Verbal and Bodily Rituals of Greeting and Parting," in *The Interpretation of Ritual: Essays in Honor of A. I. Richards*, ed. J. S. La Fontaine (London: Tavistock, 1973). On the omission of politeness formulae by members of the Society of Friends as a political and religious act, see Richard Bauman, *Let Your Words Be Few: Symbolism of Speaking and Silence among Seventeenth-Century Quakers* (Cambridge: Cambridge University Press, 1983), 43–62. See also Charles Ferguson, "The Structure and Use of Politeness Formulas," *Language in Society* 5 (1976): 137–51.

103. ADHG 51 B 23, "Procès-verbal de Jean Bourdil" (27 May 1726), 295v.

Chapter 4

1. Early medieval confraternities were socially heterogeneous groups, including persons of both sexes, all classes, and various ages from every neighborhood of a given city. They met as seldom as once or twice each year to celebrate the feast of their patron. On the origins of the confraternal movement in Italy, see John Henderson, *Piety and Charity in Late Medieval Florence* (Oxford: Clarendon Press, 1994), 147–60. In Italy before 1500, therefore, confraternities provided a temporary suspension of particular allegiances—to family, to class, to locality. But after that date, the disruption of practice and the decline in income and in membership created by war and famine fostered diminished commitment to confraternal traditions and permitted a transformation of

these institutions. After 1500, confraternities provided a celebration of the very allegiances they had once ritually undermined, and membership was restricted by personal status and parish of residence. See Ronald Weissman, *Ritual Brotherhood in Renaissance Florence* (New York: Academic Press, 1982), 64–80.

There is a large literature on devotional confraternities. Seminal works on French confraternities include the following: Gabriel Le Bras, "Les confréries chrétiennes—problèmes et propositions," *Revue historique de droit français et étranger* 19–20 (1940–41): 310–63; Maurice Agulhon, *Pénitents et francs-maçons de l'ancienne provence: Essai sur la sociabilité méridionale* (Paris: Fayard, 1968); Timothy Tackett, *Priest and Parish in Eighteenth-Century France* (Princeton: Princeton University Press, 1977); Maurice Bordes, "Contribution à l'étude des confréries de pénitents à Nice au XVIIe–XVIIIe siècles," *Annales du Midi* 19, no. 139 (July–December 1978): 377–88; Robert R. Harding, "The Mobilization of Confraternities against the Reformation in France," *Sixteenth Century Journal* 11, no. 2 (1980): 85–107; Philip Benedict, *Rouen during the Wars of Religion* (Cambridge: Cambridge University Press, 1981); Philip T. Hoffman, *Church and Community in the Diocese of Lyon, 1500–1789* (New Haven, Conn.: Yale University Press, 1984); Kathryn Norberg, *Rich and Poor in Grenoble, 1600–1814* (Berkeley: University of California Press, 1985); Keith P. Luria, *Territories of Grace: Cultural Change in the Seventeenth-Century Diocese of Grenoble* (Berkeley: University of California, 1991); and Andrew E. Barnes, *The Social Dimension of Piety: Associative Life and Devotional Change in the Penitent Confraternities of Marseilles (1499–1792)* (New York: Paulist Press, 1994). On lay piety, see Kaspar von Greyerz, *Religion and Society in Early Modern Europe, 1500–1800* (London: George Allen & Unwin, 1984).

2. Surveys of the Roman Catholic response to the reformations of the sixteenth century include H. O. Evennett, *The Spirit of the Counter-Reformation* (Cambridge: Cambridge University Press, 1968); A. D. Wright, *The Counter-Reformation* (New York: Harcourt, Brace & World, Inc., 1969); Michael Mullett, *The Counter-Reformation and the Catholic Reformation in Early Modern Europe* (New York: Methuen, 1984); N. S. Davidson, *The Counter Reformation* (New York: Basil Blackwell, 1987).

3. The struggle to preserve the body intact seems to be have been at the core of these doctrines. Doctrines of clerical celibacy, of the Incarnation, and of the Resurrection all insisted upon the preservation of bodily integrity in the maintenance of priestly virginity, in the persistence of Marian virginity, and in the restoration of the flesh after death. Doctrine held forth an ideal and eternal body that stood outside of time, unchanged by desire and decay, as the image of holiness. On the doctrine of clerical celibacy, see Peter Brown, *The Body and Society: Men, Women, and Sexual Renunciation in Early Christianity* (New York: Columbia University Press, 1988); on the virgin birth and the Virgin Mary, see Marina Warner, *Alone of All Her Sex: The Myth and Cult of the Virgin Mary* (New York: Knopf, 1976); and on the Resurrection, see Bynum, *Resurrection of the Body*.

New devotions took up the theme of the body in another key. Bodily change rather than bodily integrity was the focus of devotional worship. Very gradually, over the course of the medieval and early modern periods, Christ became the central focus of pious devotion, as is revealed by the development of the devotion of the Stations of the Cross, of cults including the Five Wounds, the True Blood, and the Sacred Heart, and of Eucharistic ceremonies and festivals. In Christocentric devotions, it was the Passion that received the most intense interest and attention. It was the moment of death and transfiguration, when the dual nature of Christ was first and finally revealed not only to his apostles but also to the world, that was celebrated in these devotions. It was the body in the process of change that these devotions sought to capture. On the decline of cults of the saints and the corresponding growth in Christocentric piety, see William A. Christian, Jr., *Local Religion in Sixteenth-Century Spain* (Princeton, N.J.: Princeton University Press, 1981); Maureen Flynn, *Sacred Charity: Confraternities and Social Welfare in Spain, 1400–1700* (Ithaca, N.Y.: Cornell University Press, 1989), 125–26; and Donald Weinstein and Rudolph Bell, *Saints and Society: The Two Worlds of Western Christendom, 1000–1700* (Chicago: University of Chicago Press, 1982). On cults of the Sacred Heart, see Louis Gougaud, *Devotional and Ascetic Practices in the Middle Ages,* trans. G. C. Bateman (London: Burns Oates & Washbourne Ltd., 1927), 75–130. On Eucharistic devotions, see Bynum, *Holy Feast and Holy Fast;* Beckwith, *Christ's Body;* and Rubin, *Corpus Christi.* On the growth in numbers of crucifixes and on visual representations of the Passion, see James Marrow, *Passion Iconography in Northern European Art* (Kortrijk, Belgium: Van Gheminert Publishing Co., 1979).

The laity often failed to grasp these doctrines to the satisfaction of the clerical hierarchy—or rejected them outright. In the sixteenth century, English Lollards rejected the notion of the real presence of Christ in the Eucharist; and the Spanish Inquisition investigated members of the laity who denied the virginity of Mary and who expressed incredulity as to the concept of the Eucharist. In each case, those charged were expressing disbelief as to the nature of holy bodies, bodies that endured change without changing, whether the transformations were of birth or of death. On England, see Beckwith, *Christ's Body,* and Rubin, *Corpus Christi.* On Spain, see Christian, *Local Religion in Sixteenth-Century Spain,* 148. Christopher F. Black, *Italian Confraternities in the Sixteenth Century* (Cambridge: Cambridge University Press, 1989), 96–97, notes the popular belief that Christ's sufferings are renewed in the act of Communion by chewing.

4. The essential connection had been established by God in the person of Jesus Christ, who embodied both humanity and divinity. His body, born into human misery, suffering death, resurrected, and shared among his followers through the mystery of the Eucharist, served to unite the separate bodies of the faithful within the body of the church. Roper, *Oedipus and the Devil,* 171–98, explores distinctively Protestant understandings of the body.

5. Judith Perkins argues that this emphasis on the human being as essentially embodied and suffering was central to the establishment and institutionalization of Christianity in the second century. See Judith Perkins, *The Suffering Self: Pain and Narrative Representation in the Early Christian Era* (New York: Routledge, 1995).

6. Schneider, *Public Life in Toulouse,* 172. This phenomenon was replicated across France; see Elizabeth Rapley, *The Dévotes: Women and Church in Seventeenth-Century France* (Montreal: McGill-Queen's University Press, 1990), 19–21.

7. On French mysticism, see Marie-Florine Bruneau, *Women Mystics Confront the Modern World: Marie de L'Incarnation (1599–1672) and Madame Guyon (1648–1717)* (Albany: State University of New York Press, 1998); and Michel de Certeau, *The Mystic Fable,* trans. Michael B. Smith (Chicago: University of Chicago Press, 1992).

8. For details concerning the *Reddes,* see BMT MS 693, Lacombe, "Traité de l'audience du Parlement de Toulouse," (1654); BMT MS 1789, Resseguier, "Mémoires chronologiques pour servir à l'histoire du parlement de Toulouse" (1732). Only one document produced by the annual visit has survived: see ADHG 51 B 76 (1700).

9. See ADHG 51 B 76, "Reddes" (1700). On this occasion at the prisons of the

conciergerie, three cases were heard: in two cases prisoners were released and informed that they must present themselves within a week.

10. See BMT MS 693, Lacombe, "Traité de l'audience du Parlement de Toulouse" (1654), 148.

11. See BMT MS 1789, Resseguier, "Mémoires chronologiques pour servir à l'histoire du parlement de Toulouse" (1732), 14.

12. On traditional Christian practice, see John Bossy, *Christianity in the West, 1400–1700* (Oxford: Oxford University Press, 1985). On religious life in France during the wars of religion, see Benedict, *Rouen during the Wars of Religion;* Diefendorf, *Beneath the Cross;* and J. H. M. Salmon, *Society in Crisis: France in the Sixteenth Century* (London: Methuen, 1975).

13. Confraternities were prohibited by an edict of Francis I. Mystery plays had been banned in Rome in 1536. See Black, *Italian Confraternities in the Sixteenth Century,* 114. The performance of mystery plays was then prohibited by the *parlement* of Paris on 17 November 1548, although they continued to be performed outside the jurisdiction of the *parlement.* See J. S. Street, *French Sacred Drama from Bèze to Corneille: Dramatic Forms and Their Purposes in the Early Modern Theatre* (Cambridge: Cambridge University Press, 1983), 7.

14. The argument that religion created community is made by John Bossy, "The Mass as a Social Institution, 1200–1700," *Past and Present* 100 (1983): 29–61, among many others. A critique of this position can be found in Rubin, *Corpus Christi,* 2. However much or little religion may have been a source of community in France before the sixteenth century, it is plainly the case that the arrival of the Reformation in France provoked serious regional, religious, and political divisions that had not previously been articulated with such intensity. See Davis, "The Rites of Violence," in *Society and Culture in Early Modern Europe;* and Diefendorf, *Beneath the Cross,* especially chapter 3.

15. See A. N. Galpern, *The Religions of the People in Sixteenth-Century Champagne* (Cambridge, Mass.: Harvard University Press, 1976), 94.

16. On the decline of confraternities in the sixteenth century, see Galpern, *Religions of the People,* 99.

17. See Barnes, *Social Dimension of Piety* (New York: Paulist Press, 1994), 12–18.

18. In Rouen, the *pénitents* were founded in 1588 and did not survive the wars of religion. See Bordes, "Contribution," 200.

19. Many Italian confraternities seem to have been inspired by calamities, most particularly by political crisis, and they became an increasingly important vehicle through which the laity could express social, political, and religious concerns. The Italian *disciplinati,* for example, first emerged during the period of Guelph-Ghibelline struggle. In this context, the members of Italian flagellant confraternities were deeply involved in promoting peace. They traveled from town to town, publicly flagellating themselves. Their activity was invested with a variety of goals: as penance for and purgation from personal sin, as a sharing in the sufferings of Christ, a demonstration of love for and solidarity with Christ, and as expiation for the sins of humanity. In addition to their practice of flagellation, these groups staged public processions at which they exhibited miraculous relics, like crucifixes that wept or bled. See John Henderson, "The Flagellant Movement and Flagellant Confraternities in Central Italy, 1260–1400," in *Religious Motivation: Biographical and Sociological Problems for the Church Historian,* ed. Derek Baker (Oxford: Basil Blackwell, 1978), 147–60. In Spain, the pattern of the establishment of penitential confraternities is different still. There, the height of peni-

tential observations coincided not with a moment of crisis but with one of prosperity. See Christian, *Local Religion in Sixteenth-Century Spain*, 200.

20. See Natalie Zemon Davis, "City Women and Religious Change" and "The Rites of Violence," in *Society and Culture in Early Modern Europe*, 86, 158, 170–72.

21. See Andrew E. Barnes, "Cliques and Participation in a Pre-Modern French Voluntary Association: The Pénitents Bourras of Marseille in the Eighteenth Century," *Journal of Interdisciplinary History* 19, no. 1 (summer 1988): 391.

22. See Barnes, *Social Dimension of Piety*, 19.

23. See Tackett, *Priest and Parish*, 195–98, and Hoffman, *Church and Community*, 145.

24. See Jean de Viguerie, *Le Catholicisme des Français dans l'ancienne France* (Paris: Nouvelles Éditions Latines, 1988), 163.

25. See Luria, *Territories of Grace*, 32.

26. See Hoffman, *Church and Community*, 85–86; Luria, *Territories of Grace*, 35–36.

27. See Tackett, *Priest and Parish*, 199.

28. Research into the Italian confraternities suggests that those groups possessing their own buildings were least likely to submit completely to clerical control. See Black, *Italian Confraternities in the Sixteenth Century*, 8. For Spain, see Flynn, *Sacred Charity*, 137–38.

29. Harding finds little support for the confraternities from the political elite, which feared their political potential—potential that they had seen realized during the wars of religion. See Harding, "Mobilization of Confraternities," 103.

30. The following numbers are drawn from Philippe Wolff, *Le Diocèse de Toulouse*, Histoire Des Diocèses de France, vol. 15 (Paris: Beauchesne, 1983), 107–14.

31. See Mark Greengrass, "The Anatomy of a Religious Riot in Toulouse in May 1562," *Journal of Ecclesiastical History* 34, no. 3 (July 1983): 367–91; and Joan Davies, "Persecution and Protestantism: Toulouse, 1562–1575," *The Historical Journal* 22, no. 1 (March 1979): 31–52.

32. See Viguerie, *Le Catholicisme des Français dans l'ancienne France*, 162.

33. See P. E. Ousset, *La confrérie des pénitents bleus de Toulouse* (Toulouse: Imprimerie Saint-Cyprien, 1927), 17.

34. Flynn has found that confraternal membership in Spain did not contract in the seventeenth and eighteenth centuries, evidence that she takes to indicate that the Counter-Reformation did not greatly alter the attitude of the Spanish laity as regards the efficacy of penitential acts, among other manifestations of the sacred. See Flynn, *Sacred Charity*, 141.

35. See ADHG E 918, no. 142, an eighteenth-century inventory of papers belonging to the *Pénitents Bleus*, which lists three books of receptions into the confraternity. These books of receptions were lost over the course of the nineteenth century. See Ousset, *La confrérie des pénitents bleus*, 4.

36. On membership in the Toulousain penitential confraternities, see J. L. Boursiquot, "Pénitents et sociétés religieuses au siècle des lumières," *Annales du Midi* 88 (April–June 1976): 159–75. Primary sources that provide information about the *Pénitents Bleus* include manuscripts in ADHG E 917–925; Etienne Molinier, *Des confrairies pénitents, où il est traicté de leur institution, règles et exercices* (Toulouse: Raymond Colomiez, 1625); *Processionnaire à l'usage de la congrégation royale de messieurs les pénitens bleus de Toulouze, avec les prières qu'ils disent dans leurs exercices du vendredy, & un abregé de leurs devoirs & des privilèges spirituels dont Ils jouïssent* (Toulouse: Chez Raymond Bosc,

1675); Jean-François Thouron, *Histoire de la royale compagnie de messieurs les pénitents bleus de Toulouse* (Toulouse, 1688); and [Un confrere Toulousain], *L'Esprit de l'institut de la congrégation royale de messieurs les pénitens bleus, divisée en douze instructions, avec les offices, & les prières que les confrères doivent réciter dans leurs saints exercises conformement à ce même esprit* (Toulouse: Jean Auridan, 1727).

37. See Berlanstein, *Barristers of Toulouse,* 29–30.

38. See Schneider, *Public Life in Toulouse,* 228.

39. See Boursiquot, "Pénitents et sociétés religieuses," 159–75.

40. "Nobility of the *Pénitents Bleus,* wealth of the *Pénitents Noirs,* antiquity of the *Pénitents Gris,* poverty of the *Pénitents Blancs.*"

41. The oldest of the Toulousain penitents were the *Pénitents Blancs,* founded in May 1571. In 1578, the company had 114 active members; in 1644, 258 members; in 1700, more than 500 members. By the end of the eighteenth century, only 177 members remained. When the company was established, its founders wanted to model themselves on the companies of Provence, but the wars of religion had made the highways too dangerous for travel, and they could not receive a copy of the statutes of those groups. So it was left to one of the founders, a native of Avignon, to recall for his *confrères* the essentials of confraternal life. On the *Pénitents Blancs,* see Marguerite Pecquet, "La compagnie des pénitents blancs de Toulouse," *Annales du Midi* 84 (April–June 1972): 213–24; Marguerite Pecquet, "La fondation des pénitents blancs de Toulouse," *Annales du Midi* 85 (July–September 1973): 335–47; and J. Adher, *Les confréries de pénitents de Toulouse avant 1789* (Toulouse: Imprimerie Lagarde et Sebille, 1897).

The *Pénitents Noirs* also modeled themselves after groups of *pénitents* that existed in Avignon and Italy. In 1578, they had 118 members and, therefore, began as the largest of the penitential companies. In 1578, the *Pénitents Gris* had only 32 members. On the *Pénitents Noirs* and *Gris,* see Jean Gaston, *La dévote compagnie des pénitents gris de Toulouse* (Toulouse: Eche, 1983).

42. Thouron, *Histoire de la royale compagnie,* 5–9.

43. Pecquet, "La fondation des pénitents blancs," 335–47.

44. Gaston, *La dévote compagnie des pénitents gris,* 52.

45. Schneider, *Public Life in Toulouse,* 227. The population of the city at this time was under 50,000. See Benedict, *Cities and Social Change,* 24.

46. See Boursiquot, "Pénitents et sociétés religieuses," 159–75. Exhaustive membership lists are no longer available for the other three penitential companies.

47. See Lenard Berlanstein, "The Advocates of Toulouse in the Eighteenth Century, 1750–1799" (Ph.D. diss., Johns Hopkins University, 1973), 331.

48. The names of the fifty-eight judges who heard cases involving sentences to torture in 1770 were drawn from the registers of the *parlement.* These names were checked against the "Liste des confrères pénitents bleus, et des dames confresses residans à Toulouse," ADHG E 921, no. 1. The eighteen judges who both heard cases involving sentences to torture and were members of the *Pénitents Bleus* were as follows: M. Blanc; Jean-Pierre Cassanclairac; *Président* Daspe; Charles-Pie d'Azemar; *Président* de Lespinasse; M. de Iost; M. du Regne; Guillaume de Lacaze; Jean-Guy-Marie de Lalo; Christophe-Suzanne de Lamothe; Marc-Bertrand-François de Lassus de Nestier; Jean-François de Montegut; François-Marguerite Delherm de Novital; Jerome-François Dufaur de Pibrac; Joseph de Raynal; Jean-François de Rochefort; Pierre-Henri-Izaac de Rudelle d'Alzon; and Louis-Emmanuel de Boyer de Sauveterre. The name of Jean-Antoine-Madelaine de Niquet, who also heard cases involving torture, does not appear

on this list, but his name is included in printed handbills advertising the results of confraternal elections in 1778, 1780, 1781, 1787, and 1788. For these handbills, see ADHG E 921 and E 922. In addition, his wife and the wife of *conseillier* Montgazin were confraternal members independently of their husbands.

Eight of these men—M. Blanc; *Président* Daspe; Guillaume de Lacaze; Christophe-Suzanne de Lamothe; Marc-Bertrand-François de Lassus de Nestier; *Président* de Lespinasse; Jean-François de Montegut; Jean-François de Rochefort—were executed during the French Revolution in An II, on 1 Floreal, 26 Prairial, and 18 Messidor, with a further fifteen of their colleagues in the *parlement*, five of whom had heard cases involving sentences to torture in the 1770s and 1780s. Note that the ratio of judges who were members of the *Pénitents Bleus* to their more secular colleagues remains consistent with the prerevolutionary peacetime ratio of roughly one-third. See P. E. Ousset, *La chapelle des pénitents bleus et l'eglise Saint-Jerome: Histoire et description* (Toulouse: Imprimerie J.-M. Caussé, 1925).

49. Each of the penitential confraternities had a complex hierarchy of officers. On the specific titles of responsibilities of these offices, see Adher, *Les confréries de pénitents de Toulouse*. These offices provided the democratic framework of these associations and access to power for the men who filled them.

50. Pecquet, "La fondation des pénitents blancs de Toulouse," 338.

51. Thouron, *Histoire de la royale compagnie, passim.*

52. Pierre Desplats had in fact served twice before, when he was an *avocat* in 1613 and again as a *conseiller* in 1619. See Thouron, *Histoire de la royale compagnie*. It should be noted that Thouron identifies him as the *premier président* of the *parlement*, whereas both Etienne Malenfant, in "Mémoires de Malenfant," (ADHG MS 149) and the anonymous author of the manuscript "Parlement de Toulouse" (ADHG MS 193) identify him as a *président à mortier*. Confraternal records of 1646 identify him as *second président à mortier*. See ADHG E 917, 146–47.

53. Funeral services that were held from the 1630s on included those held for M. Duplex, a local *avocat* and founder of the confraternity who died in the odor of sanctity; for the Cardinal de Lavalete; for the Cardinal Richelieu; for Louis XIII; for Monsieur le Prince; for Gaston, the brother of Louis XIII; for the Prince de Conti; for the archbishop of Toulouse; for Queen Marie-Therese; and for the Prince de Condé. See Thouron, *Histoire de la royale compagnie, passim.*

54. See *L'esprit de l'institut*, 5.

55. Bien, *The Calas Affair*, 3.

56. Thouron, *Histoire de la royale compagnie, passim.*

57. Molinier, *Des confrairies pénitents*, 104–105.

58. The *Pénitents Blancs* swore on their knees before the altar of the chapel to observe the statutes of the company and "to keep secret and not to tell anyone what happens in this place," in a phrase reminiscent of the torture chamber. See Pecquet, "La compagnie des pénitents blancs de Toulouse," 217. On ceremonies of admission among other penitential confraternities, see Pecquet, "La fondation des pénitents blancs de Toulouse," 216–17.

59. Ousset, *La confrérie des pénitents bleus*, 35.

60. *Processionnaire*, 153. Those who failed to observe the statutes would first be warned by the prior in the presence of the other officers. If such warnings did not alter the *confrère's* behavior, he would be sanctioned. And if the sanction too failed to have effect, he would be declared unworthy of membership before the entire confraternity,

his name struck from the register, his robes returned for the use of the company, and he would be expelled. Such a one could request readmission. Once returned to the company, he was to be completely accepted by his brothers—but only one such expulsion and return was permissible.

61. For Spain, see Flynn, *Sacred Charity*, 9.

62. *Processionnaire*, 153.

63. *Processionnaire*, 153.

64. *Processionnaire*, 155.

65. Flynn, *Sacred Charity*, 44–47.

66. For the statutes of the *Pénitents Bleus*, see *Processionnaire*, 153–55.

67. *Processionnaire*, 153.

68. Molinier, *Des confrairies pénitents*, 46.

69. Molinier, *Des confrairies pénitents*, 46.

70. *Processionnaire*, 150.

71. *Processionnaire*, 154.

72. *Processionnaire*, 154.

73. *Processionnaire*, 154.

74. *Processionnaire*, 154.

75. Molinier, *Des confrairies pénitents*, 47–48.

76. *Processionnaire*, i–iii.

77. Thouron, *Histoire de la royale compagnie*, 207–10.

78. See John Locke, *Locke's Travels in France*, ed. John Lough (Cambridge: Cambridge University Press, 1953), 82.

79. Among the *Pénitents Bleus*, plenary and lesser indulgences were liberally granted. See *Processionnaire*, 156–58. On the use of indulgences to support Eucharistic practices in the late medieval period, see Rubin, *Corpus Christi*, 211–12.

80. Although in Italy processions were narrowly intended for the good of *confrères* alone, it is clear that an appropriate public response was also anticipated. See James R. Banker, *Death in the Community: Memorialization and Confraternities in an Italian Commune in the Late Middle Ages* (Athens: University of Georgia Press, 1988), 164, 183. In Spain, passersby fell to their knees and struck their breasts. See Flynn, *Sacred Charity*, 123.

81. *Processionnaire*, 1–2.

82. See ADHG E 919, no. 18 (March–September 1633), no. 54 (October 1633), and no. 58 (November 1633).

83. Black, *Italian Confraternities in the Sixteenth Century*, 100–102.

84. Christian, *Local Religion in Sixteenth-Century Spain*, 189; and Flynn, *Sacred Charity*, 128.

85. Bordes, "Contribution à l'étude des confréries de pénitents," 386.

86. See Adher, *Les confréries de pénitents de Toulouse*, 9.

87. See Ronald Weissman, *Ritual Brotherhood in Renaissance Florence* (New York: Academic Press, 1982), 58–80. Schneider notes both the citywide recruitment of the penitents and the persistence of social and occupational segregation in recruitment practices, *Public Life in Toulouse*, 228, 230.

88. Tackett, *Priest and Parish*, 194–202.

89. See Bordes, "Contribution à l'étude des confréries de pénitents," 386.

90. See Tackett, *Priest and Parish*, 197–98; Harding, "The Mobilization of Confraternities against the Reformation in France," 92.

91. For Italy, see Banker, *Death in the Community*, 149, 182–84; Black, *Italian Confraternities in the Sixteenth Century*, 34–38, 100–103; Henderson, *Piety and Charity*, 154; Nicholas Terpstra, "Women in the Brotherhood: Gender, Class, and Politics in Renaissance Bolognese Confraternities," *Renaissance and Reformation* 26, no. 3 (1990): 193–212; and Weissman, *Ritual Brotherhood in Renaissance Florence*, 213. For Spain, see Flynn, *Sacred Charity*, 133.

92. Those who have done so include Mary Ann Clawson, "Early Modern Fraternalism and the Patriarchal Family," *Feminist Studies* 6, no. 2 (summer 1980): 368–91; Davis, "City Women and Religious Change," in *Society and Culture in Early Modern France*, 65–96; Norberg, *Rich and Poor in Grenoble;* and Terpstra, "Women in the Brotherhood," 193–212.

93. See ADHG E 921 and E 922.

94. For Italy, see Black, *Italian Confraternities in the Sixteenth Century*, 101.

95. The importance of the practice is suggested by the presence of an undated document in the records of the *Pénitents Blancs* entitled "De la discipline" (ADHG E 927, no. 73), which sets out the rules regulating the employment of flagellation. It specifies that *confrères* may process barefoot, that they may flagellate themselves while contemplating the Passion on Holy Thursday, and that the procession will culminate in an all-night vigil in the confraternal chapel, during which time *confrères* may continue to flagellate themselves.

96. The same was true in Italy, where penitents were known as *della frustra, dei battuti, di disciplina*. Black, *Italian Confraternities in the Sixteenth Century*, 100.

97. John Henderson, "The Flagellant Movement and Flagellant Confraternities," 154; and Black, *Italian Confraternities in the Sixteenth Century*, 36. Contemporary illustrations of Spanish flagellants show flagellants in various states of undress; Flynn, *Sacred Charity*, 129–30.

98. Banker, *Death in the Community*, 182.

99. Banker, *Death in the Community*, 149.

100. On the relative accuracy of his assessment of the place of women in developing market economies of the late medieval and early modern period, see, for example, Alice Clark, *Working Life of Women in the Seventeenth Century* (New York: Routledge, 1992); Martha Howell, *Women, Production, and Patriarchy in Late Medieval Cities* (Chicago: University of Chicago Press, 1986); Barbara Hanawalt, ed., *Women and Work in Preindustrial Europe* (Bloomington: Indiana University Press, 1986).

101. Black, *Italian Confraternities in the Sixteenth Century*, 80.

102. See Weissman, *Ritual Brotherhood in Renaissance Florence*, 92–95, for an analysis of confraternal liturgy. The act of flagellation stands at the center of the service.

103. Benedict, *Rouen during the Wars of Religion*, 197; Flynn, *Sacred Charity*, 131.

104. Molinier, *Des confrairies pénitents*, 256, 259.

105. It is true that, just as men who had unsexed themselves through suffering deprivations of the flesh, from chastity to flagellation, so too might women who had unsexed themselves in the same manner voluntarily choose to suffer. Freed from *dolor* by their chastity, female religious might legitimately flagellate themselves, legitimately choose to suffer. But even in this instance their chosen suffering was hidden from the world, given the requirements of *clausura*. On the regulation of female self-mortification in the early modern period, see Rapley, "Her Body the Enemy," 25–35.

106. See Georges Duby, "Réflexions sur la douleur physique au moyen âge," in *Mâle Moyen Âge* (Paris: Flammarion, 1988), 203–209.

107. On the origins of the confraternal movement in Italy, see Henderson, "The Flagellant Movement and Flagellant Confraternities in Central Italy, 1260–1400," 147–60; Black, *Italian Confraternities in the Sixteenth Century*, 23–32. Flagellation was not a widespread monastic practice until the eleventh century. It was soon after taken up by the laity, though the numbers of persons involved in the practice are difficult to determine, because it was a private practice until circa 1260. Flagellant confraternities were associated with an ascetic and Christocentric style of piety.

108. During the research for this chapter, I tried to provide quantitative answers to these questions by cross-checking membership lists for the *Pénitents Bleus* against the names of judges listed in cases of torture in order to determine whether or not judges belonging to confraternities seemed to be involved more often in cases of torture than their nonconfraternal peers. While I did find a slightly higher rate of confraternal judges participating in sentences to torture, I also noticed that these judges had often served on the court slightly longer than their nonconfraternal peers; in other words, differences in sentencing between these two groups may be accounted for by nothing other than length of service.

Chapter 5

1. Blaise Pascal, *Prière pour demander à Dieu le bon usage des maladies* (Paris: Librairie de L'Art Catholique, 1917); Wendy Perkins, "The Presentation of Illness in the Memoirs of Mme. de Motteville and of Bussy-Rabutin," *Seventeenth-Century French Studies* 12 (1990): 32–33; BMT MS 884, "Catalogue des livres de feu Messire Philippe de Caminade, président à mortier au parlement de Toulouse, de feu Messire Bertrand de Caminade, Abbé de Belleperche, et de feu Messire Jean-George de Garaud de Duranty et de Donneville, aussy président à mortier audit Toulouse"; Barthélemy Saviard, *Nouveau recueil d'observations chirurgicales* (Paris, 1702), 301.

2. Discussions of theories of the physiology of pain can be found in Vila, *Enlightenment and Pathology*, especially chapter 1; and Roselyne Rey, *The History of Pain*, trans. Louise Elliott Wallace and J. A. and S. W. Cadden (Cambridge, Mass.: Harvard University Press, 1995).

3. Untrained healers included, among others, midwives, empirics, and herbalists. On the professionalization of midwives, see Nina Gelbart, *The King's Midwife: A History and Mystery of Madame du Coudray* (Berkeley and Los Angeles: University of California Press, 1998).

4. For information on medical theory and practice, including medical training in France, see L. W. B. Brockliss and Colin Jones, *The Medical World of Early Modern France* (Oxford: Clarendon Press, 1997).

5. The resultant inferiority of surgeons' status relative to physicians was reflected in their dress: physicians wore long gowns; surgeons, short capes. In 1772, the crown elevated surgery to the status of a liberal profession, abolished the system of formal apprenticeship, and required that surgical students participate in university studies while serving as assistants to master surgeons. See Brockliss and Jones, *Medical World of Early Modern France*, 174, 188–89, 490.

6. Brockliss and Jones, *Medical World of Early Modern France*, 555, 559, 560.

7. Brockliss and Jones, *Medical World of Early Modern France*, 554.

8. Although most surgical procedures were carried out in private, public toothpulling was common. See Robert Isherwood, *Farce and Fantasy: Popular Entertainment in Eighteenth-Century Paris* (Oxford: Oxford University Press, 1986), 18–21. On physi-

cians' reluctance to touch their patients and their reliance on reporting of symptoms, sometimes through intermediaries, see Duden, *The Woman beneath the Skin*, 81–87.

9. Pierre Dionis, *Course of Chirurgical Operations* (London, 1733), 8: "'Tis customary to send to the patient's chamber (some time before the surgeon comes) a servant to dispose all things in order; but frequently, by the quantity of bits of linen which they cut, the heaps of lint which they make, and the spreading shew of numerous instruments, they strike fear and terror into the mind of the patient, by giving him a cruel idea of the operation which they are going about. I would that the chirurgeons would not shew themselves to their patients, till the moment appointed for the operation; and that all things which they want, were ready prepared at their own houses, or in a chamber near the patient, in order to spare him the sight of those preparatives, which only inspire him with a horror for those who make them." This reliance on the patient to provide some of the accouterments of surgery persisted into the nineteenth century. See *The Journals and Letters of Fanny Burney*, vol. 6, ed. Joyce Hemlow (Oxford: Clarendon Press, 1975), 609–10, for Burney's account of the preparations that she undertook in her home for her 1811 mastectomy.

10. On the careful attention paid by physicians to the problem of fear, see Antonie Luyendijk-Elshout, "Of Masks and Mills: The Enlightened Doctor and His Frightened Patient," in *The Languages of Psyche: Mind and Body in Enlightened Thought*, ed. G. S. Rousseau (Berkeley and Los Angeles: University of California Press, 1990), 186–230.

11. See Saviard, *Nouveau recueil*, 345–46, 125–31, 382–85, 275–77.

12. Jacques Daran, *Observations chirurgicales sur les maladies de l'urethre* (Paris, 1748), 116.

13. Dionis, *Course of Chirurgical Operations*, 247.

14. The examples that follow are most often drawn from eighteenth-century books and journals. Surgeons authoring texts in the seventeenth century only rarely offered case histories, tending to confirm Thomas Laqueur's thesis that the case history is a peculiarly eighteenth-century genre. See Laqueur, "Bodies, Details, and the Humanitarian Narrative," 176–204. For the specific cases cited here, see Saviard, *Nouveau recueil*, 175–79, 211–15, 187–90, 56–57.

15. Saviard, *Nouveau recueil*, 143.

16. Pierre Fauchard, *Le chirurgien dentiste, ou traité des dents* (Paris, 1728), 378.

17. Fauchard, *Le chirurgien dentiste*, 380.

18. See Daran, *Observations chirurgicales*, 202–207. Daran reports what we would see as recurrent episodes of a continuing illness as distinct and separate infections.

19. Robert James, *A Medicinal Dictionary*, 3 vols. (London: 1743–45), cf. "Dolor." This is the most succinct analysis of the nature of pain written in the eighteenth century. James's work quickly passed into French, having been offered to Diderot for translation in 1745, who passed the project on to his friends Marc-Antoine Eidous and François-Vincent Toussaint. See P. N. Furbank, *Diderot: A Critical Biography* (New York: Knopf, 1992), 28. James anticipated twentieth-century pain measurement scales, most notably the McGill Pain Questionnaire, which employs four major categories (sensory, affective, evaluative, and miscellaneous) and twenty groups of words to assist patients and doctors in evaluating pain. Copies of the McGill Pain Questionnaire are often reproduced in medical texts; see, for example, Suzanne M. Skevington, *Psychology of Pain* (New York: John Wiley & Sons, 1995), 50. Many of the McGill Pain Questionnaire categories and descriptive words correspond to those employed here by James, but

the eighteenth-century descriptive words are richer and more varied in their evocation of the emotional qualities of pain.

On the diagnostic value of pain, see, for example, Henri-François Le Dran, *The Operations in Surgery of M. Le Dran*, trans. Mr. Gataker, 3d ed. (London, 1757), 50–51, who suggests that pain is useful in establishing the location of deep abdominal wounds: "If the wound is in the epigastrium. . . . [T]he pain in this case will be violent. . . . The liver is not very quick of sensation, and therefore may be wounded without our being made immediately sensible of it by any violent pain; but though the pain may be very slight at first, it may grow very severe afterwards by the inflammation of its external membrane. . . . If the direction of the wound should tend towards the diaphragm, it is probable that may be affected, and the pain will then be more or less acute, according as the wound has penetrated either into its fleshy, or tendinous part, in the last of which it would be most violent."

20. See Dionis, *Course of Chirurgical Operations*, 50, 89, 104, 106, 156, 165; Le Dran, *The Operations in Surgery*, 50, 291; Elie Col de Villars, *Dictionnaire françois-latin des termes de médecine et de chirurgie* (Paris, 1747), 296. It should be noted that the "feeble" pains mentioned by Dionis occurred during a woman's labor and were, therefore, interpreted as a sign of danger, her attendants fearing she would not have the strength to survive her delivery. English authors characterized pains as "very great torture." See Samuel Sharp, *A Treatise on the Operations of Surgery* (London, 1739), 19.

21. See Col de Villars, *Dictionnaire françois-latin*, 232, 290; Dionis, *Course of Chirurgical Operations*, 50, 227, 237, 238; Le Dran, *The Operations in Surgery*, 291; Paul Dubé, *Le médecin des pauvres et le chirurgien des pauvres*, 4th ed. (Paris, 1674), 148, 239; and Sharp, *A Treatise on the Operations of Surgery*, ix, xxiii. Other terms used to describe pain include "burning," Dionis, *Course of Chirurgical Operations*, 458, which is opposed to the growing coldness of gangrene; "stinging," Col de Villars, *Dictionnaire françois-latin*, 232; "cutting," Col de Villars, *Dictionnaire françois-latin*, 333; and "gripping," Dionis, *Course of Chirurgical Operations*, 212.

22. On the transformation of consciousness, see Dionis, *Course of Chirurgical Operations*, 65. Le Dran, *The Operations in Surgery*, 8, in a discussion of surgical preparations, commented on the phenomenon of time distortion with great compassion: "Everything being thus got ready, the surgeon begins the operation; which should be done expeditiously, and effectually; expeditiously, because every moment of suffering seems long; nevertheless, the operator must allow himself sufficient time; and when I used the word expeditiously, I only meant that he should not lose time, taking great care not to be over hasty, lest his hand outrun his judgement, which should direct it: an operation is always soon enough done that is well done."

23. Dionis, *Course of Chirurgical Operations*, 67, 68, 105, 118, 135, 212; René-Jacques Croissant de Garengeot, *Traité des opérations de chirurgie*, 2 vols., 3d ed. (Trevoux, 1748), 2: 425.

24. Saviard, *Nouveau recueil*, 56.

25. Dionis, *Course of Chirurgical Operations*, 320.

26. Jacques Guillemeau, *The Nursing of Children, Wherein Is Set Down the Ordering and Government of Them from Their Birth* (London, 1635), 58–59.

27. Gélis, *History of Childbirth*, 69, 71, 115, 149.

28. Dubé, *Le médecin des pauvres*, 114, for bleeding and for milk infused with opium and saffron; Nicholas L'Emery, *Nouveau recueil des plus beaux secrets de médecine pour la*

guérisin de toutes sortes de maladies, new ed., 3 vols. (Paris, 1737), 39, for infused oils; and Mme. Fouquet, *Les remèdes charitables* (Paris, 1684), 36, for alcohol and vegetable juices.

29. Col de Villars, *Dictionnaire françois-latin,* 359, 372.

30. Dionis, *Course of Chirurgical Operations,* 414.

31. On spiritual intercession for healing, see Brockliss and Jones, *Medical World of Early Modern France,* 73, who note the use of prayer to saints dedicated to specific illnesses.

32. Sharp, *Treatise,* 26.

33. Garengeot, *Traité des opérations de chirurgie,* 2: 48.

34. Saviard, *Nouveau recueil,* 403–404.

35. Saviard, *Nouveau recueil,* 405.

36. Dionis, *Course of Chirurgical Operations,* 190.

37. Saviard, *Nouveau recueil,* 34.

38. Numerous patients complained of iatrogenic conditions arising from bleedings, from lithotomies, and from other surgical interventions. Saviard, *Nouveau recueil,* 118–19, makes mention of a patient who was lithotomized without success and who "complained strenuously of the discomfort he felt."

39. Saviard, *Nouveau recueil,* 154.

40. James, *Medicinal Dictionary,* cf. "Amputation." In 1811, Fanny Burney reported on her experience of her mastectomy as follows: "I began a scream that lasted unintermittingly during the whole time of the incision"; for the duration of the surgery, which she estimates lasted twenty minutes, "I bore it with all the courage I could exert, & never moved, nor stopt them, nor resisted, nor remonstrated, nor spoke—except once or twice, during the dressings, to say 'Ah Messieurs! Que je vous plains!—' . . . Except this, I uttered not a syllable, save, when so often they recommenced, calling out 'Avertissez moi, Messieurs! Avertissez moi!—'" She fainted twice during that time. Her surgeons sought to prepare her for the surgery by warning her of the extreme suffering she would endure, by urging her to cry out during its performance, and by arranging to send a note four hours in advance of the surgery—in other words, to give her little time within which to prepare herself. In fact, the note arrived two hours before the appointed time, but the surgeons were then delayed. Burney spent the time after her receipt of this note in practical preparations and in walking "backwards and forwards till I quieted all emotion, & became, by degrees, nearly stupid—torpid, without sentiment or consciousness." The only ways in which these surgeons could spare her the pain of surgery was to give her a wine cordial beforehand and to cover her face with a handkerchief, to obscure her view of the proceedings. See *Letters and Journals of Fanny Burney,* 604, 609–13.

41. Again, the exception to this rule pertains to the relief of pain during childbirth. In this case, some surgeons argued that pain was necessary, either because pain was ordained by God or because pain served a necessary function. On pain as ordained by God, see the epitaph containing the text of Genesis 3:16 in Jean Astruc, *L'art d'accoucher* (Paris, 1766). On debates about the relative necessity of pain and the desirability of pain relief, see Dionis, *Course of Chirurgical Operations,* 250; Pierre Dionis, *A General Treatise of Midwifery* (London, 1719), 256, 260, 315, 320; and Jacques Guillemeau, *Childbirth, or The Happy Delivery of Women* (London, 1635), 103.

42. Dionis, *Course of Chirurgical Operations,* 10.

43. Alexandre Dienert, *Introduction à la matière médicale* (Paris, 1753), 225.

44. Laurent Joubert, *Popular Errors*, 2 vols., trans. Gregory David de Rocher (1578; reprint, Tuscaloosa: University of Alabama Press, 1989), 1: 84.

45. Daran, *Observations chirurgicales*, 186–87.

46. Fouquet, *Remèdes charitables*, 2–4. For simple headaches, the book suggests that the patient take a tile, heat it in the fire, douse it with vinegar, and breathe in the smoke. Migraines, evidently less susceptible to purely chemical remedies, are best cured by drinking three big glasses of water and walking for a little while, or by grilling the head of a crow and eating its brains.

47. Dubé, *Le médecin des pauvres*, 50–51.

48. Fouquet, *Remèdes charitables*, 45, 60–61, 329.

49. Fouquet, *Remèdes charitables*, 31–32.

50. Symphorien Champier, *Le myrouel des appotiquaires et pharmacopoles*, ed. P. Dorveaux (1532; reprint, Paris: H. Welter, 1895), 51–52. He also cautions against opium, which causes stupefaction, languor, a pale face, several other ills, and very often sudden death, and against hyoscyamus, in three of its known varieties, all of which cause stupefaction and intoxication.

51. The possible efficacy of these sponges has aroused considerable debate among and experimentation by modern physicians. See, for example, J. F. Nunn, "Anesthesia in Ancient Times—Fact and Fable," in *The History of Anesthesia*, ed. Richard Atkinson and Thomas Boulton (New York: Parthenon, 1989).

52. Daniel de Moulin, *The History of Surgery* (Boston: Kluwer Academic Publishers, 1988), 87, referring to Ambroise Paré's *Apologie et traité* (1580).

53. De Moulin, *History of Surgery*, 91.

54. De Moulin, *History of Surgery*, 79, 81.

55. Dionis, *Course of Chirurgical Operations*, 411.

56. De Moulin, *History of Surgery*, 57.

57. In modern medicine, opioids are administered in a variety of ways: orally; by injection; sublingually in a candy base; rectally by suppository; intranasally by spray; and transdermally by patch. See Paula Bakule, ed., *Expert Pain Management* (Springhouse, Pa.: Springhouse Corporation, 1997). It is therefore possible that topical applications of opium in solution could have achieved an analgesic effect quite apart from the placebo effect. It is also worth noting that different analgesics are now considered to be most effective in relieving different kinds of pain. Opioids, for example, are believed to relieve dull constant pains more effectively than sharp stabbing pains. Were such distinctions made in early modern pharmacology? Certainly, different remedies were employed for different pains, but further study is required to determine if there was a consistent correlation of remedies to illnesses.

58. See, for example, Brockliss and Jones, *Medical World of Early Modern France*, 66. Gélis, *A History of Childbirth*, 153, hints at the same phenomenon of a universally high pain threshold. By contrast, see Daniel de Moulin, "A Historical-Phenomenological Study of Bodily Pain in Western Man," *Bulletin of the History of Medicine* 48 (1974): 540–70, who asserts that pain is suffered transhistorically and cross-culturally and that doctors have always sought to relieve it.

59. Le Dran, *The Operations in Surgery*, 303, 313, 332. Saviard, *Nouveau recueil*, 239.

60. Dionis, *Course of Chirurgical Operations*, 446–47.

61. Joseph Capuron, *Nouveau dictionnaire de médecine, de chirurgie, de physique, de chimie, et d'histoire naturelle* (Paris: J.-A. Brosson, 1806), 106, described pain as itself

causative of disease. Note, however, that surgeons were remarkably uninvolved in the debate around sensibility and its relationship to irritability, pleasure, and pain conducted by French physicians in the eighteenth century. For further discussion of sensibility, see G. S. Rousseau, "Nerves, Spirits and Fibres: Towards Defining the Origins of Sensibility," *The Blue Guitar* 2 (1976): 125–53; Janet M. Todd, *Sensibility: An Introduction* (New York: Methuen, 1986); John Mullan, *Sentiment and Sociability: The Language of Feeling in the Eighteenth Century* (Oxford: Clarendon Press, 1988); Barker-Benfield, *The Culture of Sensibility;* Ann Jessie Van Sant, *Eighteenth-Century Sensibility and the Novel: The Senses in Social Context* (Cambridge: Cambridge University Press, 1993); and Vila, *Enlightenment and Pathology,* especially chapters 1–3.

62. Joubert, *Popular Errors,* 1: 84.

63. Dionis, *Course of Chirurgical Operations,* 250.

64. Dionis, *Course of Chirurgical Operations,* 10.

65. Saviard, *Nouveau recueil,* 239.

66. Dionis, *Course of Chirurgical Operations,* 6. Dionis spoke at moving length on this subject; see Dionis, *Course of Chirurgical Operations,* 96, 213, 216, 402, 431.

67. Ambroise Paré, *The Apologie and Treatise of Ambroise Pare,* trans. Thomas Johnson, ed. Geoffrey Keynes (1634; Chicago: University of Chicago Press, 1952), 10–11.

68. Dionis, *Course of Chirurgical Operations,* 5.

69. Sauveur-François Morand, *Opuscules de chirurgie* (Paris, 1768), 177. Earlier in the century, Dionis recorded his strong objections to this surgery; see Dionis, *Course of Chirurgical Operations,* 87: "Its sole idea [that of cesarean section] will force the most intrepid to tremble. Judge also what resolution one ought to have to qualify one to open the belly of a living woman, making in it an incision about a half a foot long; then groping in the cavity of the abdomen, cut like a wound in the body of the matrix [uterus]; then pierce the membranes, and draw out a child through all these apertures. This operation terrifies and affrights the chirurgeon, even when performed after the death of the woman. What horror then should it not excite, when accompanied with the cries of a mother, which we force to suffer with unparallel'd cruelty, and the effusion of a prodigious quantity of blood, which flowing out by the great wounds, may kill her in an instant, while in the hands of the operator?"

The horrified response to surgery was recorded by English surgeons as well. Martin Lister recorded the following in his journal: "I see [Pere Jacques] cut a second time [for the stone] in the *Hostel-Dieu;* and he perform'd it upon nine Persons in three quarters of an Hour, very dextrously. He seemed to venture at all; and put me in some disorder with the cruelty of the Operation, and a stouter *Englishman* than myself." Martin Lister, *A Journey to Paris in the Year 1698,* ed. Raymond Phineas Stearns (Chicago: University of Illinois Press, 1967), 237. And as noted above, Robert James addressed the effect of patients' sufferings on surgeons, and urged surgeons to suppress their feelings: "'Tis therefore absolutely necessary in this case, that the surgeon, as Celsus directs, be intrepid, and acquit himself in all the steps of his operation, in such a manner, as if he was deaf to the moving groans, and piercing shrieks, of the tortur'd patient." James, *Medicinal Dictionary,* cf. "Amputation." Yet de Moulin notes that the celebrated English surgeon William Cheselden (1688–1752) felt ill the night before surgeries. See de Moulin, "A Historical-Phenomenological Study of Bodily Pain," 545–46. Fanny Burney observed the effect of her own mastectomy on her French surgeon; after the conclusion of the surgery, Burney reports: "I then saw my good Dr. Larry, pale nearly as myself, his face streaked with blood, & its expression depicting grief, apprehension, & almost horrour." See *Journals and Letters of Fanny Burney*, 614. Here again the emotion inspired by the sight of suffering is horror.

70. For the therapeutic uses of pain, see L. J. Rather, *Mind and Body in Eighteenth-Century Medicine* (London: Wellcome Historical Medical Library, 1965), 109–10, 188–89; and Carol Houlihan Flynn, "Running Out of Matter: The Body Exercised in Eighteenth-Century Fiction," in G. S. Rousseau, ed., *The Languages of Psyche* (Berkeley: University of California Press, 1990), 162–63.

Chapter 6

1. Michel de Montaigne, "On Conscience," in *Essays*, trans. Jacob Zeitlin (New York: Alfred A. Knopf, 1935), 2: 34–35: "The rack is a dangerous invention, and seems to be rather a test of endurance than of truth. But he who is able to bear it and he who is not alike conceal the truth. For why should pain sooner make me confess what really is than force me to say what is not? And, on the other hand, if he who is not guilty of what he is accused has the fortitude to undergo those tortures, why should not he who is guilty also have it, when so fair a reward as life is offered to him?" Ambroise Paré, *Ten Books of Surgery* (1564; reprint, Athens: University of Georgia Press, 1969), 90–91: "Now we shall treat of contusions and bruises, which are made in diverse manners . . . by an extreme tension as is that of the rack"; and *The Apologie and Treatise*, 16: "But I do not show any such way of giving the strappado to men, but I show the chirurgeon in my works, the way to reduce them [outward laxation of the spondills] surely, and without great pain." Molière, *L'Avare* (1668; reprint, Paris: Éditions du Seuil, 1946), act IV, scene vii, 144: "I want to go and fetch the law to give the *question* to my entire household: the servants, valets, my son and daughter, and to myself as well." Jean de La Bruyère, *Les caractères, ou, Les moeurs de ce siècle* (1696; reprint, Paris: Éditions Garnier Frères, 1960), 373: "The *question* is a marvelous invention and one absolutely certain to condemn an innocent person of a weak constitution and to rescue a guilty person who was born robust." Jean Racine, *Les Plaideurs* (1697; reprint, Paris: Imprimerie Nationale, 1995), act III, scene iv, 397: "Dandin: Have you ever seen them give the *question?* Isabelle: No, and I think I will not, on my life. Dandin: Come, I want to make you lose the desire. Isabelle: Monsieur! Can one see the suffering of the wretched! Dandin: It always serves to pass an hour or two."

2. Richer, *Causes célèbres et intéressantes*, 3: 31, 4: 280–82, 5: 410.

3. Richer, *Causes célèbres et intéressantes*, 1: 56–57.

4. Richer, *Causes célèbres et intéressantes*, 3: 27–29.

5. This difficulty of observation stands in marked contrast to other rituals of old regime justice. Both the gibbet and the galleys attracted the attention of numerous observers throughout the early modern period. In the 1550s, Felix Platter frequently noted the exhibition of bodies in the gibbet and on the wheel in France. See Platter, *Beloved Son Felix*, 36, 43, 64, 76, 77, 93. In fact, Platter's journal is a veritable catalog of punishments, including observations of shaming rituals, floggings, galley sentences and banishments, mutilations, and executions by hanging, burning, beheading, breaking on the wheel, and exposure in cages as well as executions in effigy. For examples of each of these in turn, see 121, 128, 72, 128, 68, 99, 59, 64, 85, 83, and 77, respectively. The public nature of these punishments is what at once permits these observations and creates in Platter such sophistication of observation. In 1554, for example, he remarked on the execution of a man for murder by breaking on a Saint Andrew's cross, which, he

wrote, "resembles our punishment of the wheel, and is here called *massarrer*," Platter, *Beloved Son Felix*, 85.

John Locke visited the galleys at Marseilles in 1676 and commented on the general health of the galley slaves. See Locke, *Locke's Travels in France*. In the 1760s, Tobias Smollett noted seeing bodies hanging in the *fourches patibulaires*, a type of gallows, and plying broken on the wheel. John Boswell remarked on his visit to and discussion with French galley slaves in Nice and Marseilles. See Smollett, *Travels through France and Italy*, 128–31, 330–31; and John Boswell, *Boswell on the Grand Tour: Italy, Corsica and France, 1765–1766*, ed. Frank Brady and Frederick Pottle (New York: McGraw-Hill Book Company, 1955), 243.

6. See Evelyn, *Diary*, 3: 28–29.

7. Mme. de Sévigné, Marie de Rabutin-Chantal, *Correspondance*, 3 vols., ed. Roger Duchêne (Paris: Gallimard, 1974–78), 2: 343 (letter 528, 17 July 1676).

8. Mme. de Sévigné, *Correspondance*, 2: 354 (letter 531, 29 July 1676).

9. Mme. de Sévigné, *Correspondance*, 2: 345 (letter 529, 22 July 1676).

10. See BMT MS 609–706, Pierre Barthès, "Les heures perdues de Pierre Barthès, Répétiteur en Toulouse, ou Recueil des Choses Dignes d'être transmises à la postérité arrivées en cette ville ou prés d'icy, 1737–1780." Biographical information concerning Barthès can be found in Edmond Lamouzele, *Toulouse au dix-huitième siècle, d'après les heures perdues de Pierre Barthès* (Toulouse: J. Marqueste, 1914).

11. See BMT MS 705, Pierre Barthès, "Les heures perdues de Pierre Barthès" (September 1760–August 1773), 6: 184: "The son hung and the father broken alive: Saturday the twelfth of this month at ten at night in the ordinary place was hung a young man of 18 or 20, an assassin, murderer, and thief native to a place near the city of Auch, accused of having robbed a hermit in his cell, and then to have crushed his skull with a hammer blow. He was seized by the *maréchaussée* with his father, his brother-in-law, some women and children, and other accomplices numbering seventeen or eighteen. Having the double *question* he bore all the horrors of the first without saying anything; but during the *question extraordinaire* after the second pitcher of water, having asked to be released and to change his shirt, he named his father who was confronting him at that moment, charging him with complicity, and this man, having sworn that he had given the hermit the first blow with his fist and then had left to keep watch at the door, while his son struck a blow at the unfortunate victim. Today Wednesday the fifteenth of this month at the same place the father was broken alive and exposed on the wheel for two hours then strangled, and exposed in the gibbet, to the sound of terrible thunder and a storm already brewing that did not break. The son would no doubt have suffered the same, but he was judged, and all finished thus."

12. ADHG 51 B 27, "Procès-verbal de Jean Begue" (11 July 1772), 78r.

13. ADHG 51 B 27, "Procès-verbal de Jean Begue" (11 July 1772), 82r.

14. BMT MS 705, Barthès, "Les heures perdues de Pierre Barthès," 7: 18 (August 1773–July 1779), and ADHG B 3861 (22 March 1774).

15. ADHG B 3861 (22 March 1774).

16. BMT MS 705, Barthès, "Les heures perdues de Pierre Barthès," 7: 18 (March 1774).

17. See BMT MS 705, Barthès, "Les heures perdues de Pierre Barthès," 7: 147–48.

18. Approval was by no means universal. Restif de La Bretonne, for example, noted, "As I crossed the square I caught sight of a poor wretch, pale, half-dead, wracked by the pains of the interrogation inflicted on him twenty hours earlier; he was stumbling

down from the *hôtel de ville* supported by the *exécuteur de la haute justice* and the confessor. These two men, so completely different, inspired an inexpressible emotion in me!"
See Restif de La Bretonne, *Les nuits de Paris, or The Nocturnal Spectator,* trans. L. Asher
and E. Fertig (New York: Random House, 1964), 7. Note also, however, that the author's emotional attention is taken up by the *exécuteur de la haute justice* and the confessor, the representatives of the state and church, and by their role in the justice system;
the victim of torture merely provides the occasion for reflection, rather than himself
becoming the object of philosophical reflection.

19. The case has been explored at length in many works, most notably Bien, *The
Calas Affair,* which provides a useful bibliography. See also F. H. Maugham, *The Case
of Jean Calas* (London: Heinemann, 1928); Marc Chassaigne, *The Calas Case,* trans.
Ragland Somerset (London: Hutchinson & Co., 1929); Alexandre Coutet, *Jean Calas,
roué vif et innocent* (Anduze: Musée du désert en Cévennes, 1933); Edna Nixon, *Voltaire
and the Calas Case* (London: Gollancz, 1961); Gilbert Collard, *Voltaire, l'affaire Calas et
nous* (Paris: Les Belles Lettres, 1994).

20. ADHG B 3850 (9 March 1762).

21. Voltaire, *L'histoire d'Elisabeth Canning et Jean Calas* (Paris, 1762), and *Traité sur
la tolérance* (Paris, 1763).

22. See Louis, *Mémoire sur une question relative à la jurisprudence.*

23. See [Anon], *Calas, sur l'échaufaud, à ses juges* (n.p., 1765); Adrien Michel Hyacin-
the Blin de Sainmore, *Lettre de Jean Calas à sa femme et à ses enfans, héroïde* (Paris, 1765);
and Etienne Simon, *Histoire des malheurs de la famille de Calas, procédé de Marc Antoine
Calas, le suicide, à l'univers, héroide* (Paris, 1765). The essay by Nougaret was entitled
*L'ombre de Calas: Le suicide, à sa famille et à son ami dans les fers, precédée d'une lettre a
M. de Voltaire* (Amsterdam, 1765). The sermons were published under the name of
Apompée de Tragopome, *Sermons prechés à Toulouse* ([Toulouse?], 1772).

24. See Sebastien Roch Nicholas Chamfort, "Jean Calas," *Mercure* (29 October
1791), 182–89; M. J. Chenier, *Jean Calas, ou l'ecole des juges* (Paris, 1791); Jean Louis
Laya, *Jean Calas, tragédie en cinq actes, en vers* (Avignon, 1791); Auguste Jacques Le-
mierre d'Argy, *Calas, ou le fanatisme* (Paris, 1791); Jean Baptiste Pujoulx, *La veuve Calas
à Paris, ou le triomphe de Voltaire, pièce en un acte, en prose* (Paris, 1791). Two more plays
were published in the early nineteenth century: Victor Ducange, *Calas* (Paris, 1819),
and Du Voisin-Calas, *Un déjeuner* (Paris, 1822).

25. See Nina Rattner Gelbart, *Feminine and Opposition Journalism in Old Regime
France: Le Journal des Dames* (Berkeley: University of California Press, 1987), 151; and
see, for example, his letter to D'Alembert, cited in Nixon, *Voltaire and the Calas Case,*
132.

26. At least eighteen English translations of the *Commentaire sur le livre des délits et
des peines* were published between 1763 and 1793. The *Traité sur la tolérance* was printed
in at least five English editions between 1764 and 1779, and *L'histoire d'Elisabeth Canning et Jean Calas* in at least one, in 1762.

27. See Christian Felix Weisse, *Der Fanatismus; oder, Jean Calas* (Leipzig, 1774). Another edition was published in 1780.

28. See ADHG MS 147, "Mémoires de Malenfant," 206.

29. The paucity of such evidence was noted by none other than Brissot de Warville.
In a discussion of Dupaty in his *Mémoires,* Brissot de Warville wrote that "[H]e participated regularly in the sessions of the *Tournelle,* although the strange discussions deprived him of the deliberative voice in the judgments which he rendered, and he wrote

every evening of what of interest had passed before his eyes." See Jean-Pierre Brissot de Warville, *Mémoires* (Paris: Firmin-Didot et Cie., 1877), 205.

30. See ADHG MS 46, "Procès-verbal de la conférence tenue entre les commissaires du Roi et les commissaires du Parlement, députés pour l'examen des articles de l'ordonnance de 1670, sur la procédure et instruction criminelle," 275v–276r. This was the only edition available to me, hence this citation.

31. The only other work from this period at all critical of torture was an essay written by Jacques Tourreil, a Toulousain *avocat* who became a member of the *Academie Française*, entitled "Si la torture est une bonne voie pour découvrir la vérité," in *Essais de jurisprudence* (Paris, 1694). It was an exercise in style that concluded that, while torture did not always achieve the truth, good is known only by comparison to its counterpart, and that for that reason torture should be maintained. All citations to this essay are to the edition republished in Jean-Pierre Brissot de Warville, *Bibliothèque philosophique du législateur, du politique, du jurisconsulte; ou Choix des meilleurs discours, dissertations, essais, fragmens, composés sur la législation criminelle*, 10 vols. (Berlin, 1782–85).

32. Nicolas, *Si la torture est un moyen seur*, 7.

33. Nicolas, *Si la torture est un moyen seur*, 22.

34. Nicolas, *Si la torture est un moyen seur*, 19, 169, 179.

35. Nicolas, *Si la torture est un moyen seur*, 17.

36. Nicolas, *Si la torture est un moyen seur*, 16.

37. Nicolas, *Si la torture est un moyen seur*, 53.

38. Nicolas, *Si la torture est un moyen seur*, 213.

39. Nicolas, *Si la torture est un moyen seur*, 110.

40. Nicolas, *Si la torture est un moyen seur*, 94.

41. Nicolas, *Si la torture est un moyen seur*, 15.

42. See *Encyclopédie*, 5: 83–87.

43. *Encyclopédie*, 5: 84.

44. *Encyclopédie*, 5: 83.

45. See *Encyclopédie*, 13: 703–705. A third unsigned article, entitled "Torture ou Question (Jurisprudence)," addressed the practice, but added nothing new to these two longer ones. See 16: 439–40.

46. See *Encyclopédie*, 13: 704.

47. See Montaigne, "On Conscience," in *Essais*, 2: 34–35.

48. Tourreil, "Si la torture est une voie," in Brissot de Warville, *Bibliothèque du législateur*, 4: 191: "They attack the constitution of the accused rather than his untruthfulness." Cesare Beccaria, *On Crimes and Punishments*, trans. Henry Paolucci (1764; reprint, New York: Macmillan, 1963), 32: "Torture is an infallible means indeed—for absolving robust scoundrels and for condemning innocent persons who happen to be weak." Letrosne, "Vues sur la justice criminelle," in Brissot de Warville, *Bibliothèque philosophique du législateur*, 2: 288–89: "It is the strength of the accused, the texture of his muscles, and their degree of sensibility, on which hangs his lot! It is his temperament, rather than his innocence, that is put to the test. If he is robust and guilty, he will save himself; but who can bear this option without shuddering? He might be weak and innocent, and perish." Voltaire, "Prix de la justice et de l'humanité," in Brissot de Warville, *Bibliothèque philosophique du législateur*, 5: 364: "You know that it is a certain secret to cause an innocent man with delicate muscles to say everything you wish, and to save a robust guilty man." Brissot de Warville, "Discours," in Brissot de Warville, *Bibliothèque philosophique du législateur*, 6: 153–54: "Let us forever abjure this invention of a barba-

rous century, which has no other goal, as is so often said, than to save a robust guilty man in order to cause an innocent man of weak constitution to perish."

49. *Encyclopédie,* 13: 704–705.

50. See, for example, Alan Charles Kors, *D'Holbach's Coterie: An Enlightenment in Paris* (Princeton: Princeton University Press, 1976) and Frank Kafker, *The Encyclopedists as a Group: A collective biography of the authors of the Encyclopédie* (Oxford: Voltaire Foundation, 1996).

51. To take but one example: Brissot de Warville was desperate for Voltaire's approval of his first piece of writing on criminal law reform, his *Théorie des loix criminelles,* and offered the introduction to him with great trepidation, yet later expressed little admiration for Voltaire's coldness of style when writing on penal reform. Brissot de Warville's volatile relationship with Marat is well known. During the revolution, Morellet penned several attacks on Brissot de Warville. Yet all four lent their support to the abolition of torture. See Eloise Ellery, *Brissot de Warville: A Study in the History of the French Revolution* (New York: Houghton Mifflin, 1915); Louis R. Gottschalk, *Jean Paul Marat: A Study in Radicalism* (New York: Benjamin Bloom, 1927).

52. Others writing before the abolition of the *question préparatoire* included Paul Risi, *Observations sur des matières de jurisprudence criminelle. Traduit du latin de M. Paul Risi [de 1766] . . . par M. S[eigneux] D[e] C[orrevon]* (Lausanne, 1768); François Seigneux de Correvon, *Essai sur l'usage, l'abus et les inconvéniens de la torture dans la procédure criminelle, par Mr S. D. C.* (Lausanne, 1768); Joseph Michel Antoine Servan, *Discours sur les moeurs* ([Paris], 1769); and M. Letrosne, *Vues sur la justice criminelle* (Orleans, 1771). All of these works were reprinted in Brissot de Warville, *Bibliothèque philosophique du législateur,* and all citations are to that collection.

53. See the *National Union Catalogue* and the catalogue of the Bibliothèque Nationale, which together list nine French editions, all preceded by Voltaire's commentary: Lausanne, 1766; Paris, 1766; Philadelphia, 1766; Paris, 1773; Philadelphia, 1775; Amsterdam, 1776; Philadelphia, 1778; Paris, An III (1794–95); Paris, 1796; and Paris, 1797. Eighteen English editions were published between 1763 and 1793.

54. Beccaria, *On Crimes and Punishments,* 8.

55. Beccaria, *On Crimes and Punishments,* 31.

56. Beccaria, *On Crimes and Punishments,* 32.

57. See also Risi, *Observations sur des matières de jurisprudence criminelle,* in Brissot de Warville, *Bibliothèque philosophique du législateur,* 2: 390.

58. Voltaire, *Commentaire sur le livre des délits et des peines* (1766; reprint, Paris, 1879).

59. Voltaire, *Prix de la justice et de l'humanité,* in Brissot de Warville, *Bibliothèque philosophique du législateur.*

60. See Voltaire, *Prix de la justice et de l'humanité,* in Brissot de Warville, *Bibliothèque philosophique du législateur,* 5: 94: "You have no proof, and for two hours you punish a wretch with a thousand deaths to give yourself the right to give him one that will last a moment."

61. Letrosne also suggested that there might be reasons to retain the *question préalable,* though he saw the procedure as fraught with legal and epistemological difficulties. See Letrosne, "Vues sur la justice criminelle," in Brissot de Warville, *Bibliothèque philosophique du législateur,* 2: 294–97.

62. Letrosne, "Vues sur la justice criminelle," in Brissot de Warville, *Bibliothèque philosophique du législateur,* 2: 296.

63. See Voltaire, *Commentaire sur le livre des délits et des peines,* 63.

64. See Brissot de Warville, *Mémoires*, 207: "The true object, which I could not show overtly, was to spread the principles of liberty which guided the English and the Americans, by inserting in this collection several pieces which only had a place in the great political reform."

65. Brissot de Warville, *Mémoires*, 202.

66. Brissot de Warville, *Bibliothèque philosophique du législateur*, 10: 69. Brissot de Warville identifies the author as the brother of Seigneux de Correvon, the latter of whom wrote but never published a translation of Beccaria, and then translated and published the work of Paul Risi in 1768, and comments that it was difficult for him to find this work, locating one by chance in London, bound with the work of Sonnenfels on torture.

67. See Brissot de Warville, *Bibliothèque philosophique du législateur*, 10: 69.

68. See Brissot de Warville, *Bibliothèque philosophique du législateur*, 10: 71.

69. Brissot de Warville, "Discours," in Brissot de Warville, *Bibliothèque philosophique du législateur*, 6: 154.

70. See Brissot de Warville, *Bibliothèque philosophique du législateur*, 7: 268.

71. Servan, *Discours sur les moeurs*, in Brissot de Warville, *Bibliothèque philosophique du législateur*, 7: 267–68.

72. Bernardi, *Discours*, in Brissot de Warville, *Bibliothèque philosophique du législateur*, 8: 197.

73. Risi, *Observations sur des matières de jurisprudence criminelle*, in Brissot de Warville, *Bibliothèque philosophique du législateur*, 2: 29.

74. Brissot de Warville, "Discours," in Brissot de Warville, *Bibliothèque philosophique du législateur*, 8: 159 (italics in the original).

75. See, for example, Bernardi, "Discours," in Brissot de Warville, *Bibliothèque philosophique du législateur*, 8: 196: "Torture is an invention of tyranny."

76. Sonnenfels, "Mémoire sur l'ábolition de la torture," in Brissot de Warville, *Bibliothèque philosophique du législateur*, 4: 254 (ellipses in original).

77. Sonnenfels, "Mémoire sur l'ábolition de la torture," in Brissot de Warville, *Bibliothèque philosophique du législateur*, 4: 220.

78. Seigneux de Correvon, "Essai sur l'usage," in Brissot de Warville, *Bibliothèque philosophique du législateur*, 10: 32.

79. Letrosne, "Vues sur la justice criminelle," in Brissot de Warville, *Bibliothèque philosophique du législateur*, 2: 290.

80. Apologists for torture agreed that one effect of pain was the diminution of the exercise of the will. Muyart des Vouglans, for example, noted that pain—like other hot and violent passions including anger, love, and drunkenness—diminishes criminal responsibility. Crimes committed in a state of hot and violent passion would therefore result in lesser charges than those committed in the grip of the cooler passions of hate, jealousy, and cupidity. See Muyart des Vouglans, *Les lois criminelles de la France dans leur ordre naturel* (Paris, 1780), 13. Note that this analysis depends upon a humoral theory of medicine; for the implications of the humoral theory within the legal realm, see Natalie Zemon Davis, *Fiction in the Archives: Pardon Tales and Their Tellers in Sixteenth-Century France* (Stanford, Calif.: Stanford University Press, 1987).

81. Seigneux de Correvon, "Essai sur l'usage, l'abus et les inconvéniens de la torture," in Brissot de Warville, *Bibliothèque philosophique du législateur*, 10: 58: "They apply this man to the *question* to clarify his variations, or in order to reconcile the contradictions into which he has fallen through the trouble of his soul; and they augment this trouble through a frightful machine, and still more through cruel pains."

82. "Instruction pour le code de la Russie," in Brissot de Warville, *Bibliothèque philosophique du législateur*, 3: 94.

83. Sonnenfels, "Mémoire sur l'ábolition de la torture," in Brissot de Warville, *Bibliothèque philosophique du législateur*, 4: 220–21. Note that in this formulation, speaking and self-condemnation under torture is no longer natural or inevitable, but is rather described and derided as "weakness." Henceforth, to remain silent under torture is represented as heroic.

84. Sonnenfels, "Mémoire sur l'ábolition de la torture," in Brissot de Warville, *Bibliothèque philosophique du législateur*, 4: 246.

85. Laqueur, "Bodies, Details and the Humanitarian Narrative."

86. Risi, "Observations sur des matières de jurisprudence criminelle," in Brissot de Warville, *Bibliothèque philosophique du législateur*, 2: 41.

87. A variety of rhetorical strategies are associated with the literature of sensibility, including the employment of words which are conventional, repetitive, and mannered; the predictable association of nouns and adjectives; and the use of terms and structures which are repeated to heighten intensity, with words in pairs or triplets. Likewise, a variety of narrative strategies, including conventional situations, stock characters, and dramatic plot reversals are associated with this style. The emphasis is on the communication of common feeling from writer to reader, through the medium of the subject matter. Nor is language found adequate to this task, as a variety of typographical strategies are employed: "In the sentimental work words are not left to carry a message alone, but are augmented by other heightening devices. Exclamation marks, brackets, italics and capitals pepper and disturb the flow of sentences. At the same time they are shunted into declaring their inadequacy and their subordination to gesture." See Todd, *Sensibility*, 5; R. F. Brissenden, *Virtue in Distress: Studies in the Novel of Sentiment from Richardson to Sade* (New York: Harper & Row, 1974), chapter 2.

88. See Norman Fiering, "Irresistible Compassion: An Aspect of Eighteenth-Century Sympathy and Humanitarianism," *Journal of the History of Ideas* 37 (April–June 1976), 195–218. The corollary to the naturalness of humane and humanitarian feeling was the absolute alienness of evil. For the sensible style was also a signal of the change in the assessment of crime. With the doctrine of sensibility—of natural benevolence—the criminal became a moral alien; and the crime, a meaningless act without redemption. For brilliant expositions of this shift in perception, see Cynthia Herrup, "Law and Morality in Seventeenth-Century England," *Past and Present* 106 (1985): 102–23; and Karen Halttunen, "Early American Murder Narratives: The Birth of Horror," in *The Power of Culture: Critical Essays in American History*, ed. Richard Wightman Fox and T. J. Jackson Lears (Chicago: University of Chicago Press, 1993). Both the descriptive and prescriptive literatures of crimes struggled to encompass the incomprehensibility of evil.

89. On the tensions among empathy, compassion, and pity, and the consequences of these emotions for political action, see Elizabeth V. Spelman, *Fruits of Sorrow: Framing Our Attention to Suffering* (Boston: Beacon Press, 1997).

Epilogue

1. Pierre François Muyart des Vouglans, "Réfutation du traité des délits et peines," in *Les lois criminelles de la France dans leur ordre naturel* (Paris, 1780), 811.

2. See Feitlowitz, *A Lexicon of Terror*, 212, who quotes the Argentine torturer Julio Simón as follows: "Look, torture is eternal. It has always existed and it always will. It is an essential part of the human being."

BIBLIOGRAPHY

Primary Sources

Unpublished Sources

ARCHIVES DÉPARTEMENTALES DE LA HAUTE-GARONNE (ADHG)

B 3540–3876, Arrêts du parlement (1600–1785)

51 B 21–27, Procès-verbaux d'exécution et de torture (1633–1788)

51 B 76, "Reddes" (1700)

101 B 2, 3, 104–286, Dossiers of the *capitoulat* (1689–1766)

C 92, "Prisons: Wages of the Executioner"

C 94, "Prisons: Prison Doctors and Surgeons"

E 917–925, *Pénitents bleus*

E 926–933, *Pénitents blancs*

E 941–954, *Pénitents noirs*

3 E 12058, no. 272, "Inventory of G.-M. Douvrier, *président à mortier* of the *parlement* of Toulouse"

3 E 12060, no. 276, "Inventory of J.-C. de Fajolle, *conseiller au parlement* of Toulouse"

3 E 12450, *Parlement* de Toulouse (1567–1725)

3 E 12678, *pénitents* (1590–1780)

MS 46, "Procès-verbal de la conférence tenue entre les commissaires du Roi et les commissaires du Parlement, députés pour l'examen des articles de l'ordonnance de 1670, sur la procédure et instruction criminelle"

MSS 147–149, "Etienne de Malenfant, Mémoires, collections et remarques du Palais faites par moi Etienne de Malenfant, Greffier civil de la Cour de Parlement de Toulouse, depuis le 2 jour de mars 1602 auquel jour je fus reçu en l'office de Greffier civil"

MS 193, "Parlement de Toulouse: Recueil de documents concernant son institution, ses officiers, ses actes, sa juridiction, sa composition, son ressort, attribué au greffier en chef, dernier en exercice, en 1685"

BIBLIOTHÈQUE MUNICIPALE DE TOULOUSE (BMT)

MSS 609–706, Barthès, Pierre. "Les heures perdues de Pierre Barthès, Répétiteur en Toulouse; ou, Recueil des Choses Dignes d'être transmises à la postérité arrivées en cette ville ou prés d'icy, 1737–1780"

MS 692, "Liste des premiers présidents"

MS 693, Pierre Lacombe, "Traité de l'audience du Parlement de Toulouse" (1654)

MS 884, "Catalogue des livres de feu Messire Philippe de Caminade, président à mortier au parlement de Toulouse, de feu Messire Bertrand de Caminade, Abbé de Belleperche, et de feu Messire Jean-George de Garaud de Duranty et de Donneville, aussy président à mortier audit Toulouse"

MS 952, "Pièces fugitives"

MS 1255, "Livre de délibérations des Pénitents Bleus"

MS 1564, "Mémoire sur l'état du parlement de Toulouse en l'année 1678" (1678)

MS 1788, "Mémoire de ce qui se fera dans le Palais de plus considérable depuis 1690"

MS 1789, Resseguier, "Mémoires chronologiques pour servir à l'histoire du parlement de Toulouse" (1732)

Published Sources

Académie Française. *Le dictionnaire de l'Académie Française*. 2 vols. Paris, 1694.

———. *Le dictionnaire de l'Académie Française*. 2 vols. Third edition. Paris, 1740.

Astruc, Jean. *L'art d'accoucher*. Paris, 1766.

Beccaria, Cesare. *On Crimes and Punishments*. 1764. Translated by Henry Paolucci. New York: Macmillan, 1963.

———. *Traité des délits et des peines*. 1764. Translated by Maurice Chevallier. Paris: G. F. Flammarion, 1965.

Bergasse, Nicolas. *Discours sur l'humanité des juges*. [Paris?], 1780.

Blin de Sainmore, Adrien Michel Hyacinthe. *Lettre de Jean Calas à sa femme et à ses enfans, héroïde*. Paris, 1765.

Bornier, Philippe. *Conférences des nouvelles ordonnances de Louis XIV*. 2 vols. Paris, 1678.

Boswell, John. *Boswell on the Grand Tour: Italy, Corsica and France, 1765–1766*. Edited by Frank Brady and Frederick Pottle. New York: McGraw-Hill Book Company, 1955.

Bouchel, Laurent. *La bibliothèque; ou, Trésor du droit français*. 3 vols. Paris, 1671.

Brillon, Pierre Jacques. *Dictionnaire des arrêsts; ou, Jurisprudence universelle des parlements de France et autres tribunaux*. 6 vols. Paris, 1727.

Brissot de Warville, Jean Pierre. *Bibliothèque philosophique du législateur, du politique, du jurisconsulte; ou, Choix des meilleurs discours, dissertations, essais, fragmens, composés sur la législation criminelle*. 10 vols. Berlin, 1782–85.

———. *Mémoires*. Paris: Firmin-Didot et Cie., 1877.

[Anon]. *Calas, sur l'échaufaud, à ses juges*. N.p., 1765.

Calendrier de la cour de parlement pour l'année 1749. Toulouse, 1749.

Cambolas, Jean de. *Décisions notables sur les diverses questions du droit, jugées par plusieurs arrêts du Parlement de Toulouse*. 5th edition. Toulouse, 1735.

Camus, Armand-Gaston. *Lettre sur la profession d'avocat*. Paris, 1777.

Capuron, Joseph. *Nouveau dictionnaire de médecine, de chirurgie, de physique, de chimie, et d'histoire naturelle*. Paris: J.-A. Brosson, 1806.

Cayron, Gabriel. *Le parfait praticien*. Toulouse, 1655.

———. *Stil et forme de procéder, tant en la cour de parlement de Toulouse, et chambre des requêtes d'icelle, qu'en toutes les courtes inférieures du ressort*. Toulouse, 1611.

Chamfort, Sébastien Roch Nicolas. "Jean Calas." *Mercure* (29 October 1791): 182–89.

Champier, Symphorien. *Le myroeul des apothecaires et pharmacopoles*. 1532. Reprint, Paris: H. Welter, 1894.

Chenier, M. J. *Jean Calas; ou, L'ecole des juges*. Paris, 1791.

Col de Villars, Elie. *Dictionnaire françois-latin des termes de médecine et de chirurgie*. Paris, 1747.

Convention Nationale. "Portant qu'il sera élevé une colonne sur la place où le fanatisme a fait périr Calas." *Décret de la Convention,* no. 1907. Du 29 jour de Brumaire, An II. Paris, 1793.

Coras, Jean de. *Arrest memorable du parlement de Tolose.* Lyon, 1561.

Daran, Jacques. *Observations chirurgicales sur les maladies de l'urethre.* Paris, 1748.

Despeisses, Antoine. *Oeuvres de M. Antoine D'Espeisses, avocat et jurisconsulte de Montpellier.* 3 vols. Lyon, 1750.

Dictionnaire universel françois et latin, vulgairement appelé Dictionnaire de Trévoux. Seventh edition. 8 vols. Paris, 1771.

Diderot, Denis, and Jean Le Rond d'Alembert, eds. *Encyclopédie; ou, Dictionnaire raisonné des sciences, des arts et des métiers par une société de gens des lettres.* 34 vols. Paris, 1751–80.

Dienert, Alexandre. *Introduction à la matière médicale.* Paris, 1753.

Dionis, Pierre. *Cours d'opérations de chirurgie.* Sixth edition. Paris, 1765.

———. *A Course of Surgical Operations.* Translated from the second French edition. London, 1733.

———. *A General Treatise of Midwifery.* London, 1719.

Le Dran, Henri-François. *The Operations in Surgery of M. Le Dran.* Translated by Mr. Gataker. Third edition. London, 1757.

Dubé, Paul. *Le medecin et le chirurgien des pauvres.* Second edition. Paris, 1674.

Eloy, Nicholas Joseph François. *Dictionnaire historique de la médecine ancienne et moderne.* 4 vols. Mons, 1778.

L'Emery, Nicholas. *Nouveau recueil des plus beaux secrets de médecine pour la guérison de toutes sortes de maladies, nouvelle édition.* 3 vols. Paris, 1737.

[Un confrere Toulousain.] *L'esprit de l'institut de la congrégation royale de messieurs les pénitens bleus, divisée en douze instructions, avec les offices, & les prières que les confrères doivent réciter dans leurs saints exercices conformément a ce même Esprit.* Toulouse: Jean Auridan, 1727.

Evelyn, John. *The Diary of John Evelyn.* Edited by E. S. de Beer. 6 vols. Oxford: Clarendon Press, 1955.

Fauchard, Pierre. *Le chirurgien dentiste; ou, Traité des dents.* Paris, 1728.

Ferrière, Claude Joseph de. *Dictionnaire de droit et de pratique.* 2 vols. Paris, 1758.

———. *Dictionnaire de droit et de pratique.* 2 vols. New edition. Toulouse, 1779.

———. *La science parfaite des notaires; ou, Le moyen de fair un farfait notaire.* New, revised, and augmented edition. Lyon, 1701.

Fouquet, Marie de Maupeou. *Les remèdes charitables de Madame Fouquet.* Paris, 1681.

Furetiere, Antoine. *Dictionnaire universel.* 2 vols. La Haye, 1690.

Garengeot, René-Jacques Croissant de. *Traité des opérations de chirurgie.* 2 vols. Third edition. Trévoux, 1748.

———. *A Treatise of Chirurgical Operations.* Translated by Mr. St. Andre. London: 1723.

Garsault, F. A. P. *Faits des causes célèbres et intéressantes augmentés de quelques causes.* Amsterdam, 1757.

Gayot de Pitaval, François. *Causes célèbres et intéressantes, avec les jugemens qui les ont décidées.* 20 vols. New edition. Paris, 1738–46.

Guillemeau, Jacques. *Childbirth; or, The Happy Delivery of Women.* London, 1635.

———. *De l'heureux accouchement des femmes.* Paris, 1609.

———. *The Nursing of Children, wherein Is Set Down the Ordering and Government of Them from Their Birth.* London, 1635.

Guybert, Philippe. *Toutes les oeuvres charitables.* Rouen, 1651.

Hazon, Jacques-Albert. *Notice des hommes les plus célèbres de la faculté de médecine.* Paris, 1778.

Isambert, François-André, ed. *Recueil général des anciennes lois françaises depuis l'an 420 jusqu'à la révolution de 1789.* 29 vols. Paris, 1821–33.

James, Robert. *A Medicinal Dictionary.* 3 vols. London, 1743–46.

Joubert, Laurent. *Popular Errors.* 2 vols. Translated by Gregory David de Rocher. Tuscaloosa: University of Alabama Press, 1989.

Jourdain, Anselme. *Traité des dépôts dans le sinus maxillaire, des fractures, et des caries de l'une et l'autre mâchoire; suivis de réflexions & d'observations sur toutes les opérations de l'art de dentiste.* Paris, 1760.

Jousse, Daniel. *Nouveau commentaire sur l'ordonnance criminelle de 1670.* Paris, 1763.

———. *Traité de la justice criminelle de France.* 4 vols. Paris, 1771.

La Bruyère, Jean de. *Les caractères; ou, Le moeurs de ce siècle.* 1696. Reprint, Paris: Éditions Garnier Frères, 1960.

La Roche Flavin, Bernard de. *Arrests notables du parlement de Toulouse.* Lyon, 1619.

———. *Treze livres des parlemens de France.* Bordeaux, 1617.

Laya, Jean Louis. *Jean Calas, tragédie en cinq actes, en vers.* Avignon, 1791.

Le Brun de la Rochette, Claude. *Les procez civil et criminel.* Lyon, 1643.

Le Roux, Joseph. *Dictionnaire français comique.* New edition. Pamplune, 1786.

Lister, Martin. *A Journey to Paris in the Year 1698.* Edited by Raymond Phineas Stearns. Chicago: University of Illinois Press, 1967.

Locke, John. *Locke's Travels in France.* Edited by John Lough. Cambridge: Cambridge University Press, 1953.

Louet, Georges. *Recueil de plusieurs arrêts notables du parlement de Paris.* 2 vols. Paris, 1742.

Louis, Antoine. *Mémoire sur une question relative à la jurisprudence; dans lequel on établit les principes pour distinguer, à l'inspection d'un corps trouvé pendu, les signes du suicide d'avec ceux de l'assassinat.* 1763. Reprinted in Jacques-Pierre Brissot de Warville, *Bibliothèque philosophique de législateur, du politique, du jurisconsulte; ou, Choix des meilleurs discours, dissertations, essais, fragmens, composés sur la législation criminelle,* vol. 7: 177–279. Berlin, 1782–85.

Louis XVI. *Déclaration du roi concernant la procédure criminelle.* Auch, 1788.

Malessaigne, Jean. *La forme et ordre judiciaire observé en la cour de parlement de Toulouse.* [Toulouse?], 1625.

Maynard, Geraud de. *Notables et singulières questions.* 2 vols. Toulouse, 1604.

Merville, Pierre Biarnoy de. *Règles pour former un avocat . . . avec un index des livres de jurisprudence les plus nécessaires à un avocat.* New edition. Paris, 1753.

Milles de Souvigny, Jean. *Pratique criminelle.* Translated from the Latin by Arlette Lebigre. 1541. Reprint, Moulins: Les Marmousets, 1983.

Molinier, Étienne. *Des confrairies pénitents, où il est traicté de leur institution, règles et exercices.* Toulouse, 1625.

Montaigne, Michel de. *Essays.* 3 vols. Translated by Jacob Zeitlin. New York: Alfred A. Knopf, 1935.

Molière. *L'Avare de Molière.* 1668; reprint, Paris: Éditions du Seuil, 1946.

Morand, Sauveur-François. *Opuscules de chirurgie.* Paris, 1768.

Muyart des Vouglans, Pierre François. *Les lois criminelles de la France dans leur ordre naturel.* Paris, 1780.

Nicolas, Augustin. *Si la torture est un moyen seur à vérifier les crimes.* 1682. Reprint, Marseille: Laffitte Reprints, 1982.

Nougaret, Pierre Jean Baptiste. *L'ombre de Calas: Le suicide, à sa famille et à son ami dans les fers, precédée d'une lettre a M. de Voltaire.* Amsterdam, 1765.

Paré, Ambroise. *The Apologie and Treatise of Ambroise Paré.* Translated by Thomas Johnson [1634]. Edited by Geoffrey Keynes. Chicago: University of Chicago Press, 1952.

———. *Ten Books of Surgery.* 1564. Reprint, Athens: University of Georgia Press, 1969.

Pasquier, Etienne. *Les recherches de la France.* Paris, 1633.

Petit, Jean-Louis. *Traité des maladies chirurgicales, et des opérations qui leur conviennent, ouvrage posthume de J.-L. Petit, mis au jour par M. Lesne, ancien directeur de l'Académie Royale de Chirurgie, nouvelle édition corrigée.* 3 vols. Paris, 1790.

Platter, Felix. *Beloved Son Felix: The Journal of Felix Platter, a Medical Student in Montpellier in the Sixteenth Century.* Translated by Sean Jennett. London: F. Muller, 1962.

Pomet, Pierre. *A Compleat History of Drugs.* Second edition. London, 1725.

Processionnaire a l'usage de la Congrégation Royale de Messieurs les Pénitens Bleus de Toulouze, avec les prières qu'ils disent dans leurs exercices du vendredy, & un abrégé de leurs devoirs & des privilèges spirituels dont ils jouïssent. Toulouse, Chez Raymond Bosc, 1675.

Procès-verbal de la conférence tenue entre les commissaires du roi et les commissaires du parlement, députés pour l'examen des articles de l'ordonnance de 1670, sur la procédure et instruction criminelle. Paris, 1757.

Pujoulx, Jean Baptiste. *La veuve Calas à Paris; ou, Le triomphe de Voltaire, pièce en un acte, en prose.* Paris, 1791.

Quesnay, Francois. *Recherches critiques et historiques sur l'origine sur les divers etat sur les progrès de la chirurgie.* Paris, 1744.

Racine, Jean. *Les plaideurs.* 1697. Reprint, Paris: Imprimerie Nationale, 1995.

Raynal, Jean. *Histoire de la ville de Toulouse, avec une notice des hommes illustrés.* Toulouse, 1759.

Restif de La Bretonne. *Les nuits de Paris; or, The Nocturnal Spectator.* Translated by L. Asher and E. Fertig. New York: Random House, 1964.

Richelet, Pierre. *Dictionnaire français, contenant les mots et les choses.* New edition. Geneva, 1690.

Richer, François. *Causes célèbres et intéressantes, avec les jugements qui les ont décidées. Rédigées de nouveau par M. Richer, ancien avocat au parlement.* 22 vols. Amsterdam, 1772–88.

Rousseaud de la Combe, Guy du. *Traité des matières criminelles suivant l'ordonnance de 1670.* Paris, 1740.

Rozoi, Barnabé Farmien de. *Annales de la ville de Toulouse.* Paris, 1771–76.

Saviard, Barthélemy. *Nouveau recueil d'observations chirurgicales.* Paris, 1702.

Segla, Guillaume de. *Histoire tragique et arrests de la cour de parlement de Toulouse.* Paris, 1613.

Seigneux de Correvon, François. *Essai sur l'usage, l'abus et les inconvéniens de la torture, dans la procédure criminelle.* Lausanne, 1768.

Serpillon, François. *Code criminel; ou, Commentaire sur l'ordonnance de 1670.* New edition. 2 vols. Lyon, 1788.

Servan, Joseph-Michel-Antoine. *Discours sur les moeurs prononcé au parlement de Grenoble, en 1769.* Lyon, 1769.

Servin, Louis. *Actions notables et plaidoyez de Messire Louys Servin, conseiller du roy. Dernière édition.* Paris, 1631.

Sévigné, Marie de Rabutin-Chantal. *Correspondance.* 3 vols. Edited by Roger Duchêne. Paris: Gallimard, 1972–78.

Sharp, Samuel. *A Treatise on the Operations of Surgery.* London, 1739.

Simon, Etienne. *Histoire des malheurs de la famille de Calas, procédé de Marc Antoine Calas, le suicide, à l'univers, héroide.* Paris, 1765.

Smollett, Tobias. *Travels through France and Italy.* 1766. Reprint, New York: Praeger, 1970.

Thouron, Jean-François. *Histoire de la royale compagnie de messieurs les pénitents bleus de Toulouse.* Toulouse, 1688.

Tragopome, Apompée de. *Sermons prechés à Toulouse.* [Toulouse?], 1772.

Voltaire. *Commentaire sur le livre des délits et des peines.* 1766. Reprint, Paris: Garnier Frères, 1879.

———. *Histoire d'Elisabeth Canning et de Jean Calas.* Paris, 1762.

———. "Prix de la justice et de l'humanité." In Jean Pierre Brissot de Warville, *Bibliothèque philosophique du législateur, du politique, du jurisconsulte; ou Choix des meilleurs discours, dissertations, essais, fragmens, composés sur la législation criminelle,* vol. 5: 1–108. Berlin, 1782–85.

———. *Traité sur la tolérance.* Paris, 1763. Reprint, Paris: Flammarion, 1989.

———. *Voltaire's Correspondence.* 107 vols. Edited by Theodore Besterman (Geneva: Institut et musée Voltaire, 1953–67).

Secondary Sources

Abbiateci, André. *Crimes et criminalité en France sous l'ancien régime.* Paris: Armand Colin, 1971.

Adher, J. *Les confréries de pénitents de Toulouse avant 1789.* Toulouse: Imprimerie Lagarde et Sebille, 1897.

Agulhon, Maurice. *Pénitents et Francs-maçons de l'ancienne provence: Essai sur la sociabilité méridionale.* Paris: Fayard, 1968.

Alleg, Henri. *The Question.* Introduction by Jean-Paul Sartre. Translated by John Calder. New York: George Braziller, 1958.

Améry, Jean. *At the Mind's Limits: Contemplations by a Survivor on Auschwitz and Its Realities.* Translated and edited by Sidney Rosenfeld and Stella P. Rosenfeld. Bloomington: Indiana University Press, 1980.

Amilhau, Henri. *Nos premiers présidents: Revue historique, politique et juridique du parlement de Toulouse.* Toulouse: L. Sistac & J. Boubée, 1882.

Anchel, Robert. *Crimes et châtiments au XVIIIe siècle.* Paris: Perrin, 1933.

Andrews, Richard Mowery. *Law, Magistracy, and Crime in Old Regime Paris, 1735–1789.* Cambridge: Cambridge University Press, 1994.

Asad, Talal. "Notes on Body Pain and Truth in Medieval Christian Ritual." *Economy and Society* 12 (1983): 287–327.

Aubry, Gérard. *La jurisprudence criminelle du châtelet de Paris sous le règne de Louis XVI.* Paris: Librairie Générale de Droit et de Jurisprudence, 1971.

Augustin, Jean-Marie. "Les Capitouls, juges des causes criminelles et de police à la fin de l'ancien régime." *Annales du Midi* 84 (1972): 183–211.

Bakan, David. *Disease, Pain and Sacrifice: Towards a Psychology of Suffering.* Boston: Beacon Press, 1968.

Bakhtin, Mikhail M. *Rabelais and His World.* Translated by Hélène Iswolsky. Bloomington: Indiana University Press, 1984.

Banker, James R. *Death in the Community: Memorialization and Confraternities in an Italian Commune in the Late Middle Ages.* Athens: University of Georgia Press, 1988.

Barasch, Moshe. *Gestures of Despair in Medieval and Early Renaissance Art.* New York: New York University Press, 1976.

Barker-Benfield, G. J. *The Culture of Sensibility: Sex and Society in Eighteenth-Century Britain.* Chicago: University of Chicago Press, 1992.

Barnes, Andrew E. "Cliques and Participation in a Pre-Modern French Voluntary Association: The Pénitents Bourras of Marseille in the Eighteenth Century." *Journal of Interdisciplinary History* 19, no. 1 (summer 1988): 25–54.

———. *The Social Dimension of Piety: Associative Life and Devotional Change in the Penitent Confraternities of Marseilles (1499–1792).* New York: Paulist Press, 1994.

Bartlett, Robert. *Trial by Fire and Water: The Medieval Judicial Ordeal.* Oxford: Clarendon Press, 1986.

Bastard-d'Etang, Henri Bruno. *Les parlements de France: Essai historique sur leurs usages, leur organisation et leur autorité.* 2 vols. Paris: Didier, 1857.

Bauman, Richard. *Let Your Words Be Few: Symbolism of Speaking and Silence among Seventeenth-Century Quakers.* Cambridge: Cambridge University Press, 1983.

Bayne, Sheila. "Le rôle des larmes dans le discours sur la conversion." In *La conversion au XVIIe siècle: Actes du XIIe colloque de Marseille,* edited by Roger Duchêne, 417–27. Marseilles: CMR, 1983.

Beckwith, Sarah. *Christ's Body: Identity, Culture, and Society in Late Medieval Writings.* New York: Routledge, 1993.

Bée, Michel. "Le spectacle de l'exécution dans la France d'ancien régime." *Annales Economie, Sociétés, Civilizations* 38 (July–August 1983): 843–62.

Beik, William H. "Magistrates and Popular Uprisings in France before the Fronde: The Case of Toulouse." *Journal of Modern History* 46 (December 1974): 585–608.

———. *Urban Protest in Seventeenth-Century France: The Culture of Retribution.* Cambridge: Cambridge University Press, 1997.

Bell, David A. *Lawyers and Citizens: The Making of a Political Elite in Old Regime France.* Oxford: Oxford University Press, 1994.

Bell, Rudolph. *Holy Anorexia.* Chicago: University of Chicago Press, 1985.

Belton, Neil. *The Good Listener: Helen Bamber, A Life against Cruelty.* London: Weidenfeld & Nicholson, 1998.

Benedict, Philip. *Rouen during the Wars of Religion.* Cambridge: Cambridge University Press, 1981.

Benedict, Philip, ed. *Cities and Social Change in Early Modern France.* London: Unwin Hyman, 1989.

Berlanstein, Lenard R. "The Advocates of Toulouse in the Eighteenth Century, 1750–1799." Ph.D. diss., Johns Hopkins University, 1973.

———. *The Barristers of Toulouse in the Eighteenth Century, 1740–1793.* Baltimore, Md.: Johns Hopkins University Press, 1975.

Bien, David. *The Calas Affair: Persecution, Toleration and Heresy in Eighteenth-Century Toulouse.* Princeton, N.J.: Princeton University Press, 1960.

Billaçois, François. "Pour une enquête sur la criminalité dans la France d'ancien régime." *Annales Economie, Sociétés, Civilizations* 22 (March–April 1967): 340–49.

Black, Christopher F. *Italian Confraternities in the Sixteenth Century.* Cambridge: Cambridge University Press, 1989.

Bloch, Marc. *The Royal Touch: Sacred Monarchy and Scrofula in France and England.* Translated by J. E. Anderson. London: Routledge & Kegan Paul, 1973.

Bloch, R. Howard. *Medieval French Literature and Law.* Berkeley and Los Angeles: University of California Press, 1977.

Böckle, Franz, and Jacques Pohier, eds. *The Death Penalty and Torture.* New York: Seabury Press, 1979.

Bok, Sissela. *Secrets: On the Ethics of Concealment and Revelation.* New York: Vintage Books, 1983.

Bondois, Paul. "La torture dans le ressort du parlement de Paris aux XVIIIe siècle." *Annales historiques de la révolution française* 5 (1928): 322–37.

Bordes, Maurice. "Contribution à l'étude des confreries de pénitents à Nice au XVIIe–XVIIIe siècles." *Annales du Midi* 19, no. 139 (July–December 1978): 377–88.

Bossy, John. *Christianity in the West, 1400–1700.* Oxford: Oxford University Press, 1985.

———. "The Mass as a Social Institution." *Past and Present* 100 (1983): 29–61.

———. "The Social History of Confession in the Age of the Reformation." *Transactions of the Royal Historical Society,* 5th ser., 25 (1975): 21–38.

Boursiquot, J. L. "Pénitents et sociétés religieuses au siècle des lumières." *Annales du Midi* 88 (April–June 1976): 159–75.

Bouwsma, William. "Lawyers and Early Modern Culture." *American Historical Review* 78 (April 1973): 303–27.

Bras, Gabriel, Le. "Les confréries chrétiennes—problèmes et propositions." *Revue historique de droit français et étranger,* 4th ser., 19–20 (1940–41): 310–63.

Bremmer, Jan, and Herman Roodenburg, eds. *A Cultural History of Gesture.* Ithaca, N.Y.: Cornell University Press, 1992.

Briggs, Robin. *Communities of Belief: Cultural and Social Tension in Early Modern France.* Oxford: Clarendon Press, 1989.

Brissenden, F. *Virtue in Distress: Studies in the Novel of Sentiment from Richardson to Sade.* New York: Harper & Row, 1974.

Brockliss, L. W. B. *French Higher Education in the Seventeenth and Eighteenth Centuries: A Cultural History.* Oxford: Clarendon Press, 1987.

———. "The Medico-Religious Universe of an Early Eighteenth-Century Parisian Doctor: The Case of Philippe Hecquet." In *The Medical Revolution of the Seventeenth Century,* edited by Roger French and Andrew Wear. Cambridge: Cambridge University Press, 1989.

Brockliss, L. W. B., and Colin Jones. *The Medical World of Early Modern France.* Oxford: Clarendon Press, 1997.

Brown, Roger, and Albert Gilman. "The Pronouns of Power and Solidarity." In *Style in Language,* edited by Thomas A. Sebeok, 253–76. Cambridge, Mass.: MIT Press, 1960.

Brown, Penelope, and Stephen Levinson. "Universals in Language Usage: Politeness Phenomena." In *Questions and Politeness: Strategies in Social Interaction,* edited by Esther N. Goody. Cambridge: Cambridge University Press, 1978.

Brown, Peter. *The Body and Society: Men, Women, and Sexual Renunciation in Early Christianity.* New York: Columbia University Press, 1988.

Broyard, Anatole. *Intoxicated by My Illness, and Other Writings on Life and Death.* New York: Fawcett Columbine, 1992.

Bruneau, Marie-Florine. *Women Mystics Confront the Modern World: Marie de L'Incarnation (1599–1672) and Madame Guyon (1648–1717).* Albany: State University of New York Press, 1998.

Bryant, Lawrence. *The King and the City in the Parisian Royal Entry Ceremony: Politics, Art and Ritual in the Renaissance.* Geneva: Librairie Droz, 1986.

Burke, Peter. "Insult and Blasphemy in Early Modern Italy." In *The Historical Anthropology of Early Modern Italy: Essays on Perception and Communication,* 95–109. Cambridge: Cambridge University Press, 1987.

———. *Popular Culture in Early Modern Europe.* New York: Harper & Row, 1978.

Burke, Peter, ed. *New Perspectives on Historical Writing.* University Park: Pennsylvania State University Press, 1992.

Burney, Fanny. *The Journals and Letters of Fanny Burney.* 12 vols. Edited by Joyce Hemlow and Althea Douglas. Oxford: Clarendon Press, 1972–84.

Bynum, Caroline Walker. *Holy Feast and Holy Fast: The Religious Significance of Food to Medieval Women.* Berkeley and Los Angeles: University of California Press, 1987.

———. *The Resurrection of the Body in Western Christianity, 200–1336.* New York: Columbia University Press, 1995.

Byman, Seymour. "Ritualistic Acts and Compulsive Behaviour." *American Historical Review* 83 (June 1978): 625–43.

Cameron, Iain A. *Crime and Repression in the Auvergne and the Guyenne, 1720–1790.* Cambridge: Cambridge University Press, 1981.

———. "The Police of Eighteenth-Century France." *European Studies Review* 7 (1977): 47–75.

Castan, Nicole. "Crime and Justice in Languedoc: The Critical Years, 1750–90." *Criminal Justice History* 1 (1980): 175–84.

Castan, Yves. *Honnêteté et relations sociales en Languedoc, 1715–1780.* Paris: Plon, 1974.

Catte, Tabatha, Tobia Delmolino, and Robert Held, eds. *Catalogo della mostra di strumenti di tortura, 1400–1800.* Florence, Qua d'Arno, 1985.

Certeau, Michel de. *The Mystic Fable.* Translated by Michael B. Smith. Chicago: University of Chicago Press, 1992.

Chalande, Jules. *Histoire des rues de Toulouse: Monuments, institutions, habitants.* 1919–29. Reprint, Marseille: Laffitte, 1982.

Charon, Rita. "Doctor-Patient/Reader-Writer: Learning to Find the Text." *Soundings* 72 (spring 1989): 137–52.

Chassaigne, Marc. *The Calas Case.* Translated by Ragland Somerset. London: Hutchinson & Co., 1929.

Chaytor, Miranda. "Household and Kinship: Ryton in the Late Sixteenth and Early Seventeenth Centuries." *History Workshop Journal* (1980): 24–60.

Christian, William A., Jr. *Local Religion in Sixteenth-Century Spain.* Princeton, N.J.: Princeton University Press, 1981.

———. "Provoked Religious Weeping in Early Modern Spain." In *Religious Organization and Religious Experience,* edited by John Davis. London: Academic Press, 1982.

Church, William. "The Decline of French Jurists as Political Theorists, 1660–1789." *French Historical Studies* 5 (1967): 1–40.

Clanchy, M. T. *From Memory to Written Record: England, 1066–1307.* Cambridge, Mass.: Harvard University Press, 1979.

Clark, Alice. *Working Life of Women in the Seventeenth Century.* New York: Routledge, 1992.

Clark, Stuart. "French Historians and Early Modern Popular Culture." *Past and Present* 100 (1983): 62–99.

Cobb, Richard. *Death in Paris.* Oxford: Oxford University Press, 1978.

Cobban, Alfred. "Cruelty as a Political Problem." *Encounter* 4 (1955): 32–39.

———. "The *Parlements* of France in the Eighteenth Century." In *Aspects of the French Revolution.* New York: George Braziller, 1968.

Cohen, Esther. *The Crossroads of Justice: Law and Culture in Late Medieval France.* Leiden: E. J. Brill, 1993.

Cohen, Thomas V., and Elizabeth S. Cohen. *Words and Deeds in Renaissance Rome: Trials before the Papal Magistrates.* Toronto: University of Toronto Press, 1993.

Cohn, Norman R. C. *The Pursuit of the Millennium: Revolutionary Millenarians and Mystical Anarchists of the Middle Ages.* Revised and expanded edition. New York: Oxford University Press, 1970.

Cohn, Samuel K., Jr. *Death and Property in Siena, 1205–1800: Strategies for the Afterlife.* Baltimore, Md.: Johns Hopkins University Press, 1988.

Collard, Gilbert. *Voltaire, l'affaire Calas et nous.* Paris: Les Belles Lettres, 1994.

Collins, James. "Geographic and Social Mobility in Early Modern France." *Journal of Social History* 24, no. 3 (spring 1991): 563–77.

Constable, Giles. *Attitudes towards Self-inflicted Suffering in the Middle Ages.* Brookline, Mass.: Hellenic College Press, 1982.

Coutet, Alexandre. *Jean Calas, roué vif et innocent.* Anduze: Musée du désert en Cévennes, 1933.

Cox, Stephen. "Sensibility as Argument." In *Sensibility in Transformation: Creative Resistance to Sentiment from the Augustans to the Romantics,* edited by Syndy McMillen Conger. London: Associated University Press, 1990.

Curran, Patricia. *Grace before Meals: Food Ritual and Body Discipline in Convent Culture.* Urbana: University of Illinois Press, 1989.

Curzon, Alfred de. "L'énseignement du droit français dans les universités de France au XVII et XVIII siècles." *Nouvelle revue historique de droit français et étranger* 44 (1919): 209–69.

Damaska, Mirjan. "The Death of Legal Torture." *Yale Law Journal* 87 (1978): 860–90.

Darnton, Robert. *The Great Cat Massacre and Other Episodes in French Cultural History.* New York: Basic Books, 1984.

———. *The Literary Underground of the Old Regime.* Cambridge, Mass.: Harvard University Press, 1982.

———. *Mesmerism and the End of the Enlightenment in France.* Cambridge, Mass.: Harvard University Press, 1968.

Daston, Lorraine, and Katherine Park. "Hermaphrodites in Renaissance France." *Critical Matrix* 1 (1985): 1–19.

Davidson, N. S. *The Counter Reformation.* New York: Basil Blackwell, 1987.

Davies, Joan. "Persecution and Protestantism: Toulouse, 1562–1575." *The Historical Journal* 22, no. 1 (March 1979): 31–52.

Davis, Natalie Zemon. "Boundaries and the Sense of Self in Sixteenth-Century France." In *Reconstructing Individualism: Autonomy, Individuality, and the Self in Western Thought*, edited by T. C. Heller. Stanford, Calif.: Stanford University Press, 1986.

———. *Fiction in the Archives: Pardon Tales and Their Tellers in Sixteenth-Century France*. Stanford, Calif.: Stanford University Press, 1987.

———. "Ghosts, Kin, and Progeny: Some Features of Family Life in Early Modern France." *Daedalus* 106 (spring 1977): 87–114.

———. *The Return of Martin Guerre*. Cambridge, Mass.: Harvard University Press, 1983.

———. *Society and Culture in Early Modern France: Eight Essays*. Stanford, Calif.: Stanford University Press, 1975.

Delbèke, Francis. *L'action politique et sociale des avocats au XVIIe siècle*. Paris and Louvain: Librairie Universitaire, 1927.

Delcambre, Etienne. "The Psychology of Lorraine Witchcraft Suspects." In *European Witchcraft*. Edited by E. William Monter. New York: John Wiley & Sons, Inc., 1969.

———. "Witchcraft Trials in Lorraine: Psychology of the Judges." In *European Witchcraft*. Edited by E. William Monter. New York: John Wiley & Sons, Inc., 1969.

Detourbet, Edmond. *La procédure criminelle aux XVIIe siècle*. Paris: Arthur Rousseau, 1881.

Dewald, Jonathan. "'The Perfect Magistrate': *Parlementaires* and Crime in Sixteenth-Century Rouen." *Archive for Reformation History* 67 (1976): 284–300.

Diefendorf, Barbara B. *Beneath the Cross: Catholics and Huguenots in Sixteenth-Century Paris*. New York: Oxford University Press, 1991.

Diefendorf, Barbara B., and Carla Hesse, eds. *Culture and Identity in Early Modern Europe (1500–1800): Essays in Honor of Natalie Zemon Davis*. Ann Arbor: University of Michigan Press, 1993.

Dixon, Laurinda S. *Perilous Chastity: Women and Illness in Pre-Enlightenment Art and Medicine*. Ithaca, N.Y.: Cornell University Press, 1995.

Doyle, William. *The Parlement of Bordeaux and the End of the Old Regime, 1771–1790*. New York: St. Martin's Press, 1974.

Dubedat, M. *Histoire du parlement de Toulouse*. 2 vols. Paris: Arthur Rousseau, 1885.

DuBois, Page. *Torture and Truth*. New York: Routledge, 1990.

Dubus, Andre. *Broken Vessels*. Boston: David R. Godine, 1991.

Duby, Georges. "Réflexions sur la douleur physique au moyen âge." In *Mâle moyen âge*, 203–209. Paris: Flammarion, 1988.

Duden, Barbara. *The Woman beneath the Skin: A Doctor's Patients in Eighteenth-Century Germany*. Translated by Thomas Dunlap. Cambridge: Harvard University Press, 1991.

Durand, Bernard. "Arbitraire du juge et le droit de la torture: L'exemple du conseil souverain de Roussillon." *Recueil des mémoires et travaux publié par la société d'histoire du droit et des institutions des anciens pays de droit ecrit*, fasc. 10 (1979): 141–79.

Edgerton, Samuel Y., Jr. *Pictures and Punishment: Art and Criminal Prosecution during the Florentine Renaissance*. Ithaca, N.Y.: Cornell University Press, 1985.

Elias, Norbert. *The Civilizing Process*. Translated by Edmund Jephcott. 2 vols. New York: Pantheon Press, 1978–82.

———. *The History of Manners*. Vol. 1 of *The Civilizing Process*. Translated by Edmund Jephcott. New York: Pantheon Books, 1978.

Esmein, Adhemar. *A History of Continental Criminal Procedure, with Special Reference to France*. Translated by John Simpson. Boston: Little, Brown and Company, 1913.

Estes, J. Worth. *Dictionary of Protopharmacology, Therapeutic Practices, 1700–1850*. Canton, Mass.: Science History Publications, 1990.

Evans, Richard J. *Rituals of Retribution: Capital Punishment in Germany, 1600–1987*. Oxford: Oxford University Press, 1996.

Evennett, H. O. *The Spirit of the Counter-Reformation*. Cambridge: Cambridge University Press, 1968.

Fairchilds, Cissie. *Domestic Enemies: Masters and Servants in Old Regime France*. Baltimore, Md.: Johns Hopkins University Press, 1984.

Farge, Arlette. "Les artisans malade de leur travail." *Annales Economie, Sociétés, Civilizations* 32, no. 5 (September–October 1977): 993–1006.

Farge, Arlette, and Jacques Revel. *The Vanishing Children of Paris: Rumor and Politics before the French Revolution*. Translated by Claudia Miéville. Cambridge, Mass.: Harvard University Press, 1991.

Farr, James R. *Hands of Honor: Artisans and Their World in Dijon, 1550–1650*. Ithaca, N.Y.: Cornell University Press, 1988.

———. "The Pure and Disciplined Body: Hierarchy, Morality, and Symbolism in France during the Catholic Reformation." *Journal of Interdisciplinary History* 21 (winter 1991): 391–414.

Feitlowitz, Marguerite. *A Lexicon of Terror: Argentina and the Legacies of Torture*. New York: Oxford University Press, 1998.

Ferguson, Charles. "The Structure and Use of Politeness Formulas." *Language in Society* 5 (1976): 137–51.

Fiering, Norman S. "Irresistible Compassion: An Aspect of Eighteenth-Century Sympathy and Humanitarianism." *Journal of the History of Ideas* 37 (April–June 1976): 195–218.

Firth, Raymond. "Verbal and Bodily Rituals of Greeting and Parting." In *The Interpretation of Ritual: Essays in Honor of A. I. Richards*, edited by J. S. La Fontaine. London: Tavistock, 1972.

Floutard, Gilbert, and Marc Miguet. *La justice à Toulouse au XVIIIème siècle*. Toulouse: Service d'Action Culturelle et Educative, 1986.

Flynn, Maureen. *Sacred Charity: Confraternities and Social Welfare in Spain, 1400–1700*. Ithaca, N.Y.: Cornell University Press, 1989.

———. "The Spectacle of Suffering in Spanish Streets." In *City and Spectacle in Medieval Europe*, edited by Barbara A. Hanawalt and Kathryn L. Reyerson, 153–70. Minneapolis: University of Minnesota Press, 1993.

Forster, Robert. *The Nobility of Toulouse: A Social and Economic Study*. Baltimore, Md.: Johns Hopkins University Press, 1960.

Foucault, Michel. *Discipline and Punish: The Birth of the Prison*. Translated by Alan Sheridan. New York: Vintage Books, 1979.

Frêche, Georges. *Toulouse et la région midi-pyrénées au siècle des lumières vers 1670–1789*. Paris: Cujas, 1974.

Froeschlé-Chopard, Marie. *La religion populaire en Provence orientale au XVIIIe siècle*. Paris: Beauchesne, 1980.

Furbank, P. N. *Diderot: A Critical Biography*. New York: Knopf, 1992.

Galpern, A. N. *The Religions of the People in Sixteenth-Century Champagne*. Cambridge, Mass.: Harvard University Press, 1976.

Garfinkel, Harold. "Conditions of Successful Degradation Ceremonies." *American Journal of Sociology* 61 (1956): 420–24.

Garrioch, David. "Verbal Insults in Eighteenth-Century Paris." In *The Social History of Language*, edited by Peter Burke and Roy Porter, 104–19. Cambridge: Cambridge University Press, 1987.

Gaston, Jean. *La dévote compagnie des pénitents gris de Toulouse.* Toulouse: Eche, 1983.

Gatrell, V. A. C., and T. B. Hadden. "Criminal Statistics and Their Interpretation." In *Nineteenth-Century Society: Essays in the Use of Quantitative Methods for the Study of Social Data*, edited by E. A. Wrigley. Cambridge: Cambridge University Press, 1972.

Gatrell, V. A. C., Bruce Lenman, and Geoffrey Parker, eds. *Crime and the Law: The Social History of Crime in Western Europe since 1500.* London: Europa Publications, 1980.

Geertz, Clifford. "Centers, Kings and Charisma: Reflections on the Symbolics of Power." In *Culture and Its Creators: Essays in Honor of Edward Shils*, edited by Joseph Ben-David and Terry Nichols Clark. Chicago: University of Chicago Press, 1977.

———. *The Interpretation of Cultures.* New York: Basic Books, 1973.

Gelbart, Nina Rattner. *Feminine and Opposition Journalism in Old Regime France:* Le Journal des Dames. Berkeley: University of California Press, 1987.

———. *The King's Midwife: A History and Mystery of Madame du Coudray.* Berkeley and Los Angeles: University of California Press, 1998.

Gélis, Jacques. *History of Childbirth: Fertility, Pregnancy, and Birth in Early Modern Europe.* Translated by Rosemary Morris. Boston: Northeastern University Press, 1991.

Gennep, Arnold van. *Manuel de folklore français contemporain.* 7 vols. Paris: Picard, 1947.

———. *The Rites of Passage.* Translated by Monika B. Vizedom and Gabrielle L. Caffee. London: Routledge & Kegan Paul, 1960.

Giesey, Ralph E. *The Royal Funeral Ceremony in Renaissance France.* Geneva: E. Droz, 1960.

Gilman, Sander. *Making the Body Beautiful: A Cultural History of Aesthetic Surgery.* Princeton, N.J.: Princeton University Press, 1999.

Ginzburg, Carlo. *The Cheese and the Worms: The Cosmos of a Sixteenth-Century Miller.* Translated by John and Anne C. Tedeschi. New York: Penguin, 1980.

———. "The Inquisitor as Anthropologist." In *Clues, Myths and the Historical Method.* Translated by John and Anne C. Tedeschi. Baltimore, Md.: Johns Hopkins University Press, 1989.

Gittings, Clare. *Death, Burial and the Individual in Early Modern England.* London: Croom Helm, 1984.

Given, James B. "The Inquisitors of Languedoc and the Medieval Technology of Power." *American Historical Review* 94, no. 2 (April 1989): 336–59.

———. *State and Society in Medieval Europe: Gwynedd and Languedoc under outside Rule.* Ithaca, N.Y.: Cornell University Press, 1990.

Gluckman, Max. *Custom and Conflict in Africa.* Oxford: Basil Blackwell, 1966.

Goffman, Erving. *Interaction Ritual: Essays on Face to Face Behaviour.* New York: Doubleday, 1967.

Good, Mary-Jo DelVecchio, et al., ed. *Pain as Human Experience: An Anthropological Perspective.* Berkeley and Los Angeles: University of California Press, 1992.

Goodman, Dena. *The Republic of Letters: A Cultural History of the French Enlightenment.* Ithaca, N.Y.: Cornell University Press, 1994.

Goody, Esther N. "'Greeting,' 'Begging' and the Presentation of Respect." In *The Interpretation of Ritual: Essays in Honor of A. I. Richards*, edited by J. S. La Fontaine. London: Tavistock, 1972.

———. "Towards a Theory of Questions." In *Questions and Politeness*, edited by Esther N. Goody. Cambridge: Cambridge University Press, 1978.

Goody, Jack. "Religion and Ritual: The Definitional Problem." *The British Journal of Sociology* 12 (1961): 142–64.

Goubert, Pierre. "Les officiers royaux des présidiaux, bailliages et élections dans la société française du XVII siècle." *Dix-septième siècle* 52–53 (1959): 54–75.

Gougaud, Louis. *Devotional and Ascetic Practices in the Middle Ages*. Translated by G. C. Bateman. London: Burns Oates and Washbourne Ltd., 1927.

Gowing, Laura. "Gender and the Language of Insult in Early Modern London." *History Workshop Journal* 35 (1993): 1–21.

Grealy, Lucy. *Autobiography of a Face*. Boston: Houghton Mifflin Co., 1994.

Greenblatt, Stephen. "Toward a Universal Language of Motion: Reflections on a Seventeenth-Century Muscle Man." In *Choreographing History*, edited by Susan Leigh Foster, 25–31. Bloomington: Indiana University Press, 1995.

Greengrass, Mark. "The Anatomy of a Religious Riot in Toulouse in May 1562." *Journal of Ecclesiastical History* 34, no. 3 (July 1983): 367–91.

Greenshields, Malcolm. *An Economy of Violence in Early Modern France: Crime and Justice in the Haute Auvergne, 1587–1664*. University Park: Pennsylvania State University Press, 1994.

———. "Women, Violence, and Criminal Justice Records in Early Modern Auvergne (1587–1664)." *Canadian Journal of History* 22 (August 1987): 175–94.

Gresset, Maurice. "La justice répressive aux XVII et XVIII siècles." *Bulletin d'histoire moderne et contemporaine* 13 (1982): 143–52.

Greyerz, Kaspar von. *Religion and Society in Early Modern Europe, 1500–1800*. London: George Allen & Unwin, 1984.

Groebner, Valentin. "Losing Face, Saving Face: Noses and Honour in the Late Medieval Town." *History Workshop Journal* 40 (1995): 1–15.

Guyon, Gérard. "L'information criminelle et la détention avant jugement du Moyen Age au XVIII siècle." *Cahiers du droit* (1985): 47–75.

Hallpike, C. R. "Social Hair," *Man* 4 (1969): 259–61.

Halttunen, Karen. "Early American Murder Narratives: The Birth of Horror." In *The Power of Culture: Critical Essays in American History*, edited by Richard Wightman Fox and T. J. Jackson Lears. Chicago: University of Chicago Press, 1993.

Hanawalt, Barbara, ed. *Women and Work in Preindustrial Europe*. Bloomington: Indiana University Press, 1986.

Hanlon, Gregory. "Les rituels d'agression en Aquitaine au XVII siècle." *Annales Economie, Sociétés, Civilizations* 40, no. 2 (1985): 244–68.

Hanson, Elizabeth. "Torture and Truth in Renaissance England." *Representations* 34 (spring 1991): 53–84.

Harding, Robert R. "The Mobilization of Confraternities against the Reformation in France." *Sixteenth Century Journal* 11, no. 2 (1980): 85–107.

Hardwick, Julie. *The Practice of Patriarchy: Gender and the Politics of Household Authority in Early Modern France*. University Park: Pennsylvania State University Press, 1998.

Hargreaves-Mawdsley, W. H. *A History of Legal Dress in Europe until the End of the Eighteenth Century*. Oxford: Clarendon Press, 1963.

Hawkins, Anne Hunsaker. *Reconstructing Illness: Studies in Pathography.* West Lafayette, Ind.: Purdue University Press, 1993.

Held, Robert. *Inquisition: A Bilingual Guide to the Exhibition of Torture Instruments from the Middle Ages to the Industrial Era, Presented in Various European Cities in 1983–87* (in English and Spanish). Florence: Qua d'Arno, 1985.

Henderson, John. "The Flagellant Movement and Flagellant Confraternities in Central Italy, 1260–1400." In *Religious Motivation: Biographical and Sociological Problems for the Church Historian,* edited by Derek Baker. Oxford: Basil Blackwell, 1978.

———. *Piety and Charity in Late Medieval Florence.* Oxford: Clarendon Press, 1994.

Hepworth, Mike, and Bryan Turner. *Confession: Studies in Deviance and Religion.* New York: Routledge and Kegan Paul, 1982.

Herrup, Cynthia. "Law and Morality in Seventeenth-Century England." *Past and Present* 106 (1985): 102–23.

Hoffman, Philip T. *Church and Community in the Diocese of Lyon, 1500–1789.* New Haven, Conn.: Yale University Press, 1984.

Horten, Gerd. "'Bearing Truth': Single Women, Childbirth and Torture in English and New England Courts, 1575–1860." Paper presented at the annual meeting of the International Association for Philosophy and Literature in Irvine, California, 26–28 April 1990.

Howell, Martha. *Women, Production, and Patriarchy in Late Medieval Cities.* Chicago: University of Chicago Press, 1986.

Hufton, Olwen H. "Attitudes towards Authority in Eighteenth-Century Languedoc." *Social History* 3 (1978): 281–302.

———. *The Poor of Eighteenth-Century France, 1750–1789.* Oxford: Clarendon Press, 1974.

Ignatieff, Michael. "Torture's Dead Simplicity." *New Statesman* 110 (20 September 1985): 24–26.

Illich, Ivan. "A Plea for Body History." *Michigan Quarterly Review* 26 (spring 1987): 342–48.

Imbert, Jean. *Quelques procès criminels des XVIIe et XVIIIe siècles.* Paris: Presses Universitaires de France, 1964.

Isherwood, Robert. *Farce and Fantasy: Popular Entertainment in Eighteenth-Century Paris.* Oxford: Oxford University Press, 1986.

Jacobson, David Yale. "The Politics of Criminal Law Reform in Pre-Revolutionary France." Ph.D. diss., Brown University, 1976.

———. "The *Trois Roués* Case." *Proceedings of the Annual Meeting of the Western Society for French History* 4 (1976): 168–73.

Kafker, Frank A. *The Encyclopedists as a Group: A Collective Biography of the Authors of the Encyclopédie.* Oxford: Voltaire Foundation, 1996.

Kafker, Frank A., and Serena L. Kafker. *The Encyclopedists as Individuals: A Biographical Dictionary of the Authors of the Encyclopédie.* Oxford: Voltaire Foundation, 1988.

Kagan, Richard. "Law Students and Legal Careers in Eighteenth-Century France." *Past and Present* 68 (August 1975): 38–72.

Kantorowicz, Ernst H. *The King's Two Bodies: A Study in Mediaeval Political Theology.* Princeton, N.J.: Princeton University Press, 1957.

Kaufmann, Joanne. "The Critique of Criminal Justice in Eighteenth-Century France: A Study in the Changing Social Ethics of Crime and Punishment." Ph.D. diss., Harvard University, 1976.

————. "In Search of Obedience: The Critique of Criminal Justice in Eighteenth-Century France." *Proceedings of the Annual Meeting of the Western Society for French History* 6 (1978): 188–95.

Keele, Kenneth B. *Anatomies of Pain*. Oxford: Blackwell Scientific Publications, 1957.

Kerr, Margaret H., Richard D. Forsyth, and Michael J. Plyley. "Cold Water and Hot Iron: Trial by Ordeal in England." *Journal of Interdisciplinary History* 22, no. 4 (spring 1992): 573–95.

Klaits, Joseph. *Servants of Satan: The Age of the Witch Hunts*. Bloomington: Indiana University Press, 1985.

Kleinman, Arthur. *The Illness Narratives: Suffering, Healing and the Human Condition*. New York: Basic Books, 1988.

Knowlson, John. "The Idea of Gesture as a Universal Language in the Seventeenth and Eighteenth Centuries." *Journal of the History of Ideas* 26 (1965): 495–508.

Kors, Alan Charles. *D'Holbach's Coterie: An Enlightenment in Paris*. Princeton, N.J.: Princeton University Press, 1976.

Labov, William. "Rules for Ritual Insults." In *Studies in Social Interaction*, edited by David Sudnow, 120–69. New York: The Free Press, 1972.

Laget, Mireille. "Childbirth in Seventeenth- and Eighteenth-Century France: Obstetrical Practices and Collective Attitudes." In *Medicine and Society in France*, edited by Robert Forster and Orest Ranum. Baltimore, Md.: Johns Hopkins University Press, 1980.

Lamouzele, Edmond. *Toulouse au dix-huitième siècle, d'après les heures perdues de Pierre Barthès*. Toulouse: J. Marqueste, 1914.

Landon, Lana Hartman. "Suffering over Time: Six Varieties of Pain." *Soundings* 72 (spring 1989): 75–82.

Langbein, John H. *Prosecuting Crime in the Renaissance: England, Germany, France*. Cambridge, Mass.: Harvard University Press, 1974.

————. *Torture and the Law of Proof: Europe and England in the Ancien Régime*. Chicago: University of Chicago Press, 1977.

Lapierre, Eugene. *La parlement de Toulouse: son ressort, ses attributions, et ses archives*. Toulouse: Typographie de Bonnal et Gibrac, 1860.

Laqueur, Thomas. "Bodies, Details, and the Humanitarian Narrative." In *The New Cultural History*, edited by Lynn Hunt. Berkeley: University of California Press, 1989.

————. *Making Sex: The Body and Sex from the Greeks to Freud*. Cambridge, Mass.: Harvard University Press, 1990.

Lawrence, Christopher. "The Nervous System and Society in the Scottish Enlightenment." In *Natural Order: Historical Studies of Scientific Culture*, edited by Barry Barnes and Steven Shapin. Beverly Hills, Calif.: Sage Publications, 1979.

Lea, Henry Charles. *Torture*. Vol. 4 of *Superstition and Force: Essays on the Wager of Law, the Wager of Battle, the Ordeal, Torture*, edited by Edward Peters. 1866. Reprint, Philadelphia: University of Pennsylvania Press, 1973.

Lewis, Gilbert. *Day of Shining Red: An Essay on Understanding Ritual*. Cambridge: Cambridge University Press, 1980.

Lough, John. *France Observed in the Seventeenth Century by British Travelers*. Boston: Oriel Press, 1985.

————. "Louis, Chevalier de Jaucourt (1704–1780): A Biographical Sketch." In *The*

Encyclopédie in Eighteenth Century England and Other Studies. Newcastle upon Tyne: Oriel Press, 1970.

Luria, Keith P. "Rituals of Conversion: Catholics and Protestants in Seventeenth-Century Poitou." In *Culture and Identity in Early Modern Europe (1500–1800): Essays in Honor of Natalie Zemon Davis,* edited by Barbara B. Diefendorf and Carla Hesse. Ann Arbor: University of Michigan Press, 1993.

———. *Territories of Grace: Cultural Change in the Seventeenth-Century Diocese of Grenoble.* Berkeley: University of California, 1991.

Luyendijk-Elshout, Antonie. "Of Masks and Mills: The Enlightened Doctor and His Frightened Patient." In *The Languages of Psyche: Mind and Body in Enlightened Thought,* ed. G. S. Rousseau, 186–230. Berkeley and Los Angeles: University of California Press, 1990.

Maugham, F. H. *The Case of Jean Calas.* London: Heinemann, 1928.

McCullough, Lawrence B. "The Abstract Character and Transforming Power of Medical Language." *Soundings* 72 (spring 1989): 111–26.

MacDonald, Michael. *Mystical Bedlam: Madness, Anxiety, and Healing in Seventeenth-Century England.* Cambridge: Cambridge University Press, 1981.

McManners, John. *Death and the Enlightenment.* Oxford: Oxford University Press, 1981.

Mackrell, John. "Criticism of Seigneurial Justice in Eighteenth-Century France." In *French Government and Society, 1500–1800: Essays in Memory of Alfred Cobban,* edited by J. F. Bosher. London: Athlone Press, 1973.

Maes, L. T. "Empoisonnement, procédure, inquisitoriale, torture, et peine de mort au début de XVIII siècle." *Revue historique de droit français et étranger* 55 (1977): 59–72.

Maestro, M. *Voltaire and Beccaria as Reformers of the Criminal Law.* New York: Octagon, 1972.

Mairs, Nancy. *Plaintext: Essays.* Tucson: University of Arizona Press, 1986.

———. "The Literature of Personal Disaster." In *Voice Lessons,* edited by Nancy Mairs, 123–35. Boston: Beacon Press, 1994.

Mahoney, Michael Sean. *The Mathematical Career of Pierre de Fermat, 1601–1665.* Second edition. Princeton, N.J.: Princeton University Press, 1994.

Mandrou, Robert. *Magistrats et sorciers en France aux XVIIe siècle. Une analyse de psychologie historique.* Paris: Plon, 1968.

Mann, R. D., ed. *The History of the Management of Pain: From Early Principles to Present Practice.* Park Ridge, N.J.: Pantheon, 1988.

Marion, Marcel. *Dictionnaire des institutions de la France aux dix-septième et dix-huitième siècles.* 1923. Reprint, Paris: Éditions A. & J. Picard, 1984.

Martin, Daniel. "Justice parisienne et justice provinciale au dix-huitième siècle." *Bulletin de la société d'histoire moderne,* 15th ser., 15 (1976): 3–12.

Marrow, James. *Passion Iconography in Northern European Art.* Kortrijk, Belgium: Van Gheminert Publishing Co., 1979.

Maury, Alfred. "La législation criminelle sous l'ancien régime." *Revue de deux mondes* 23 (1877): 580–617.

Mauss, Marcel. "Body Techniques." In *Sociology and Pyschology: Essays.* Translated by Ben Brewster. Boston: Routledge & Kegan Paul, 1979.

Maza, Sarah. *Private Lives and Public Affairs: The Causes Célèbres of Prerevolutionary France.* Berkeley and Los Angeles: University of California Press, 1993.

Mellor, Alec. *La torture*. Paris: Horizons littéraires, 1949.

Melzack, Ronald, and Patrick D. Wall. *The Challenge of Pain*. New York: Basic Books, 1983.

Mentzer, Raymond A. *Heresy Proceedings in Languedoc, 1500–1560*. Philadelphia: American Philosophical Society, 1984.

———. "The Self-Image of the Magistrate in Sixteenth-Century France." *Criminal Justice History* 5 (1984): 23–43.

Mer, L. B. "La procédure criminelle au XVIIIe siècle: l'enseignement des archives bretonnes." *Revue historique* 555 (July–September 1985): 9–42.

Merback, Mitchell B. *The Thief, the Cross, and the Wheel: Pain and the Spectacle of Punishment in Medieval and Renaissance Europe*. Chicago: University of Chicago Press, 1998.

Mesuret, Robert. *Évocation du vieux Toulouse*. Paris: Éditions de Minuit, 1960.

Meyer, Jean. *La noblesse bretonne au XVIIIe siècle*. Paris: S.E.V.P.E.N., 1966.

Mogensen, Wayne. "Crimes and Punishments in Eighteenth-Century France." *Social History/Histoire Sociale* 10 (1977): 337–53.

Montrose, Louis A. *"A Midsummer Night's Dream* and the Shaping Fantasies of Elizabethan Culture: Gender, Power, Form." In *Rewriting the Renaissance: The Discourses of Sexual Difference in Early Modern Europe*. Edited by Margaret Ferguson, Maureen Quilligan, and Nancy Vickers. Chicago: University of Chicago Press, 1986.

Moogk, Peter N. "'Thieving Buggers' and 'Stupid Sluts': Insults and Popular Culture in New France." *William and Mary Quarterly* 36 (1979): 524–47.

Mornet, Daniel. "Les enseignements des bibliothèques privées, 1750–1780." *Revue d'histoire littéraire de France* 17 (1910): 449–97.

Morris, David B. *The Culture of Pain*. Berkeley: University of California Press, 1991.

Moulin, Daniel de. "A Historical-Phenomenological Study of Bodily Pain in Western Man." *Bulletin of the History of Medicine* 48 (1974): 540–70.

———. *The History of Surgery*. Boston: Kluwer Academic Publishers, 1988.

Mousnier, Roland E. *Society and the State*. Vol. 1 of *The Institutions of France under the Absolute Monarchy, 1598–1789*. Translated by Brian Pearce. Chicago: University of Chicago Press, 1979.

———. *The Organs of State and Society*. Vol. 2 of *The Institutions of France under the Absolute Monarchy, 1598–1789*. Translated by Arthur Goldhammer. Chicago: University of Chicago Press, 1984.

Muchembled, Robert. "Pour une histoire des gestes (XVe–XVIIIe siècle)." *Revue d'histoire moderne et contemporaine* 34 (1987): 87–101.

Muir, Edward, and Guido Ruggiero. Introduction to *History from Crime*, edited by Edward Muir and Guido Ruggiero. Baltimore, Md.: Johns Hopkins University Press, 1994.

Mullan, John. "Hypochondria and Hysteria: Sensibility and the Physicians." *The Eighteenth Century: Theory and Interpretation* 25 (1984): 141–74.

———. *Sentiment and Sociability: The Language of Feeling in the Eighteenth Century*. Oxford: Clarendon Press, 1988.

Mullett, Michael. *The Counter-Reformation and the Catholic Reformation in Early Modern Europe*. New York: Methuen, 1984.

Mundy, John Hine. *Liberty and Political Power in Toulouse, 1050–1230*. New York: Columbia University Press, 1954.

Musée des Augustins. *La réforme à Toulouse, de 1562 à 1762*. Toulouse: n.p., 1962.

Neuschel, Kristen. *Word of Honor: Interpreting Noble Culture in Sixteenth-Century France*. Ithaca, N.Y.: Cornell University Press, 1989.

Nixon, Edna. *Voltaire and the Calas Case*. London: Gollancz, 1961.

Norberg, Kathryn. *Rich and Poor in Grenoble, 1600–1814*. Berkeley: University of California Press, 1985.

Nunn, J. F. "Anesthesia in Ancient Times—Fact and Fable." In *The History of Anesthesia*, edited by Richard Atkinson and Thomas Boulton. New York: Parthenon, 1989.

Ong, Walter. *Orality and Literacy: The Technologizing of the Word*. London: Methuen, 1982.

Otis, Leah. *Prostitution in Medieval Society: The History of an Urban Institution in Languedoc*. Chicago: University of Chicago Press, 1985.

Ousset, P. E. *La chapelle des pénitents bleus et l'eglise Saint-Jerome: Histoire et description*. Toulouse: Imprimerie J.-M. Caussé, 1925.

———. *La Confrérie des pénitents bleus de Toulouse*. Toulouse: Imprimerie Saint-Cyprien, 1927.

Outram, Dorinda. *The Body and the French Revolution: Sex, Class and Political Culture*. New Haven, Conn.: Yale University Press, 1989.

———. *The Enlightenment*. Cambridge: Cambridge University Press, 1995.

Paster, Gail Kern. *The Body Embarrassed: Drama and the Disciplines of Shame in Early Modern England*. Ithaca, N.Y.: Cornell University Press, 1993.

Paulhet, Jean Claude. "Les parlementaires Toulousains à la fin du dix-huitième siècle." *Annales du Midi* 76 (1964): 189–204.

Pecquet, Marguerite. "La Compagnie Des Pénitents Blancs de Toulouse." *Annales du Midi* 84 (April–June 1972): 213–24.

———. "La fondation des pénitents blancs de Toulouse." *Annales du Midi* 85 (July–September 1973): 335–47.

Perkins, Judith. *The Suffering Self: Pain and Narrative Representation in the Early Christian Era*. New York: Routledge, 1995.

Perkins, Wendy. "The Presentation of Illness in the Memoirs of Mme. de Motteville and of Bussy-Rabutin." *Seventeenth-Century French Studies* 12 (1990): 26–37.

Pernick, Martin S. *A Calculus of Suffering: Pain, Professionalism, and Anesthesia in Nineteenth-Century America*. New York: Columbia University Press, 1985.

Peters, Edward. *Torture*. New York: Basil Blackwell, 1985.

Pinson-Ramin, Véronique. "La torture judiciaire en Bretagne au XVIIe siècle." *Revue historique de droit français et étranger* 72 (1994): 549–68.

Pitt-Rivers, Julian. "Honor and Social Status." In *Honour and Shame: The Values of Mediterranean Society*, edited by J. G. Peristiany. Chicago: University of Chicago Press, 1966.

Price, Reynolds. *A Whole New Life*. New York: Atheneum, 1994.

Puppi, Lionello. *Torment in Art: Pain, Violence, and Martyrdom*. New York: Rizzoli, 1990.

Ranum, Orest. "Courtesy, Absolutism and the Rise of the French State, 1630–1660." *Journal of Modern History* 52 (September 1980): 426–51.

———. "Lèse-Majesté Divine: Transgressing Boundaries." *Proceedings of the Annual Meeting of the Western Society for French History* 9 (1981): 68–80.

Rapley, Elizabeth. *The Dévotes: Women and Church in Seventeenth-Century France*. Montreal: McGill-Queen's University Press, 1990.

———. "Her Body the Enemy: Self-Mortification in Seventeenth-Century Convents." *Proceedings of the Annual Meeting of the Western Society for French History* 21 (1994): 25–35.

Rateau, Marguerite. "Les peines capitales et corporelles en France sous l'ancien régime (1670–1789)." *Annales internationales de criminologie* (1963): 276–308.

Rather, L. J. *Mind and Body in Eighteenth-Century Medicine.* London: Wellcome Historical Medical Library, 1965.

Reich, Warren Thomas. "Speaking of Suffering: A Moral Account of Compassion." *Soundings* 72 (spring 1989): 83–110.

Reinhardt, Steven G. "Crime and Royal Justice in Ancien Régime France: Modes of Analysis." *Journal of Interdisciplinary History* 13 (winter 1983): 437–60.

———. *Justice in the Sarladais, 1770–1790.* Baton Rouge: Louisiana State University Press, 1991.

———. "The Selective Prosecution of Crime in Ancien Régime France." *European History Quarterly* 16 (January 1986): 3–24.

Rejali, Darius. *Torture and Modernity: Self, Society, and State in Modern Iran.* Boulder, Colo.: Westview Press, 1994.

Rey, Roselyne. *The History of Pain.* Translated by Louise Elliott Wallace and J. A. and S. W. Cadden. Cambridge, Mass.: Harvard University Press, 1995.

Ribeiro, Aileen. *Dress in Eighteenth-Century Europe, 1715–1789.* New York: Holmes & Meier, 1984.

Richardson, Ruth. *Death, Dissection and the Destitute.* London: Penguin, 1988.

Rizzo, Tracey. "Sexual Violence in the Enlightenment: The State, the Bourgeoisie, and the Cult of the Victimized Woman." *Proceedings of the Annual Meeting of the Western Society for French History* 15 (1988): 122–29.

Roche, Daniel. *Le siècle des lumières en province: Académies et académiciens provinciaux, 1680–1789.* 2 vols. Paris: Mouton, 1978.

Rogozinski, Jan. *Power, Caste, and Law: Social Conflict in Fourteenth-Century Montpellier.* Cambridge, Mass.: Medieval Academy of America, 1982.

Roper, Lyndal. *Oedipus and the Devil: Witchcraft, Sexuality and Religion in Early Modern Europe.* New York: Routledge, 1994.

Rousseau, G. S. "Nerves, Spirits and Fibres: Towards Defining the Origins of Sensibility." *The Blue Guitar* 2 (1976): 125–53.

Rousseau, G. S., ed. *The Languages of Psyche: Mind and Body in Enlightenment Thought.* Berkeley: University of California Press, 1990.

Rubin, Miri. *Corpus Christi: The Eucharist in Late Medieval Culture.* Cambridge: Cambridge University Press, 1991.

Ruff, Julius R. *Crime, Justice, and Public Order in Old Regime France: The Sénéchaussées of Libourne and Bazas, 1696–1789.* London: Croom Helm, 1984.

———. "Rural Feuds and the Control of Conflict in the Guyenne, 1696–1789." *Proceedings of the Annual Meeting of the Western Society for French History* 14 (1987): 21–29.

Rule, John. *The Experience of Labour in Eighteenth-Century English Industry.* New York: St. Martin's Press, 1981.

Sacks, Oliver. *Awakenings.* New York: E. P. Dutton, 1973.

———. *A Leg to Stand On.* New York: Harper and Row, 1984.

———. *The Man Who Mistook His Wife for a Hat and Other Clinical Tales.* New York: Harper and Row, 1970.

Sáez, Nacuñán. "Torture: A Discourse on Practice." In *Tattoo, Torture, Mutilation, and Adornment: The Denaturalization of the Body in Culture and Text.* Edited by Frances E. Mascia-Lees and Patricia Sharpe. Albany: State University of New York Press, 1992.

Salmon, J. H. M. *Society in Crisis: France in the Sixteenth Century.* London: Methuen, 1975.

Sanday, Peggy Reeves. *Divine Hunger: Cannibalism as a Cultural System.* Cambridge: Cambridge University Press, 1986.

Scarry, Elaine. *The Body in Pain: The Making and Unmaking of the World.* New York: Oxford University Press, 1985.

Schnapper, Bernard. "La justice criminelle rendue par le parlement de Paris sous le règne de François I." *Revue historique de droit français et étranger* 52 (1974): 252–84.

Schneider, Robert A. *The Ceremonial City: Toulouse Observed, 1737–1780.* Princeton, N.J.: Princeton University Press, 1995.

———. "Crown and Capitoulat: Municipal Government in Toulouse, 1500–1789." In *Cities and Social Change in Early Modern France,* edited by Philip Benedict. London: Unwin Hyman, 1989.

———. "Mortification on Parade: Penitential Processions in Sixteenth- and Seventeenth-Century France." *Renaissance and Reformation* 10, no. 1 (February 1986): 123–46.

———. *Public Life in Toulouse, 1463–1789: From Municipal Republic to Cosmopolitan City.* Ithaca, N.Y.: Cornell University Press, 1989.

Schwartz, Robert. *Policing the Poor in Eighteenth-Century France.* Chapel Hill: University of North Carolina Press, 1988.

Sgard, Jean. "La littérature des causes célèbres." In *Approches des lumières: Mélanges offerts à Jean Fabre.* Paris: Klincksieck, 1974.

Shapiro, Barbara J. *Beyond Reasonable Doubt and Probable Cause: Historical Perspectives on the Anglo-American Law of Evidence.* Berkeley and Los Angeles: University of California Press, 1991.

———. *Probability and Certainty in Seventeenth-Century England: A Study of the Relationships between Natural Science, Religion, History, Law and Literature.* Princeton, N.J.: Princeton University Press, 1983.

Shennan, J. H. *The Parlement of Paris.* Ithaca, N.Y.: Cornell University Press, 1968.

Shklar, Judith. "Putting Cruelty First." *Daedalus* 111 (summer 1982): 17–27.

Shostak, Marjorie. *Nisa: The Life and Words of a !Kung Woman.* New York: Vintage Books, 1981.

Skevington, Suzanne M. *Psychology of Pain.* New York: John Wiley & Sons, 1995.

Shue, Henry. "Torture." *Philosophy and Public Affairs* 7 (1978): 124–43.

Soman, Alfred. "Criminal Jurisprudence in *Ancien-régime* France: The *Parlement* of Paris in the Sixteenth and Seventeenth Centuries." In *Crime and Criminal Justice in Europe and Canada.* Edited by Louis A. Knafla. Waterloo, Ontario: Wilfred Laurier University Press, 1981.

———. "Deviance and Criminal Justice in Western Europe, 1300–1800: An Essay on Structure." *Criminal Justice History* 1 (1980): 3–28.

———. *Sorcellerie et justice criminelle: Le parlement de Paris, 16e–18e siècles.* Hampshire: Variorum, 1992.

Sonenscher, Michael. *The Hatters of Eighteenth-Century France.* Berkeley: University of California Press, 1987.

Spelman, Elizabeth V. *Fruits of Sorrow: Framing Our Attention to Suffering.* Boston: Beacon Press, 1997.

Spierenburg, Pieter. *The Spectacle of Suffering: Executions and the Evolution of Repression from a Preindustrial Metropolis to the European Experience.* Cambridge: Cambridge University Press, 1984.

Starr, June, and Jane F. Collier, eds. *History and Power in the Study of Law.* Ithaca, N.Y.: Cornell University Press, 1989.

Stock, Brian. *Listening for the Text: On the Uses of the Past.* Baltimore, Md.: Johns Hopkins University Press, 1990.

Street, J. S. *French Sacred Drama from Bèze to Corneille: Dramatic Forms and Their Purposes in the Early Modern Theatre.* Cambridge: Cambridge University Press, 1983.

Tackett, Timothy. *Priest and Parish in Eighteenth-century France.* Princeton, N.J.: Princeton University Press, 1977.

Terpstra, Nicholas. "Women in the Brotherhood: Gender, Class, and Politics in Renaissance Bolognese Confraternities." *Renaissance and Reformation* 26, no. 3 (1990): 193–212.

Thomas, Keith. *Religion and the Decline of Magic.* London: Penguin, 1973.

Thomson, Rosemarie Garland. "Redrawing the Boundaries of Feminist Disability Studies." *Feminist Studies* 20, no. 3 (fall 1994): 583–95.

Thoumas-Schapira, Micheline. "La bourgeoisie toulousaine à la fin du dix-septième siècle." *Annales du Midi* 67 (1955): 313–29.

Timerman, Jacobo. *Prisoner without a Name, Cell without a Number.* Translated by Toby Talbot. New York: Vintage Books, 1981.

Todd, Janet. *Sensibility: An Introduction.* New York: Methuen, 1986.

Trachtenberg, Joshua. *Jewish Magic and Superstition: A Study in Folk Religion.* New York: Behrman's Jewish Book House, 1939.

Turner, Victor. *The Ritual Process: Structure and Anti-structure.* Ithaca, N.Y.: Cornell University Press, 1977.

Ullmann, Walter. "Reflections on Medieval Torture." *Juridical Review* 56 (1944): 123–37.

Ulrich, D. "La répression en Bourgogne au XVIIIe siècle." *Revue historique de droit français et étranger* 50 (1972): 398–437.

Van Sant, Ann Jessie. *Eighteenth-Century Sensibility and the Novel: The Senses in Social Context.* Cambridge, Mass.: Cambridge University Press, 1993.

Vigarello, Georges. *Concepts of Cleanliness: Changing Attitudes in France since the Middle Ages.* Translated by Jean Birrell. Cambridge: Cambridge University Press, 1988.

Viguerie, Jean de. *Le catholicisme des français dans l'ancienne France.* Paris: Nouvelles Éditions Latines, 1988.

Vila, Anne C. *Enlightenment and Pathology: Sensibility in the Literature and Medicine of Eighteenth-Century France.* Baltimore, Md.: Johns Hopkins University Press, 1998.

Vincent-Buffault, Anne. *The History of Tears: Sensibility and Sentimentality in France.* Translated by Teresa Bridgeman. New York: St. Martin's Press, 1991.

Wakefield, Walter L. *Heresy, Crusade, and Inquisition in Southern France, 1100–1250.* Berkeley: University of California Press, 1974.

Warner, Marina. *Alone of All Her Sex: The Myth and Cult of the Virgin Mary.* New York: Knopf, 1976.

Weisner, Merry. *Working Women in Renaissance Germany.* New Brunswick, N.J.: Rutgers University Press, 1986.

Weisser, Michael. *Crime and Punishment in Early Modern Europe.* Atlantic Highlands, N.J.: Humanities Press, 1979.

Weissman, Ronald. *Ritual Brotherhood in Renaissance Florence.* New York: Academic Press, 1982.

Wellman, Kathleen Anne. *La Mettrie: Medicine, Philosophy and Enlightenment.* Durham: Duke University Press, 1992.

Weschler, Lawrence. *A Miracle, A Universe: Settling Accounts with Torturers.* New York: Pantheon, 1990.

Wills, Antoinette. *Crime and Punishment in Revolutionary Paris.* Westport, Conn.: Greenwood Press, 1981.

Wilson, Lindsay B. *Women and Medicine in the French Enlightenment: The Debate over "Maladies des Femmes."* Baltimore, Md.: Johns Hopkins University Press, 1993.

Wolff, Philippe. *Le Diocèse de Toulouse.* Histoire Des Diocèses de France, vol. 15. Paris: Beauchesne, 1983.

———. *Histoire de Toulouse.* Second edition. Toulouse: Private, 1970.

Wright, A. D. *The Counter-Reformation.* New York: Harcourt, Brace & World, Inc., 1969.

Yates, Frances. *The Art of Memory.* London: Routledge & Kegan Paul, 1966.

Zborowski, Mark. *People in Pain.* Foreword by Margaret Mead. San Francisco: Jossey-Bass, 1969.

INDEX

Page numbers for illustrations are in italics